The Impact of GAAP
on Financial Analysis

The Impact of GAAP on Financial Analysis

Interpretations and Applications for Commercial and Investment Banking

ALEXANDER JOHN SANNELLA

Q

Quorum Books
New York • Westport, Connecticut • London

Library of Congress Cataloging-in-Publication Data

Sannella, Alexander John.
  The Impact of GAAP on Financial analysis : interpretations and
applications for commercial and investment banking / Alexander John
Sannella.
    p.   cm.
  Includes index.
  ISBN 0-89930-607-1 (alk. paper)
    1. Corporations—United States—Accounting.   2. Accounting—
Standards—United States.   3. Financial statements.   I. Title.
  HF5686.C7S316   1991
  657'.48—dc20   90-25742

British Library Cataloguing in Publication Data is available.

Library of Congress Catalog Card Number: 90-25742
ISBN: 0-89930-607-1

First published in 1991

Quorum Books, One Madison Avenue, New York, NY 10010
An imprint of Greenwood Publishing Group, Inc.

Printed in the United States of America

The paper used in this book complies with the
Permanent Paper Standard issued by the National
Information Standards Organization (Z39.48-1984).

10 9 8 7 6 5 4 3 2 1

Copyright Acknowledgments

The author and publisher gratefully acknowledge permission to reprint
material from the American Institute of Certified Public Accountants, Inc.
and the Financial Accounting Standards Board. Copyright © 1973 by the
American Institute of Certified Public Accountants, Inc., 1211 Avenue of
the Americas, New York, New York 10036-8775. Copies are available
directly from the AICPA. Copyright by Financial Accounting Standards
Board, 401 Merritt 7, PO Box 5116, Norwalk, Connecticut 06856-5116,
U.S.A. Reprinted with permission. Copies of the complete document are
available from the FASB.

Dedicated to

Ann, Christopher, Eric, Anthony and Marissa

and to

My Teachers and Students

Contents

Contents

Contents

Exhibits

Chapter 1

Chapter 2

Chapter 3

Chapter 4

Chapter 5

Chapter 6

Chapter 7

Chapter 8

Chapter 9

Preface and Acknowledgements

This book is based on my experience of over seven years in teaching financial accounting and statement analysis to participants of training seminars for investment banks and commercial banks.

In the development of this book, my primary objective was to provide comprehensive coverage of all accounting and reporting issues that are critical to the financial and credit analyst in understanding and interpreting financial information generated in today's current reporting environment. In order to accomplish this objective and, at the same time, to make this book a useful tool for both the accountant and the nonaccountant, the material is presented in an analytical rather than a mechanical fashion.

Each topic is discussed in full, beginning with the most basic concepts and accounting issues and building up to highly complex analytical issues relating to the specific reporting area. The fact that the basics of financial accounting are presented throughout this book does not imply that this book is intended to be a primer or a self-study program. The more basic sections could be omitted by a reader who is very familiar with accounting. However, the basic issues presented are available to those readers who would like to review some of the basics or obtain a solid foundation in a particular accounting area.

Although the book does not utilize a standard bookkeeping approach (i.e., journal entries and t-accounts are not used), the financial statement effects of a particular accounting standard are illustrated through the use of an equation analysis. The equation presents a model of the balance sheet and the income statement, and illustrates the impact of a transaction on cash flows, if any. The equation model provides the reader with a framework that supports the analytical exposition used throughout this book.

In summary, the objectives of this book are to provide an analytical explanation of Generally Accepted Accounting Principles (GAAP) and to provide practical applications of GAAP for the financial and credit analyst. The book presents

GAAP in a clear, lucid style which places emphasis on understanding financial information for purposes of making sound credit and investment decisions.

As noted above, the book provides an exposition of GAAP without the use of mechanical bookkeeping procedures. This type of presentation is accomplished through a five step approach.

1. An analysis and discussion of the financial accounting issue. This includes a presentation of the solution prescribed by the accounting profession and a clear indication of how current accounting practice either enhances or impairs user understanding and effective decision making (i.e., what is the accounting risk and quality of accounting information).

2. An indication of the effects of the application of GAAP on the three basic financial statements: the balance sheet, the income statement and the statement of cash flows. This will be accomplished by the equation analysis noted above, and through illustrations from published annual reports and filings with the Securities and Exchange Commission.

3. A numerical illustration of the application of GAAP.

4. Where possible, an analytical restatement to reflect an alternative accounting treatment of an event or transaction. Although not GAAP, the alternative approach may be preferred by the financial and credit analyst in assessing accounting risk and quality of accounting information.

5. The impact of the application of GAAP on financial ratios and other analytical statistics, both before and after the analytical restatement.

ORGANIZATION OF THE TEXT

As noted earlier, the primary purpose of this book is to provide an analysis and understanding of publicly available financial information. I believe that this understanding begins with the theory underlying published financial statements prepared in accordance with GAAP. Therefore, the first section of this work provides a survey of the basic financial statements, related footnote disclosures and the conceptual framework underlying each financial statement.

The subsequent sections of the book are presented in financial statement order. In each section, a basic introduction to the topic and an in-depth analysis of specific financial statement items are presented. This exposition intends to highlight four key issues:

1. Recognition of an economic event or transaction;

2. Measurement or valuation of the economic event or transaction;

3. Presentation or classification of the event on the financial statement(s);

4. The cash flow effect of the event or transaction.

The first three chapters of this book discuss the conceptual foundation underlying the three basic financial statements, current assets, noncurrent assets, an analysis of liabilities, and stockholders' equity.

The remaining chapters of the book focus on more complex accounting and reporting problems. These issues include accounting for income taxes, computing earnings per share, accounting for intercorporate investments and business combinations, and accounting for leases.

In the final two chapters of the text, issues relating to full disclosure are presented. Full disclosure issues include extraordinary items, accounting changes, discontinued operations, and the statement of cash flows.

Cases are provided at the ends of certain chapters. The cases provide an application of the text to real-world examples and problems, and draw from actual business experience. Solutions to the cases are provided in an appendix.

ACKNOWLEDGEMENTS

I appreciate the unparalleled support and professional commitment given by Eric Valentine, William Neenan, Jay Rozgonyi and Maureen Melino at the Greenwood Publishing Group.

I would also like to give a special note of thanks to Roger Tully and Carolyn Kilponen of United Jersey Bank for providing me with their invaluable professional insight into real-world issues and problems in credit analysis. In addition, I would like to thank the participants of the Morgan Stanley & Company and Kidder Peabody & Company training seminars for their comments and suggestions on the lecture notes used over the last seven years that provided the basis for this book. Finally, the completed version of this book would not have been possible without the computer assistance provided by Dermod Wood of Rutgers University.

Alexander John Sannella

The Impact of GAAP
on Financial Analysis

1

An Introduction to Generally Accepted Accounting Principles and Their Implications for Credit and Financial Analysis

INTRODUCTION

The implications of Generally Accepted Accounting Principles (GAAP) for users' understanding and the analysis of published financial statements are the central points of this book. The book incorporates the theory and assumptions underlying financial statements and uses detailed illustrations and case studies to enhance the reader's understanding of fundamental accounting and reporting issues. Throughout the book, the material is presented without utilizing a mechanical accounting framework (i.e., debit and credit bookkeeping procedures). Instead, the theoretical foundation underlying a particular accounting issue is presented along with detailed illustrations and, where appropriate, an equation analysis which provides the financial statement impact of the economic event or transaction. This approach provides an intuitive understanding of critical accounting and reporting issues facing the analyst.

This chapter begins by presenting the definition of GAAP to be used throughout the text. In addition, the issues of accounting risk and the quality of accounting numbers are related to this definition of GAAP. In the next section of this chapter, the primary sources of GAAP are identified. The following section provides an overview of the three basic financial statements and the articulation between these statements. The conceptual foundation underlying the three basic financial statements is also discussed. In the final section of this chapter, the organization of the text is outlined.

Those readers familiar with the introductory accounting and reporting issues noted in the preceding paragraph should omit chapter 1.

GAAP DEFINED

As used throughout this book, Generally Accepted Accounting Principles are defined as broad reporting guidelines representing the "best" method or methods from many possible alternatives. Although only broad guidelines, the use of GAAP in financial reporting is essential in enhancing user confidence in published financial information. In addition, financial information based on GAAP assists in satisfying the primary objective of financial accounting: to provide information that enables users to make rational, economic decisions (e.g., credit and investment decisions). [1]

GAAP versus Tax Accounting

It should be noted that the terms *financial accounting* and *financial information* used above specifically highlight the fact that the primary focus of GAAP is financial accounting and reporting rather than tax accounting and reporting. As will be discussed in a later section of this book, there are different accounting methods for financial and tax accounting (i.e., the proverbial "two sets of books"). The use of different accounting methods should be expected, given the contrasting objectives of financial and tax accounting.

As indicated above, the primary objective of financial accounting is to provide information useful in making rational economic decisions. On the other hand, the objectives of tax accounting are

1. To raise revenues;

2. To achieve stated economic objectives (for example, tax credits are granted to stimulate investment in research and development activities);

3. To achieve stated social objectives (for example, tax credits are granted for the rehabilitation of certain nonresidential, real property).

From the financial accounting standpoint, taxes are only considered to the extent that they impact published financial information. However, the manner in which the accountant reflects the impact of taxation is usually different from the information presented on the entity's income tax returns. Regardless of the accountant's treatment of income taxes, the analyst must be able to utilize the information provided in the annual report to assess the present and potential future cash flow consequences of the firm's tax information reported in the financial statements.

Reference to GAAP in the Annual Report

The fact that the financial statements are presented in accordance with GAAP is clearly stated in the independent auditors' report. An independent auditors' report for the General Electric Company is presented in Exhibit 1.1. In the third or opinion paragraph of the auditors' report, the accountant states that the financial statements were presented in conformity with GAAP. In addition, the independent auditors' report will indicate if GAAP has been applied consistently, period to period, or if there has been a change in accounting method. The last paragraph of the auditors' report presented in Exhibit 1.1 indicates that there have been changes

EXHIBIT 1.1

Sample Disclosure: General Electric Company: Independent Auditor's Report

----

To Share Owners and Board of Directors of General Electric Company

We have audited the accompanying statement of financial position of General Electric Company and consolidated affiliates as of December 31, 1988 and 1987 and the related statements of earnings and cash flows for each of the years in the three-year period ended December 31, 1988. These consolidated financial statements are the responsibility of the Company's management. Our responsibility is to express an opinion on these consolidated financial statements based on our audits.

We conducted our audits in accordance with generally accepted auditing standards. Those standards require that we plan and perform the audit to obtain reasonable assurance about whether the financial statements are free of material misstatement. An audit includes examining, on a test basis, evidence supporting the amounts and disclosures in the financial statements. An audit also includes assessing the accounting principles used and significant estimates made by management, as well as evaluating the overall financial statement presentation. We believe that our audits provide a reasonable basis for our opinion.

In our opinion, the aforementioned financial statements appearing on pages 24-29 and 44-70 present fairly, in all material respects, the financial position of General Electric Company and consolidated affiliates at December 31, 1988 and 1987, and the results of their operations and their cash flows for each of the years in the three-year period ended December 31, 1988, in conformity with generally accepted accounting principles.

As discussed in note 1 to the consolidated financial statements, in 1988 the Company changed its method of inclusion of previously unconsolidated affiliates; and in 1987 the Company changed its methods of accounting for income taxes and overhead recorded in inventory. We concur with these accounting changes.

Peat Marwick Main & Co.

Peat Marwick Main & Co.
Stamford, Connecticut
February 10, 1989

----

in certain GAAP methods used by General Electric. This information provided in the fourth or explanatory paragraph of the auditors' report provides a signal to the analyst that certain financial information may no longer be comparable with prior years due to the change in GAAP method.

The first footnote to the financial statements provides the summary of significant accounting policies (i.e., the GAAP) used by a firm. By reviewing the first footnote, the credit and financial analyst can identify the GAAP used by a firm and determine if these methods are consistent each period and if the GAAP methods are comparable with other firms in the same industry. Knowledge of the GAAP methods used is essential for understanding and interpreting the valuation of the economic resources and the measurement of profit or loss for the firm. The accounting policies footnote for General Electric Company is presented in Exhibit 1.2. Note that in the footnote section entitled "GE Accounting Policies" the reader is informed as to the GAAP methods of accounting used for revenue recognition, inventory, depreciation, etc.

THE QUALITY OF ACCOUNTING INFORMATION AND ACCOUNTING RISK

In the definition of GAAP and in a review of the independent auditors' report, several terms were couched in vague language such as "broad reporting guidelines", "best alternative method" and "presents fairly". The use of broad terminology indicates that accounting is not an exact science. In fact, accounting has often been criticized for the significant amount of flexibility, judgement and subjectivity afforded to management in three key areas:

1. The initial choice of a GAAP method;

2. A change from one GAAP method to another;

3. Discretion and judgement in the application of GAAP (e.g., the use of estimates).

The latitude afforded to management within these three areas implies that the analyst may have some difficulty in comparing the financial information reported for two firms in the same industry, if a different set of GAAP accounting methods or estimation techniques were used by the individual firms. In addition, the analyst may not be able to compare the same firm over time if that firm changes GAAP methods or modifies the estimation techniques used in the consistent application of a particular GAAP method.

Discretion in selection and application, and changes in GAAP, also provide management with an invaluable tool for smoothing or manipulating income by shifting reported income numbers between accounting periods. Depending on management's reporting objectives, an income-increasing or an income-reducing reporting strategy may be adopted.

These issues raise questions regarding the quality of the accounting numbers reported and subjects the analyst to "accounting risk", in addition to business and market risk, when making credit and investment decisions. A major portion of this

EXHIBIT 1.2

Sample Disclosure: General Electric Company: Accounting Policies Footnote

----

Note 1   Summary of Significant Accounting Policies

Consolidation and financial statement presentation

In 1988, GE was required to adopt two new Statements of Financial Accounting Standards (SFAS): SFAS No. 94 — "Consolidation of All Majority-Owned Subsidiaries"; and SFAS No. 95 — "Statement of Cash Flows." These changes are in addition to changes made in 1987 to implement SFAS No. 96 — "Accounting for Income Taxes" and to modify GE's accounting procedures to include in inventory certain manufacturing overhead costs previously charged directly to expense.

Consolidation. The consolidated financial statements now represent the adding together of all companies in which General Electric Company directly or indirectly has a majority ownership or otherwise controls ("affiliated companies"). In the past, results of financial services affiliates — the principal one being General Electric Financial Services, Inc. (GEFS or GE Financial Services) and its affiliated companies — were included on the equity basis as one line in total earnings and net assets. This was permissible under prior rules and, because financial services operations are so different in nature from and essentially unrelated to operations of other GE businesses, management believed that financial statements were more understandable if GEFS' statements were shown separately. It should be emphasized that, using the new consolidation procedure, consolidated net earnings and share owners' equity are unchanged for all periods presented. However, substantially more detail is required under the new standard than under rules previously in effect. Also as a result of this change, the Company adopted an unclassified consolidated statement of financial position.

Management believes it is important to preserve as much as possible the identity of the principal financial data and related measurements to which share owners and others have become accustomed over the years. Accordingly, consolidated financial statements and notes now are generally presented in a format that includes data grouped basically as follows.

- **GE** — this is essentially the former basis of consolidation except that it includes some very small financial services affiliates previously not consolidated. The effect of transactions among companies within this group has been eliminated. Where appropriate for clarification or emphasis, particularly in the notes, this group of entities also is referred to as "GE except GEFS."

- **GEFS** — this affiliate owns all of the common stock of General Electric Capital Corporation (GECC or GE Capital) and of Employers Reinsurance Corporation (ERC)

----

and 80% of the stock of Kidder, Peabody Group Inc. (Kidder, Peabody). These affiliates and their respective affiliates are consolidated in the GEFS columns with the effect of transactions among them eliminated before the consolidated presentation.

- **Consolidated** — these columns represent the adding together of GE and GEFS. However, it is necessary to remove the effect of transactions between GE except GEFS and GEFS to arrive at a consolidated total. The "eliminations" used to arrive at these consolidated totals are summarized below.

Eliminations

(In millions)	1988	1987	1986
Statement of Earnings			
Sales of goods	$ (5)	$ —	$ —
Sales of services	(26)	(8)	(5)
Other income	(5)	6	6
Earnings of GEFS	(788)	(552)	(504)
Earned income	(34)	(29)	(23)
Total revenues	(858)	(583)	(526)
Cost of goods sold	(5)	—	—
Cost of services sold	(26)	(8)	(5)
Interest and other financial charges	(29)	(10)	(9)
Other costs and expenses	(10)	(13)	(8)
Total costs and expenses	(70)	(31)	(22)
Earnings before income taxes, extraordinary item and cumulative effect of accounting changes	(788)	(552)	(504)
Extraordinary item	—	62	—
Income tax accounting change	—	(518)	—
Net earnings	$ (788)	$(1,008)	$ (504)
Statement of Financial Position			
GE current receivables	$ (330)	$ (37)	
GEFS financing receivables	(107)	(92)	
Other GEFS receivables	(107)	(183)	
Investment in GEFS	(4,819)	(3,980)	
Total assets	$(5,363)	$(4,292)	
Short-term borrowings	$ (170)	$ (85)	
Accounts payable	(264)	(216)	
Long-term borrowings	(110)	(11)	
Total liabilities	(544)	(312)	
GEFS equity	(4,819)	(3,980)	
Total liabilities and equity	$(5,363)	$(4,292)	
Statement of Cash Flows			
Net earnings (operating activities)	$ (13)	$ (213)	$ 483
Investing activities	(171)	243	(508)
Financing activities	184	(30)	25
Total	$ —	$ —	$ —

Virtually all products financed by GECC are manufactured by companies other than GE.

There is no change in method for consolidating companies in which GE or GEFS owns between 20% and 50% ("associated companies"). Results of these companies are still included on a one-line basis.

Cash flows. SFAS No. 95 now requires a Statement of Cash Flows in place of the former Statement of Changes in Financial Position. The principal result (in addition to consolidation) is to present analytical data of cash flow items rather than the former focus on changes in cash and marketable securities less short-term borrowings for GE other than GEFS. For purposes of implementing this standard, marketable securities of GE except GEFS are treated as cash equivalents. Certain of the securities so treated have maturities ranging between 90 and 365 days; but, as part of GE's cash management program, maturities are scheduled based on contemplated cash needs for the ensuing 12 months. GEFS' amounts classified as "marketable securities carried at cost" and "marketable securities carried at market" are not treated as cash equivalents in the Statement of Cash Flows.

Prior-year statements have been restated or reclassified as appropriate to conform them to the presentations required by SFAS Nos. 94 and 95.

Pensions and other retirement benefits. Accounting policies for pensions and other retirement benefits are discussed in note 7.

Income taxes. SFAS No. 96 — "Accounting for Income Taxes" was issued by the Financial Accounting Standards Board in December 1987. A requirement of SFAS No. 96 is that deferred tax liabilities or assets at the end of each period be determined using the tax rate expected to be in effect when taxes are actually paid or recovered. Accordingly, under SFAS No. 96 rules, income tax expense provisions will increase or decrease in the same period in which a change in tax rates is enacted. Previous rules required providing deferred taxes using rates in effect when the tax asset or liability was first recorded without subsequent adjustment solely for tax-rate changes (except with respect to leveraged leases).

In conformity with SFAS No. 96 transition rules, the Company elected to adopt the new income tax accounting during 1987. The cumulative effect to January 1, 1987 ($577 million, including $518 million for GEFS) of the change is shown in the 1987 columns of the Statement of Earnings. Also, as required, quarterly earnings reported for 1987 were restated for the effect of this change on interim quarters in 1987 as if it had occurred at January 1. Restated quarterly amounts can be found in note 35.

Exhibit 1.2, continued

GE accounting policies

Sales. A sale is recorded when title passes to the customer or when services are performed in accordance with contracts.

Investment tax credit (ITC). The ITC was repealed, with some transitional exceptions, effective January 1, 1986. However, for financial reporting purposes, GE has deferred recognition of the ITC each year and continues to amortize ITC as a reduction of the provision for income taxes over the lives of the facilities to which the credit applies.

Inventories. The values of most inventories are determined on a last-in first-out, or LIFO, basis and do not exceed realizable values. Effective January 1, 1987, GE changed its accounting procedures to include in inventory certain manufacturing overhead costs previously charged directly to expense. Among the more significant types of manufacturing overhead included in inventory as a result of the change are: depreciation of plant and equipment; pension and other benefits of manufacturing employees; and certain product-related engineering expenses. The Company believes this change was preferable because it provides a better matching of production costs with related revenues in reporting operating results. In accordance with generally accepted accounting principles, the cumulative effect of this change for periods prior to January 1, 1987 ($281 million after providing for taxes of $215 million) is shown separately in 1987 in the Statement of Earnings on page 24. There was virtually no effect from this change on 1987 results after recording the cumulative effect, and the pro forma effect on prior-years results was immaterial.

Depreciation, depletion and amortization. The cost of most manufacturing plant and equipment is depreciated using an accelerated method based primarily on a sum-of-the-years digits formula. If manufacturing plant and equipment is subject to abnormal economic conditions or obsolescence, additional depreciation is provided.

GEFS accounting policies

Methods of recording earned income. Income on all loans is earned on the interest method. For loan contracts on which finance charges are precomputed, finance charges are deferred at the time of contract acquisition. For loan contracts on which finance charges are not precomputed but are billed to customers, income is recorded when earned. Accrual of interest income is suspended when collection of an account becomes doubtful, generally after the account becomes 90 days delinquent.

Financing lease income that includes related investment tax credits and residual values is recorded on the interest method so as to produce a level yield on funds not yet recovered. Unguaranteed residual values included in lease income are based primarily on independent appraisals of the values of leased assets remaining at expiration of the lease terms.

Origination, commitment and other nonrefundable fees related to fundings are deferred and recorded in earned income on the interest method. Commitment fees related to loans not expected to be funded and line-of-credit fees are deferred and recorded in earned income on a straight-line basis over the period to which the fees relate. Syndication fees are recorded in earned income at the time the related services are performed unless significant contingencies exist.

In 1987, GEFS adopted Statement of Financial Accounting Standards No. 91 — "Accounting for Nonrefundable Fees and Costs Associated with Originating or Acquiring Loans and Initial Direct Costs of Leases," which modified certain accounting principles that apply to nonrefundable fees and costs associated with lending and leasing activities. GEFS' accounting practices with respect to such fees and costs already conformed substantially to the requirements of SFAS No. 91, and, accordingly, the effect of adopting the new accounting standard in 1987 was not material.

Kidder, Peabody's proprietary securities and commodities transactions are recorded on a trade-date basis. Trading and investment securities are valued at market or estimated fair value. Unrealized gains and losses on open contractual commitments, principally financial futures, when-issued securities and forward contracts on U.S. government and federal agency securities, are reflected in the Statement of Earnings on a trade-date basis. Customers' transactions and the related revenues and expenses are reflected in the financial statements on a settlement-date basis. Revenues and expenses on a trade-date basis are not materially different. Investment banking revenues from management fees, sales concessions and underwriting fees are recorded on settlement date. Advisory fee revenue is recorded when services are substantially completed and the revenue is reasonably determinable.

See "insurance affiliates" on page 47 for information with respect to earned income of these businesses.

Allowance for losses on financing receivables. GEFS maintains an allowance for losses on financing receivables at an amount which it believes is sufficient to provide adequate protection against future losses in the portfolio. For small-balance and certain large-balance receivables, the allowance for losses is determined principally on the basis of actual experience during the preceding three years. Additional allowances are also recorded to reflect management's judgment of additional loss potential. For other receivables, principally the larger loans and leases, the

7

Exhibit 1.2, continued

----

allowance for losses is determined primarily on the basis of management's judgment of net loss potential, including specific allowances for known troubled accounts.

All accounts or portions thereof deemed to be uncollectible or to require an excessive collection cost are written off to the allowance for losses. Small-balance accounts are progressively written down (from 10% when more than three months delinquent to 100% when more than 12 months delinquent) to record the balances at estimated realizable value. However, if at any time during that period an account is judged to be uncollectible, such as in the case of a bankruptcy, the remaining balance is written off. Larger-balance accounts are reviewed at least quarterly, and those accounts which are more than three months delinquent are written down, if necessary, to record the balances at estimated realizable value.

Marketable securities. Marketable securities of Kidder, Peabody are carried at market value with the difference between cost and market value included in operations. Marketable debt securities held by all other GEFS affiliates are carried at amortized cost. Marketable equity securities of insurance affiliates are carried at market value, and unrealized gains or losses, less applicable deferred income taxes, are recognized in equity.

Securities purchased under agreements to resell (reverse repurchase agreements) and securities sold under agreements to repurchase (repurchase agreements). Repurchase and reverse repurchase agreements are treated as financing transactions and are carried at the contract amount at which the securities subsequently will be resold or reacquired. Repurchase agreements relate either to marketable securities, which are carried at market value, or to securities obtained pursuant to reverse repurchase agreements. It is GEFS' policy to take possession of securities subject to reverse repurchase agreements. GEFS monitors the market value of the underlying securities in relation to the related receivable, including accrued interest, and requests additional collateral if appropriate.

Depreciation and amortization. The cost of equipment leased to others on operating leases is amortized, principally on a straight-line basis, to estimated net salvage value over the lease term or the estimated economic life of the equipment. Depreciation of property and equipment for GEFS' own use is recorded on either a sum-of-the-years digits or a straight-line basis over the lives of the assets.

Investment tax credit (ITC). ITC associated with equipment on operating leases and buildings and equipment is deferred and amortized over the lives of the underlying assets.

Insurance affiliates. The accounts of insurance affiliates are adjusted from accounting practices prescribed by state insurance regulatory authorities to a "generally accepted accounting principles" basis. The principal adjustments reflect deferral and amortization of costs (primarily commissions) of acquiring premiums, and net the effects of certain specialty reinsurance transactions.

Premiums on short-duration insurance contracts are reported as earned income over the terms of the related reinsurance treaties or insurance policies. In general, earned premiums are calculated on a pro-rata basis or are determined based on reports received from reinsureds. Premium adjustments under retrospectively rated reinsurance contracts are recorded based on estimated losses and loss expenses, including both case and incurred-but-not-reported (IBNR) reserves. Revenues on long-duration contracts are reported as earned when due.

Deferred insurance acquisition costs are amortized as the related premiums are earned for property and casualty business or over the premium-paying periods of the contracts in proportion to anticipated premium income for life insurance business. Deferred insurance acquisition costs are reviewed for recoverability, and, for short duration contracts, anticipated investment income is considered in making recoverability evaluations.

The estimated liability for outstanding losses and loss expenses consists of case reserves based on reports and estimates of losses and an IBNR reserve based primarily on experience, except where experience is not sufficient, in which case industry averages for the particular insurance products are used. Estimated amounts of salvage and subrogation recoverable on paid and unpaid losses are deducted from outstanding losses. The liability for future policy benefits of the life insurance affiliates has been computed mainly by a net-level-premium method based on assumptions for investment yields, mortality and terminations that were appropriate at date of purchase or at the time the policies were developed, including provisions for adverse deviations.

----

book addresses these issues and is devoted to providing the analyst with the background needed to better assess the quality of accounting numbers and to minimize the accounting risk associated with an investment choice or a credit-granting decision. By presenting controversial GAAP accounting and reporting issues from the user's perspective, this book will provide the analyst with the tools needed to convert one GAAP method to another. Although it is not always possible to convert from one GAAP method to another on a quantitative basis, at a minimum the analyst should be able to understand the direction in which "subjective" adjustments should be made, in order to compare the financial statements of two firms in the same industry or for making comparisons of the financial information provided by the same firm over time.

SOURCES OF GAAP

As noted in the General Electric footnote, "Summary of Significant Accounting Policies" (Exhibit 1.2), there were references to the sources of GAAP used. For example, the footnote states that the company was required to adopt two new standards of accounting, SFAS 94, "Consolidation of All Majority-Owned Subsidiaries", and SFAS 95, "Statement of Cash Flows". These standards are required by the Financial Accounting Standards Board (FASB), which is the current standard setting body. In addition to the FASB, other sources of GAAP include the pronouncements of the Accounting Principles Board (APB) and the Committee on Accounting Procedure (CAP) that are still in effect or have not been superseded by a subsequent FASB standard. These standard setting bodies and other sources of GAAP are briefly discussed in the next section.

The Financial Accounting Standards Board (FASB): (1973-Present)

The FASB is a seven-member, full-time board that issues authoritative pronouncements called "Statements of Financial Accounting Standards" (SFAS), or simply "Statements" or "FASBs". To date, over 105 Statements have been issued. In addition, the FASB issues Interpretations of its authoritative pronouncements.

The issuance of an FASB Statement is a public process implemented through a "due process" system consisting of ten steps.

1. A topic is placed on the FASB's agenda.

2. A task force carefully defines the problems and accounting alternatives.

3. Research and analysis of the issue is conducted by the FASB's technical staff.

4. A Discussion Memorandum (DM) is released. The DM presents the issues, the rationale, and the advantages and disadvantages of alternative accounting and reporting solutions to the problem.

5. A public hearing is held.

6. The results of the public hearing are analyzed.

7. An exposure draft of the Statement is issued.

8. Public comment is requested for a 30-day period after the issuance of the exposure draft.

9. The public comments are evaluated.

10. The final Statement is issued.[2]

This "due process" allows management, members of the financial and accounting community and academicians to lobby for those standards they support, and to "vote" against those standards they oppose. It is interesting to note that the due process system does not end with the issuance of the final Statement. Several cases will be noted throughout this book which illustrate how various interest groups have lobbied the FASB, as well as the government, to suspend the effective dates or completely eliminate the requirements of a particular standard. In addition, if a standard is issued but is not used by the accounting profession, it is not "generally accepted". The lack of general acceptance, even without direct opposition and lobbying, could result in the suspension or elimination of a particular accounting standard. Therefore, GAAP consists of all standards issued by the FASB, or by the former authoritative bodies that have not been superseded by the FASB, which have the general support of the members of the accounting profession.

The Accounting Principles Board (APB): (1959-1973)

The APB, a part-time board, issued pronouncements known as "Opinions". Over the period of its existence, the APB issued 31 Opinions, many of which have not been superseded by an FASB Statement, and therefore are still considered part of GAAP and have authoritative support.

The Committee on Accounting Procedure (CAP): (1939-1959)

The Committee on Accounting Procedure was primarily established to reduce the number of accounting alternatives in practice and to develop uniform standards of accounting, reporting and disclosure. The CAP issued pronouncements known as "Bulletins". There were a total of 51 Bulletins, many of which remain in force today. Specific references to the Bulletins are rare because they have become the basic foundation of GAAP.

Other Sources of GAAP

In addition to the semipublic (or semiprivate) bodies specifically designated by the accounting profession to promulgate accounting standards, there are other influential organizations that effect GAAP. These organizations include:

1. The Securities and Exchange Commission (SEC). The SEC's GAAP are found in Regulation S-X, Staff Accounting Bulletins (SABs), and Financial Reporting Releases (FRRs) (previously known as Accounting Series Releases [ASRs]). Filings with the SEC include Form 10-K (annual), Form 10-Q (quarterly) and Form 8-K, which must be filed within 15 days after the occurrence of a "material" event.

   Legally, the SEC has the authority to dictate accounting principles but historically has allowed the accounting profession to issue its own standards. Nonetheless, the SEC has used its power in limited cases and frequently exerts pressure on the FASB to issue or adopt certain standards of accounting, reporting and disclosure.

2. The Internal Revenue Service (IRS). In many cases accounting principles are based on a corresponding tax method. The IRS can also force the use of certain tax accounting principles for financial reporting purposes. However, only in the case of inventory accounting has the IRS required conformity between the income tax and financial reporting method used.

3. The American Institute of Certified Public Accountants (AICPA). Today, the AICPA is no longer directly involved in the standard setting process. However, the Accounting Standard Executive Committee (AcSEC) of the AICPA continues to issue pronouncements called Statements of Position (SOPs) and Issue Papers which present accounting problems and issues and proposed accounting alternatives that are not currently being addressed by the FASB. Although not considered part of GAAP, SOPs and Issue Papers can be deemed GAAP by the SEC or the FASB, and will thereby have the same authoritative support as all other parts of GAAP.

   The AICPA also issues Statements on Auditing Standards (SASs), which provide the basis of the Generally Accepted Auditing Standards (GAAS) which must be followed in order for the accountant to render an opinion on the financial statements, taken as a whole. In the auditor's opinion presented in Exhibit 1.1, there is a reference to GAAS. As is the case in the use of GAAP, a clear statement that the accountant followed GAAS in the examination of financial statements provides the reader with certain assurances as to the quality of the audit work performed and the validity of the conclusions reached, as to the fair presentation of financial position, results of operations, and statement of cash flows. Auditing is a specialized field of accounting and therefore auditing standards are not considered in this text.

THE THREE BASIC GENERAL PURPOSE FINANCIAL STATEMENTS AND THEIR RELATED CONCEPTS

The Three Basic General Purpose Financial Statements

In order to present financial statements in accordance with GAAP, published financial statements must include the three basic general purpose financial statements: the balance sheet or the statement of financial position; the income statement, the statement of profit and loss or the statement of operations; and the cash flow statement. In addition, a complete set of financial statements requires full disclosure in the form of footnotes.

The three basic financial statements are said to be general purpose financial statements because they are designed to satisfy the needs of a wide spectrum of user groups, including investors, creditors, financial and credit analysts, insurance companies, labor unions, employees and government agencies. Although considered general purpose, most financial information is provided to satisfy users with limited ability and authority to obtain additional information.[3] Usually, the primary users are identified as investors and creditors. However, from a practical standpoint, the investors are probably the primary user group addressed by the accounting profession in published annual reports. For the most part, the other user groups can demand and obtain additional information or request clarification of data included in the annual report. For example, if a firm wants to obtain additional financing, it would probably not hesitate to satisfy a potential creditor's demand for additional information.

The Balance Sheet or Statement of Financial Position. The balance sheet is a listing of the assets, liabilities and capital of the entity at a point in time. From an economic standpoint, the balance sheet presents the stock of wealth of the firm.

The assets of the firm have been defined as economic resources owned or controlled by the firm and having future service potential (economic benefit) to the firm. Notice that the assets of the firm do not have to be owned. As long as the economic resources are controlled and provide future economic benefit, they can be included among the assets of the entity. As will be discussed in a later chapter, under certain conditions leased equipment can be included among the assets of the firm (i.e., "capitalized"), even if not owned.

Liabilities are the debts owed to outsiders (i.e., creditors) by the firm. Liabilities are also known as "creditors' equity" or the creditors' claim against the assets of the firm.

The capital of the firm represents the owners' wealth which is a residual claim to the assets of the firm, or the owners' equity. Because the creditors' claims must be satisfied first, the owners' equity has also been called net worth or net assets.

A balance sheet or statement of financial position for the General Electric Company is presented in Exhibit 1.3.

As noted in Exhibit 1.3, the balance sheet is based on the fundamental accounting or balance sheet equation: Assets = Equities, or Assets = Liabilities + Stockholders' Equity.

In the asset section of the balance sheet, assets are listed in the "order of liquidity" (where liquidity is defined as the ability to convert an economic resource into

EXHIBIT 1.3

Sample Disclosure: General Electric Company: Statement of Financial Position

---

At December 31 (In millions)	General Electric Company and consolidated affiliates 1988	1987
Assets		
Cash (note 12)	$ 2,187	$ 2,543
Marketable securities carried at cost (note 13)	5,779	5,353
Marketable securities carried at market (note 14)	5,089	4,000
Securities purchased under agreements to resell	13,811	12,889
Current receivables (note 15)	6,780	6,745
Inventories (note 16)	6,486	6,265
GEFS financing receivables (investment in time sales, loans and financing leases) — net (note 17)	35,832	27,839
Other GEFS receivables (note 18)	4,699	4,458
Property, plant and equipment (including equipment leased to others) — net (note 19)	13,611	12,973
Investment in GEFS	—	—
Intangible assets (note 20)	8,552	5,748
All other assets (note 21)	8,039	6,601
Total assets	**$110,865**	**$ 95,414**
Liabilities and equity		
Short-term borrowings (note 22)	$ 30,422	$ 23,873
Accounts payable (note 23)	6,004	5,728
Securities sold under agreements to repurchase	13,864	13,187
Securities sold but not yet purchased, at market (note 24)	2,088	1,407
Progress collections and price adjustments accrued	3,504	3,760
Dividends payable	369	319
All other GE current costs and expenses accrued (note 25)	5,549	4,867
Long-term borrowings (note 26)	15,082	12,517
Reserves of insurance affiliates	4,177	3,549
All other liabilities (note 27)	6,986	6,325
Deferred income taxes	3,373	3,100
Total liabilities	91,418	78,632
Minority interest in equity of consolidated affiliates (note 28)	981	302
Common stock (926,564,000 shares issued)	584	584
Other capital	823	878
Retained earnings	17,950	15,878
Less common stock held in treasury	(891)	(860)
Total share owners' equity (notes 29 and 30)	18,466	16,480
Total liabilities and equity	**$110,865**	**$ 95,414**

Commitments and contingent liabilities (note 31)

---

cash with minimal risk of loss). It is common practice to report financial position through the use of a classified balance sheet. In the classified balance sheet assets are classified as current if the economic resource is expected to be used or consumed in operations or converted into cash within one year from the balance sheet or one operating cycle, whichever is longer. The operating cycle is the "cash-to-cash" cycle of the firm. For some operations, such as those requiring an aging process, a single operating cycle may extend beyond one year. In general, however, assets meeting the one-year criterion are classified as current. Conversely, if the asset is expected to provide economic benefit for a period longer than one year from the balance sheet date, it would be classified as a long-term or noncurrent asset.

Liabilities are listed in the "order of maturity". It is common reporting practice to classify liabilities as current if due within one year of the balance sheet date, and noncurrent or long term if payable in a period greater than one year from the balance sheet date. In theory, a current liability is properly defined as an obligation whose liquidation will require the use of economic resources properly classified as current assets or the creation of other current liabilities. Although the latter definition captures the operating cycle concept used in the discussion of current and noncurrent assets, the one-year criterion for the classification of liabilities is generally sufficient in practice.

The classification of assets and liabilities is useful for the analyst in "matching maturities" of assets and liabilities. The excess of current assets over current liabilities, or working capital, is an important concept in the assessment of a firm's liquidity in the analysis of financial statements.

Finally, captial is classified as stockholders' equity on the corporate balance sheet. The stockholders' equity section of the balance sheet consists of two major components: contributed or paid-in capital and retained earnings.

Contributed or paid-in capital includes the capital stock (either common or preferred) issued by the entity at par or face value, and the amounts received above par value. The amounts received over par value are called additional paid-in capital or paid-in capital in excess of par. Retained earnings represent the historical record of earnings or losses that have not been paid out or distributed as dividends.

The Income Statement, Statement of Profit and Loss or Statement of Operations. The income statement is a listing of revenues, expenses, and net income or net loss over a period of time. The income statement presents the change in owners' wealth or the flow of wealth for the accounting period (e.g., one month, one quarter or one year). The model of the income statement is simply Net Income (Loss) = Revenues - Expenses. A sample income statement or statement of earnings for the General Electric Company is presented in Exhibit 1.4.

Because the balance sheet is the stock of wealth at a point in time, it is a cumulative statement. On the other hand, the income statement is the flow of wealth or the change in capital resulting from the operations of the firm over a particular period of time. Therefore, the balance sheet is a permanent statement while the income statement is only a temporary statement. As a result, at the end of each accounting period, the change in owners' wealth from the income statement must be transferred to capital (specifically retained earnings) on the balance sheet. This transfer or "closing" process is illustrated in the following diagram.

```
-------------------------------------------------------------------------
Balance Sheet at 12/31/XX
----------------------------

Assets   =   Liabilities   +            Stockholders' Equity
                                -------------------------------------------
                                                       Beginning
                             Contributed Capital  +  Retained Earnings
                             --------------------     -----------------
                                         ---------> Net Income <Loss>
                                         |            - Dividends
                                         ^          --------------------
                                         |            Change in Retained
                                         |            Earnings for the
                                         ^            Year
                                         |          --------------------
                                         |            Ending Retained
                                         |            Earnings
                                         ^          ====================
Income Statement for the Year Ended 12/31/XX:  |
---------------------------------------------  |
                                               ^
         Transfer or "Closed Out to Capital"   |
         |----->----->----->----->----->----->------->|
         |
         ^
         |
         |
Net Income <Loss>  = Revenues  -  Expenses
-------------------------------------------------------------------------
```

Due to the fact that net income or loss is transferred or closed out to capital (i.e., retained earnings) at the end of each accounting period, all revenue and expense accounts begin each period with a zero balance. It is for this reason that income statement accounts are sometimes known as temporary accounts, and the income statement is said to reflect "completed accounting cycles". On the other hand, the balance sheet is said to consist of permanent accounts because their balances are cumulative and are carried forward period to period. Because of the cumulative nature of the balance sheet accounts, the balance sheet is said to reflect "incomplete accounting cycles". The balance sheet cycles will be completed when the economic resources of the firm generate revenues which are matched on the income statement with the expenses incurred to produce those revenues.

The Statement of Cash Flows. The primary objectives of the cash flow statement are:

1. To provide information about the firm's cash receipts and cash payments from operating activities;

2. To provide information about the firm's financing and investing activities over a period of time.

EXHIBIT 1.4

Sample Disclosure: General Electric Company: Statement of Earnings

For the years ended December 31 (In millions)	General Electric Company and consolidated affiliates		
	1988	1987	1986
Revenues			
Sales of goods	$28,953	$29,937	$28,139
Sales of services	9,840	9,370	7,067
Other income (note 4)	675	655	1,016
Earnings of GEFS	—	—	—
GEFS earned income from operations (note 5)	10,621	8,196	5,963
Effect of change in tax-rate assumptions for leveraged leases (note 5)	—	—	(172)
Total revenues	50,089	48,158	42,013
Costs and expenses (note 6)			
Cost of goods sold	21,155	22,359	20,707
Cost of services sold	7,676	7,290	5,425
Interest and other financial charges (note 8)	4,817	3,912	2,679
Insurance policy holder losses and benefits	1,501	1,560	1,439
Provision for losses on financing receivables (note 9)	434	290	558
Other costs and expenses	9,724	8,406	7,760
Unusual expenses, including provisions for business restructurings (note 10)	—	1,118	311
Minority interest in net earnings (loss) of consolidated affiliates	61	(4)	7
Total costs and expenses	45,368	44,931	38,886
Earnings (loss) before income taxes, extraordinary item and cumulative effect of accounting changes	4,721	3,227	3,127
(Provision) credit for income taxes (note 11)	(1,335)	(1,108)	(1,027)
Effect of change in tax-rate assumptions for leveraged leases (note 5)	—	—	392
Earnings before extraordinary item and cumulative effect of accounting changes	3,386	2,119	2,492
Extraordinary item (note 26)	—	(62)	—
Cumulative effect to January 1, 1987 of accounting changes			
Initial application of Statement of Financial Accounting Standards No. 96 — "Accounting for Income Taxes" (note 1)	—	577	—
Change in overhead recorded in inventory (note 1)	—	281	—
Net earnings	$ 3,386	$ 2,915	$ 2,492
Net earnings per share (in dollars)			
Before extraordinary item and cumulative effect of accounting changes	$ 3.75	$ 2.33	$ 2.73
Extraordinary item (note 26)	—	(.07)	—
Cumulative effect to January 1, 1987 of accounting changes			
Initial application of Statement of Financial Accounting Standards No. 96 — "Accounting for Income Taxes" (note 1)	—	.63	—
Change in overhead recorded in inventory (note 1)	—	.31	—
Net earnings per share	$ 3.75	$ 3.20	$ 2.73
Dividends declared per share (in dollars)	$ 1.46	$ 1.32½	$ 1.18½

Source: General Electric Company 1988 Annual Report. Copyright, 1989, by The General Electric Company. Reprinted with permission.

In addition, an analysis of the cash flow statement, along with the income statement and footnote disclosures, enables the analyst to explain or reconcile the change in cash as well as other elements of the balance sheet. This interrelationship or "articulation" between the three basic general purpose financial statements is illustrated in the following diagram.

```
|---------------|
|Income Statement|
|  for the Year |
|  Ended 12/31/92|
|----------------|                        |-------------|        |"Flow of Wealth"|-------->| Balance Sheet |
| Balance Sheet  |-------->|(with footnotes)|         | at 12/31/92   |
| at 12/31/91    |         |----------------|         | "Stock of     |
| "Stock of      |                                    | Wealth"       |
| Wealth"        |                                    |-------------|
|----------------|
        |                   |---------------|                |
        |                   |  Statement of |                |
        |                   |  Cash Flows   |                |
        |------------------>|  for the Year |-------------->|
                            |  Ended 12/31/92|
                            |(with footnotes)|
                            |---------------|
```

The statement of cash flows for the General Electric Company is presented in Exhibit 1.5.

The above diagram illustrates how the income statement and the statement of cash flows, with adequate footnote disclosure, can be used to explain or reconcile changes from one balance sheet to another. The ability to link or relate financial information contained on different financial statements is known as "articulation". Specifically, articulation refers to the interaction between assets, liabilities and equity elements with revenues and expenses. In other words, the elements of the three basic general purpose financial statements are intrinsically interrelated so that the elements of the balance sheet are dependent on the elements of the income statement and the elements of the income statement are dependent on the elements of the balance sheet.

An illustration of the concept of articulation for the General Electric financial statements is presented below.

Illustration of Articulation Between the General Electric Financial Statements

In order to illustrate the concept of articulation, the data contained in Exhibits 1.3, 1.4 and 1.5 will be used. The following illustrations will reconcile or explain the change in treasury stock and retained earnings on the General Electric balance

EXHIBIT 1.5

Sample Disclosure: General Electric Company: Statement of Cash Flows

	General Electric Company and consolidated affiliates		
For the years ended December 31 (In millions)	1988	1987	1986
Cash flows from operating activities			
Net earnings	**$ 3,386**	$ 2,915	$ 2,492
Adjustments to reconcile net earnings to cash provided from operating activities			
Extraordinary item and cumulative effect of changes in accounting principles	—	(796)	—
Depreciation, depletion and amortization	**2,266**	1,913	1,825
Earnings retained by GEFS	—	—	—
Deferred income taxes	**124**	37	103
Decrease (increase) in GE current receivables	**123**	138	624
Decrease (increase) in GE inventories	**(209)**	375	(317)
Increase in insurance reserves	**315**	669	852
Provision for losses on financing receivables	**434**	290	558
Net change in certain broker-dealer accounts	**(573)**	(103)	(1,298)
All other operating activities	**1,236**	401	1,124
Cash provided from operating activities	**7,102**	5,839	5,963
Cash flows from investing activities			
Property, plant and equipment including equipment leased to others			
– additions	**(3,681)**	(2,277)	(2,806)
– dispositions	**470**	890	694
Net increase in GEFS financing receivables	**(6,057)**	(4,575)	(4,203)
Payments for principal businesses purchased, net of cash acquired	**(3,504)**	(555)	(6,730)
Proceeds from principal business dispositions	**880**	646	1,386
All other investing activities	**(1,772)**	(1,084)	(1,821)
Cash used for investing activities	**(13,664)**	(6,955)	(13,480)
Cash flows from financing activities			
Net change in borrowings (less than 90-day maturities)	**3,868**	2,519	4,536
Debt having maturities more than 90 days			
– newly issued	**11,324**	8,219	9,576
– repayments and other reductions	**(8,801)**	(6,883)	(6,214)
Sale of preferred stock by GECC	**600**	—	—
Disposition of GE shares from treasury	**356**	361	283
Purchase of GE shares for treasury	**(387)**	(846)	(348)
Dividends paid to GE share owners	**(1,263)**	(1,177)	(1,058)
Cash provided from (used for) financing activities	**5,697**	2,193	6,775
Total cash flows — increase (decrease) in cash and equivalents	**$ (865)**	$ 1,077	$ (742)

Source: General Electric Company 1988 Annual Report. Copyright, 1989 by The General Electric Company. Reprinted with permission.

sheets.

Reconciliation of the Change in Treasury Stock

Exhibit 1.3: Statement of Financial Position:	1987	1988	Increase
Common stock held in the treasury..........	<$891>	<$860>	<$31>

Net
Cash
Outflow

To Reconcile: Exhibit 1.5: Statement of Cash Flows:	1988

Financing Activities:

Disposition of GE shares from treasury (cash inflow)..............	$356
Purchase of GE shares for treasury (cash outflow).................	<387>
Net cash outflow....................................	<$31>

Reconciliation of the Change in Retained Earnings

Exhibit 1.3: Statement of Financial Position:	1988	1987	Increase
Retained earnings...........................	$17,950	$15,878	$ 2,072

To Reconcile: All three statements must be used (Exhibits 1.3, 1.4 and 1.5):

	1988
Net income (Exhibit 1.4)...	$ 3,386
Less: Dividends paid to GE shareholders (Exhibit 1.5; Financing Activities)...	<1,263>
Less: Dividends declared but unpaid as measured by the increase in dividends payable on the balance sheet (Exhibit 1.3), (i.e., $369 - 319 = $50 + $1 rounding error)..............	<51>
Increase in retained earnings for 1988.................	$ 2,072

Note that this reconciliation illustrates the point that the statement of cash flows does not include all changes in the balance sheet, but only those changes that result in a cash receipt or a cash disbursement. This is due to the fact that financial statements presented in accordance with GAAP are prepared on the accrual basis and not on the cash basis. These issues will be discussed in the next section, which presents the basic conceptual foundation underlying the balance sheet and the income statement.

THE CONCEPTUAL FOUNDATION FOR FINANCIAL STATEMENTS PREPARED IN ACCORDANCE WITH GENERALLY ACCEPTED ACCOUNTING PRINCIPLES

Concepts Related to the Balance Sheet

Although applicable to all financial information, the following concepts are generally identified with the balance sheet. These concepts include the historical cost concept, the going concern concept, conservatism, and the business entity concept.

The Historical Cost Concept. This principle states that assets are to be initially recorded at cost, and remain at cost until sold, consumed in operations or otherwise disposed of by the entity. Cost is the agreed upon acquisition price arrived at objectively through a bargained or "arms-length" transaction which involves a buyer and seller both attempting to maximize their own wealth.

This concept also requires that cost is the ceiling on asset valuation and assets are never carried on the financial statements at market or appraisal values, nor are they adjusted for inflation. However, if there are declines in market values, asset values can be written down under certain circumstances due to conservatism (to be discussed). It should be noted that certain industry practices (e.g., insurance), permit investment securities to be carried at their market values.

Although unrelated to current market values and irrelevant in a period of inflation, accountants continue to use historical cost valuation because it is objectively determined and subject to independent verification.

The Going Concern Concept. The going concern concept provides justification for the use of historical cost valuation. It states that, unless there is evidence to the contrary, accountants will record and report the results of transactions "as if" the entity will continue to operate for an indefinite period of time. That is, the entity will continue to operate for a period of time long enough to carry out contemplated operations, utilize existing productive capacity and liquidate outstanding obligations. This concept justifies accounting practices such as the long-term and short-term categories on a classified balance sheet, and the depreciation of plant assets for an extended period of time, such as 30 years.

As noted above, the going concern concept also justifies the use of the historical cost valuation. If the business is going to exist for an indefinite period of time, productive assets are not for sale. If the firm's productive assets are not for sale, then current market values are not relevant. Therefore, if current market values are not relevant, only historical cost-based information is useful to the reader of financial statements. Of course, if there is evidence that the business will not continue to exist (e.g., bankruptcy), then liquidation values should be used as the basis of financial statement presentation.

Conservatism. In its basic form, conservatism means that if an accountant is faced with two alternative valuation bases or different accounting methods, the accountant should select that basis or method that is least likely to overstate assets and income.

Conservatism supports historical cost in that market values above original cost cannot be used. Conservatism also represents an exception to cost because as noted above, write-downs below cost are permitted under certain conditions. Thus, the accountant would rather understate assets and income than overstate assets and income.

Nonetheless, "over-conservatism" should be avoided. In many cases a firm may take excessive write-downs to smooth income or engage in "big bath accounting", and justify this action by the principle of conservatism. For example, if a firm expects a decrease in profits or a loss in the next accounting period, they could take write-downs today in order to make next year's decrease in profit or the loss appear less dramatic, or to keep earnings on a smooth trend. In addition, if a firm is going to report a loss in the current year, they may take excessive write-downs and increase the loss even further (i.e., take a "big bath"), so as to look better or make a significant improvement in the subsequent accounting period. The philosophy underlying big bath accounting is that a two million dollar loss is just as bad as a one million dollar loss. In any event, income smoothing and big bath accounting cannot be justified by conservatism because these techniques are essentially tools used to manipulate reported earnings or to shift accounting income numbers between reporting periods.

The Business Entity Concept. The business or accounting entity concept states that all transactions and events related to the reporting entity must be kept separate and distinct from the personal affairs of the owner(s), related businesses or other outside business interests of the owner(s) of the entity.

Although disclosures of related parties and financial information of affiliated businesses may be provided in the financial statements, these entities may be kept "off-balance sheet" and make the resulting analysis of financial statements difficult.

Concepts Related to the Income Statement

The concepts relating to the income statement are concerned with revenue and expense recognition and are fundamentally integrated with the accrual basis of accounting.

The Revenue Realization Concept. According to the revenue realization concept, revenue is recognized when:

1. An exchange has taken place and

2. The earning process is "essentially complete".

The earning process is considered to be essentially complete when there are no material uncertainties as to future costs to be incurred with respect to the transaction and as to collection.

The Matching Principle. The matching principle states that expenses (costs) are to be recognized only in the period in which the related revenues (benefits) are received. For example, this principle would justify the deferral or "capitalization" of the cost of a productive asset (e.g., delivery van), and expense (i.e., depreciate) this cost only in the future when the deliveries are made and revenues are generated. In this way, the capitalized or deferred costs are allocated (matched) to future periods of expected benefit. However, if an economic resource is determined to have no future benefit, it should be expensed immediately in the period in which this determination is made. The capitalization-expense alternative will be a critical issue to be discussed throughout this book.

The Cash versus the Accrual Basis of Accounting. Under GAAP, only the accrual basis of accounting is acceptable. However, the cash basis of accounting can be used under limited circumstances or when the financial statement effect of the transaction is not material.

Under the cash basis, revenues are recognized only when cash is received and expenses are recognized only when cash is paid. This approach to revenue and expense recognition is not acceptable because it only measures cash receipts and disbursements, and does not reflect economic activity. In addition, cash basis net income can be manipulated through management or the timing of cash flows.

Under the accrual basis of accounting, revenues are recognized when earned in accordance with the revenue realization concept, and expenses are recognized when incurred in accordance with the matching principle, regardless of when the cash is received or paid. The accrual basis gives rise to accruals (i.e., the economic event is recognized before the cash event) and deferrals (i.e., the economic event is recognized after the cash event).

It should be noted that the statement of cash flows is not a violation of the accrual basis of accounting. Rather, this statement should be viewed as presenting the cash flows that result from the firm's economic activities properly recognized under the accrual basis of accounting.

ORGANIZATION OF THE TEXT

Part I of this book provides a detailed analysis of corporate financial position. The corporate balance sheet is disaggregated and an in-depth discussion of assets, debt and stockholders' equity is provided.

In Part II, a discussion of critical issues in current corporate financial reporting is provided. In this discussion, complex areas such as accounting for income taxes, earnings per share, intercorporate investments and business combinations, and accounting for leases are presented.

Finally, in Part III, issues relating to full disclosure are discussed. Areas such as accounting changes and discontinued operations are analyzed in detail. The statement of cash flows is examined in the last chapter of this book.

Throughout the discussion of these areas, detailed illustrations are provided and an equation analysis is used to reflect the impact of a particular event or transaction on the three basic general purpose financial statements where appropriate. In addition, cases are provided at the end of each chapter. The cases are designed to provide practical application of the analytical issues addressed in the chapter.

NOTES

1. For a detailed discussion of this topic see American Institute of Certified Public Accountants, <u>Objectives of Financial Statements</u> (New York: AICPA, 1973) and Financial Accounting Standards Board, Statement of Financial Accounting Concepts No. 1, <u>Objectives of Financial Reporting by Business Enterprises</u> (Stamford, CT: FASB, 1978).

2. Donald E. Kieso and Jerry J. Weygandt, <u>Intermediate Accounting</u> (New York: John Wiley & Sons, Inc., 1989), 8 - 9.

3. American Institute of Certified Public Accountants, <u>Objectives of Financial Statements</u> (New York: AICPA, 1973), 17.

Part I

An Analysis of Corporate Financial Position

2

Corporate Assets: Special
Accounting and Reporting Issues

INTRODUCTION

The classified balance sheet is the most common means of reporting corporate financial position. On the classified balance sheet, assets and liabilities are segregated into their current and noncurrent components. This classification assists the analyst in determining liquidity through matching the maturities of current assets with current liabilities.

The present chapter focuses on special accounting and reporting issues relating to corporate assets. In the analysis of corporate assets, a review of the basic principles of accounting for areas such as accounts receivable, inventory and plant assets is provided. Readers familiar with the more basic accounting areas can omit these sections of the chapter. After the basic review, more complex issues such as the LIFO-FIFO switch and capitalization of interest will be discussed. Corporate debt will be presented in the next chapter.

THE CURRENT ASSET SECTION OF THE BALANCE SHEET

Current assets are defined as assets that are reasonably expected to be converted into cash, sold or consumed within one year or operating cycle, whichever is longer. The operating cycle is the "cash-to-cash" cycle of the firm. A typical operating cycle is illustrated in the following diagram.

```
     |----|   |---------|   |----|   |-------------------|   |----|
|--->|Cash|-->|Inventory|-->|Sale|-->|Accounts Receivable|-->|Cash|--->|
|    |----|   |---------|   |----|   |-------------------|   |----|    |
|                                                                      |
|<----------<-----------<-----------<----------<----------<----------<--|
                 \
                  \                |-------------------|
                   \               |   Excess Cash is  |
                    \<---------->| Invested in       |
                                   |Marketable Securities|
                                   |-------------------|
```

A firm will usually complete more than one operating cycle per year. However, in some industries such as distilling or shipbuilding it may take longer than one year to complete a single operating cycle.

The operating cycle is a critical concept in the analysis of financial statements and can be measured through the application of some basic financial ratios. Converting the inventory turnover ratio into the number of days supply on hand or the "holding interval", and converting the accounts receivable turnover ratio into number of days sales in receivables or the "collection interval", provides the analyst with the variables needed to determine the length of the operating cycle. The holding interval measures the number of days from the acquisition or production of inventory to the point of sale. The collection interval measures the number of days required to convert the accounts receivable back into cash. The length of the operating cycle is the sum of the holding interval and the collection interval. The holding interval, the collection interval and the length of the operating cycle should be compared for the same firm over time, and it should also be assessed through comparison with some industry standard.

Due to the importance of the operating cycle, the key topics in the analysis of current assets are cash, accounts receivable and the bad debt expense, investments in marketable securities, and accounting for inventory.

Cash

Cash is the only asset without valuation problems. However, proper classification can be an issue. Cash is classified as current unless it is restricted from use in the current operating cycle. Restrictions on withdrawal, and therefore limitations on use, in the current operating cycle include foreign bank accounts, escrow accounts and bond sinking funds. When cash is restricted from use in the current operating cycle, it must be reclassified out of the regular cash line item on the balance sheet. Generally an account entitled "restricted funds" is used to indicate that there is some limitation on the use of cash. If the restriction extends beyond one year from the balance sheet date, the restricted funds account is classified as a noncurrent asset and is included in the Other Assets section of the balance sheet. If the restriction is for less than one year, the restricted funds account could still be classified as current, but segregated from the regular cash line item in the Current Assets section of the balance sheet.

In addition to the above mentioned restrictions, cash may also be segregated due to compensating balances. Compensating balances are minimum cash balances that are "required" to be kept on deposit by debtors as support for existing credit agreements.

The key issue surrounding compensating balance requirements is also classification. According to the SEC, if the compensating balances are legally restricted, similar to an escrow account, and held against short-term debt, the cash held as a compensating balance must be reclassified as another current asset. On the other hand, if the balance is held against long-term debt, the amount of cash held as a compensating balance must be reclassified as a noncurrent asset on the balance sheet. In either case, the legally restricted compensating balances cannot be combined with regular cash on the balance sheet.

If the compensating balances are not legally restricted, the amounts, terms and length of the arrangement must be disclosed in footnotes to the financial statements. However, a classification out of regular cash is not required. A sample compensating footnote disclosure is presented in Exhibit 2.1.

In those cases where compensating balances exist but the amount of cash is not legally restricted, the amount of available cash and liquidity may be overstated by use of conventional measures of liquidity. Although firms consider compensating balances as part of their minimum operating cash balances, these funds may not actually be available for use in the current operating cycle. That is, even if the compensating balances are not legally restricted from withdrawal, the firm may be reluctant to draw down a compensating balance because this action may result in technical default of the loan agreement or may seriously impair the firm's future credit standing. In the case of the Newell Company and Subsidiaries in Exhibit 2.1, the extent of "restricted" cash can be estimated by multiplying the compensating balance percentage by the amount of the lines of credit subject to compensating balance requirements. For the Newell Company, $251,050 (i.e., 5% x $5,021,000) of the total cash balance reported as regular cash in the current asset section of the balance sheet at year end may not be available for use in the current operating cycle, or from a conservative standpoint, may not be considered by the analyst to be as "liquid" as regular cash. The analyst can also use this information to obtain a range of available cash balances in the assessment of liquidity (i.e., cash with and without the compensating balance requirement). In any event, the existence of compensating balance restrictions indicates some deterioration of the firm's credit rating.

Accounts Receivable and the Bad Debt Expense

In accounting for accounts receivable, or any asset with valuation issues, there are two major purposes or objectives.

1. The Balance Sheet Purpose: to properly value the asset at its net realizable value (NRV), which is the amount that is reasonably expected to be realized in cash. In addition, this objective includes proper classification as either current or noncurrent, depending on the expected timing of the cash

EXHIBIT 2.1

Credit Arrangements

The Company has lines of credit with various banks
to provide short-term financing.

Under the line of credit arrangements, the Company
may borrow up to $52,500,000 (of which $47,500,000 was
available at December 31, 1987), based on such terms as the
Company and the respective banks have mutually agreed
upon. While the arrangements do not have termination
dates, the terms are reviewed and revised periodically.

In connection with $21,000,000 of these line of credit
arrangements, the Company has agreed to maintain compensating balances, generally at 5% of the line of credit.
Compensating balances are not legally restricted as to with-
drawals and serve as part of the Company's minimum
operating cash balances.

A summary of short-term borrowing activity follows:

$ in Thousands	1987	1986	1985
Notes payable to banks:			
Outstanding at year-end			
—borrowing	$ 5,021	$ 8,861	$ 9,540
—average interest rate	7.9%	7.3%	9.4%
Average for the year			
—borrowing	$21,061	$15,615	$ 4,237
—average interest rate	6.9%	9.4%	10.0%
Maximum borrowing out-			
standing during the year	$53,075	$46,000	$23,250
Commercial paper:			
Outstanding at year-end			
—borrowing	—	$ 8,430	$10,561
—average interest rate	—	6.3%	8.1%
Average for the year			
—borrowing	$ 4,086	$ 7,463	$ 8,778
—average interest rate	6.5%	7.1%	7.9%
Maximum borrowing out-			
standing during the year	$13,000	$11,488	$11,018

----

realization.

2. The Income Statement Purpose: to properly match costs with revenues.

As will be noted throughout the discussion of corporate assets, there is generally a trade-off between these two objectives.

Specifically for accounts receivable, the valuation issue relates to the amount of cash ultimately expected to be collected. For all sales on credit, a firm must reasonably expect some uncollectible accounts. This is a cost or expense of doing business on credit. The loss from uncollectible accounts is known as the bad debt expense.

There are two methods to account for the bad debt expense:

1. The direct write-off method (the tax method);

2. The allowance method (the GAAP method).

The Direct Write-Off Method. Under the direct write-off, no provision is made for the expected losses from uncollectible accounts in the year of the sale. The bad debt expense is only recognized during the period in which the account is actually determined to be uncollectible. This could be several accounting periods after the sale was made.

The direct write-off method is only used for tax purposes. It can be used for financial reporting only if accounts receivable and the bad debt expense are immaterial to the financial position and operating results of the firm. However, in most cases the direct write-off method is not generally accepted. The direct write-off method is not used for GAAP purposes because it is said to violate the two objectives of accounting for receivables as noted above. In the year of the sale, the direct write-off method overstates assets by failing to provide a provision against the balance of accounts receivable to reduce its net realizable value, and overstates reported profit by not charging income for the expected loss from bad debts. For these reasons, the direct write-off method does not properly value the receivable and it does not match costs with revenues in the year of the sale. In addition, in the year of the write-off, income is reduced for a bad debt relating to sales revenue generated in a prior period. Again, there is a mismatch of costs and revenues. It is for these reasons that GAAP requires the use of the allowance method.

The Allowance Method. The allowance method is required under GAAP. It is not acceptable for income tax purposes, except for commercial banks with assets under $500 million dollars.

Under the allowance method, the bad debt expense is estimated and charged against income in the year of the sale in order to match costs with revenues. This is considered proper matching because the cost of selling on credit is matched with the additional sales generated only because the firm extends credit to its customers. The other side of the bad debt expense estimate is to create an allowance (i.e., a provision, a "cushion" or a "reserve") for the ultimate failure to collect the receivable. The allowance account is deducted from the gross accounts receivable balance so as to properly value accounts receivable at its net realizable value (i.e., the amount reasonably expected to be realized in cash). The allowance account is considered a "contra asset account" and must be offset against accounts receivable on the balance sheet so that "accounts receivable, net" is reported in the financial statements.

The allowance account provides a cushion against future write-offs. In the year in which an account is actually determined to be uncollectible, the account is written off against the allowance. The write-off under the allowance method reduces the allowance account and the balance of accounts receivable (i.e., it has no effect on net realizable value). However, there is no income statement impact from the write-off under the allowance method because income was already reduced by the estimated bad debt expense in the year of the sale. The differences between the direct write-off method and the allowance method are illustrated in the following equation analysis.

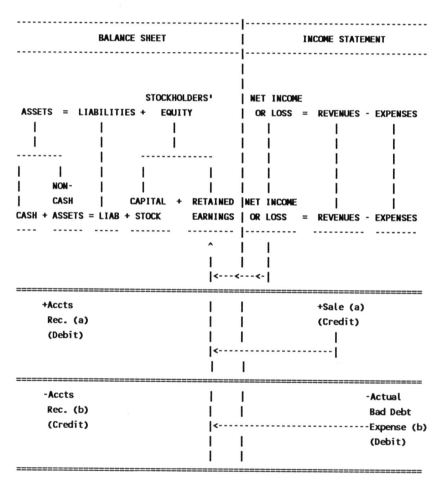

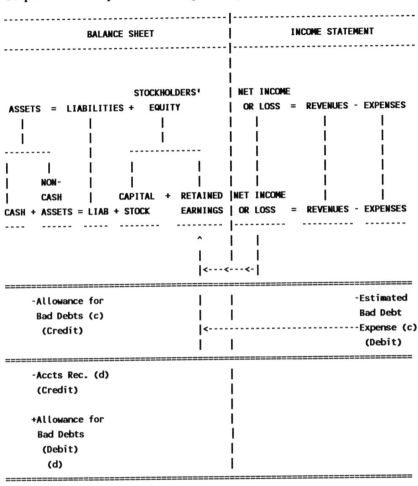

(a) Entry to record the sale of merchandise on credit.
(b) Entry to write-off a bad debt under the direct write-off method in the
     year in which the account is determined to be uncollectible.
(c) Entry to record the estimated bad debt provision under the allowance
     method in the year of the sale.
(d) Entry to write-off an account under the allowance method in the year in
     which the account is determined to be uncollectible.

A simple numerical illustration of accounting for bad debts under the direct
write-off and allowance methods is presented in Exhibit 2.2. Note that in both the
above equation analysis and in Exhibit 2.2 there are no cash flow implications for
accounting for uncollectible accounts.

In Exhibit 2.2 it is assumed that $1,000 in credit sales are made in 1988 and
there is no business activity in 1989. The bad debt expense is the firm's only operating expense. It is also assumed that a customer owing $10 declares bankruptcy in

EXHIBIT 2.2

Illustration: Comparison of the Direct Write-Off and the Allowance Methods of Accounting for the Bad Debts Expense

---

Partial Financial Statements:

	Direct Write-Off Method (TAX)		Allowance Method (GAAP)	
Income Statements	---	---	---	---
------------------	1988	1989	1988	1989
Credit Sales......	$1,000	$ 0	$1,000	$ 0
Less: Bad Debts				
Expense.....	< 0 >	<10> Actual	< 10> Est.	0 (c)
	-------	------- (a)	-------- (b) -----	
Net Income <Loss>.	$1,000	$<10>	$ 990	$ 0
	======	=====	=======	=====
Balance Sheets	1988	1989	1988	1989

Accounts Rec......	$1,000	$ 990 (a)	$1,000	$ 990 (c)
Less: Allowance				
for Bad				
Debts.......	N/A	N/A	< 10> (b)	< 0 >(c)
	-------	--------	--------	-------
Net Realizable				
Value.............	$1,000	$ 990	$ 990	$ 990
	======	======	=======	=======
Stockholders'				
Equity Section:				
Retained Earnings.	$1,000	$ 990	$ 990	$ 990
	======	======	=======	=======

(a) A write-off of a bad debt under the direct write-off method reduces both income and accounts receivable in the year in which the account is determined to be uncollectible. No adjustment is made in the year of sale.

(b) Under the allowance method, an estimate of the uncollectible accounts is made in the year of the sale and is charged against income and retained earnings. The estimate is also provided for in the allowance for bad debts and is deducted from accounts receivable to carry accounts receivable at net realizable value.

Exhibit 2.2, continued

(c) A write-off of a bad debt under the allowance method reduces the allowance (i.e., provision) for bad debts and accounts receivable. As a result, when an account is written off under the allowance method, there is no effect on income and the net realizable value of accounts receivable remains unchanged. The write-off is made against a provision or cushion that was created in the year of the sale, at which time an expense was charged against income so as to match costs and revenues.

1989. If we assume that the direct write-off method is used, the 1988 financial statements reflect $1,000 in both income and assets. In 1989, the firm reports a net loss of $10 under the direct write-off method, although there is no economic activity during this year. Not only are assets and income overstated in 1988, but income is understated in 1989. Thus the use of the direct write-off method results in improper asset valuation and a mismatching of costs with revenues.

If the allowance method is used, a provision for estimated bad debts is made in 1988, the year of the sale, which reduces both assets and reported income. In 1989, when the account actually becomes uncollectible, the customer's account is written off against the provision created in 1988. The income statement correctly reflects no activity in 1989 and the balance sheet for the period is unchanged. This approach properly matches costs and revenues and carries the balance of accounts receivable at its net realizable value.

This illustration assumed that there were no estimation errors under the allowance method. However, estimation errors would not affect the basic principles of accounting for bad debts. If estimation errors occur, they would be corrected on a prospective basis where the future year's provision for bad debts would reflect both the current year's requirements as well as an adjustment for prior period estimation errors.

Although the allowance method is favored under GAAP because it better satisfies accounting and reporting objectives, the use of the allowance method results in several problems for analysts. First, there is a great deal of judgement and subjectivity in the bad debt estimate. This problem is compounded by the fact that there are no GAAP methods of estimation. In other words, GAAP is satisfied if the allowance method is used but the method used to estimate the bad debt expense is at the discretion of management. Common estimation methods used in practice include a percentage of credit sales, a percentage of the accounts receivable balance, an analysis of an aging of accounts receivable and a combination of several methods. The method used to estimate the bad debt expense can significantly affect reported net income and the net realizable value of accounts receivable on the balance sheet. However, no matter which method is used to account for the bad debt expense or to estimate the allowance for bad debts, there is no effect on cash flow.

Second, there are usually inadequate disclosures regarding the techniques used to estimate the allowance for bad debts. A footnote disclosure would be required only if the firm changes its estimation method and if that change results in a material effect on reported income. The lack of adequate disclosures coupled with the highly subjective nature of the estimation used increases the accounting risk and reduces the quality of reported earnings associated with the accounting for uncollectible accounts.

Other Issues in Accounting for Receivables

Pledging, Assigning and Factoring Accounts Receivable. Pledging, assigning or factoring of accounts receivable can be used by a firm to convert their receivables into immediate cash.

When a firm "pledges" accounts receivable, the accounts receivable are pledged as collateral for a financing arrangement. The "assignment" of accounts receivable is also used in a borrowing arrangement, except that when accounts receivable are assigned, the receivables are still pledged as collateral for the loan but the receipts on collection of the receivables are used to pay down the debt. In either case, the accounts receivable are not removed from the current asset section of the balance sheet. Instead, footnotes to the financial statements indicate the contingent liability related to the transfer of the accounts receivable rights to others. Nevertheless, the analyst must consider the potential adverse effects on liquidity from a default on the debt relating to the receivables pledged or assigned to third parties.

In the case of a "factoring" of accounts receivable, the accounts receivable are sold at a discount to a third party called a factor. Here, customers are instructed to remit payments directly to the factor. The accounting and reporting issues for factoring accounts receivable depend on whether the receivables are sold with or without recourse.

If the receivables are sold without recourse, the transaction is considered an outright sale and the accounts receivable are removed from the books and the related gain or loss on the transaction is recorded. The gain or loss is measured as the difference between the net proceeds on the sale and the face amount of the receivables factored. If the receivables are factored with recourse, the risk of loss and collection remains with the seller. Here there is a question as to the underlying nature of the transaction. Is it a sale or a loan? The answer to this question is provided by FASB Statement No. 77, "Reporting by Transferors for Transfers of Receivables with Recourse".

Under SFAS 77, paragraph 5, a transfer of accounts receivable with recourse can be accounted for and reported as a sale with the gain or loss recognized, if all three of the following criteria are met:

1. The seller transfers all control of the economic benefits from the receivables. An option requiring the seller to repurchase the receivables at some future date would violate the criterion of surrendering all control to the factor.

2. The seller's obligation under the recourse provisions can be reasonably estimated.

3. The purchaser of the receivables cannot require the seller to repurchase the receivables.

If the seller does not meet all three criteria, the amount of the proceeds for the transfer of the receivables is recorded and is reported as a liability. A sale cannot be recorded and the amount of receivables transferred remains in the current asset section of the balance sheet.

For the factoring of accounts receivable with recourse accounted for as a sale, SFAS 77, paragraph 9, requires the following disclosures:

1. The proceeds received for each income statement presented;

2. If the information is available, the balance of the factored receivables that remains uncollected at the date of each balance sheet presented.

Although the provisions of SFAS 77 provide guidance as to the appropriate accounting and reporting of a transfer of receivables with recourse, it sanctions a form of off-balance sheet financing.[1] When a transfer is made with recourse and that transfer is recorded as a sale, the liability is never reflected on the balance sheet. However, the seller's exposure to the risk on the transaction is no different from a primary debtor in a lending agreement. As a result, the analyst should carefully examine the footnotes to the financial statements in order to determine the extent of off-balance sheet financing resulting from factoring of accounts receivable with recourse.

Imputed Interest on Sales Using Notes Receivable. According to APB Opinion No. 21, "Interest on Receivables and Payables", when goods and services are exchanged for a note receivable, the interest rate is assumed to be fair unless:

1. No interest rate is stated;

2. The stated amount of interest is unreasonable;

3. The face amount of the note receivable is materially different from the cash price of the goods or services provided or from the market value of the note.

When any of these conditions exist, it is difficult to determine the separate amounts of the sales revenue and financing income earned on the transaction. Opinion 21 provides guidance as to the appropriate accounting for these types of notes receivable transactions.

If the current cash price of the goods or services provided is known, the sales revenue is set equal to the cash price. The difference between the face amount of the note receivable and the sales value is considered to be deferred interest income (i.e., discount on notes receivable) and is amortized to interest income over the life of the loan. At the end of each accounting period, the carrying value of the note receivable is reported as the face amount of the note less the unamortized balance of the deferred interest income.

If the goods or services have no established market so that a cash price cannot be determined, the sales value recorded is set equal to the present value of the note. The present value of the note is determined by discounting the principal and interest (if any) at an imputed rate of interest. The imputed interest rate is a rate of interest that approximates that rate which would have resulted from an independent transaction under similar circumstances. Therefore, the imputation of a rate of interest requires consideration of factors such as the debtor's credit rating, the prime rate, and the rate on similar sources of financing by the debtor.

The difference between the face amount of the note receivable and the sales value (i.e., the present value of the note discounted at the imputed rate of interest) is considered deferred interest income (i.e., discount on notes receivable). The deferred interest income is amortized to income over the life of the loan. At each balance sheet date, the notes receivable are presented net of the unamortized discount. According to Opinion 21, the deferred interest income should be amortized by using the effective interest rate method of amortization. This method of amortization will be illustrated in the discussion of long-term debt in the next chapter.

Investments in Marketable Securities

The standards of accounting and reporting for investments in marketable securities are set forth in FASB Statement No. 12, "Accounting for Certain Marketable Securities". SFAS 12 is required only for investments in equity securities but may be applied to investments in debt securities on a voluntary basis. The provisions of SFAS 12, paragraph 8, require the valuation of the aggregate portfolio of investments in marketable securities at the lower of cost or market (LCM). Because the provisions of SFAS 12 apply equally to the short-term and the long-term aggregate portfolios, the accounting and reporting standards for both the current and noncurrent portfolios will be discussed in this section.

Portfolio Classification. The classification of a portfolio of marketable securities depends on management's intention or purpose for the investment. Short-term or temporary investments are acquired by using excess cash from the operating cycle without disrupting normal operations. Here, it is management's intention to liquidate these investments and return the cash to operations when needed. The investment is made in order to receive a greater rate of return than if the cash is held idle.

The long-term or permanent portfolio is acquired for a specific purpose, such as a permanent source of dividend or interest income. It is management's intention to hold these securities for an extended period of time.

As noted above, both portfolios must be accounted for at LCM. At acquisition, the investments are recorded at cost, which includes the purchase price plus commissions and all other transaction costs. At the end of each accounting period subsequent to acquisition, the valuation of the portfolio must be adjusted for both temporary fluctuations in the value of the aggregate portfolio and permanent and significant declines in the value of an individual security within a portfolio.

Temporary Market Fluctuations in the Value of the Aggregate Portfolio. In the application of the SFAS 12 LCM rules, the accountant must compare the aggregate cost to the aggregate market value of the portfolio at the end of each accounting period. The aggregate market value is determined by multiplying the closing stock prices from the Wall Street Journal by the number of shares held of each security included in the portfolio at the balance sheet date. The comparison of aggregate cost to aggregate market results in the application of the following procedures.

1. If the aggregate market exceeds the aggregate cost, no adjustment is made and the portfolio is carried at cost. However, the market value is disclosed either parenthetically on the balance sheet or in a footnote to the financial statements.

2. If the aggregate cost exceeds the aggregate market value of the portfolio, a write-down to market is required. On the balance sheet, an allowance (i.e., a contra-asset account) is created and offsets the cost of the portfolio to bring the portfolio down to market. If the portfolio is classified as short-term, an unrealized loss is recognized on the current income statement. In

the case of the noncurrent portfolio, management does not intend to liquidate the portfolio in the short run, and as a result, the probability of realization of the loss is minimal. Therefore, the unrealized loss for the long-
term portfolio is reported as a negative element of stockholders' equity on
the balance sheet. This negative stockholders' equity account is usually
called an "unrealized loss on marketable securities, noncurrent". This is one
of several valuation adjustment accounts reported as an element of stockholders' equity.

With the portfolio carried at market, the historical cost is disclosed either
parenthetically on the balance sheet or in a footnote to the financial statements.

3. After a write-down to market, subsequent recoveries are permitted, but
   only to the extent of previously recognized unrealized losses. That is, the
   portfolio cannot be written up above original historical cost. If there is a
   market recovery, the allowance account is reduced on the balance sheet
   (increasing the carrying value of the portfolio). An unrealized gain is
   recognized on the income statement if the portfolio is classified as short-
   term. If the portfolio is classified as long-term, the market recovery is given
   recognition through a reduction of the unrealized loss account in the
   stockholders' equity section of the balance sheet. Because management
   does not intend to liquidate the long-term portfolio there is a small probability of realizing the gain in cash in the short run. Therefore, the gain
   should not be reported as income and is reflected as a reduction of the
   unrealized loss account in the stockholders' equity section.

4. If an individual security is sold from either the short-term or the long-term
   portfolio, the difference between the net proceeds on the sale (i.e., selling
   price less transactions costs) and the original historical cost is recognized
   on the income statement as a realized gain or loss. The allowance account
   is not affected at the time of the sale because the allowance is applied
   against the aggregate portfolio and not against any individual security. The
   fact that a security is no longer in the portfolio will impact the year end
   adjustment in applying the SFAS 12 LCM rules.

Permanent and Significant Declines in the Value of an Individual Security. If
there is a permanent and significant decline in the market value of an individual
security within either portfolio, a realized loss is recognized on the income statement and the security is written down directly without regard to the allowance
account. Subsequent recoveries are not permitted for write-downs resulting from
permanent and significant declines.

It should be noted that if investments in marketable debt securities are not
voluntarily accounted for under the provisions of SFAS 12, they must be carried at
cost, unless there has been a permanent and significant decline in their market
value.

Transfers of Individual Securities Between Portfolios. The transfer of an individual security between the short-term and long-term portfolios must be made at LCM. According to SFAS 12, paragraph 10, if a write-down to market is required on the transfer, it must be accounted for as a realized loss as if it was a permanent and significant decline.

The financial statement effects of accounting for marketable securities are presented in the following equation analysis.

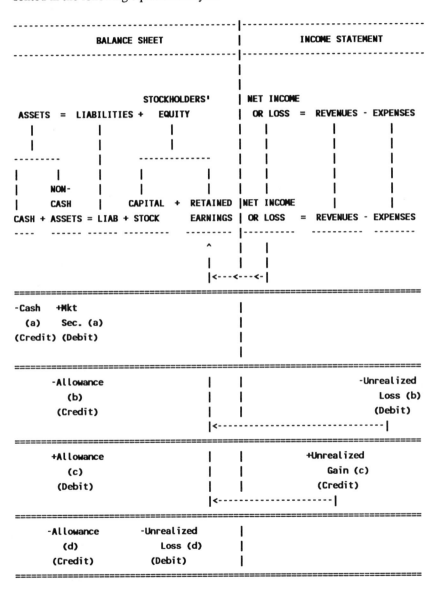

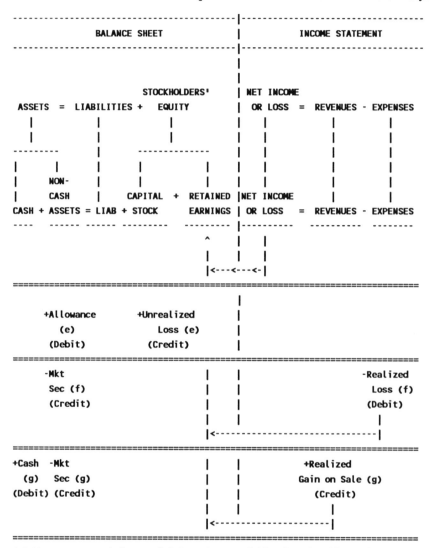

(a) Entry to record the acquisition of a portfolio of marketable equity
    securities.
(b) Entry to record an unrealized loss on the aggregate short-term portfolio.
(c) Entry to record an unrealized gain (i.e., a market recovery) on the
    aggregate short-term portfolio.
(d) Entry to record an unrealized loss on the aggregate long-term portfolio.
    Note that for the long-term portfolio, the unrealized loss is a deduction
    from total stockholders' equity.
(e) Entry to record an unrealized gain (i.e., a market recovery) on the
    aggregate long-term portfolio. Note that for the long-term portfolio, a
    market recovery is recorded as a reduction of the unrealized loss account.
    There is no unrealized gain account. However, the effect of the market

recovery is to increase total stockholders' equity.
(f) Entry to record a realized loss on a permanent and significant decline for an individual security in either portfolio or to record a realized loss on a transfer between portfolios.
(g) Entry to record the sale of an individual security from either portfolio at a gain. If the sale was at a loss, both income and retained earnings would be reduced.
==

A numerical illustration for the SFAS 12 lower of cost or market rules is presented in Exhibit 2.3. Sample balance sheet and footnote disclosures for the short-term and long-term portfolios of marketable securities for the Loral Corporation and Subsidiaries are presented in Exhibit 2.4.

The Mark-to-Market Proposal. The SFAS 12 lower of cost or market rules are generally applicable to nonregulated companies. Insurance companies are permitted to value investment portfolios at market. When valuing the portfolio of securites at market changes in the market value of the investment, both above and below historical cost, are recognized in the financial statements.

Many financial institutions carry their portfolios of investment securities at historical cost or lower of cost or market. With the recent debacle in the savings and loan industry, regulators have expressed concern over the practice of carrying investment portfolios at historical cost. Although the difference between the market value of investments and original cost is disclosed in the footnotes to the financial statements, losses are not reflected on the income statement. Many security analysts are concerned with this practice because banks could adopt the cost approach used by many savings and loans and bury securities whose price had declined by placing them in the aggregate portfolio of marketable securities.

As a result of a recent study conducted by the American Institute of Certified Public Accountants (AICPA), the SEC has recommended a change from the historical cost model to "mark-to-market" or market-based accounting for financial institutions. The primary objective of the SEC proposal is to have investment securities held by financial institutions carried at market value rather than at historical cost or lower of cost or market, and to recognize all losses on security investments in the current income statement.

Inventories

In the analysis of inventory, the primary accounting and reporting issues focus on the components of the total inventory. The components of total inventory consist of the units to be included in the ending inventory, the composition of unit cost, the allocation of unit cost to the units in ending inventory and to the units sold, a change in the allocation method used, and the amount of obsolete or slow-moving items included in ending inventory. These issues will be discussed in the following sections of this chapter.

Units Included in Ending Inventory. The units to be included in ending inventory are ultimately determined by physical count. Either a perpetual or periodic inventory system can be used for the determination and control of the physical quantities in

EXHIBIT 2.3

Illustration: The Lower of Cost or Market Rule for Marketable Equity Securities

---

Portfolio of Marketable Equity Securities (MES):

Security	Acquisition Cost At 6/11/90	Market Value at 12/31/90	Market Value at 12/31/91	Market Value at 12/31/92
IBM.............	$ 5,000	$ 6,500	$ 4,000	$ 5,000
GM..............	8,000	7,000	6,000	8,000
Mobil...........	3,000	4,000	2,000	2,000
Xerox...........	10,000	5,500	13,000	15,000
Aggregate Portfolio	$26,000	$23,000	$25,000	$30,000

```
                   |              |            |           |
                   |   <$3,000>   |   $2,000   |   $1,000  |
                   |--------------|------------|-----------|
                   | Unrealized Loss |    Market Recoveries  |
                   |-------------------------------------------|
```

Balance Sheet Presentation for Both the Short-Term and Long-Term Portfolios:

LCM Valuation:	1990	1991	1992
Cost.......................................	$26,000	$26,000	$26,000
Less: Valuation Allowance (To Write MES Down to Market).....................	<3,000>	<1,000>	< 0 >
LCM Valuation on the Balance Sheet........	$23,000	$25,000	$26,000
	Market	Market	Cost

44

Exhibit 2.3, continued

Parenthetical or Footnote Disclosure:

	1990	1991	1992
	$26,000	$26,000	$30,000
	Cost	Cost	Market
	=======	=======	=======

Presentation of Unrealized Loss or Gain:

	1990	1991	1992
If the portfolio is Short Term:			
Other Income <Expense> on the Income Statement	<$3,000>	$ 2,000	$ 1,000
	=======	=======	=======
	Unrealized	Unrealized	
	Loss	Gains	

If the portfolio is Long Term:
Cumulative Valuation Adjustment to Stockholders'
Equity (Unrealized Loss or Contra-Equity

Account)	<$3,000>	<$1,000>	$ 0
	=======	=======	=======

EXHIBIT 2.4

Sample Disclosure: Loral Corporation and Subsidiaries: Balance Sheet and Footnote Disclosures of Marketable Securities

Loral Corporation And Subsidiaries As Of March 31, 1985 and 1984
CONSOLIDATED BALANCE SHEETS

Assets:	1985	1984
Current assets:		
Cash and marketable securities (Note 3)	$ 48,293,000	$ 39,674,000
Accounts receivable on U.S. Government and other defense contracts	59,930,000	61,004,000
Accounts receivable	19,730,000	13,233,000
Unbilled contract receivables (Notes 1 and 4)	36,697,000	21,696,000
Inventories (Notes 1 and 4):		
Costs accumulated under contracts, less progress payments	86,816,000	75,240,000
Industrial	21,958,000	19,493,000
Other current assets	4,058,000	3,089,000
Total current assets	277,482,000	233,429,000
Marketable securities, non-current (Note 3)	26,089,000	27,303,000
Property, plant and equipment (Notes 1 and 5)	212,525,000	171,789,000
Less accumulated depreciation and amortization	68,324,000	52,607,000
	144,201,000	119,182,000
Cost in excess of net assets acquired, less amortization (Notes 1 and 2)	29,072,000	21,004,000
Other assets (Note 8)	14,294,000	11,909,000
	$491,138,000	$412,827,000

Liabilities and Shareholders' Equity:	1985	1984
Current liabilities:		
Current portion of long-term debt (Note 6)	$ 1,113,000	$ 464,000
Accounts payable, trade	44,486,000	40,620,000
Contract advances in excess of cost	17,568,000	13,980,000
Accrued salaries and wages	19,768,000	17,434,000
Other current liabilities	15,586,000	13,379,000
Income taxes (Note 7)	70,278,000	39,152,000
Total current liabilities	168,799,000	125,029,000
Deferred income taxes (Note 7)	29,816,000	30,527,000
Long-term debt (Note 6)	32,408,000	32,325,000
Commitments (Note 9)		
Shareholders' equity (Note 8):		
Common stock, $.25 par value; authorized, 30,000,000 shares, issued 23,540,398 and 23,272,284 shares	5,885,000	5,818,000
Capital surplus	104,070,000	98,581,000
Retained earnings	156,755,000	125,634,000
	266,710,000	230,033,000
Less:		
Treasury stock, at cost (185,119 and 168,389 shares)	4,674,000	4,380,000
Unrealized loss on marketable securities, non-current (Note 3)	1,921,000	707,000
Total shareholders' equity	260,115,000	224,946,000
	$491,138,000	$412,827,000

See notes to consolidated financial statements.

46

Exhibit 2.4, continued

NOTES TO CONSOLIDATED FINANCIAL STATEMENTS (Continued)

---

3 Cash and Marketable Securities:

At March 31, 1985 and 1984, cash and marketable securities consisted of the following:

	1985	1984
Cash	$ 2,361,000	$ 6,139,000
Marketable securities:		
Current, at cost which approximates market:		
U.S. Government Securities		11,854,000
Time and Certificates of Deposit	20,103,000	
Commercial paper (General Motors Acceptance Corporation: $11,985,000 at March 31, 1965)	14,670,000	12,550,000
Other	11,159,000	9,131,000
	$48,293,000	$39,674,000
Non-current, at lower of cost or market (Cost: $28,010,000)	$26,089,000	$27,303,000

Non-current marketable securities represent investments, made during 1983, in adjustable rate preferred stock issued by various large financial institutions. A valuation allowance, representing the unrealized excess of cost over market value of these equity securities, was charged to shareholders' equity. This valuation allowance of $1,921,000 at March 31, 1985, reflects unrealized losses of $2,281,000 offset by unrealized gains of $360,000. The valuation allowance increased by $1,214,000 during 1985, and was charged to shareholders' equity. The potential tax benefit of the unrealized capital loss has not been recognized.

Source: Loral Corporation 1985 Annual Report. Copyright, 1985, by the Loral Corporation. Reprinted with permission.

inventory throughout the accounting period.

Under a perpetual inventory system, inventory accounts are continually updated for acquisitions and sales of inventory, and the cost of goods sold is determined and charged against income after each sale. Regardless of how reliable the perpetual system is, a physical count of inventory must be taken at least once a year to verify the accuracy of the perpetual records.

If a periodic inventory system is used, the balance in inventory is only determined at the end of the accounting period by physical count and the cost of goods sold is determined by the formula to be discussed below. Obviously, a pure periodic system is not very effective in controlling inventory. Therefore, a hybrid system is usually employed whereby inventory is controlled internally by management through the use of a perpetual system, and a periodic system is used for financial reporting purposes.

Determination of Unit Cost. The unit cost of an item in inventory consists of the invoice price or manufacturing costs, plus all "reasonable and necessary" expenditures required to have the inventory item in its existing condition and location. Reasonable and necessary expenditures include transportation costs, packaging, etc. There is a great deal of discretion as to what constitutes a reasonable and necessary expenditure. If management considers a cost to be reasonable and necessary, it is capitalized as part of the unit cost of inventory. On the other hand, if the expenditure is not considered reasonable and necessary, it is charged to expense immediately.

When these costs are capitalized, current assets (i.e., inventory) increase and there will be no effect on reported profit until the item is sold. If the cost is expensed as incurred, income is reduced in the current period. As a result, identical firms taking different positions as to what is considered a reasonable and necessary expenditure will report different net incomes and different inventory values. A firm's capitalization policy may influence decision making because inventory could be the basis for collateral on a loan. In addition, the increased earnings resulting from capitalization could be used in the determination of a firm's ability to repay debt and to distribute dividends. Unfortunately for the analyst, there is generally little disclosure as to the composition of the unit cost of inventory. However, a footnote would be required if the firm changed its capitalization policy with respect to inventory costs, and that change had a material effect on inventory valuation and reported net income and earnings per share.

The Allocation of Unit Cost to the Items Included in Ending Inventory. The "allocation problem in inventory" is one of the most important issues in accounting. The allocation problem consists of identification of the units remaining in ending inventory and the units sold, and the assignment or allocation of a unit cost to the units in ending inventory and to the units sold. The allocation problem is illustrated in Exhibit 2.5.

The allocation problem can also be illustrated by the cost of goods sold formula used in a periodic inventory system.

```
Beginning inventory........................$  2,000

Add: Purchases or the cost of goods
     manufactured.............................  58,000
                                            ----------
Goods available for sale...................$ 60,000

Less: Ending inventory.........................  <  ?  >
                                            ----------

Cost of goods sold........................$    ?
                                            =========
```

The above formula points out the significance of the valuation assigned to ending inventory. Depending on management's reporting objectives, an allocation method can be used to overstate or understate inventory, which in turn will be directly related to reported net income and earnings per share.

If management selects an allocation method that increases ending inventory, assets will be increased, cost of goods sold will be reduced and reported income will increase. Conversely, an allocation method that reduces the valuation of ending inventory will reduce total assets, overstate cost of goods sold and understate net income. It should be noted that the ending inventory of the current year becomes the beginning inventory of the next year. Therefore, depending on the level of inventory and unit costs in the subsequent year, the income effects could reverse in the next accounting period. Management may also have quite different objectives in selecting an allocation method for tax purposes. The tax consequences relating to the choice of inventory valuation method will be discussed in a subsequent section of this chapter.

If unit prices were constant over time or if it were possible to specifically identify the exact cost of the units in inventory and units sold, there would be no allocation problem and the choice of inventory method would be irrelevant. However, unit prices of inventory are normally not stable and specific identification may not be possible. Even if specific identification is possible, management may wish to select another method of inventory valuation in order to satisfy some financial reporting or tax objective. In these situations, management is permitted to make certain cost flow assumptions.

There are three GAAP cost flow assumptions that can be used to allocate the total cost of goods available to ending inventory and cost of goods sold. These are:

1.   The average cost method;

2.   The first-in, first-out method (FIFO);

3.   The last-in, first-out method (LIFO).

Originally, sound accounting theory dictated that each cost flow assumption should be designed to match the cost flow to the unit flow of the items in inventory.

EXHIBIT 2.5

Illustration: Diagram of the Allocation Problem in Inventory

```
        Balance                                          Balance
     Sheet (Asset)                                    Sheet (Asset)
|------------------|                             |------------------|
|    Beginning     |                             |                  |
|    Inventory     |                             |     Ending       |
|    1,000 units   |                             |    Inventory     |
|  a $2  = $2,000  |                             |    5,500 units   |
|------------------|                             |       a ?        |
        |                                        |------------------|
        |                                                 |
        |                                                 |
        |                  |------------------|           |
        |----------------->|   Cost of Goods  |---------->|
                           |   Available for  |
              +            |      Sale        |      +
                           |16,000 units at a |
        |----------------->|   $60,000 total  |---------->|
        |                  |      cost        |           |
        |                  |------------------|           |
        |                                                 |
        |                                                 |
|----------------------------------|          |------------------|
|   Purchases or Production         |          |   Cost of Goods  |
|                                   |          |      Sold        |
| 6,000 units a $3.00 = $18,000     |          |   10,500 units   |
| 4,000 units a $4.00 =  16,000     |          |       a ?        |
| 2,000 units a $4.50 =   9,000     |          |------------------|
| 3,000 units a $5.00 =  15,000     |               Income
|------                -------- |                 Statement
|15,000 units            $58,000    |           (Costs or Expense)
|======                ======  |
|----------------------------------|
```

Thus, the average cost approach is appropriate for a firm selling a high volume of homogeneous goods. For example, the operations of a distributor of home heating oil may be well suited for the use of the average cost method. The FIFO method is most useful for a firm selling a product subject to rapid obsolescence, style changes or perishability. Retail outlets would probably find that the FIFO cost flow assumption best matched their actual unit flow. Finally, the LIFO approach would be appropriate for a firm with operations requiring a base stock. For example, a coal mining operation would maintain a base level in a pile of coal. All subsequent mining would be added to the top of the pile and all sales would be from the top of the pile. Sales would draw down the inventory level until the base stock level was reached.

The theoretical objectives of matching unit flow and cost flow are no longer relevant. In today's accounting and reporting environment, the financial reporting objectives focus on balance sheet (i.e., inventory) valuation and income determination. As indicated in the discussion of accounts receivable and the bad debt expense, there is generally a trade-off between these two objectives. This trade-off of objectives will be more evident in the case of accounting for inventory. In addition, because of the IRS LIFO conformity rule, which requires that if a firm uses LIFO for tax purposes it must also be used for financial reporting, the inventory choice for financial reporting may be tied to the tax method selected and not related to the theoretical unit flow of inventory.

Exhibit 2.6 uses the same information provided in Exhibit 2.5 to illustrate the three GAAP cost flow assumptions. All of the calculations in Exhibit 2.6 assume:

1. A periodic inventory system is used;

2. There is a period of rising inventory costs;

3. Inventory levels are increasing.

The average cost method is known as the weighted average method when applied in a periodic inventory system. The weighted average method applies a weighted average unit cost of $3.75 per unit to the number of units in ending inventory and the number of units sold. As noted in the summary of inventory valuation in Exhibit 2.6, the weighted average valuation will fall between the two extreme measures, FIFO and LIFO.

The FIFO method of inventory valuation assigns the most recent costs to ending inventory and the oldest costs to the cost of goods sold. FIFO results in an inventory valuation that approximates current cost. This provides the credit analyst with the most realistic valuation for assessing the collateral of an inventory based loan, before considering the possibility of slow moving or obsolete inventory. In a period of rising prices, FIFO tends to provide the highest valuation of ending inventory. However, FIFO tends to mismatch costs with revenues in that it allocates the oldest low-unit cost to the cost of goods sold which are to be matched against inflated, current sales dollars. In a period of inflation this mismatch tends to overstate reported net income and earnings per share. The overstatement of FIFO income actually results in "phantom profits" because the additional reported income does not provide any incremental cash flows. Thus, in using the FIFO method, manage-

EXHIBIT 2.6

Illustration: Basic Inventory Methods Under a Periodic Inventory System

----

	Units	Unit Cost	Total Cost
Beginning Inventory January 1, 1992...	1,000	$2.00	$ 2,000
Purchases or Production:			
March 30, 1992....................	6,000	3.00	18,000
April 16, 1992....................	4,000	4.00	16,000
June 13, 1992.....................	2,000	4.50	9,000
October, 5, 1992.................	3,000	5.00	15,000
Total Available for Sale....	16,000		$60,000
Ending Inventory (Physical Count)			
December 31, 1992................	5,500		
Units sold during the year.......	10,500		

Ending Inventory Valuation Under the Alternative GAAP Methods:
----

(1) Weighted Average Method:

$$\text{Weighted Average Cost per Unit} = \frac{\text{Total Cost of Goods Available}}{\text{Total Number of Units Available}}$$

$$= \frac{\$60,000}{16,000} = \$3.75/\text{unit}$$

Ending Inventory = 5,500 x $3.75 = $20,625

Cost of Goods Sold = $60,000 - 20,625 = $39,375

----

(2) The First-In, First-Out Method (FIFO): Assigns the most recent costs to
ending inventory and the oldest cost to the cost of goods sold.

52

Exhibit 2.6, continued

	Units	Unit Cost	Total Cost
Most recent cost: Oct. 5th purchase........	3,000	$5.00	$15,000
Next most recent cost: June 13th purchase..	2,000	4.50	9,000
Next most recent cost: April 16th purchase.	500	4.00	2,000
FIFO Ending Inventory.................	5,500		$26,000

FIFO Cost of Goods Sold = $60,000 - 26,000 = $34,000

---

(3) The Last-In, First-Out Method (LIFO): Assigns the oldest cost to ending inventory and the most recent cost to the cost of goods sold.

	Units	Unit Cost	Total Cost
Oldest cost: Beginning inventory..........	1,000	$2.00	$ 2,000
Next oldest cost: March 30th purchase.....	4,500	3.00	13,500
LIFO Ending Inventory.................	5,500		$15,500

LIFO Cost of Goods Sold = $60,000 - 15,500 = $44,500

Summary of Inventory Valuation and Cost of Goods Sold Under the Three GAAP Accounting Alternatives

	Ending Inventory	Cost of Goods Sold
FIFO.......................	$26,000	$34,000
Weighted Average...........	$20,625	$39,375
LIFO.......................	$15,500	$44,500

NOTE: The above relationships or rankings of the three cost flow assumptions will only hold if:

1. Prices are rising for inventory acquisition or manufacturing costs,

2. Inventory levels are constant or increasing.

With declining prices or decreasing inventory levels (i.e., a LIFO liquidation), the above relationships or rankings may reverse.

---

ment trades off proper balance sheet valuation for a mismatch of costs and revenues on the income statement.

The LIFO approach allocates the oldest cost to ending inventory and the most recent costs to the cost of goods sold. During a period of rising prices and with constant or increasing inventory levels, LIFO tends to significantly understate inventory valuation. However, the resulting cost of goods sold is considered to better match costs and revenues. Improved income statement matching results from the fact that current costs are matched with higher, current sales revenues. Some believe that the use of LIFO actually adjusts the income statement for inflation. With the exception of the depreciation, depletion and amortization of old historical cost based assets, the use of LIFO in a period of inflation produces an income statement that matches current dollar revenues with current dollar operating expenses. Nonetheless, the LIFO method trades off balance sheet inventory valuation for proper matching on the income statement. In an inventory-based loan, the credit analyst must recognize the fact that the use of LIFO will result in a highly conservative valuation for the inventory to be considered as collateral.

The summary of inventory valuation under the three GAAP alternatives in Exhibit 2.6 clearly illustrates the differences between the LIFO and FIFO methods. The FIFO method provides the highest inventory valuation and the lowest cost of goods sold, while the opposite is true for the LIFO method. The $10,500 difference between the inventory valuation under FIFO and LIFO is known as the LIFO reserve. The significance and uses of the LIFO reserve will be discussed in detail below.

It is critical to recognize the fact that the rankings in this illustration will only hold if there is a period of inflation and inventory levels are constant or increasing. If inventory levels decline, it is known as a LIFO liquidation. When a LIFO liquidation occurs, old low-cost base layers of LIFO inventory are assumed to be sold. If prices are rising, the matching of old low cost LIFO layers against high inflated sales dollars will increase LIFO profits, and can even result in a LIFO net income in excess of what would have been reported if the FIFO method was used.

In order to illustrate a LIFO liquidation, assume that the June 13th and October 5th purchases or production runs in Exhibit 2.6 were not made. In addition, assume that the same number of units were sold so that the physical count of ending inventory resulted in 500 units on December 31st. Inventory levels decreased from 1,000 units at the beginning of the year to 500 units at year end. Under these assumptions, the information presented in Exhibit 2.6 would be modified as follows:

	Units	Unit Cost	Total Cost
Beginning inventory 1/1......	1,000	$2.00	$ 2,000
Purchases or Production:			
March 30..............	6,000	3.00	18,000
April 16..............	4,000	4.00	16,000
Total available for sale....	11,000		$36,000
Ending inventory (physical count) 12/31................	<500>		
Units sold..................	10,500		

Under the FIFO method of inventory valuation, the 500 units in ending inventory would be valued at the most recent cost of $4.00 per unit or a total ending inventory value of $2,000. Cost of goods sold would be $34,000 (i.e., $36,000 - 2,000), which is the same as the case of increasing inventory levels in Exhibit 2.6. Therefore, with no change in the inflation assumption, declining inventory levels do not affect reported FIFO profits.

If the LIFO method is applied to the revised information, the ending inventory of 500 units would be valued at the oldest cost, or $2.00 per unit. In this case, it is said that management has "eaten into LIFO layers" or has "released LIFO layers". This results in a total ending inventory valuation of $1,000. However, the cost of goods sold would only be $35,000 (i.e., $36,000 - 1,000). When compared to the original solution, cost of goods sold declines (and reported income before taxes increases) by $9,500 (i.e., $44,500 - 35,000). In addition, taxable income would increase by $9,500 as well.

The above comparison is not completely valid because it includes the full effect of the two subsequent purchases or production runs. Accountants will generally compute liquidation profits only based on the hypothetical, subsequent purchase or production run that would have been required to cover the number of units liquidated (i.e., to avoid the LIFO liquidation).

In this illustration, the firm is considered to have liquidation profits of $1,000. The liquidation profits are computed as the difference between the actual cost of goods sold and the cost of goods sold that would have resulted if the firm had purchased or produced the same quantity of inventory as it sold, or if the firm had purchased or produced enough units to avoid the liquidation. To avoid the liquidation, the firm would have been required to purchase or produce 10,500 units. The cost of the 10,500 units acquired and the liquidation profits are determined as follows:

```
March 30..........6,000 units at $3.00 = $18,000

April 16..........4,000 units at $4.00 =  16,000

Additional acquisition on
April 16 to avoid liquidation:

                   500 units at $4.00 =   2,000
                                        -------

Cost of sales without liquidation........ $36,000

Cost of sales with liquidation........... <35,000>
                                        ----------

Liquidation profits...................... $ 1,000
                                        ========
```

An alternative method to compute the liquidation profits is to take the difference between the old LIFO cost and the most recent cost of inventory acquired during the year and multiply that difference by the number of units liquidated (i.e., the decrease in inventory).

```
500 units x ($4.00 - 2.00) = $1,000
                            =======
```

LIFO and Taxes. The selection of the inventory method has increased significance when the tax implications of inventory valuation are considered. The consequences of selecting LIFO versus FIFO for income tax purposes is the only inventory issue that has cash flow implications for the firm. Without considering taxes, the LIFO-FIFO choice is purely a cosmetic financial reporting issue. However, with the IRS LIFO conformity rule, income tax and financial reporting issues become interrelated.

As noted earlier, the IRS LIFO conformity rule requires that if a firm uses LIFO for tax purposes, it must also use LIFO for financial reporting. In a period of rising prices and with constant or increasing inventory levels, LIFO could significantly increase cost of sales and result in large tax savings and increased cash flows for the firm, relative to the FIFO basis.

Before LIFO conformity, firms historically used FIFO or average cost for financial reporting and LIFO for tax reporting. As a result, when LIFO conformity was first enacted into law, many firms were required to switch to LIFO for financial reporting purposes. The switch to LIFO created a great deal of problems for credit and financial analysts in attempting to determine the value of inventory and to compare profitability over time and between firms in the same industry. In response to user needs, the accounting profession requires a significant amount of disclosure relating to the LIFO inventories presented on a firm's balance sheet. The major disclosure requirements from the AICPA's LIFO Issues Paper are summarized in the following paragraphs.

The AICPA's LIFO Issues Paper. In 1984, the Accounting Standards Division of the AICPA issued a position paper on various LIFO topics. The SEC subsequently declared that this paper should be viewed as part of GAAP as it addressed questions not covered in other authoritative pronouncements. Some of the disclosure requirements of the AICPA Issues Paper on LIFO topics include:

1. Disclosure of the LIFO reserve. The firm is required to disclose either the LIFO reserve (i.e., the difference between FIFO cost and the LIFO inventory value), or the replacement cost of inventory.

2. Partial adoption of LIFO. The presumption is that if a company switches to LIFO it should do so for all of its inventories. The exception would be if a company has a valid reason for not adopting LIFO for a part of their inventory or a product line. For example, if a company can anticipate a reduction of certain lines of inventory or declining prices for a particular product, a non-LIFO inventory method can be used for that portion of the total inventory.

3. Disclosure of the extent to which LIFO is used. Ideally the portion of cost of sales resulting from the use of LIFO should be provided. If this is not practical, the portion of the ending inventory valued under the LIFO method should be disclosed. The portion of inventory valued at LIFO can be disclosed as a percentage of the total inventory or as an absolute dollar amount.

4. LIFO liquidations. The effects on income from liquidating LIFO inventories should be disclosed, usually in the footnotes to the financial statements. LIFO liquidation is not considered an unusual item. It should be noted that the effect of LIFO liquidation is not reported on the face of the income statement but is "buried" in the reduced cost of goods sold.

   The disclosure of liquidation profits is important because it indicates to the analyst how much of reported net income was due to the firm's operating strength and what amount of income was simply caused by a decrease in the level of inventory on hand. In addition, the existence of liquidation profits has cash consequences because it results in a higher tax liability than would have resulted in the absence of a liquidation.

5. Disallowance of replacement reserves. In the past, if LIFO inventories were involuntarily liquidated, firms would sometimes create replacement reserves on the balance sheet which anticipated replacement in the next accounting period of the units currently liquidated. In creating the reserve, a liability or an allowance for replacement would be reported on the balance sheet and cost of goods sold would be measured as if the liquidation did not occur. As a result, income would not be increased by the liquidation. The replacement reserve approach is no longer permitted.

6. Non-LIFO disclosures. Under the first LIFO conformity requirements, in

order for LIFO to be accepted by the IRS companies were not allowed to report anything but LIFO values in their financial reports. However, in 1981 this original conformity requirement was relaxed. A company may now present non-LIFO disclosures. Non-LIFO disclosures could include proforma inventory valuation and net income and earnings per share as if the FIFO method was used. Non-LIFO disclosures enable the analyst to convert from the LIFO to the FIFO method of inventory valuation. The analytical restatement from LIFO to FIFO is important in comparing two firms in the same industry or in conducting a proforma consolidation in a proposed merger or acquisition. In addition, the disclosures assist in restoring comparability over several accounting periods in the year in which a firm changes to the LIFO method for financial reporting purposes. An analytical restatement from LIFO to FIFO will be illustrated in the next section of this chapter.

It should be noted that with the issuance of the AICPA's LIFO Issues Paper, the SEC cautioned companies that the supplemental LIFO disclosures must be considered carefully to avoid implying that FIFO earnings are the "real" earnings of a company using LIFO. The SEC believed that the risk of user misinterpretation is mitigated when such disclosures are made, if the companies that file their statements with the SEC also (a) state clearly that LIFO results in a better matching of costs and revenues; (b) indicate why the supplemental disclosures are being provided; and (c) present essential information about the supplemental income calculation to enable users to appreciate the quality of the information. In addition, the SEC believed that if companies made such disclosures, they should be made in the footnotes to the financial statements or in management's discussion and analysis.

7. Net of tax disclosures. If non-LIFO disclosures are given, the effects on net income and financial position should be reported net of tax.

8. Lower of cost or market (LCM). A company should report its inventory at the lower of cost or market. The LCM rules for inventory will be discussed in a later section of this chapter.

Restatement of Inventory from LIFO to FIFO. The LIFO disclosures are significant in that they represent a source of information that is available year after year, and which enables the analyst to restate both the inventory on the balance sheet and net income on the income statement from the LIFO basis to a proforma FIFO and/or average cost basis.

Exhibits 2.7 and 2.8 provide an illustration of restating inventory and income from the LIFO to the FIFO method for Ashland Oil, Inc. and Subsidiaries.

LIFO inventories are restated to the FIFO basis by simply adding the LIFO reserve disclosed in the footnote to the LIFO inventory values reported on the balance sheet and in Note A. Exhibit 2.7 also provides an estimation of the amount of purchases or production. This could be useful in a trend analysis. For example, if there is a decreasing trend in production and raw materials inventory, coupled with an increase in work in process and finished goods inventories, the analyst may conclude that management is expecting a slowdown in sales in the short run.

To determine the difference in pretax income, it is only necessary to compute the differences in cost of goods sold under LIFO and proforma FIFO. It should be noted that in the case of Ashland Oil, cost of sales and operating expenses are aggregated as a single line item. For purposes of this illustration it is assumed that line item only consists of the cost of goods sold.

The difference in cost of sales and therefore in pretax profit is <$131>, which means that pretax income is greater under LIFO. Part of the reason for this effect can be found in the analysis of the LIFO reserve. Note that Exhibit 2.7 presents a short-cut approach to determine the profit implications of the LIFO-FIFO switch. The difference in pretax profit is nothing more than the change in the LIFO reserve. If the LIFO reserve increases, it implies that either prices are rising, inventory levels are constant or increasing, or there is a combination of both. The existence of inflation and constant or increasing inventory levels cause the cumulative differences between LIFO and FIFO inventory values to increase, thereby resulting in a specific effect which increases the cost of sales and the resulting tax benefits under LIFO. That is, LIFO profit is less than FIFO profit. When there is a decrease in the LIFO reserve, it implies that either prices are declining or inventory levels are decreasing (i.e., there is a LIFO liquidation). Under these conditions, the cumulative difference between the LIFO and FIFO inventory valuation is reduced. In addition, the specific effect for the year results in a reduced cost of goods sold and a loss of tax benefits under LIFO. In this case, LIFO pretax profit could be greater than the FIFO proforma income before tax.

In 1982, Ashland Oil experienced a decrease in its LIFO reserve. The specific effect resulted in LIFO income in excess of proforma FIFO income of $131 million. As noted above, this specific effect could be due to declining prices and/or a liquidation. Note A to the financial statements provides information regarding the existence of a LIFO liquidation. In 1982, liquidation profits amounted to $42,500,000 or $1.41 per share, which explains part of the decrease in the LIFO reserve.

More significant is the fact that the decrease in the reserve and the liquidation provide evidence that the taxes actually paid increased substantially. In other words, LIFO resulted in significant tax disadvantages for Ashland Oil in 1982. The extent of this tax disadvantage cannot be determined by the information provided in Exhibits 2.7 and 2.8. However, the amount of the liquidation profits alone can provide some idea of the extent of the adverse tax consequences of using LIFO in 1982 relative to FIFO.

Using the Statements of Consolidated Income in Exhibit 2.8, the 1982 effective tax rate for financial reporting is 38% (i.e., income tax expense / income before tax = $111,290 / $292,154). With an effective tax rate of 38% it means that the pretax liquidation profits were $68,548,387 (i.e., $42,500,000/ [1 - .38]). If it is assumed that Ashland was subject to a 50% corporate income tax rate for tax purposes in 1982, and there were no book-tax differences relating to inventory, then the liquidation could have resulted in an increased tax burden of $34,274,193 (i.e., $68,548,387 x 50%) when compared to the results that would have been obtained in the absence of a LIFO liquidation.

Finally, the LIFO reserve will decrease if there is a reduction in the quantity of

EXHIBIT 2.7

Illustration: Restatement of Inventory from the LIFO to the FIFO Basis for Ashland Oil, Inc. and Subsidiaries

----

SEE EXHIBIT 2.8 FOR THE SOURCE DATA FOR THE FOLLOWING ILLUSTRATION.

Restatement of Crude Oil, Petroleum Products and Chemical Inventories from LIFO to FIFO:

	9/30/82	9/30/81
Inventory at LIFO, etc., as reported....	$ 358	$ 451
Add: LIFO Reserve (Excess FIFO, Current or Replacement Cost over LIFO).....	796	927
Inventory at FIFO, etc., as restated....	$1,154	$1,378

Estimation of Purchases or the Cost of Goods Manufactured:

	9/30/82
Ending Inventory.........................	$ 358
Cost of Goods Sold.......................	7,828
Cost of Goods Available for Sale........	$8,186
Less: Beginning Inventory...............	< 451>
Purchases or Cost of Goods Manufactured.	$7,735

Restatement of the 1982 Income Statement Under FIFO, etc.:

	LIFO	FIFO
Beginning Inventory....................................	$ 451	$1,378
Add: Purchases or the Cost of Goods Manufactured...	7,735	7,735
Cost of Goods Available for Sale.....................	$8,186	$9,113
Less: Ending Inventory...............................	< 358>	<1,154>
Cost of Goods Sold...................................	$7,828	$7,959

Difference in Pretax Accounting Income = $7,828 - 7,959 = <$131>

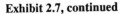

In this case, pretax accounting income would have been $131 less if the FIFO method was used by Ashland Oil.

Shortcut Approach for Determination of the Difference in Pretax Accounting Income:

The difference in pretax accounting income between the LIFO and FIFO methods is simply the change in the LIFO Reserve.

Change in the LIFO Reserve = $796 - 927 = <$131>

In this case, the LIFO Reserve declined so that pretax accounting income under LIFO is greater than under FIFO. If the LIFO Reserve increases, then the pretax accounting income under LIFO would be less than under the FIFO method.

It should be noted that the LIFO Reserve measures the cumulative effect on ending inventory of using or changing to the LIFO method at a particular point in time, relative to the FIFO method. The change in the LIFO Reserve measures the specific effect on income in a given year from using the LIFO method relative to the FIFO method of inventory valuation.

EXHIBIT 2.8

Sample Disclosure: Ashland Oil, Inc. and Subsidiaries: Consolidated Statements of Income, Assets Section of the Consolidated Balance Sheet and Inventory Footnote

----

Ashland Oil, Inc. and Subsidiaries
Statements of Consolidated Income
Years Ended September 30

(In thousands except earnings per share)	1982	1981	1980
Revenues			
Sales and operating revenues (including excise taxes)	$9,109,879	$9,506,564	$8,366,466
Interest and other income	148,649	174,766	141,462
Equity income—Notes C and L	13,157	23,188	10,775
Gain from prepayment of certain long-term debt	2,309	22,813	2,123
	9,273,994	9,727,331	8,520,826
Costs and expenses			
Cost of sales and operating expenses	7,828,146	8,453,648	7,277,835
Excise taxes on products and merchandise	245,210	244,488	247,098
Selling, general and administrative expenses	678,294	620,739	420,078
Depreciation, depletion and amortization (including capitalized leases)—Note A	179,810	153,144	131,523
Interest expense	78,569	97,710	88,691
	9,010,029	9,569,729	8,165,225
Income from operations and investments	263,965	157,602	355,601
Gain related to sales of operations—Note B	28,189	—	9,488
Income before income taxes	292,154	157,602	365,089
Income taxes—Notes A and D	111,290	67,570	159,960
Net income	$ 180,864	$ 90,032	$ 205,129
Earnings per share—Note A			
Primary	$ 5.29	$ 2.22	$ 6.80
Assuming full dilution	$ 5.27	$ 2.21	$ 6.74
Average common shares and equivalents outstanding			
Primary	30,057	26,502	27,432
Assuming full dilution	30,209	26,688	27,694

Exhibit 2.8, continued

Ashland Oil, Inc. and Subsidiaries
Consolidated Balance Sheets
September 30

(In thousands)	1982	1981
Assets		
Current assets		
Cash and short-term securities—Note A	$ 281,577	$ 396,674
Accounts receivable (less allowances for doubtful accounts of $18,875,000 in 1982 and $19,138,000 in 1981)	992,131	901,110
Construction completed and in progress—at contract prices	58,645	57,652
Inventories—Note A	358,522	451,064
Prepaid expenses	75,601	60,123
	1,766,476	1,866,623
Investments and other assets		
Investments in and advances to unconsolidated subsidiaries and affiliates—Notes B, C and L	444,031	445,875
Cost in excess of net assets of companies acquired (less accumulated amortization of $9,071,000 in 1982 and $2,979,000 in 1981)—Notes A and B	135,408	154,760
Notes and other receivables	43,551	31,934
Other assets, prepaid royalties and deferred charges	139,174	120,094
	762,164	752,663
Property, plant and equipment—at cost—Notes A, F and N		
Petroleum	1,512,900	1,310,311
Chemical	305,047	278,263
Coal	208,381	178,288
Construction	269,472	269,853
Engineering and technology	140,977	123,840
Exploration (successful efforts method)	312,268	188,704
Other	98,015	184,676
	2,847,060	2,533,935
Less accumulated depreciation, depletion and amortization	1,165,219	1,031,408
	1,681,841	1,502,527
	$4,210,481	$4,121,813

Ashland Oil, Inc. and Subsidiaries
Notes to Consolidated Financial Statements

Note A—Significant accounting policies

Principles of consolidation

The consolidated financial statements include the accounts of Ashland and all significant majority-owned subsidiaries except Integon Corporation ("Integon"), a wholly owned insurance holding company. Investments in Integon, other unconsolidated subsidiaries, 20% to 50% owned affiliates, and joint ventures are primarily accounted for on the equity method (see Note C). The remaining investments (not significant) are accounted for at cost.

Inventories

(In thousands)	1982	1981
Crude oil and petroleum products	$134,498	$227,981
Chemicals and other products	184,836	183,944
Materials and supplies	39,188	39,139
	$358,522	$451,064

Crude oil, petroleum products and chemical inventories of approximately $187,000,000 at September 30, 1982 and $247,000,000 at September 30, 1981 are valued using the last-in, first-out (LIFO) method. The replacement cost for these inventories exceeds their LIFO carrying value by approximately $796,000,000 for 1982 and $927,000,000 for 1981. The remaining inventories are stated generally at the lower of cost (using the first-in, first-out (FIFO) or average cost methods) or market.

Ashland has decreased its crude oil and petroleum product inventories in recent years as a result of the reduced domestic demand for petroleum products, the suspension of refining operations at Buffalo N.Y. and a shift away from foreign to domestic crude oil because of its lower cost. Cost of sales and operating expenses include costs for these inventories based on prior years' LIFO values which were less than current replacement costs. As a result of the crude oil, petroleum product and other inventory quantity reductions, net income was increased by approximately $42,500,000 ($1.41 per share) in 1982 and $29,750,000 ($1.08 per share) in 1980. The effect of inventory quantity reductions during 1981 was not significant.

Exploration and development costs

Oil and gas exploration and development costs are accounted for using the successful efforts method. Coal lease acquisition and development costs which are recoverable are capitalized. Coal exploration costs are expensed as incurred.

Depreciation, depletion and amortization

The cost of plant and equipment (other than capitalized exploration and development costs) is depreciated over the estimated useful lives of the assets principally by the straight-line method. Capitalized exploration and development costs are amortized by the unit-of-production method over the estimated recoverable reserves. Costs in excess of net assets of companies acquired are amortized principally over forty years by the straight-line method (see Note B).

Expenditures for maintenance, repairs and minor replacements are expensed as incurred ($168,428,000 in 1982, $182,886,000 in 1981 and $185,596,000 in 1980).

Income taxes

Deferred income taxes are provided for significant timing differences in the recognition of revenue and expense for tax and financial reporting purposes. Investment tax credit is accounted for as a reduction of the provision for income taxes in the year realized for tax purposes.

Source: Ashland Oil, Inc. and Subsidiaries 1982 Annual Report. Copyright, 1982, by Ashland Oil, Inc. Reprinted with permission.

inventory and/or declining prices. Given that the pretax effect of the LIFO liquidation (i.e., quantity reductions) on income was $68 million and the total decrease in the LIFO reserve was $131, then the remainder of the reduction of the LIFO reserve may be due to declining oil prices. The total effect of declining prices on the LIFO reserve and reported pretax income is approximately $63 million (i.e., $131 - 68).

The Lower of Cost or Market Rule for Inventory (LCM). The lower-of-cost-or-market rule for inventory is the accountant's test for obsolescence. At the end of each accounting period, auditing standards require that accountants compare the cost of the ending inventory, measured at LIFO, FIFO or average cost, with the market value of the inventory. If cost is greater than market, a write down of the inventory is required. Because LIFO tends to understate inventory cost in a period of inflation, an LCM problem is typically not expected if the firm uses the LIFO method.

Although similar in basic principle to the LCM rules for marketable securities, the LCM rules for inventory differ in several significant respects. First, the LCM rules for inventory can be applied to the aggregate inventory, product lines or individual items. The different levels of aggregation are permitted to allow for certain products in inventory that may be sold at a loss in order to stimulate sales of a related product. For example, a firm may sell pens at a loss or very low profit margin in order to generate sales of refills at excessive markups. In this case, it would not be appropriate to write off the pens as obsolete because their cost is in excess of their market values. The pens are interrelated with the refills and therefore should be evaluated together, as a single unit. This would justify the application of the LCM rules to a particular product line or to the total inventory, rather than to the individual items in inventory.

Second, the market value for inventory is not obtained by simply referring to some published price list as was the case with marketable securities. That is, the market value for inventory is not the current selling price of the item. Instead, market is the current replacement cost (CRC) subject to limitations or boundaries. These boundaries are known as the ceiling and floor, or the NRV/NRV-NP rules.

In the application of the LCM rules for inventory, CRC cannot exceed the ceiling which is defined as net realizable value (NRV). NRV is equal to the selling price of the item less any disposal costs such as commissions, packaging and freight. The NRV upper boundary or the ceiling on market is required in order to prevent overvaluation of inventory. That is, inventory should not be valued above an amount that is reasonably expected to be realized in cash from the disposal of the item. Conversely, CRC cannot fall below the floor. This lower boundary is defined as NRV less a normal profit (NP). The floor, or lower limit on the market value, is used to prevent undervaluation of inventory. Unnecessary or excessive write-offs of inventory (e.g., "big bath accounting") could result in smoothing income or reporting inflated profits in subsequent years when the undervalued inventory item is eventually sold at a normal selling price. The floor or NRV-NP represents the most reasonable lower limit at which inventory can be carried. The NRV-NP limit can be proven as follows.

```
Normal Profit = Selling Price - Cost of Inventory - Disposal Costs

Normal Profit = (Selling Price - Disposal Costs) - Cost of Inventory

Normal Profit = Net Realizable Value - Cost of Inventory

Cost of Inventory = Net Realizable Value - Normal Profit
```

An illustration of the LCM rules for inventory is presented in Exhibit 2.9.

NONCURRENT ASSETS

There are three major categories of noncurrent assets. These are:

1. Tangible fixed assets or property, plant and equipment;

2. Intangible assets;

3. Natural resources or wasting assets.

With the exception of land, all noncurrent assets have limited lives. The accountant must reflect this limited usefulness to the firm by systematic write-offs of the cost of the noncurrent asset against income. This is considered a process of allocation rather than valuation, and the cost of the noncurrent asset is allocated to the future periods of expected benefit in order to match costs with revenues.

Tangible Fixed Assets

Characteristics of Tangible Fixed Assets. In order to be classified as a tangible fixed asset, the asset must possess three characteristics. The asset must be:

1. Tangible in nature;

2. Long-lived;

3. Used in the production and sale of other assets.

The third characteristic is the most important in the analysis of financial statements because in order to make a proper analysis of fixed assets, this balance sheet category should only include active and productive assets, and therefore exclude idle plant and equipment. According to the SEC, if material in amount, idle plant assets should be disclosed in a footnote. In addition, if the plant asset is expected to be idle for an extended period of time, it should be segregated from plant assets and reclassified as "other assets" or "investments" in the noncurrent assets section of the balance sheet. If idle plant assets are not properly identified, there could be a

EXHIBIT 2.9

Illustration: Lower of Cost or Market Rule For Inventory

The following information is provided regarding an inventory consisting of four items and two product lines:

Group	Item	Cost	CRC	SP	Disposal Costs	NP
A	101	$18	$14	$20	$ 5	$ 2
A	102	15	20	25	7	3
B	110	50	50	80	20	8
B	112	72	70	95	20	10

Applying the "ceiling" and "floor" limitations on market, the valuation at LCM would be determined as follows:

Group	Item	CRC	NRV Ceiling	NRV - NP Floor	Market	Cost	LCM
A	101	$14	$15	$13	$ 14	$ 18	$14 M
A	102	20	18	15	18	15	15 C
B	110	50	60	52	52	50	50 C
B	112	70	75	65	70	72	70 M

Total Inventory.......$154 $155

The application of LCM to:

1. Total Inventory = $155 - 154 = $1 Loss or Write-down required;

2. Individual Items:

   Item 101: $18 - 14 = $4
   Item 112: 72 - 70 = 2

   Total........... $6 Loss or Write-down required;

3. Group or Product Line Basis:

   A: ($18 + 15) - ($14 + 18) = $1
   B: ($50 + 72) - ($52 + 70) = 0

   Total................... $1 Loss or Write-down required.

Exhibit 2.9, continued

```
Definitions

     CRC      =  Current Replacement Cost
     SP       =  Selling Price
     Disposal =  Costs of Completion and Disposal
     NP       =  Normal Profit
     NRV      =  Net Realizable Value = (SP - Disposal Costs)
     Cost     =  FIFO, LIFO or Average Cost
```

---

distortion of various profitability ratios and rates of return such as the ratio of pretax income to productive assets. The incorrect inclusion of idle plant assets in this computation would bias the ratio in a downward direction due to the fact that the idle plant in the denominator does not provide any contribution to production and income.

Plant Asset Accounting at Acquisition. At acquisition, plant assets must be recorded at cost, where cost includes invoice price (or production costs) plus all reasonable and necessary expenditures required to have the asset in its existing condition and location and ready for its intended use (e.g., production). Reasonable and necessary expenditures for plant assets include shipping, installation, special wiring and possibly interest charges for self-constructed assets. As was the case in the determination of the unit cost of inventory, what management considers to be reasonable and necessary depends on the firm's capitalization policy.

With respect to plant assets, capitalization policy can relate to either:

1. The types of costs to capitalize and the types of costs to be charged to expense as incurred. Depending on management's judgement and capitalization policy, a reasonable and necessary expense could be expensed or capitalized. For example, delivery charges can be expensed or capitalized depending on the theory prescribed to by management. Expensing delivery costs can be justified under the theory that the cost of shipping the item does not add to the asset's productivity or efficiency and as a result does not have any future economic benefit to the firm. Conversely, delivery costs could be capitalized as part of the cost of the item under the theory that without the required delivery, the asset could not contribute to production. Therefore, the choice is at the discretion of management and either expensing or capitalization can be justified. When a capitalization policy is selected by management, it should be followed consistently. Normally, the firm's capitalization policy is not disclosed in the footnotes to the financial statements, unless there has been a change in policy and the effect of the change on net income is material. It should be noted that the capitalization issue can also be a problem subsequent to acquisition with regard to repair and maintenance-type expenditures.

2. The magnitude of costs to capitalize. For example, some firms have a "materiality threshold" for capitalization. If an expenditure falls below a fixed dollar limit, it is expensed immediately rather than capitalized as part of the cost of an asset.

The capitalization issue is important for asset valuation and income determination. If a cost is inappropriately capitalized, both assets and income are overstated in the year of the expenditure. In subsequent accounting periods, the cost of the expenditure will be charged against income through higher depreciation charges. The effect is to understate future years' reported income. On the other hand, if an expenditure is inappropriately expensed as incurred, assets and income are understated in the year of acquisition. However, income will be overstated through lower depreciation charges over subsequent accounting periods. Although the total income reported over the life of the asset will be the same, the profit reported each year will be misstated. The capitalization-expense alternative could provide management with a valuable tool for shifting reported profit between accounting periods for purposes of smoothing income or avoiding technical default of a loan agreement. For example, improperly capitalizing costs could improve reported income in the current year so as to bring profitability ratios up to the levels required by restrictive covenants in debt agreements. Regardless of the accounting alternative selected, cash flows will be the same in total and for each year. There is only a single cash outflow in the year in which the expenditure is made. However, additional cash flow consequences could arise if certain expenditures are deducted for tax purposes rather than capitalized.

Plant Asset Accounting Subsequent to Acquisition. Subsequent to acquisition, the two major accounting issues relating to fixed assets are repairs and maintenance, and depreciation. The repairs and maintenance issue involves the capitalization-expense alternative discussed above and will not be repeated again here.

All plant assets, except land, are subject to depreciation. The accountant views depreciation as a process of allocation of the asset's cost to the expected future periods of benefit in order to properly match costs with revenues. Depreciation is not considered a process of economic valuation. This same view can be applied to the amortization of intangible assets and the depletion of natural resources.

The Nature of Depreciation. Depreciation is only an estimate and this estimation technique involves consideration of three factors:

1.   The estimated useful or productive life;

2.   The estimated scrap or residual value of the asset;

3.   The allocation method selected.

The estimated productive life of a plant asset can be estimated by consideration of factors such as past experience, IRS guidelines, industry practice, maintenance policy, the firm's usage versus normal usage, obsolescence and future inadequacy.

The estimated scrap or salvage value is the amount expected to be realized upon disposal of the asset at the termination of its productive service to the firm. Scrap value can be based on past experience or industry practice. For example, most computer leasing firms assume a zero scrap value in their depreciation computations.

The selection of an allocation method involves the choice of one of the four GAAP depreciation methods. The four GAAP depreciation methods are:

1.   The straight-line method;

2.   The units-of-output (production) method;

3.   The sum-of-the-years digits method;

4.   The declining-balance method.

The sum-of-the-years digits and the declining balance methods are also known as accelerated or decreasing charge methods.

The GAAP depreciation methods can also be used for most state and local taxes. However, the IRS requires the use of the Modified Accelerated Cost Recovery System (MACRS). The MACRS system will be considered in the chapter dealing with accounting for income taxes.

Originally, good accounting theory prescribed that the depreciation method selected by management should reflect the operating and economic conditions facing the firm as well as the manner in which the asset was used. Therefore, the straight-line method should be used in those cases where there is relatively uniform periodic usage of the asset and a low obsolescence factor. The units of production or the activity method should be used when physical wear is the primary cause of depreciation and asset utilization varies year to year. Finally, the two accelerated methods should be used when the asset generates greater usefulness in the earlier years of its life than in its later years. This is usually true for assets with a high obsolescence factor in earlier years and a high maintenance factor in later years. Due to the increased maintenance factor in later years, many believe that the accelerated methods result in a relatively constant charge against income for each year of the asset's life. In the earlier years the charge against income would primarily consist of the higher accelerated depreciation expense and a lower maintenance factor. In the later years of the asset's life, the total charge against income would consist of lower depreciation expense but increased maintenance costs. As a result, the cost of using the asset would be relatively constant year to year.

As was the case in selecting an inventory method, the choice of depreciation method in today's accounting and reporting environment will depend on management's reporting objectives--an income-increasing or income- reducing reporting strategy. Unlike the inventory valuation choice, there is no IRS conformity rule for depreciation. Therefore, the selection of depreciation method for financial reporting is typically independent from the method used for income tax purposes.

Regardless of the method selected, depreciation is usually recorded as an end of the period adjustment. Depreciation is charged against income on the income statement. On the balance sheet, the carrying value of the plant asset is reduced by increasing a contra-asset account called accumulated depreciation or the allowance for depreciation. The allowance for depreciation is netted or offset against the cost of the plant asset and the difference, the net book value (NBV), is reported in the noncurrent asset section of the balance sheet.

The use of the contra-asset account is necessary due to the fact that depreciation is only an estimate and may be revised. The only objectively determined information is the original historical cost of the asset. As a result, the accountant attempts to preserve the historical cost and records the estimated depreciation of the plant asset in the accumulated depreciation account. Nevertheless, the two accounts cannot be separated and must be viewed as a single unit, net book value. Regardless of the depreciation method used, the charge for depreciation is a noncash expense and the annual depreciation expense is an add-back in the reconciliation of accrual basis net income and cash generated from operations in the statement of cash flows.

Illustration of the GAAP Depreciation Methods. The four GAAP depreciation methods are illustrated in Exhibit 2.10. In addition, the exhibit presents an example of the optimal time to switch methods for state and local income tax purposes.

Under the straight-line method, depreciable cost (i.e., cost less estimated scrap value) is divided by the estimated useful life of the asset. In this illustration, the depreciation expense of $24,000 would be charged against income in each of the five years of the asset's life. At the end of the asset's life the total in the accumulated depreciation account is $120,000 (i.e., $24,000 x 5 years). Therefore, the net book value is equal to the estimated scrap value of $5,000.

The straight-line method can also be viewed as depreciating a constant depreciable cost at a constant rate. The straight-line rate is computed as one over the estimated useful life. In this case, the straight-line rate is 20% (i.e., 1/5 years). Thus, each year 20% of the $120,000 depreciable cost, or $24,000, is charged against income as depreciation expense.

Under the units-of-production method, depreciable cost is divided by the estimated life in terms of productive output. The result is a rate of depreciation per unit of output. In Exhibit 2.10, the rate of depreciation is $1.20 per unit. For each unit produced, up to 100,000 units, $1.20 will be charged against income. After 100,000 units of production, the asset is fully depreciated and the accumulated depreciation account will equal $120,000. At this point, the net book value is equal to the estimated scrap value of $5,000.

The first accelerated method illustrated in Exhibit 2.10 is the sum-of-the-years digits method. The-sum-of-the-years digits method applies a declining rate of depreciation against a constant depreciable cost. The-sum-of-the-years digits rate for each year of the asset's life is determined as the ratio of the number of years of useful life remaining at the beginning of the year divided by the sum of the years. The acceleration of the depreciation charge is achieved through the declining sum-of-the-years digits fraction. As with the straight-line and the units-of-output methods, the sum-of-the-years digits method depreciates the asset down to its estimated scrap value of $5,000.

The last accelerated depreciation method illustrated is the declining-balance method. Originally developed for income tax purposes, there are a series of declining balance methods based on the straight-line rate. There is single declining balance (i.e., one times the straight-line rate), one and one-half declining balance (i.e., one and one-half times the straight-line rate), and double declining balance (i.e., twice the straight-line rate). Double declining balance is the most common approach and is illustrated in Exhibit 2.10.

The double declining balance method applies a constant rate of depreciation against a declining net book value. The constant rate of depreciation is computed at twice the straight-line rate. In this case the straight-line rate is 20% so that the double declining-balance rate is 40%. The 40% is then applied against the net book value of the asset. Note that the net book value of the asset is equal to cost less accumulated depreciation. Acceleration is achieved due to the declining net book value over time. Even more significant is the fact that the double declining-balance method is the only depreciation method that does not consider the estimated scrap value. As a result, at the end of the asset's useful life, the remaining net book value may be greater than or less than the estimated salvage value. In Exhibit 2.10, the remaining net book value is $9,720, which exceeds the planned scrap value of $5,000. When this occurs, the accountant has three alternatives. First, the final net book value that results from the double declining-balance method can be maintained as the imputed scrap value. Second, the remaining net book value at the

EXHIBIT 2.10

Illustration: Basic GAAP Depreciation Methods and the Optimal Point to Switch Depreciation Methods for State and Local Tax Purposes

----

Information provided from the accounting records:

    Equipment Cost....................$125,000
    Estimated Useful Life............. 5 years or 100,000 units of output
    Estimated Scrap or Salvage Value..$5,000
    Date of Acquisition: January 2, 1992

----

(1) Straight-Line Method:

$$\text{Annual Depreciation Expense} = \frac{\text{Cost - Estimated Scrap Value}}{\text{Estimated Useful Life}}$$

$$= \frac{\$125,000 - 5,000}{5 \text{ years}} = \$24,000/\text{year}$$

----

(2) Units-of-Production Method:

$$\text{Depreciation Expense per Unit} = \frac{\text{Cost - Estimated Scrap Value}}{\text{Estimated Units of Output}}$$

$$= \frac{\$125,000 - 5,000}{100,000 \text{ units}} = \$1.20/\text{unit}$$

If the firm manufactures 27,500 units in its first year of operation, the depreciation expense for the year is $33,000 (i.e., $1.20 x 27,500).

----

(3) The Sum-Of-The-Years-Digits Method (SYD): Applies a declining rate of depreciation against a constant depreciable cost (defined as cost less estimated scrap value).

$$\text{SYD Rate} = \frac{\text{Number of Years Remaining at the Beginning of the Year}}{\text{Sum of the Years}}$$

Exhibit 2.10, continued

Where,

Sum of the Years = n((n + 1)/2) = 5((5 + 1)/2) = 15 = 5 + 4 + 3 + 2 + 1

SYD Depreciation Schedule:

Year	Depreciable Cost (Cost - Scrap Value)	SYD Fraction Deprecation Rate	Deprecation Expense
1	$120,000	5/15	$ 40,000
2	120,000	4/15	32,000
3	120,000	3/15	24,000
4	120,000	2/15	16,000
5	120,000	1/15	8,000

			$120,000
			========

----

(4) Double Declining-Balance Method (DDB): Applies a constant rate of depreciation against a declining net book value (defined as cost less accumulated depreciation).

DDB Rate = "Twice the straight line rate"

Straight line rate = 1/Useful life = 1/5 = 20%

DDB Rate = 2 x 20% = 40%

DDB Depreciation Schedule: (c)

Beginning of the Year	Cost	Accumulated Depreciation	Net Book Value	DDB %	Depreciation Expense
1	$125,000	$ 0	$125,000	40%	$50,000
2	125,000	50,000	75,000	40%	30,000
3	125,000	80,000	45,000	40%	18,000
4	125,000	98,000	27,000	40%	10,800
5	125,000	108,800	16,200	40%	6,480
6 (a)	125,000	115,280	9,720 (b)		

(a) This is the beginning of year six or the end of year five.
(b) The ending net book value is greater than the planned scrap value of $5,000. There are three alternatives in this case. First, the $9,720 can be treated as an imputed scrap value and no further depreciation is taken.

74

Exhibit 2.10, continued

Second, the $9,720 or $9,720 less the $5,000 scrap value can be depreciated over some estimated remaining life. Third, the depreciation in year five is increased to $11,200 so that the net book value at the end of year five is exactly equal to the original estimated scrap value of $5,000.

(c) The declining balance methods are the only methods to ignore scrap value. This fact results in the additional analysis required in the last year of the asset's life as noted in (b) above.

===

Optimal Point to Switch from DDB to Straight-Line for State and Local Tax Purposes. The objective is to minimize the adverse tax effects from reversal.

End of Year	Beginning of the Year	DDB Remaining NBV	DDB Depr. Expense	Modified Straight-Line (Assuming No Scrap Value)
0	1	$125,000	$50,000	$125,000/5Yrs. = $25,000
1	2	75,000	30,000	75,000/4Yrs. = 18,750
2	3	45,000	18,000	45,000/3Yrs. = 15,000
3	4 ***	27,000	10,800	27,000/2Yrs. = 13,500

***Optimal time to switch to straight line because modified straight line exceeds the original DDB depreciation expense.

Graph:

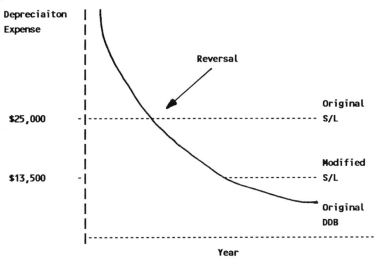

It should be noted that the switch to straight-line does not prevent reversal but slows down the rate of reversal.

---

end of the asset's life can be depreciated over some estimated period of re
maining life. Finally, the last year's depreciation expense can be "forced" so that
the remaining net book value is exactly equal to the original estimated salvage
value.

Optimal Point to Switch from Accelerated to Straight Line Depreciation. The last
section of Exhibit 2.10 illustrates the determination of the optimal point to switch
from accelerated to straight-line depreciation for state or local income tax purposes. In order to determine the optimal switch point, the actual accelerated depreciation (double declining-balance in this case) is compared to a revised or modified
straight line. The modified straight-line depreciation is determined by dividing the
remaining net book value at the beginning of each year, determined under double
declining balance, by the number of years of useful life remaining at the beginning
of each year. It is assumed that the firm would not use a scrap value for income tax
purposes because a scrap value reduces the amount of the available tax deductions
for depreciation.

Based on the computations in Exhibit 2.10, the optimal time to switch is at the
beginning of year four. This will result in a modified straight-line depreciation of
$13,500 in years four and five. If the double declining-balance method was still
employed, only $10,800 and $6,480 would be available for tax deductions in years
four and five, respectively. Note that in the early years of the asset's life, there are
tax advantages in using double declining balance over straight line. In the later
years, reversal takes place causing the use of the accelerated method to be a tax
disadvantage when compared to the straight-line method. The switch to straight line
does not prevent reversal from taking place, but it slows down the rate of reversal.
In most cases, firms would elect to switch to straight line at the time it is optimal to
do so. In fact, the IRS MACRS tables actually build in a switch to straight line in
the last few years of the asset's life.

Estimated Measures of Plant Age.[2] Depreciation expense can result in a significant charge against income, but because depreciation is a noncash expense, it is
added back to net income in the reconciliation of accrual basis net income and
operating cash flows on the cash flow statement. However, depreciation should not
be ignored by the analyst simply because it is a noncash expense. Eventually,
equipment will have to be replaced in order to maintain current operating capacity.
At the point replacement takes place, there could be a significant cash drain on the
firm or it may require additional financing. This information is useful in the projec-
tion of future cash flows for input into discounted cash flow models that may be
designed to predict the timing of additional financing requirements.

In order to estimate when mandatory replacement of plant and equipment will
take place, measures of plant age can be developed. An illustration of estimated
measures of plant age for the General Electric Company in 1983 is presented in
Exhibit 2.11. It should be noted that the measures of plant age utilized in Exhibit
2.11 assume that the straight-line method is used and there is no estimated salvage
value. The footnotes to the financial statements should provide information regarding the firm's depreciation policy. If a method other than straight line is used and if
a scrap value is included in the firm's computations, these estimated measures
become less accurate.

The measure of average remaining life on Exhibit 2.11 provides the analyst with
an estimate of when the full replacement of capacity becomes mandatory. In a

EXHIBIT 2.11

Illustration: Analytical Measures of Plant Age for General Electric Company

----

Footnote No. 11, Property, Plant and Equipment (PP&E), from the 1983 General
----

Electric Annual Report:
----

11 Property, plant and equipment

(In millions)	1983	1982
Major classes at December 31:		
Manufacturing plant and equipment		
Land and improvements	$ 192	$ 188
Buildings, structures and related equipment	2,965	2,851
Machinery and equipment	8,533	7,884
Leasehold costs and manufacturing plant under construction	578	424
Mineral property, plant and equipment	2,538	2,496
	$14,806	$13,843
Cost at January 1	$13,843	$12,705
Additions	1,721	1,608
Dispositions	(758)	(470)
Cost at December 31	$14,806	$13,843
Accumulated depreciation, depletion and amortization		
Balance at January 1	$ 6,535	$ 5,861
Current-year provision	1,084	984
Dispositions	(507)	(304)
Other changes	(3)	(6)
Balance at December 31	$ 7,109	$ 6,535
Property, plant and equipment less depreciation, depletion and amortization at December 31	$ 7,697	$ 7,308

Exhibit 2.11, continued

Measures of Plant Age:

$$\text{Average Total Life Span} = \frac{\text{Gross PP\&E (a)} \quad \$14,806}{\text{Current Depreciation Expense} \quad \$ 1,084} = 13.6 \text{ years}$$

(a) Although not excluded in this illustration, it is probably more correct to
exclude land from the computation because land does not depreciate. In
this case, land could not be separately identified from the land
improvements.

Disaggregation

$$\text{Average Age} = \frac{\text{Accumulated Depreciation} \quad \$7,109}{\text{Current Depreciation Expense} \quad \$1,084} = 6.5 \text{ years}$$

$$\text{Average Remaining Life} = \frac{\text{Net PP\&E} \quad \$7,697}{\text{Current Depreciation Expense} \quad \$1,084} = 7.1 \text{ years}$$

Average Total Life Span as above.................... 13.6 years

---

comparison of different firms, a capital intensive firm with older facilities (as determined by the average age on Exhibit 2.11) may report higher income, profit margins and returns on total assets than a firm with more current acquisitions of plant and equipment. The upward bias for the older firm results from the lower depreciation charges and the reduced net book values of plant assets towards the end of their useful lives. By comparing the average age of plant and equipment of the two firms, the analyst is able to identify the potential bias in the comparison of the firm's financial ratios. Once identified, the analyst can control for that bias when drawing conclusions about the overall financial condition and operating strength of the two firms.

Capitalization of Interest

A critical issue in accounting for certain acquisitions of plant assets is the determination of the proper treatment of the interest incurred on financing the plant asset acquisition or construction. Specifically, the accountant must determine if the interest on financing the acquisition is a cost of acquisition or construction or a pure finance charge. If the interest incurred is considered a cost of acquisition or construction it should be capitalized as part of the cost of the asset. On the other hand, if the interest incurred is considered a finance charge it should be expensed immediately on the current income statement.

FASB Statement No. 34, "Capitalization of Interest Cost", requires the capitalization of "material" interest charges incurred in the acquisition or construction of certain assets. The interest capitalized is known as "avoidable interest". Avoidable interest is an opportunity cost concept because it represents the interest that could have been avoided if the plant asset had not been acquired or constructed.

SFAS 34, paragraph 7, concluded that capitalization of interest on certain assets was necessary in order to properly value the acquisition cost of the asset and to properly match costs with revenues by allocating the interest cost over the asset's productive life through higher depreciation charges. The provisions of SFAS 34 are simply reinforcing the balance sheet and income statement objectives of accounting for current and noncurrent assets.

The following equation analysis illustrates the typical events involved in a capitalization of interest transaction.

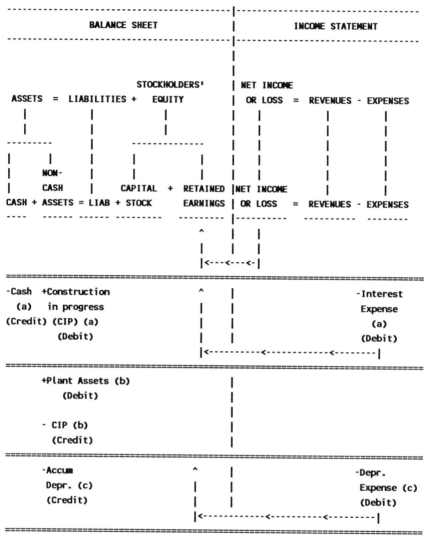

(a) Entry to record the payment of interest on borrowed funds and the allocation of interest to be expensed and the interest to be capitalized as Construction in Progress (CIP), a fixed asset account.

(b) Entry to record the reclassification of cost from CIP to Plant Assets upon completion of construction.

(c) Entry to record depreciation for the year.

There are four major considerations in the application of the SFAS 34 interest capitalization requirements. These are:

1. The assets that qualify for interest capitalization;

2. The expenditures on which interest should be computed;

3. The rate of interest to be used in the computations;

4. The period of capitalization.

Qualifying Assets.[3] According to SFAS 34, paragraph 9, if material, interest charges relating to the following projects should be capitalized:

1. "Assets constructed or otherwise produced for the firm's own use (including assets constructed or produced for the enterprise by others for which deposits or progress payments have been made)" (e.g., a self-constructed power plant by a public utility). This category does not include the manufacture of inventory or other routine production.

2. "Assets intended for sale or lease that are constructed or otherwise produced as discrete projects" (e.g., office buildings, land purchased for future development).

3. Paragraph 5 of SFAS 58, "Capitalization of Interest Costs in Financial Statements that Include Investments Accounted for by the Equity Method", amends SFAS 34 to include as a qualifying asset.

   Investments (equity, loans and advances) accounted for by the equity method while the investee has activities in progress necessary to commence its planned principal operations provided that the investee's activities include the use of funds to acquire qualifying assets for its operations.

Of course, interest accrued after the planned operations begin cannot be capitalized. In addition, interest cannot be capitalized on assets that are ready for intended use, even if held idle.

Expenditures on Which Interest Should be Computed. If the assets qualify for capitalization, SFAS 34, paragraph 13, states that interest should be computed on the "weighted average accumulated expenditures" for the year or the accounting period for which interest capitalization is required. The average accumulated expenditure is a measure of the amount of "outstanding debt" associated with the project, either directly or indirectly, for which the firm incurs finance charges. From the opportunity cost standpoint, debt could have been avoided or retired if the average expenditures for the period were not made.

There are two approaches used in practice to determine the average accumulated expenditure. The following example will illustrate these two methods.

Assume a firm is constructing its own plant. During the first year of construction, the firm incurred expenditures equal to $3,000,000. The $3,000,000 was paid in four equal installments of $750,000 at the end of each quarter. There are two ways to determine the weighted average accumulated expenditure.

First, the firm could weight each expenditure by the number of months each payment was "outstanding". That is,

```
March 31...............$  750,000  x  9/12  =  $  562,500
June 30...............    750,000  x  6/12  =     375,000
Sept. 30..............    750,000  x  3/12  =     187,500
Dec. 31...............    750,000  x  0/12  =           0
                       ------------              ------------
                        $3,000,000               $1,125,000
                       ============              ============
```

The $1,125,000 becomes the "principal" on which avoidable interest is computed.

Second, if it is reasonable to assume that expenditures are made on a uniform basis throughout the accounting period, then the weighted average accumulated expenditure can be estimated by a simple averaging process.

```
(Ending Balance of CIP  -  Beginning Balance of CIP) / 2
```

In this case the average expenditure would be $1,500,000 (i.e., [$3,000,000 - 0] / 2), and avoidable interest would be determined on this amount.

The Rate of Interest.[4] In determining the rate of interest to use for capitalization, a distinction must be made between "direct debt" and "indirect debt". Direct debt is debt incurred specifically to finance the project (e.g., a state bond issue is passed to finance construction of a nuclear power plant). If the weighted average accumulated expenditure for the accounting period is less than or equal to the face amount of the direct debt, then the actual coupon rate of interest on the direct debt is multiplied against the weighted average accumulated expenditure for the period to determine the amount of interest to capitalize.

However, if the weighted average accumulated expenditure exceeds the outstanding balance of the direct debt, the accountant assumes that by undertaking the project, the firm foregoes the opportunity to liquidate all other outstanding debt. This other debt is the so-called indirect debt. Since this is only an assumption, the accountant cannot determine the order in which the indirect debt would have been liquidated. As a result, a weighted average interest rate for the all indirect debt is calculated and is applied against the excess of the weighted average accumulated expenditure over the amount of direct debt outstanding.

In recent practice, many firms have been using a single weighted average rate of interest determined by averaging the rates of interest on the direct debt and all of the indirect debt. This single average rate of interest is multiplied by the average accumulated expenditure for the period in order to determine the amount of interest to be capitalized.

Period of Interest Capitalization. According to SFAS 34, paragraph 17, interest is to be capitalized from the time of the initial expenditure up to the time the asset is ready for its intended use. Therefore, if construction is completed but the asset is idle (e.g., protests blocking the operation of a nuclear power plant), interest incurred after the completion of the project must be charged to expense and cannot be capitalized.

Other Issues. Other requirements relating to interest capitalization include the following.

1. If direct debt is obtained but remains idle until construction begins, or during the construction period, the debt proceeds may be invested in interest earning assets on a temporary basis. According to FASB Technical Bulletin No. 81-5, any interest earned cannot be offset against the amount of interest capitalized and the amount of interest expensed. That is, the construction and financing decision must be accounted for separately from any subsequent investment decisions.

2. Due to the accountant's assumptions and the averaging procedures used in the SFAS 34 computations, it is possible that there could be an amount of interest to be capitalized in excess of the actual debt service for the period. This is not permitted. The maximum amount of interest to be capitalized under SFAS 34, paragraph 15, is equal to the actual interest incurred during the accounting period.

3. As indicated in the equation analysis above, when interest is capitalized it is added to the cost of construction or production and is charged to a noncurrent asset account on the balance sheet, construction in progress. When construction is completed and the asset is ready for its intended use, it is reclassified out of construction in progress and into plant assets. The plant asset account is now subject to depreciation. The depreciation charges will be increased by including part of the write-off of the interest previously capitalized. As a result, interest previously capitalized is ultimately charged against income via depreciation expense over the useful life of the asset.

4. When interest is capitalized as an asset on the balance sheet, the amount of interest expense charged against income on the income statement is not the total debt service for the period. However, SFAS 34, paragraph 21, requires that the firm must disclose the amount of interest capitalized for the year, either in the financial statements or in the related footnotes. By adding the interest capitalized per the footnote to the interest expense charged on the income statement, the analyst can determine the total interest incurred for the year. This information is required in the computation of financial statistics such as the times-interest-earned ratio and other fixed charge coverage ratios. If the analyst only uses the interest expense reported on the income statement, these ratios and other statistics could be significantly misstated.

Illustration of Interest Capitalization. Assume that a firm is constructing its own plant. The total expenditures for the first year of construction amounted to $3,000,000. Using the estimation technique, the average accumulated expenditure for the year is $1,500,000 (i.e., [$3,000,000 - 0] / 2).

It is assumed that the firm had the following debt structure.

Debt directly related to the project..........$1,000,000, 10% Note

Debt not directly related to the project...... $200,000, 12% Note

Debt not directly related to the project......$1,000,000, 9% Bonds

The amount of interest to be capitalized for the year is determined as follows:

1. Determine the weighted average rate of interest on indirect debt.

The weighted average rate of interest is required because $500,000 of the indirect debt is needed to cover the expenditures for the year. That is, the average expenditure for the year was determined to be $1,500,000, but there is only $1,000,000 of direct debt available to finance these expenditures. Therefore, an additional $500,000 (i.e., $1,500,000 - 1,000,000) is assumed to have been financed from the indirect sources.

Principal	Rate	Interest	Weighted Average Rate
$ 200,000	12%	$ 24,000 (a)	
1,000,000	9%	90,000 (b)	
$1,200,000		$114,000	$114,000 / $1,200,000 = 9 1/2%

2. Compute the total interest to be capitalized for the year.

Direct debt..........$1,000,000 x   10% = $100,000 (c)

Indirect debt........ 500,000 x 9 1/2% =   47,500

Avoidable interest to be capitalized........ $147,500

Note that the maximum interest that can be capitalized for the year is equal to the actual interest of $214,000 (i.e., a + b + c).

3. Determine the interest expense to be reported on the income statement.

Total interest paid...........$214,000

Less: Interest capitalized....<147,500>

Interest expense..............$ 66,500

The amount of interest capitalized for the period will be disclosed in the footnotes to the financial statements. A sample footnote disclosure of interest capitalized by General Electric in 1988 is presented in Exhibit 2.12. This disclosure is critical for the analyst because it may be the only source of information available relating to the actual debt service for the year.

Other Noncurrent Assets: Deferred Charges

Prepaid expenses are advance payments for goods and services to be received in the future (e.g., prepaid rent, prepaid insurance). Generally, prepaid expenses are capitalized as current assets on the balance sheet until expired. When expired, usually with the passage of time, they are charged to expense on the income statement. The analysts must consider the fact that prepaid expenses are not highly liquid assets because, even if classified as current, they are incapable of satisfying creditor claims or being converted into cash.

Deferred charges are essentially long-term prepaid expenses. Specifically, they are charges already incurred but are capitalized as assets. Therefore, the charge against income is deferred to future periods when management expects to receive the benefits from these current expenditures. This is justified by the matching principle. For example, if a firm pays for a significant amount of advertising towards the end of an accounting period and management believes that the impact of the ad campaign will extend for approximately two years, management will defer the cost of advertising as a long-term prepaid asset and amortize it over two years so as to match the cost against the increased sales resulting from the advertisements.

As noted in the discussion of the capitalization-expense alternative for the cost of a plant asset, management has a great deal of discretion in determining which costs should be expensed and which costs should be capitalized. In addition, there is supporting theoretical justification for either alternative treatment. Therefore, care must be taken in the analysis of deferred expenses because many of these long-term "assets" may actually have no future economic value to the firm and may be nothing more than expenses erroneously capitalized as assets. Not only does this misclassification overstate asset value, none of which is available for collateral or for generating future income and cash flow, it also overstates income and earnings per common share.

INTANGIBLE ASSETS

Introduction

Intangible assets are defined as assets without physical substance but which have economic value to the firm because of the rights they confer upon the holder. There are basically two classifications of intangible assets:

1. Specifically identifiable intangible assets. This group includes intangible

EXHIBIT 2.12

Sample Disclosure: General Electric Company: Footnote Disclosure of
Capitalized Interest

Note 8 Interest and Other Financial Charges

GE. Interest capitalized, principally on major property,
plant and equipment projects, was $11 million in 1988,
$23 million in 1987 and $38 million in 1986.

GEFS. GEFS interest and discount expense reported in the
Statement of Earnings is net of interest income on temporary investments of excess funds ($285 million, $165 million and $53 million in 1988, 1987 and 1986, respectively)
and capitalized interest of $16 million, $4 million and
$8 million, respectively, for 1988, 1987 and 1986.

Source: General Electric Company 1988 Annual Report. Copyright, 1989, by
The General Electric Company. Reprinted with permission.

assets such as patents, copyrights, trademarks, trade names, leaseholds, leasehold improvements and franchises. Specifically identifiable intangible assets have definite and determinable lives (e.g., the legal life of a patent is seventeen years).

2. Intangible assets that are not specifically identifiable. This classification only includes goodwill. As will be discussed in the chapter on intercorporate investments and business combinations, goodwill is usually determined as the excess of acquisition cost over the fair market value of the net assets acquired. Goodwill has an indefinite life and is tied to the continued existence of the acquired entity. Therefore, goodwill cannot be recorded unless the entity is purchased. As a result, an entity could be expending resources to develop, maintain or restore such intangible value, but it would not be reported on the balance sheet until "paid for" in an objectively determined transaction. For example, expenditures on training programs must be expensed as incurred. However, the firm must expect some future economic benefit from management training, otherwise the costs would not be incurred. Regardless of their future economic benefit, these expenditures and their related intangible values cannot be recorded as assets until an independent party pays for them in an acquisition of the entity.

Amortization of Intangible Assets

According to APB Opinion No. 17, "Intangible Assets", all intangible assets, including goodwill, are subject to amortization. The intangible must be amortized over its economic life or legal life, whichever is shorter, not to exceed forty years. The straight-line method of amortization should be used, unless some other systematic method is found to be preferable under the circumstances. Straight-line amortization is identical to straight-line depreciation with the exception that an accumulated amortization account is generally not used in practice. Instead, the intangible asset (e.g., copyright) is reduced directly.

It should be noted that because Opinion 17 was only effective from 1970, financial statements reporting pre-1970 goodwill are not subject to amortization. However, firms can amortize pre-1970 goodwill on a voluntary basis. As would be the case for any asset, in the event that management determines that recorded goodwill is of no economic value, it must be written off immediately as a charge against income.

Special Cases: Research and Development Costs and Computer Software Costs

Research and Development Costs (R&D). According to paragraph 12 of FASB Statement No. 2, "Accounting for Research and Development Costs", "all R&D costs must be expensed as incurred", unless reimbursed under contract. If to be reimbursed, the R&D costs would be capitalized as a receivable. SFAS 2, paragraph 13, also requires the disclosure of the level of R&D expenditures in the financial statements.

Prior to SFAS 2, R&D costs were capitalized as an intangible asset under the theory that these costs represented future economic benefit to the firm when a patented product was developed. For the most part, this theoretical justification is valid. However, accountants found it difficult to determine the asset value related to the R&D costs in practice. Specifically, it was difficult to estimate which R&D costs were going to result in successful products and which costs would become worthless. Due to the insurmountable problems involved in assessing potential marketability and value of these expenditures, accountants adopted a conservative position in that they decided to understate asset value and income (i.e., all R&D expenditures were assumed to be fully expired without any economic benefit) rather than overstate assets and income (i.e., by capitalizing R&D costs as an intangible asset). With expensing all R&D as incurred, the costs included in a patent account are now minimal (e.g., legal costs and registration fees). A patent can only include R&D costs if the reporting entity purchases the research leading to the patent from an outside research firm.

The fact that all R&D costs are expensed immediately is a result of a pragmatic solution by the FASB and does not literally imply that these expenditures have no future service potential. Actually, for certain industries, R&D is probably one of the most important investments made by the firm. This is precisely one of the reasons why SFAS 2 requires the disclosure of the firm's R&D activity. Sample disclosures of R&D activity are presented in Exhibits 2.13 and 2.14.

The disclosure of R&D activity can assist the analyst in estimating the value of the unrecorded asset related to a firm's research activity. This estimation cannot be made in the case of a firm's other significant unrecorded asset, goodwill. If an analyst believes that R&D is a significant investment for the firm, the disclosure of its R&D activity can be used to restate the financial statements on a proforma basis, under the assumption that the firm capitalizes R&D costs and amortizes these costs over the expected period of benefit. An analytical capitalization of the R&D costs for Data General Corporation is presented in Exhibit 2.15.

The proforma financial information presented in Exhibit 2.15 assumes that the firm's R&D activity began in 1982 and that all R&D costs are assumed to have a three-year economic life. After the restatement, the intangible asset account, deferred R&D of $95,902, is included among the firm's noncurrent assets. In addition, the 1984 proforma income before extraordinary gain and income taxes is $120,881. The actual 1984 income before extraordinary gain and income taxes was $109,601. The difference is $11,280, which is exactly the difference between the $101,520 R&D expensed under SFAS 2 and the 1984 proforma amortization of the capitalized R&D of $90,240.

After the issuance of SFAS 2, many firms attempted to circumvent the requirement to expense R&D as incurred by creating a limited partnership to conduct research for the parent or related company. Under the limited partnership treatment, the parent would treat the R&D as purchased and capitalize it as an asset, possibly in the patent account. The limited partnership would have its R&D reimbursed so that according to SFAS 2, it could be capitalized as a receivable from the parent. Under this scenario, neither party to the transaction would recognize the R&D expense as required by SFAS 2.

To resolve this problem, the FASB issued Statement No. 68, "Research and

EXHIBIT 2.13

Sample Disclosure: Data General Corporation: Disclosure of Research and Development Expense on the Statement of Income

----

Consolidated Statements of Income

Data General Corporation

	Year Ended		
In thousands except income per share	**Sept. 29, 1984 (53 Weeks)**	Sept. 24, 1983 (52 Weeks)	Sept. 25, 1982 (52 Weeks)
Revenues:			
Equipment sales	**$ 884,375**	$595,618	$617,183
Service and other revenues billed separately	**276,440**	233,286	188,727
Total revenues	**1,160,815**	828,904	805,910
Costs and expenses:			
Cost of equipment sales, service, and other revenues	**659,121**	476,391	457,414
Research and development	**101,520**	84,662	84,538
Selling, general, and administrative	**297,549**	231,321	228,052
Total costs and expenses	**1,058,190**	792,374	770,004
Income from operations	**102,625**	36,530	35,906
Other income, principally interest	**23,662**	21,290	18,727
Interest expense	**(16,686)**	(16,810)	(17,582)
Income before extraordinary gain and income taxes	**109,601**	41,010	37,051
Provision for income taxes	**(42,369)**	(17,875)	(17,222)
Reversal of deferred taxes on DISC income	**12,551**	—	—
Income before extraordinary gain	**79,783**	23,135	19,829
Extraordinary gain	**3,473**	—	4,829
Net income	**$ 83,256**	$ 23,135	$ 24,658
Income per share:			
Income before extraordinary gain	**$3.08**	$ .96	$ .92
Extraordinary gain	**.13**	—	.22
Net income	**$3.21**	$ .96	$1.14
Weighted average shares outstanding including common stock equivalents	**25,939**	23,985	21,676

The company does not segregate cost data for service and other revenues billed separately to customers.

Source: Data General Corporation 1984 Annual Report. Copyright, 1984, by Data General Corporation. Reprinted with permission.

EXHIBIT 2.14

Sample Disclosure: NBI Incorporated: Footnote Disclosure of Research and Development Activity

---

NBI, Inc.
Notes to Consolidated Financial Statements
June 30, 1985, 1984 and 1983

1. Summary of significant accounting policies

Principles of consolidation: The consolidated financial statements include the accounts of the Company and its subsidiaries, which are wholly-owned. All significant intercompany accounts and profits have been eliminated.

Revenue recognition: Revenue from equipment sales and leases accounted for as sales-type leases is recognized upon shipment to the customer. For equipment installed under operating leases, rental and service revenue is recognized ratably over the term of the lease.

Equipment installed under non-cancellable sales-type leases is recorded as a sale at the discounted present value of the rental payments and the related cost of the equipment is charged to cost of sales.

Leasing arrangements: The Company leases certain of its office automation equipment to customers under non-cancellable agreements which expire within 3 years. Substantially all contracts provide for minimum rentals and require the lessee to pay executory costs. The majority of these contracts are classified as sales-type leases.

Research and development costs: All costs for product research and development are expensed as incurred and are: $12,298,000 in 1985, $10,122,000 in 1984 and $8,891,000 in 1983.

Inventories: Inventories are stated at the lower of cost (first-in, first-out method) or market. The cost of manufactured inventories includes material, labor and factory overhead.

Marketable securities: Marketable securities consist of preferred stocks which have a cost of $5,581,000, $8,483,000 and $11,180,000 as of June 30, 1985, 1984 and 1983, respectively. Marketable securities are valued at the lower of aggregate cost or market value and, at June 30, 1985 had unrealized losses of $206,000. The cost of securities sold was determined by the specific identification method.

Depreciation: Capital assets are carried at cost and depreciated on a straight-line basis over the following lives:

Asset Type	Life
Rental equipment	3 year
Buildings	40 year
Building improvements	5-15 year
Machinery and equipment	5-10 year
Furniture and fixtures	5-7 year
Leasehold improvements	lease term

Income taxes: Investment and research and experimentation tax credits are accounted for as reductions of income tax expense under the flow-through method. Income taxes have not been provided on the undistributed earnings of the Company's Foreign Sales Corporation, NBI Virgin Islands, Inc.

Deferred income taxes result from timing differences in the recognition of revenue and expense for financial statement and tax return purposes.

Source: NBI, Inc. 1985 Annual Report. Copyright, 1985, by NBI, Inc. Reprinted with permission.

EXHIBIT 2.15

Illustration: Capitalization of Research and Development Costs For
Data General Corporation

SEE EXHIBIT 2.14 FOR THE SOURCE DATA USED IN THIS ILLUSTRATION

Deferral or Capitalization of R&D Costs:

```
        1982...............$ 84,538
        1983...............  84,662
        1984............... 101,520
                           ---------
        Total..............$270,720
```

Less: Accumulated Amortization....<174,818> See schedule below.
```
                                   ---------
     Net Book Value at 9/24/84....$ 95,902
                                   =========
```

Amortization Table: (Assumes a three-year life and all R&D acquisitions were made as of the beginning of the year.)

	Expensed In			
Acquired In	1982	1983	1984	Accumulated
1982: ($ 84,538/3yrs)....	$28,179	$28,179	$28,179	$ 84,538
1983: ($ 84,662/3yrs)....	N/A	28,220	28,220	56,440
1984: ($101,520/3yrs)....	N/A	N/A	33,840	33,840
			$90,240	$174,818

Balance Sheet Restatement in 1984:

Noncurrent Assets:

```
   Deferred R&D Costs (net of accumulated
      amortization of $174,818)...............+ $95,202
```

Stockholders' Equity:

```
   Retained Earnings (to balance)...............+ $95,202
```

Exhibit 2.15, continued

Income Statement Restatement in 1984:

Income before extraordinary gain and income taxes (as reported)......$109,601

Add Back: R&D Costs expensed during the year......................... 101,520

Less: Amortization expense (Proforma).............................< 90,240>

Income before extraordinary gain and income taxes (as restated)......$120,881
                                                                       =========

Development Arrangements", in 1982. According to SFAS 68 and the SEC, these arrangements are in substance lending agreements in which the parent has borrowed funds from the limited partnership and is using this financing to cover its R&D costs, which must be charged to expense. In general, the accountant must expense the R&D on the books of the entity that received the primary benefit from the research activity. Normally, the parent company would be required to charge income for the R&D expenditures and record the liability to the limited partnership. The limited partnership would record the receivable from the parent for reimbursement of the cash expended on its R&D activities.

Research Costs and Patents. As noted above, unless a firm purchases research from another entity in an objectively determined transaction, the amounts capitalized in the patent account on the balance sheet will be minimal. The patent account will normally only consist of registration fees and the legal costs involved with the successful defense of the patent.

Computer Software Costs. In recent years, questions have been raised regarding the nature of computer software costs incurred by firms that sell or lease software to outside entities. Specifically, it was uncertain if computer software costs were R&D, an intangible asset or a cost of inventory. Of course, the costs of software, systems and programs developed internally, and exclusively for internal use, are expensed as incurred in the form of salaries and supplies.

The nature of computer software costs was clearly defined by the FASB in Statement No. 86, "Accounting for the Costs of Computer Software to be Sold, Leased, or Otherwise Marketed". According to SFAS 86, computer software costs for firms that develop software for external use are incurred in three distinct stages. At each stage, a different accounting treatment is required.

1. Computer software costs expensed as research and development. According to SFAS 86, paragraph 3, all costs incurred to establish the software's "technological feasibility" are classified as R&D and therefore must be expensed as incurred. These costs are considered necessary to determine the firm's ability to produce the software according to specification. This category of computer software costs would include the costs of planning, designing, coding and testing.

2. Computer software costs capitalized as an intangible asset. According to paragraph 5 of SFAS 86, after the technological feasibility of the software has been established, the remainder of the costs needed to generate product masters are to be capitalized as an intangible asset, "computer software production costs". The term *product masters* includes the completed versionsof the software, documentation and training materials.

3. Computer software costs included in inventory. The costs incurred to duplicate and package the software, the documentation and the training materials are to be capitalized as part of the cost of inventory according to SFAS 86, paragraph 9.

It should be noted that if computer software is purchased and it has alternative future uses, it may also be capitalized. Without alternative future use, the cost of purchased software must be expensed as incurred. The alternative future use test should also be applied to the acquisition of software that will be integrated with a product or process in which the R&D phase is not complete.

For those computer software costs capitalized as an intangible asset, SFAS 86, paragraph 8, requires that a firm amortize these costs by using the greater of:

1. The ratio of current gross revenues to the total current and expected future gross revenues (i.e., the percent of revenue approach), or

2. The straight-line method over the remaining useful life of the asset.

SFAS 86 adopted a conservative approach in that all costs preceding the establishment of technological feasibility must be expensed as incurred. In addition, the Board expressed great concern over the valuation of the capitalized software costs presented in the balance sheet. As a result, SFAS 86, paragraph 10, requires that the capitalized costs be carried at the lower of the net unamortized cost at year end or net realizable value. Although not specified in SFAS 86, net realizable value is usually defined as expected revenues less expected costs of disposal. If cost (i.e., the net unamortized cost of the intangible) exceeds net realizable value, the intangible asset must be written down to net realizable value without subsequent recovery. Of course, the costs included in inventory would be carried at either LIFO, FIFO or average cost, and would be subject to the LCM test for obsolescence discussed earlier in this chapter.

SFAS 86, paragraph 11, requires a separate disclosure of a firm's software development activity. The disclosure should include the balance of the unamortized computer software costs included in each balance sheet presented, and the total amount charged to expense in each income statement presented for the amounts amortized and the amounts written down to net realizable value. The SFAS 2 disclosure requirements also apply to those computer software costs expensed as R&D. A sample disclosure for the adoption of SFAS 86 by Wang Laboratories, Inc. for the year ended June 30, 1986 is presented in Exhibit 2.16.

Finally, SFAS 86, paragraph 6, requires that the costs of improvement, maintenance and customer support should be charged to expense at the point at which the related revenue is recognized or when those costs are incurred, whichever comes first.

NATURAL RESOURCES

Introduction

Natural resources include oil and gas deposits, timberlands, and mineral deposits. Natural resources are recorded at cost and depleted over their economic lives. As in the case of depreciation and amortization, the cost of a natural resource is allocated to the expected future periods of benefit through systematic charges against income.

For financial reporting purposes, the natural resource is normally depleted by

EXHIBIT 2.16

Sample Disclosure: Wang Laboratories Incorporated: Footnote Disclosure of Deferred Computer Software Costs

----

Note B — Deferred Software Production Costs

Effective July 1, 1985, the Company adopted a change in accounting for costs of computer software. The change was made in accordance with the provisions of Statement of Finan- cial Accounting Standards No. 86, which specifies that certain costs in- curred in the development of com- puter software to be sold or leased to customers are to be capitalized and amortized over the economic useful life of the software product. Total costs capitalized and deferred during the year ended June 30, 1986 ap- proximated $21.1 million, of which $1.8 million has been amortized and charged to expense. The net effect of the change ($19.3 million) was re- corded in the fourth quarter of Fiscal 1986.

----

the units-of-production method. The depreciation of related costs (e.g., tunnels, shafts and offshore platforms) would be depreciated over the expected useful life of the natural resource if these assets were not movable or did not have alternative future uses. If the assets are movable and have an alternative future use, they would be depreciated over their own expected useful lives or the life of the natural resource, whichever is shorter.

For tax purposes, firms can deduct the greater of cost or percentage depletion. Percentage depletion can only be used under highly restrictive conditions. Under percentage or statutory depletion, the firm is allowed a depletion deduction from between 5% and 22% of the gross revenue generated from the resource. The percentage allowed depends on the natural resource in question. Because percentage depletion is based on gross revenues rather than cost, depletion could be in excess of the total cost of the natural resource. Even if the firm uses a cost-based depletion method for tax purposes, it may not be the same as the deduction for financial reporting purposes due to other book-tax differences, such as the determination of the costs to be capitalized in the determination of the cost of the natural resource (i.e., the depletion base).

Accounting for Natural Resources

Generally, accounting for natural resources is straightforward. However, there are several controversial accounting and reporting issues relating to oil and gas producing firms. The issues relating to proper accounting and reporting in the oil and gas industry is sometimes known as the "oil and gas controversy". As part of this controversy, the primary point of discussion centers around the proper treatment of the costs incurred in the exploration of nonproducing wells (i.e., dry holes). Once again, the argument is based on the capitalization-expense alternative facing management. That is, which costs incurred in the exploration activities of an oil and gas producing entity should be capitalized as part of the cost of the natural resource (i.e., the depletion base) and which costs should be expensed immediately. The nature of the costs associated with oil and gas producing activities and the alternative accounting methods are presented below.

The Cost of a Natural Resource: The Depletion Base. The cost of a natural resource in the oil and gas industry consists of three elements:

1. Acquisition cost of the deposit. The acquisition cost is the price paid to obtain the property or the right to search and explore.

2. Development costs. The development costs include intangible development costs such as grading the land, construction of tunnels and shafts and the costs of constructing offshore drilling platforms. As noted earlier, some of these costs relate to individual assets that can be moved to be utilized in alternative future locations.

3. Exploration costs. These are the costs of staffing and drilling for oil and gas. The proper accounting treatment of exploration costs is the primary component of the oil and gas controversy.

Alternative Accounting Treatments of Exploration Costs. There are two methods of accounting for costs of exploration activities. These methods are known as full-costs and successful efforts.

Under the full-cost method, all costs associated with successful and producing wells, as well as unsuccessful or dry holes, are capitalized as part of the cost of the natural resource. The full-cost method's capitalization treatment of the cost of dry wells is justified by the theory that the costs of exploring and drilling dry wells are a "reasonable and necessary" expenditure required for the discovery of successful and producing wells from the same offshore tract of land. Of course, if the entire tract of land is found to be unproductive, all costs should be written off in the year in which the loss of value becomes evident.

The full-cost method is an income increasing alternative in the early years of the natural resource's useful life. By capitalizing the costs of dry wells, both assets and income are initially increased. However, in the later years, income will be reduced through recognition of higher depletion charges.

The full-cost method is normally used by the smaller, more aggressive oil and gas firms, "the independents", who are interested in initially reporting higher profits for purposes of raising capital by either debt or equity financing.

Under the successful-efforts method, only those costs associated with exploring successful and producing wells are capitalized as part of the depletion base. All costs associated with dry wells are expensed as incurred. By expensing all costs incurred in exploring the unsuccessful project, the successful-efforts method becomes the income reducing accounting alternative in the early years of the life of the natural resource. In the later years of the life of the natural resource, the depletion charges would be lower and reported profits would be higher relative to the full-cost method. The use of the successful-efforts method is justified by the theory that dry wells produce no oil and gas and provide no future economic benefit. Therefore, the costs associated with the dry wells should be expensed at the point at which the particular deposit is determined to be nonproductive. As noted above, if all of the property is found to be unproductive, all costs associated with the project should be written off against income in the year in which the project is determined to be worthless.

The successful-efforts method is used by larger, established firms in an attempt to reduce reported profits. The large oil and gas firms tend to employ an overall income reducing reporting strategy in an attempt to reduce their "size" so as to minimize public criticism and possible government interference.

The Oil and Gas Controversy. The oil and gas controversy began in 1977 with the FASB's issuance of Statement No. 19, "Financial Accounting and Reporting by Oil and Gas Producing Companies". Under SFAS 19, paragraph 19, only the successful-efforts method of accounting was permitted. The restriction of the use of the full-cost method raised significant protests and lobbying in Congress from the smaller oil and gas companies. Due to this pressure, in 1979 the FASB issued Statement No. 25, "Suspension of Certain Accounting Requirements for Oil and Gas Producing Companies". SFAS 25, paragraph 4, suspended the effective date of SFAS 19. However, SFAS 25 has never been amended, so that both methods of accounting are currently accepted in practice.

Even with both the full-cost and successful-efforts methods in use by 1979, the

SEC was not satisfied with the accounting and reporting standards for oil and gas producing activities. As a result, the SEC proposed the implementation of reserve recognition accounting (RRA). Under the RRA proposal, as soon as oil is discovered, the cost of the natural resource should be capitalized and set equal to the discounted value of the expected future net cash flows from proven oil and gas reserves. Income would also be recognized and measured by the amounts capitalized, net of the costs incurred in the acquisition, development and exploration of the natural resource. The RRA valuation would be reviewed each year. Revisions of the RRA valuation could be due to changes in interest rate assumptions, projected oil and gas prices, and proven oil and gas reserves. Changes in the discounted cash flow valuation would be reflected on the income statement as income if the RRA value increased from the prior year, and write-offs could result if the undepleted balance of the oil and gas deposit exceeded its discounted cash flow valuation.

Given the potential errors in geological surveys and interest rate assumptions, and the volatility of oil and gas prices, RRA could result in significant year-to-year fluctuations in reported profits. Therefore, the SEC abandoned its RRA proposal in 1982. As a compromise, the FASB expanded the disclosure requirements for oil and gas producing activities in 1982 with the issuance of Statement No. 69, "Disclosures about Oil and Gas Producing Activities". SFAS 69, paragraphs 6 and 7, requires the disclosure of the following information about a firm's oil and gas producing activities.

1. Both publicly traded and privately held companies engaged in significant oil and gas producing activities must disclose:

    a. "the method of accounting for costs incurred" (i.e., full-cost or successful-efforts);
    b. "the manner of disposing of capitalized costs relating to those activities" (i.e., expensing immediately or capitalization and then depleting).

2. The following additional disclosures are required for publicly traded companies only:

    a. "Proved oil and gas reserve quantities" at the beginning and the end of the period;
    b. "Capitalized costs relating to oil and gas producing activities" and the related accumulated depreciation, depletion, etc;
    c. "Costs incurred for property acquisition, exploration and development activities";
    d. "Results of operations in the aggregate and for the separate geographical areas of activity";
    e. "A standardized measure of discounted future net cash flows relating to the proved oil and gas reserve quantities".

This last disclosure requirement is similar to the SEC's RRA proposal.

For large oil and gas producing companies, the disclosures required under

SFAS 69 can be extensive. Exhibit 2.17 presents the supplemental information on oil and gas exploration and production activities by Exxon in 1984. Of particular interest to the analyst is the comparison of the net carrying value of the natural resource with the discounted cash flow measure. In Exhibit 2.17, the net capitalized costs at December 31, 1984 are equal to $22,176. The standardized measure of discounted future net cash flows relating to proved oil and gas reserve quantities are equal to $29,949 at December 31, 1984. In this case, the net carrying value of the natural resource on Exxon's balance sheet is conservative and therefore possibly undervalued. Undervaluation of the carrying value of the natural resource would be expected in Exxon's case due to its use of the successful efforts method. Nonetheless, the discounted cash flow measure is only a tentative benchmark, due to the possible errors in estimating oil and gas reserve quantities and the assumptions used in projections such as future oil and gas prices, future operating costs and the appropriate discount rate to use in the computations.

It is important to note that the SEC encouraged the FASB to require the current value disclosures in SFAS 69 due to the ceiling imposed by the SEC on the amounts to be capitalized under the full-cost method. Specifically, in 1986 the SEC sanctioned the use of full-cost accounting, but only with a ceiling on the total amount of costs to be capitalized in the carrying value of the natural resource. Costs can be capitalized, but only up to the present value of the company's reserves. All costs incurred in excess of the ceiling must be expensed as incurred. In addition, if oil and gas prices or estimated reserves decrease, capitalized costs, net of accumulated depletion at the end of the year, could exceed the present value of the company's oil and gas reserves so that write-offs could be taken if these decreases are deemed to be permanent in nature.

Thus, given the SEC's imposed ceiling on the valuation of oil and gas deposits, if the discounted cash flow valuation was significantly less than the net carrying value at historical cost, it may imply that the natural resource on the balance sheet is overstated. If the fluctuation in the discounted cash flow valuation was other than temporary (e.g., a downward revision in the original estimate of proven oil and gas reserve quantities), a write-down of the cost of the natural resource may be considered appropriate. This is a very real possibility if one considers the potential overstatement of asset value under the full-cost method.

Due to the significance of the oil and gas activities of some firms and the different valuations that could result from the full-cost and the successful-efforts methods, it is important for the analyst to consider the possibility of overstatement of the natural resource and the potential write-off in subsequent accounting periods.

Utilization of the SFAS 69 supplemental disclosures of a firm's oil and gas producing activities, along with knowledge of industry trends and projections of oil and gas prices, can provide the analyst the sufficient data to assess the propriety of the valuation of the firm's natural resource base and the firm's ability to generate income and cash flows from its oil and gas producing activities. In addition, the analyst could use this information to project the need for future write-offs of the historical cost-based valuation of the carrying value of the firm's natural resources.

EXHIBIT 2.17

Sample Disclosure: Exxon Corporation: Footnote Disclosure of Supplemental Information on Oil and Gas Exploration and Production Activities

----

Supplemental Information on Oil and Gas Exploration and Production Activities

This section provides historical revenue, cost, operating earnings and reserve information regarding Exxon's oil and gas exploration and production operations during 1982, 1983 and 1984. This information was developed in conformance with Financial Accounting Standards Board Statement No. 19 — Financial Accounting and Reporting by Oil and Gas Producing Companies, as modified by Statements No. 25 and No. 69. For most of this section, the information is shown for each of the six major geographic areas in which the company operates. Additional information on exploration and production activities can be found on pages 5 through 11.

The following pages (pages 42 and 43) show the company's crude oil and natural gas reserves at year-end 1982, 1983 and 1984 and a summary of the major changes to these reserves — such as new discoveries and production — during these years. These reserves are shown separately for consolidated affiliates, for the company's proportional interest in proved reserves of equity companies and for supplies available under long-term agreements with foreign governments. Additional production information may be found on page 50.

The second set of tables, on page 44, provides consolidated oil and gas exploration and production costs that were capitalized at the end of 1983 and 1984 and costs which were incurred by the exploration and production function during 1982, 1983 and 1984. The company's proportional interests of capitalized costs and costs incurred by equity companies are shown separately.

The fifth table, on page 45, summarizes the earnings of the oil and gas exploration and production function for 1982, 1983 and 1984.

The data discussed on pages 42 through 45 are historical information and are consistent with the other financial and operating information published by Exxon. However, the tables on pages 46 and 47, concerning the "standardized measure of discounted future net cash flows," depart significantly from historical accounting practices. Exxon has taken exception to the disclosure of these data as required by Statement No. 69.

Discussion of Standardized Measure

The standardized measure data on pages 46 and 47 are based upon estimated volumes of oil and gas reserves as well as forecasts of future production rates over the lives of the reserves. While, in management's judgment, the quantities are reasonable, there is no methodology or certification process which would permit independent verification of such volumes and rates. The standardized measure data are also based upon prices and costs at December 31, 1984, with no provision for deducting exploration expenses, amortization of acquisition costs (bonus payments), depreciation of capitalized production investments, purchase costs of royalty oil and gas or other similar payments to governments. In addition, an arbitrary 10 percent discount rate (which does not necessarily represent a cost of capital, a borrowing cost, or reflect political risk) is used in determining present values.

Thus, the data set forth on pages 46 and 47 should not be interpreted as necessarily representing current profitability or amounts Exxon will receive, or costs which will be incurred, or the manner in which oil and gas will be produced from the respective oil and gas reserves. Actual future selling prices and related production costs, development costs, production schedules, and reserves and their classifications may differ significantly from data assumed or portrayed.

As a result of these concerns, the company does not believe that the presentation on pages 46 and 47 is the proper basis to reflect the results of oil and gas operations. However, the company believes that the table on page 45, when used in conjunction with the other historical data in this section, provides relevant information to assist in an evaluation of the company's oil and gas exploration and production operations and in the development of reasonable interpretations concerning the value of the oil and natural gas reserves, and the levels of future earnings and cash flows.

Exhibit 2.17, continued

Oil and Gas Reserves*

The following information, describing changes during the years and balances of oil and gas reserves at year-end 1982, 1983 and 1984, is presented in accordance with Financial Accounting Standards Board (FASB) Statement No. 19 – Financial Accounting and Reporting by Oil and Gas Producing Companies, as amended by Statements No. 25 and No. 69. The definitions of proved reserves used in these tables are those developed by the Department of Energy for its Financial Reporting System and adopted by the FASB.

Proved reserves are the estimated quantities of oil and gas which geological and engineering data demonstrate with reasonable certainty to be recoverable in future years from known reservoirs under existing economic and operating conditions. They include some reserves which may or

may not be producible within the lives of existing agreements. In some cases, substantial new investments in additional wells and related facilities will be required to recover these proved reserves, including a major pipeline in the case of Alaskan gas reserves.

Proved reserves include 100 percent of each majority-owned affiliate's participation in proved reserves and Exxon's ownership percentage of the proved reserves of equity companies, but exclude royalties and quantities due others when produced. Gas reserves exclude the gaseous equivalent of liquids expected to be removed from the gas on leases, at field facilities and at gas processing plants. These liquids are included in the category net proved reserves of crude oil and natural gas liquids.

Net proved developed reserves are those volumes which

	Total Worldwide	United States	Canada	Other Western Hemisphere	Europe	Middle East and Africa	Australia and Far East
				(millions of barrels)			
Crude oil and natural gas liquids							
Net proved developed and undeveloped reserves							
Beginning of year 1982	6,157	2,822	489	36	1,646	7	1,157
Revisions of previous estimates	440	160	141	(13)	131	1	20
Improved recovery	48	48	—	—	—	—	—
Extensions, discoveries, and other additions	201	76	1	2	108	14	—
Production	(499)	(270)	(35)	(4)	(105)	(2)	(83)
End of year 1982	6,347	2,836	596	21	1,780	20	1,094
Revisions of previous estimates	224	44	13	7	88	2	70
Improved recovery	59	59	—	—	—	—	—
Extensions, discoveries, and other additions	405	128	156	2	118	—	1
Production	(557)	(285)	(33)	(5)	(135)	(2)	(97)
End of year 1983	6,478	2,782	732	25	1,851	20	1,068
Revisions of previous estimates	155	67	16	3	(6)	—	75
Improved recovery	104	61	43	—	—	—	—
Extensions, discoveries, and other additions	327	90	152	2	69	—	14
Production	(590)	(285)	(34)	(6)	(150)	(2)	(113)
End of year 1984	6,474	2,715	909	24	1,764	18	1,044
Net proved developed reserves (included above)							
Beginning of year 1982	3,636	2,185	408	19	470	3	551
End of year 1982	3,863	2,134	527	19	624	3	556
End of year 1983	3,962	2,115	509	19	685	5	629
End of year 1984	3,924	2,030	530	21	597	3	743
Proportional interest in proved reserves of equity companies							
End of year 1982	75	—	—	—	50	—	25
End of year 1983	57	—	—	—	47	—	10
End of year 1984	69	—	—	—	58	—	11
Supplies available under long-term agreements with foreign governments							
End of year 1982	541	—	—	—	—	541	—
Received during the year 1982	8	—	—	—	—	8	—
End of year 1983	525	—	—	—	—	525	—
Received during the year 1983	9	—	—	—	—	9	—
End of year 1984	509	—	—	—	—	509	—
Received during the year 1984	8	—	—	—	—	8	—
Oil sands reserves							
End of year 1982	187	—	187	—	—	—	—
End of year 1983	179	—	179	—	—	—	—
End of year 1984	172	—	172	—	—	—	—
Worldwide net proved developed and undeveloped reserves (including supplies and oil sands)							
End of year 1982	7,150	2,836	783	21	1,830	561	1,119
End of year 1983	7,239	2,782	911	25	1,898	545	1,078
End of year 1984	7,224	2,715	1,081	24	1,822	527	1,055

----

are expected to be recovered through existing wells with existing equipment and operating methods. Undeveloped reserves are those volumes which are expected to be recovered as a result of future investments, pending or in-progress, to drill new wells, to recomplete existing wells, and/or to install facilities to collect and deliver the production from existing and future wells.

The United States net proved oil reserves include oil attributable to a secondary recovery program which is not yet in operation in the Prudhoe Bay field in Alaska and net proved natural gas reserves include 9,294 billion cubic feet of reserves in Alaska. Reserves attributable to oil and gas discoveries reported in the Mackenzie Delta region of Canada, and certain oil and gas discoveries elsewhere in the U.S. and Canada and in Malaysia, Thailand, Indonesia,

China, Australia, the U.K., the Netherlands and Norway, were not considered proved as of year-end 1984 due to geological, technological and economic uncertainties and therefore are not included in the tabulation.

Crude oil and natural gas liquids and natural gas production quantities shown are the net volumes withdrawn from Exxon's oil and gas reserves. These differ from the quantities of oil and gas delivered for sale by the producing function and, especially in the case of natural gas, volumes consumed and/or vented. Such quantities were not significant for crude oil and natural gas liquids. For natural gas, such quantities amounted to approximately 190 billion cubic feet in 1982, 183 billion cubic feet in 1983, and 157 billion cubic feet in 1984.

	Total Worldwide	United States	Canada	Other Western Hemisphere	Europe	Middle East and Africa	Australia and Far East
Natural gas			(billions of cubic feet)				
Net proved developed and undeveloped reserves							
Beginning of year 1982	**27,785**	**16,924**	**1,293**	**280**	**5,998**	**5**	**3,285**
Revisions of previous estimates	1,538	(45)	103	(13)	689	—	804
Improved recovery	36	36	—	—	—	—	—
Extensions, discoveries, and other additions	920	581	24	3	312	—	—
Production	(1,603)	(1,035)	(70)	(29)	(349)	(1)	(119)
End of year 1982	**28,676**	**16,461**	**1,350**	**241**	**6,650**	**4**	**3,970**
Revisions of previous estimates	1,825	1,323	7	4	506	—	(15)
Improved recovery	9	9	—	—	—	—	—
Extensions, discoveries, and other additions	1,307	586	9	3	703	—	6
Production	(1,516)	(946)	(66)	(28)	(365)	(1)	(110)
Sales of minerals-in-place	(1,022)	—	—	—	—	—	(1,022)
End of year 1983	**29,279**	**17,433**	**1,300**	**220**	**7,494**	**3**	**2,829**
Revisions of previous estimates	566	68	19	19	463	3	(4)
Improved recovery	36	20	16	—	—	1	—
Extensions, discoveries, and other additions	1,526	1,340	6	2	171	—	7
Production	(1,622)	(977)	(62)	(28)	(440)	(1)	(114)
End of year 1984	**29,785**	**17,884**	**1,279**	**213**	**7,688**	**3**	**2,718**
Net proved developed reserves (included above)							
Beginning of year 1982	22,906	15,886	1,021	208	3,097	5	2,689
End of year 1982	22,498	15,378	1,153	185	3,280	4	2,498
End of year 1983	23,010	16,366	1,127	163	3,251	3	2,100
End of year 1984	23,160	16,194	1,100	157	3,568	3	2,138
Proportional interest in proved reserves of equity companies							
End of year 1982	15,666	—	—	—	15,441	—	225
End of year 1983	17,541	—	—	—	17,441	—	100
End of year 1984	17,214	—	—	—	17,123	—	91
Worldwide net proved developed and undeveloped reserves							
End of year 1982	44,342	16,461	1,350	241	22,091	4	4,195
End of year 1983	46,820	17,433	1,300	220	24,935	3	2,929
End of year 1984	46,999	17,884	1,279	213	24,811	3	2,809

*These and other tables, as noted, in this report do not include reserve, supply, cost and other data relating to Exxon's interest in the Arabian American Oil Company (Aramco) because the government of Saudi Arabia prohibits the disclosure of confidential information under a directive issued by the Minister of Petroleum and Mineral Resources bearing Number 1030/Z. During 1980, the government acquired the beneficial interest in substantially all of Aramco's assets and operations. However, Aramco continues to have access to a significant volume of Saudi Arabian crude oil.

Exhibit 2.17, continued

Oil and Gas Exploration and Production Costs

The tables below summarize the capitalized costs at December 31, 1983 and 1984 and certain costs incurred in oil and gas producing activities during 1982, 1983 and 1984. The definitions of terms used in developing these tables are consistent with those described in Financial Accounting Standards Board Statement No. 19—Financial Accounting and Reporting by Oil and Gas Producing Companies.

The amounts shown in the table for total capitalized costs less the accumulated depreciation are $2,773 million less in 1983 and $2,881 million less in 1984 than those reported as investment in property, plant and equipment—exploration and production in Note 5 on page 36 mainly due to excluding from the data certain transportation and research assets and assets related to the oil sands operations of Syncrude in Canada and including in the data accumulated site restoration costs, both as required by Statement No. 19.

The amounts reported as costs incurred in property acquisition, exploration and development activities include both capitalized costs and costs charged to expense. Exxon's 1983 costs incurred were $5,648 million, down 19 percent from 1982 mainly due to lower exploration and development costs. Exxon's 1984 costs incurred were $6,536 million, up 16 percent from 1983 mainly due to higher expenditures for exploration acreage and increased exploration drilling in the U.S.

	Total Worldwide	United States	Canada	Other Western Hemisphere	Europe	Middle East and Africa	Australia and Far East
Capitalized costs			(millions of dollars)				
As of December 31, 1983							
Property (acreage) costs							
Proved	$ 1,387	$ 1,218	$ 113	$ 6	$ 17	$ 5	$ 28
Unproved	3,827	3,602	157	7	27	16	18
Total property costs	5,214	4,820	270	13	44	21	46
Producing assets	20,818	12,422	1,170	206	5,021	67	1,932
Support facilities	932	357	106	14	135	10	310
Incomplete construction	3,809	1,702	388	3	1,162	41	513
Total capitalized costs	30,773	19,301	1,934	236	6,362	139	2,801
Accumulated depreciation, depletion, amortization and valuation provisions	10,144	7,136	622	116	1,541	40	689
Net capitalized costs	**$20,629**	**$12,165**	**$1,312**	**$120**	**$4,821**	**$ 99**	**$2,112**
Proportional interest of net capitalized costs of equity companies	$ 564	—	—	—	$ 529	—	$ 35
As of December 31, 1984							
Property (acreage) costs							
Proved	$ 1,671	$ 1,506	$ 106	$ 6	$ 14	$ 5	$ 34
Unproved	4,065	3,859	146	3	22	17	18
Total property costs	5,736	5,365	252	9	36	22	52
Producing assets	23,574	14,315	1,281	236	5,495	59	2,188
Support facilities	1,043	400	101	18	139	5	380
Incomplete construction	3,345	1,506	474	3	872	76	414
Total capitalized costs	33,698	21,586	2,108	266	6,542	162	3,034
Accumulated depreciation, depletion, amortization and valuation provisions	11,522	7,923	639	182	1,760	46	972
Net capitalized costs	**$22,176**	**$13,663**	**$1,469**	**$ 84**	**$4,782**	**$116**	**$2,062**
Proportional interest of net capitalized costs of equity companies	$ 559	—	—	—	$ 524	—	$ 35
Costs incurred in property acquisition, exploration and development activities							
During 1982							
Property acquisition costs	$ 547	$ 539	$ 6	—	$ 428	$ 79	$ 2
Exploration costs	1,897	932	76	$175			207
Development costs	4,496	2,572	179	10	1,114	14	607
Total	**$ 6,940**	**$ 4,043**	**$ 261**	**$185**	**$1,542**	**$ 93**	**$ 816**
Proportional interest of costs incurred by equity companies	$ 238	—	—	—	$ 197	—	$ 41
During 1983							
Property acquisition costs	$ 839	$ 808	$ 1	—	$ 3	$ 11	$ 16
Exploration costs	1,446	780	46	$ 50	328	25	217
Development costs	3,363	1,875	243	21	732	11	481
Total	**$ 5,648**	**$ 3,463**	**$ 290**	**$ 71**	**$1,063**	**$ 47**	**$ 714**
Proportional interest of costs incurred by equity companies	$ 193	—	—	—	$ 169	—	$ 24
During 1984							
Property acquisition costs	$ 1,332	$ 1,311	$ 4	—	—	$ 1	$ 16
Exploration costs	1,616	1,032	36	$ 31	$ 328	31	158
Development costs	3,588	1,773	304	17	1,166	29	299
Total	**$ 6,536**	**$ 4,116**	**$ 344**	**$ 48**	**$1,494**	**$ 61**	**$ 473**
Proportional interest of costs incurred by equity companies	$ 178	—	—	—	$ 163	—	$ 15

Exhibit 2.17, continued

Earnings

The table below provides historical revenue, cost and earnings data regarding Exxon's oil and gas exploration and production operations during 1982, 1983 and 1984. Total earnings shown for the exploration and production activity are the same as those reflected in the primary financial statements, and as shown on pages 4 and 5. The volumes of crude oil and natural gas liquids production associated with these earnings and the net production volumes of natural gas delivered for sale by the producing function are shown on page 50. Crude oil, natural gas liquids and natural gas volumes from equity companies' production and from supplies available under long-term agreements with foreign governments are also reported on page 50.

The company believes this table (used in conjunction with the other information in this section concerning capitalized costs, costs incurred, reserves and production—all of which are presented on a geographic basis) provides interested persons with relevant information to assist in an evaluation of the company's oil and natural gas exploration and production operations and in the development of reasonable interpretations concerning the value of the oil and natural gas reserves. It is the company's opinion that this information is more meaningful for this purpose than the standardized measure of discounted future net cash flows, as prescribed by the FASB, which is contained on the following two pages.

	Total Worldwide	United States	Canada	Other Western Hemisphere	Europe	Middle East and Africa	Australia and Far East
	(millions of dollars)						
Year 1982							
Revenue	$16,037	$8,425	$825	$ 41	$3,998	$ 62	$2,686
Less costs:							
Production costs*	6,572	3,595	335	28	931	9	1,674
Exploration expense	1,712	960	64	107	355	77	149
Depreciation, depletion and amortization expense	1,934	1,276	79	9	405	19	146
	5,819	2,594	347	(103)	2,307	(43)	717
Related income tax	3,391	1,069	241	1	1,708	(2)	374
Earnings from own production	2,428	1,525	106	(104)	599	(41)	343
Proportional interest in earnings of equity companies	670	—	—	—	579	62	29
Other earnings**	333	345	4	7	(37)	(17)	31
Total earnings from exploration and production	$ 3,431	$1,870	$110	$ (97)	$1,141	$ 4	$ 403
Year 1983							
Revenue	$16,956	$8,136	$937	$ 72	$4,680	$ 45	$3,086
Less costs:							
Production costs*	6,027	3,299	304	24	600	9	1,791
Exploration expense	1,364	788	49	85	246	30	166
Depreciation, depletion and amortization expense	2,306	1,481	87	40	481	12	205
	7,259	2,568	497	(77)	3,353	(6)	924
Related income tax	4,136	1,078	316	—	2,262	3	477
Earnings from own production	3,123	1,490	181	(77)	1,091	(9)	447
Proportional interest in earnings of equity companies	567	—	—	—	538	8	21
Other earnings**	389	376	5	1	4	5	(2)
Total earnings from exploration and production	$ 4,079	$1,866	$186	$ (76)	$1,633	$ 4	$ 466
Year 1984							
Revenue	$18,236	$8,407	$930	$ 94	$5,159	$ 39	$3,607
Less costs:							
Production costs*	5,712	2,792	301	18	572	6	2,023
Exploration expense	1,328	858	33	25	245	29	138
Depreciation, depletion and amortization expense	2,704	1,762	89	54	549	10	240
	8,492	2,995	507	(3)	3,793	(6)	1,206
Related income tax	4,689	1,294	300	(5)	2,506	5	589
Earnings from own production	3,803	1,701	207	2	1,287	(11)	617
Proportional interest in earnings of equity companies	595	—	—	—	510	77	8
Other earnings**	391	311	(4)	(10)	81	12	1
Total earnings from exploration and production	$ 4,789	$2,012	$203	$ (8)	$1,878	$ 78	$ 626
Revenue							
Year 1982 – Sales to third parties	$ 4,930	$1,510	$577	$ 41	$ 700	$ 37	$2,065
Sales to consolidated affiliates	11,107	6,915	248	—	3,298	25	621
Year 1983 – Sales to third parties	5,051	1,362	611	72	785	27	2,194
Sales to consolidated affiliates	11,905	6,774	326	—	3,895	18	892
Year 1984 – Sales to third parties	7,680	1,698	594	94	2,663	24	2,607
Sales to consolidated affiliates	10,556	6,709	336	—	2,496	15	1,000

* Includes taxes other than income taxes. Specifically included are U.S. "windfall profit" tax: $1,377 (1982), $853 (1983), $692 (1984) and Australian excise tax: $1,260 (1982), $1,374 (1983), $1,510 (1984).

** Includes earnings related to transportation of oil and gas, sale of supplies from other sources including long-term agreements with foreign governments, oil sands operations and technical services agreements, and reduced by minority interests.

104

Exhibit 2.17, continued

Standardized Measure of Discounted Future Net Cash Flows Relating to Proved Oil and Gas Reserves

Please see the "Discussion of Standardized Measure" on page 41.

Except as noted in the following paragraph, the standardized measure of discounted future net cash flows relating to proved oil and gas reserves is computed by applying the year-end prices of crude oil, including condensate and natural gas liquids, and natural gas (with consideration of price changes only to the extent provided by contractual arrangements) to the estimated future production of oil and gas reserves, as shown on pages 42 and 43, less the estimated future expenditures to be incurred in developing and producing the proved reserves, assuming continuation of both the existing economic conditions and the level of current costs.

The production costs used in calculating future net cash flows are based on the average costs for the year for consolidated affiliates. Total costs are shown on page 45. Use of year-end information would not materially alter the results. Development costs are based on existing plans

for drilling, equipping and installing the actual wells and facilities, if any, required to produce the reserves held at year-end 1984. Where necessary, these existing development plans have been extrapolated, based on engineering estimates, to the end of the lease, concession, contract, etc., or to the time required to complete the recovery of the reserves, whichever is earlier. In certain instances, such as offshore platforms, existing development plans include facilities or capacity designed to produce both proved and probable reserves. These investments have been charged against proved reserves only, because the existence of the probable reserves may not be confirmed until after the investments have been made.

Related income taxes were calculated using statutory tax rates for year-end 1982, 1983 and 1984 where applicable. In some instances, particularly in foreign operations, effective income tax rates were used to estimate anticipated taxes.

The standardized measure is computed using the estimated future net cash flows and a discount factor of 10 percent per year.

	Total Worldwide	United States	Canada	Other Western Hemisphere	Europe	Middle East and Africa	Australia and Far East
				(millions of dollars)			
As of December 31, 1982							
Future cash inflows from sales of oil and gas	$224,615	$105,994	$13,821	$268	$74,648	$699	$29,185
Future production and development cash costs	101,057	57,052	6,403	192	23,312	332	13,766
Future income tax expenses	68,090	20,633	4,445	—	35,651	84	7,277
Future net cash flows	55,468	28,309	2,973	76	15,685	283	8,142
Effect of discounting net cash flows at 10%	29,565	15,724	1,967	23	7,441	127	4,283
Standardized measure of discounted future net cash flows	$ 25,903	$ 12,585	$ 1,006	$ 53	$ 8,244	$156	$ 3,859
As of December 31, 1983							
Future cash inflows from sales of oil and gas	$218,005	$ 97,212	$20,032	$353	$73,079	$578	$26,751
Future production and development cash costs	86,493	42,467	8,873	234	23,448	275	11,196
Future income tax expenses	70,295	24,291	6,198	—	32,628	97	7,081
Future net cash flows	61,217	30,454	4,961	119	17,003	206	8,474
Effect of discounting net cash flows at 10%	34,358	18,408	3,278	30	8,591	101	3,950
Standardized measure of discounted future net cash flows	$ 26,859	$ 12,046	$ 1,683	$ 89	$ 8,412	$105	$ 4,524
As of December 31, 1984							
Future cash inflows from sales of oil and gas	$218,444	$100,208	$24,099	$316	$69,539	$526	$23,756
Future production and development cash costs	84,247	39,508	10,936	194	23,009	231	10,369
Future income tax expenses	68,378	26,751	7,459	22	27,461	99	6,586
Future net cash flows	65,819	33,949	5,704	100	19,069	196	6,801
Effect of discounting net cash flows at 10%	35,870	19,661	3,420	25	9,910	82	2,772
Standardized measure of discounted future net cash flows	$ 29,949	$ 14,288	$ 2,284	$ 75	$ 9,159	$114	$ 4,029

Proportional interest in the standardized measure of discounted future net cash flows related to proved reserves of equity companies*							
At December 31, 1982	$ 5,040	—	—	—	$ 4,982	—	$ 58
At December 31, 1983	4,277	—	—	—	4,224	—	53
At December 31, 1984	4,361	—	—	—	4,304	—	57

105

Exhibit 2.17, continued

Change in Standardized Measure of Discounted Future Net Cash Flows Relating to Proved Oil and Gas Reserves — Consolidated Affiliates

In 1982, the value of the previous year's reserves increased due to development expenditures incurred during the year and to upward revisions in the estimated quantities of these reserves, particularly in the U.S., Canada, Norway, and the U.K. These improvements were more than offset by sales and transfers of oil and gas during the year and by the combined effects of flat prices and higher lifting costs, especially in the U.S. and the U.K.

For 1983, the value of the previous year's reserves increased due to development expenditures incurred during the year and to revisions in the estimated quantities of these reserves, particularly in the U.S., the U.K. and Malaysia. These improvements were essentially offset by sales of oil and gas produced during the year.

In 1984, the value of previous year's reserves also increased significantly due to revisions in the estimated quantities of these reserves, to the addition of new reserves during the year and to higher forecast production rates near-term reflecting 1984 experience.

Costs capitalized in the financial statements are expensed under the standardized measure method except for costs associated with unevaluated properties and uncompleted exploration wells which totaled $1,581 million, $1,966 million and $1,869 million at the end of 1982, 1983 and 1984, respectively. These costs are deferred until the year the evaluation is completed. Current year's development expenditures have the effect of reducing the standardized measure's development costs and are shown as an increase in present value. Current year's proceeds from producing operations recognized in the historical financial statements do not affect these results if they are identical to the assumptions used in estimating the standardized measure's values in the prior year.

Related income taxes were calculated using statutory tax rates for year-end 1982, 1983 and 1984 where applicable. In some instances, particularly in foreign operations, effective income tax rates were used to estimate anticipated taxes.

	1982	1983	1984
	(millions of dollars)		
Value of reserves added during the year, due to extensions, discoveries, other additions and improved recovery, less related costs	$ 817	$ 1,300	$ 2,463
Changes in value of previous year reserves due to:			
Sales and transfers of oil and gas produced during the year, net of production costs	(9,285)	(10,929)	(12,524)
Development costs incurred during the year	4,496	3,363	3,588
Net change in prices and production costs	(5,971)	(283)	240
Revision of previous reserves estimates	2,380	3,125	981
Accretion of discount	6,154	5,829	5,855
Other changes	(1,834)	(2,156)	3,544
Net change in income taxes	1,892	707	(1,057)
Total change in the standardized measure during the year	$(1,351)	$ 956	$ 3,090

Source: Exxon Corporation 1984 Annual Report. Copyright, 1985, by the Exxon Corporation. Reprinted with permission.

NOTES

1. Donald E. Kieso and Jerry J. Weygandt, Intermediate Accounting (New York: John Wiley & Sons, 1989), 315-316.

2. For an additional discussion of this topic see Leopold A. Bernstein, Financial Statement Analysis: Theory, Application and Interpretation, 4thEdition, (Homewood, IL: Richard D. Irwin, Inc, 1989).

3. Paragraph 9 of SFAS 34 was amended by SFAS 42 by adopting the phrase "qualifying assets".

4. SFAS 34, paragraph 13, refers to the interest rate used in the computations for the capitalization of interest as the "capitalization rate".

CASE 2.1. JOHNSON AND JOHNSON AND SUBSIDIARIES: RESTATEMENT
OF LIFO TO FIFO

Johnson and Johnson, employing approximately 77,400 people worldwide, is
engaged in the manufacture and sale of a broad range of products in the health-
care and other fields in many countries of the world. The Company's primary interest, both historically and currently, has been in products related to health and well-
being. The Company's involvement in product lines outside the health-care field
generally has been a result of the application of resources, technology and products
originally designed for the health-care field.

Source: Johnson and Johnson and Subsidiaries 1983 Annual Report. Copyright,
       1984, by Johnson and Johnson and Subsidiaries. Reprinted with permission.

REQUIRED: Review the Company's Consolidated Balance Sheet, Consolidated Statement of Earnings and Retained Earnings and Note 6--Inventories.

1.   Determine the Company's LIFO Reserve for 1982 and 1983.

2.   If the Company was to convert to the FIFO basis of inventory valuation,
     determine the following for 1983:

     a. The cost of sales under the FIFO basis;

     b. Net income after tax before extraordinary items under the FIFO basis;

     c. Earnings per share before extraordinary items under the FIFO basis.

3.   Compute the current (working capital) ratio and the inventory turnover
     ratio under both the LIFO and FIFO methods of inventory valuation.
     Indicate the effect of using LIFO on the conclusions drawn from these
     ratios.

Johnson & Johnson and Subsidiaries   Consolidated Balance Sheet

At January 1, 1984 and January 2, 1983 (Dollars in Millions Except Per Share Figures)	1983	1982*
Assets		
Current assets		
Cash and cash items	$ 122.6	140.4
Marketable securities, at cost, which approximates market value	303.9	225.1
Accounts receivable, trade, less allowances $28.1 (1982, $24.8)	836.4	758.1
Inventories (Notes 1 and 6)	992.2	957.5
Prepaid expenses and other receivables	202.0	172.0
Total current assets	2,457.1	2,253.1
Marketable securities, non-current, at cost, which approximates market value	181.5	222.1
Property, plant and equipment, at cost (Note 1)		
Land and land improvements	149.9	142.2
Buildings and building equipment	1,050.0	924.7
Machinery and equipment	1,106.2	1,005.9
Construction in progress	163.6	238.6
	2,469.7	2,311.4
Less accumulated depreciation and amortization	801.5	733.5
	1,668.2	1,577.9
Other assets	154.7	156.5
Total assets	$4,461.5	4,209.6
Liabilities and Stockholders' Equity		
Current liabilities		
Loans and notes payable (Note 7)	$ 214.4	213.9
Accounts payable	311.2	312.1
Taxes on income	13.6	1.3
Salaries, wages and commissions	78.1	75.0
Miscellaneous taxes	47.7	53.6
Miscellaneous accrued liabilities	258.8	244.3
Total current liabilities	923.8	900.2
Long-term debt (Note 7)	195.6	142.2
Certificates of extra compensation (Note 11)	46.6	42.9
Deferred investment tax credits	41.0	35.3
Other liabilities and deferrals	223.1	279.8
Minority interests in international subsidiaries	4.9	9.7
Stockholders' equity		
Preferred stock—without par value (authorized and unissued 2,000,000 shares)	—	—
Common stock—par value $1.00 per share (authorized 270,000,000 shares; issued 191,562,000 and 189,361,000 shares)	191.6	189.4
Additional capital	272.1	234.5
Cumulative currency translation adjustments (Note 4)	(260.7)	(163.5)
Retained earnings	2,824.5	2,540.1
	3,027.5	2,800.5
Less common stock held in treasury, at cost (234,000 shares)	1.0	1.0
Total stockholders' equity	3,026.5	2,799.5
Total liabilities and stockholders' equity	$4,461.5	4,209.6

*Reclassified to conform to 1983 presentation.

Source: Johnson and Johnson and Subsidiaries 1983 Annual Report. Copyright, 1984, by Johnson and Johnson and Subsidiaries. Reprinted with permission.

Johnson & Johnson and Subsidiaries   Consolidated Statement of Earnings and Retained Earnings

Dollars in Millions Except Per Share Figures (Note 1)	**1983**	1982	1981
Revenues			
Sales to customers	**$5,972.9**	5,760.9	5,399.0
Other revenues			
Interest income	**82.9**	88.9	78.8
Royalties and miscellaneous	**49.4**	49.3	28.6
	132.3	138.2	107.4
Total revenues	**6,105.2**	5,899.1	5,506.4
Costs and expenses			
Cost of products sold	**2,471.8**	2,450.9	2,368.4
Selling, distribution and administrative expenses	**2,352.9**	2,248.8	2,030.6
Research expense	**405.1**	363.2	282.9
Interest expense	**88.3**	74.4	60.7
Interest expense capitalized	**(36.9)**	(46.3)	(43.5)
Other expenses including nonrecurring charge (Note 2)	**99.9**	20.9	23.4
Total costs and expenses	**5,381.1**	5,111.9	4,722.5
Earnings before provision for taxes on income and extraordinary charge	**724.1**	787.2	783.9
Provision for taxes on income (Note 3)	**235.1**	263.8	316.3
Earnings before extraordinary charge	**489.0**	523.4	467.6
Extraordinary charge—withdrawal of TYLENOL capsules (net of $50.0 taxes) (Note 2)	**—**	(50.0)	—
Net earnings	**489.0**	473.4	467.6
Retained earnings at beginning of period	**2,540.1**	2,249.1	1,940.1
Cash dividends paid (per share: 1983, $1.075; 1982, $.97; 1981, $.85)	**(204.6)**	(182.4)	(158.6)
Retained earnings at end of period	**$2,824.5**	2,540.1	2,249.1
Per share of common stock			
Earnings before extraordinary charge	**$ 2.57**	2.79	2.51
Extraordinary charge	**—**	(.27)	—
Net earnings per share	**$ 2.57**	2.52	2.51

Note 6. Inventories

At the end of 1983 and 1982, inventories comprised:

(Dollars in Millions)	1983	1982
Raw materials and supplies	$294.8	301.8
Goods in process	215.9	223.2
Finished goods	481.5	432.5
	$992.2	957.5

If all inventories were valued on the FIFO basis, total inventories would have been $1,115.2 million and $1,090.5 million at January 1, 1984 and January 2, 1983, respectively.

Source: Johnson and Johnson and Subsidiaries 1983 Annual Report. Copyright, 1984 by Johnson and Johnson and Subsidiaries. Reprinted with permission.

CASE 2.2. MATRIX CORPORATION: ACCOUNTING FOR MARKETABLE EQUITY SECURITIES

Matrix Corporation is a leading manufacturer of equipment used for electronic image acquisition, recording, processing, storage, transmission and display. Its three Optical/Electronic Business Units are Medical Imaging, Computer Graphics and Industrial Imaging.

Source: Matrix Corporation 1986 Annual Report. Copyright, 1986, by Matrix
         Corporation. Reprinted with permission.

REQUIRED: Study the Consolidated Balance Sheet and Footnote 2-- Marketable Securities.

1. Determine the historical cost, the allowance to reduce marketable securities to market and the unrealized loss for 1985 and 1986 for the Company's current portfolio of marketable equity securities. In addition, indicate where the unrealized loss is to be reported in the Company's financial statements and the cash flow effect of the unrealized loss.

2. Repeat the requirements listed in question 1 for the Company's noncurrent portfolio of marketable equity securities.

3. For the current portfolio only, assume that the certificates of deposit and time deposits were the only securities transferred (i.e., sold) in 1986. In addition, assume that there were no purchases made during the year. Determine the cash inflow from the sale of marketable securities in 1986.

MATRIX CORPORATION AND SUBSIDIARIES

CONSOLIDATED BALANCE SHEET
July 31, 1986 and August 31, 1985
(dollars in millions)

	1986	1985
ASSETS		
CURRENT ASSETS:		
Cash	$ 1.8	$ 2.6
Marketable securities	58.1	25.5
Accounts receivable, less allowance		
for doubtful accounts of $.9 and $1.1	31.9	29.5
Inventories	31.0	29.1
Prepaid expenses and other	5.7	3.3
Total current assets	128.5	90.0
Marketable securities	27.8	6.3
Investments in and advances to 50% or		
less owned companies	—	3.7
Property, plant and equipment, less accumulated		
depreciation and amortization	20.6	16.2
Excess of cost over equity in net assets of		
subsidiaries, less accumulated amortization of		
$2.0 and $1.6	16.3	10.2
Other assets	4.1	2.9
	$197.3	$129.3
LIABILITIES		
CURRENT LIABILITIES:		
Accounts payable	$ 5.3	$ 3.8
Accrued expenses and liabilities	5.5	5.0
Income taxes	1.3	1.1
Deferred income taxes	1.5	—
Total current liabilities	13.6	9.9
Long-term debt	86.3	34.5
Deferred income taxes	3.0	2.1
Total liabilities	102.9	46.5
SHAREHOLDERS' EQUITY	94.4	82.8
	$197.3	$129.3

The accompanying notes are an integral part of the consolidated financial statements.

Source: Matrix Corporation 1986 Annual Report. Copyright, 1986, by Matrix
Corporation. Reprinted with permission.

2. Marketable Securities   Marketable securities consist of notes and bonds, which are carried at amortized cost, and investments in various funds and equity securities, which are carried at the lower of cost or market. Money market funds, equity securities and securities with a fixed maturity date of 1 year or less are carried as current assets.

Current marketable securities consist of:

	July 31, 1986	August 31, 1985
Corporate notes and bonds.	$42,100,000	$15,200,000
Certificate and time deposits	3,300,000	10,000,000
Money market funds.	4,900,000	300,000
Government securities	4,700,000	—
Equity securities	3,100,000	—
	$58,100,000	$25,500,000

Non-current marketable securities consist of:

	July 31, 1986	August 31, 1985
Municipal bond fund.	$ 4,000,000	$ 4,200,000
Preferred stock funds	2,000,000	2,100,000
Government securities fund.	2,600,000	—
Partnership fund	3,900,000	—
Corporate notes and bonds.	9,000,000	—
Government securities	6,300,000	—
	$27,800,000	$ 6,300,000

At July 31, 1986, the aggregate cost of current marketable securities exceeded their market value by $100,000 (there was no unrealized loss at August 31, 1985). This amount has been recorded, through a charge to income, as a reduction in the carrying value of the assets.

At July 31, 1986 and August 31, 1985, the aggregate cost of non-current marketable securities exceeded their market value by $300,000 and $200,000, respectively. These amounts have been recorded as a reduction in the carrying value of the assets and an equivalent reduction in shareholders' equity.

Sales of marketable securities resulted in a realized gain of $1,500,000 in 1986 and a realized loss of $100,000 in 1985 (both included in other income, net), with cost determined principally on a specific identification basis.

Source: Matrix Corporation 1986 Annual Report. Copyright, 1986, by Matrix Corporation. Reprinted with permission.

3

Analytical Issues in Accounting for Corporate Debt and Stockholders' Equity

ANALYSIS OF CORPORATE DEBT

Introduction

The most recent definition of liabilities by the Financial Accounting Standards Board is found in Statement of Financial Accounting Concepts (SFAC) No. 6. Paragraph 35 of SFAC 6 defines a liability as a "probable future sacrifice of economic resources arising from the current obligations of an entity to transfer assets or to provide services to other entities in the future as a result of current or past transactions".

In the first part of this chapter, issues relating to reporting and accounting for current and long-term liabilities are discussed. For both classifications of liabilities, a basic review of accounting for corporate debt is provided. The discussion then moves on to special issues in measurement and classification of liabilities. The second part of this chapter provides a discussion of accounting for stockholders' equity.

Classification of Corporate Debt

Liabilities are presented on the balance sheet in the order of maturity. Corporate debt is further classified as either current or long term.

Current Liabilities. Current liabilities are defined as obligations that will be liquidated through the use of economic resources properly classified as current assets or through the creation of other current liabilities. From a practical standpoint, current liabilities are usually due and payable within one year from the balance sheet date. Current liabilities include:

- Trade accounts payable;

- Income and other taxes payable;

- Current portion of long-term debt (including capitalized lease obligations);

- Current deferred income taxes payable;

- Short-term notes and loans payable;

- Current obligations under pension plans;

- Allowances or reserves for repairs and maintenance or product warranties.

Within the current liability classification, special analytical issues will arise with respect to the classification of short-term debt expected to be refinanced and long-term debt callable by the creditor.

Long-Term or Noncurrent Liabilities. Long-term liabilities are generally defined as those obligations that are due and payable in a period of time more than one year from the balance sheet date. The long-term debt classification includes:

- Bonds payable;

- Long-term notes payable;

- Obligations under capital lease;

- Long-term obligations under pension plans.

Capital lease obligations will be discussed in detail in chapter 7.

Special analytical issues relating to long-term corporate debt include early retirement or extinguishment of debt, in-substance defeasance of debt, interest rate swaps, troubled debt restructuring, and analysis of pension obligations and the related pension disclosures.

"Accounting Limbo". Due to strong differences of opinion regarding the nature and proper classification of several items of corporate debt and stockholders' equity, accountants have created another section of the balance sheet located between liabilities and stockholders' equity. This grey area of the balance sheet is sometimes known as "accounting limbo". The items in this section are not specifically classified as debt or equity, but are basically left "unclassified" by the accountant. The ambiguous classification requires that the analysts classify these items according to their own judgement and interpretation of the nature of the financial statement item. The items usually found in the grey area include long-term deferred income taxes payable, minority interest and redeemable preferred stock. Deferred income taxes will be discussed in the next chapter and minority interests will be presented along with accounting for business combinations in chapter 5. Redeemable preferred

stock will be discussed in a subsequent section of this chapter.

Contingent Liabilities. Contingent liabilities are defined as potential obligations that may become actual obligations of the entity depending on certain future events occurring or not occurring. Examples include actual or threatened litigation, income tax investigations and guarantees of the debt of others.

Contingent liabilities are usually only disclosed in the footnotes to the financial statements, and are not formally recorded in the accounts. Some firms will include a line item entitled "commitments and contingencies" on the face of the balance sheet in the liabilities and stockholders' equity section, without including any dollar amounts in the financial statement totals. This disclosure will reference a footnote and at least makes the analyst aware of the potential obligations of the firm. Loss contingencies are discussed in detail in chapter 8.

Many of the classification issues discussed above are included in the liabilities and stockholders' equity section of the Ashland Oil balance sheet presented in Exhibit 3.1.

Special Issues in Accounting for Current Liabilities

The analytical issues relating to current liabilities center around the proper classification of transactions involving refinancing short-term debt and the creditor's right to call long-term obligations. The professional standards relating to short-term debt expected to be refinanced and the classification of obligations that become callable by the creditor are discussed in the following sections.

Short-Term Debt Expected to be Refinanced. Short-term debt expected to be refinanced relates to an agreement or a transaction that will take place after the date of the balance sheet but before the financial statements are issued. The period between the balance sheet date and the date the financial statements are issued is known as the "post-balance sheet" or "subsequent events period".

Post-balance sheet or subsequent events result from the fact that there is usually a two-to three-month lag between the fiscal year end and end of the auditors' field work, and the release of the annual report. During this period of time, the auditor may become aware of events that could significantly influence the judgement of an informed user of the financial statements.

The key issue here is whether the accountant is required to account for events that take place during the post-balance sheet period and possibly modify the financial statements to be issued. That is, should the accountant reflect an event that occurs in 1991 in the financial statements for the year ended in 1990? The professional standards for accounting and auditing specify that the accountant is responsible for events that take place up to the last date of field work, which is also the date of the auditor's opinion.

With respect to post-balance sheet or subsequent events, professional auditing pronouncements require the following.

1. If the 1991 subsequent event was caused by other events and conditions which existed as of the date of the 1990 balance sheet and would have been accounted for in 1990 if brought to the attention of the accountant, the

EXHIBIT 3.1

Sample Disclosure: Ashland Oil: Liabilities and Stockholders' Equity Section of the Balance Sheet

(In thousands)	1982	1981
Liabilities and Stockholders' Equity		
Current liabilities		
Short-term debt	$ 15,514	$ 31,500
Trade and other payables—Note A	1,424,025	1,456,526
Contract advances and progress billings in excess of costs incurred	88,789	99,075
Income taxes—Notes A and D	42,643	24,020
Current portion of long-term debt and capitalized lease obligations	43,091	50,423
	1,614,062	1,661,544
Noncurrent liabilities and deferred credits		
Long-term debt—less current portion—Note E	585,478	583,290
Capitalized lease obligations—less current portion—Note F	175,354	186,776
Other long-term liabilities	127,052	115,416
Deferred income taxes—Notes A and D	252,329	206,254
Minority interests in consolidated subsidiaries	56,396	38,941
Redeemable preferred stock (1982 liquidation value—$367,870,000)—Note H	352,579	357,790
Common stockholders' equity—Notes E, I and J		
Common stock, par value $1.00 per share		
Authorized—60,000,000 shares		
Issued—26,834,000 shares in 1982 and 26,813,000 shares in 1981	26,834	26,813
Paid-in capital	169,030	168,108
Retained earnings	862,295	782,060
Deferred translation adjustments—Note A	(5,749)	—
Common shares in treasury—at cost (251,000 shares)	(5,179)	(5,179)
	1,047,231	971,802
Commitments and contingencies—Notes F and G		
	$4,210,481	$4,121,813

118

Exhibit 3.1, continued

Note G—Litigation and claims	Numerous lawsuits are pending or threatened against Ashland or its subsidiaries, alleging claims for substantial amounts. Ashland has been advised by its law department that either there are meritorious defenses to substantially all such litigation and claims, or any liability which finally may be determined, in excess of amounts already provided for, should not have a material effect on Ashland's consolidated financial position.
Note H—Redeemable preferred stock	Ashland has 15,000,000 authorized shares of cumulative redeemable preferred stock, without par value, issuable in series. At September 30, 1982, 6,771,000 shares were outstanding as follows: $3.96 Series, 3,481,000 shares; 8.375% Series, 37,000 shares; 8.50% Series, 47,000 shares; and $4.50 Series, 3,206,000 shares. Except for the $4.50 Series, all shares are voting.

(In thousands)	Convertible		Nonconvertible			
	$5.00 Series of 1970	$3.96 Series of 1981	8.375% Series of 1974	8.50% Series of 1976	$4.50 Series of 1980	Total
Balance at October 1, 1979	$413	$ —	$45,000	$50,000	$ —	$ 95,413
Converted 3,000 shares and canceled 1,000 shares	(413)					(413)
Issued 3,556,000 shares in exchange for common stock					160,022	160,022
Purchased 159,000 shares					(7,150)	(7,150)
Redeemed 2,500 shares			(2,500)			(2,500)
Balance at September 30, 1980	—	—	42,500	50,000	152,872	245,372
Issued 3,482,000 shares in the acquisition of Integon		121,859				121,859
Purchased 171,000 shares					(7,713)	(7,713)
Redeemed 2,500 shares			(2,500)			(2,500)
Other changes		772				772
Balance at September 30, 1981	—	122,631	40,000	50,000	145,159	357,790
Redeemed 5,625 shares			(2,500)	(3,125)		(5,625)
Purchased 20,000 shares					(887)	(887)
Converted 1,000 shares		(33)				(33)
Other changes		1,334				1,334
Balance at September 30, 1982	$ —	$123,932	$37,500	$46,875	$144,272	$352,579

All of the above preferred stocks are carried at redemption value except for the $3.96 Series. The $3.96 Series was recorded at its $35 per share fair value at the date of issuance. The difference between the fair value and the redemption price of $40 per share is being amortized over the life of the issue. Shares of this issue are convertible into common stock on a one for one basis.

Mandatory redemption requirements for the $4.50 Series begin in 1991. Annual mandatory redemption requirements for the remaining preferred issues are $5,625,000 through 1986 and $12,544,000 in 1987.

Ashland also has 15,000,000 authorized shares of cumulative preference stock, without par value, issuable in series. None of these shares have been issued at September 30,1982.

Source: Ashland Oil, Inc. and Subsidiaries 1982 Annual Report. Copyright, 1982, by Ashland Oil, Inc. Reprinted with permission.

accountant must actually "go back" and adjust the 1990 financial statements for the subsequent event and make adequate footnote disclosures of the transaction. For example, if a major customer, with a significant outstandng receivable balance, petitions for bankruptcy in January of 1991, the accountant must write-off this receivable in the 1990 financial statements and make adequate disclosure of the event because the conditions resulting in the customer's insolvency existed as of the balance sheet date.

2.   If the 1991 subsequent event was caused by events and conditions that existed only during the post-balance sheet period, the accountant should only disclose the transaction in the footnotes to the 1990 financial statements, and would not make any adjustments to the 1990 financial statements. For example, the sale of additional stock or additional borrowing during the post-balance sheet period must be disclosed in a subsequent events footnote. Another illustration of a post-balance sheet event only requiring disclosure in the 1990 financial statements would be the bankruptcy of the major customer discussed in the example above, if that bankruptcy resulted from significant losses due to a major casualty. In this case, no adjustments would be required to the 1990 financial statements because the conditions surrounding the bankruptcy (i.e., the major casualty) did not exist as of the balance sheet date.

Short-term debt expected to be refinanced in the next accounting period may qualify as a post-balance sheet event, and if refinanced on a long-term basis, it may be reclassified as a noncurrent liability. FASB Statement No. 6 sets forth the conditions under which the short-term debt can be reclassified as long term.

Specifically, SFAS 6, paragraph 2, covers situations where the short-term debt is expected to be (a) extended or replaced by additional short-term debt that will be due beyond one year from the balance sheet date, and (b) replaced or refinanced with either long-term debt or equity securities. In either case, the short-term obligation will no longer require the use of current assets or the creation of current liabilities in its liquidation. Therefore, the obligation no longer meets the definition of a current liability, and to the extent refinanced, would be reclassified as a noncurrent liability. In addition, adequate footnote disclosure providing the particulars of the terms of the refinancing is required.

It should be noted that the firm must first refinance (i.e., obtain the additional financing), and then liquidate the short-term obligation. If the sequence of events was reversed (i.e., the firm liquidates the short-term debt and then obtains new financing), the firm would be utilizing cash from current operations and the obligation would still meet the definition of a current liability and should not be reclassified as long term.

SFAS 6, paragraphs 10 and 11, set forth two criteria that must be met in order for the firm to exclude the short-term obligation from current liabilities and to reclassify the debt as long term. Management must intend to refinance on a long-term basis, and management must demonstrate the ability to consummate the refinancing.

According to SFAS 6, paragraph 11, the ability to refinance is demonstrated by either (a) actual refinancing during the post-balance sheet period, or (b) entering into a firm agreement which permits refinancing on a long-term basis and where the terms of the agreement are readily determinable. A commercial loan agreement containing a material adverse change clause would violate the second criterion of SFAS 6.

As noted earlier, only the portion of the short-term liability refinanced can be reclassified as a noncurrent obligation. The reclassification from short-term to long-term debt will improve the firm's liquidity statistics without changing total debt and without affecting cash flow. These results are due to the fact that the application of SFAS 6 causes a simple reclassification of the short-term debt into long-term debt. The details of the new financing agreement are only disclosed in a footnote to the financial statements, and the new debt obligation and the related cash inflow are not recorded until the contract is consummated in the next accounting period.

Classification of Obligations that are Callable by the Creditor. The case where long-term debt becomes callable by the creditor due to technical default is the converse of the case of short-term debt expected to be refinanced. This second issue is concerned with obligations that, by their terms, are due on demand or will be due on demand within one year from the balance sheet date. The accounting and disclosure requirements for callable debt are set forth by FASB Statement No. 78, "Classification of Obligations that are Callable by the Creditor".

According to SFAS 78, paragraph 1, this standard is applicable to obligations that are or will be callable by the creditor either because:

1. "The debtor's violation of a provision of the debt agreement at the balance sheet date makes the debt callable". For example, the debtor is in technical default due to violation of a restrictive covenant of a commercial loan agreement requiring maintenance of a certain level of working capital.

2. If the violation is "not cured within a specified grace period", the obligation will become callable.

Under these circumstances the debt would be due and payable on demand and should be reclassified as a current liability. Nevertheless, in paragraph 5 of SFAS 78, the Board went on to specify that the callable obligation may continue to be classified as long term if one of the following conditions is met:

1. The creditor either waives or loses the right to demand payment (e.g., the violation is cured);

2. The obligation will not become callable because it is probable that the violation will be cured with the grace period.

Although still classified as long-term debt, the conditions and circumstances justifying the noncurrent classification, given the technical default, should be disclosed in a footnote to the financial statements.

Analysis of Short-Term Debt

In the review of current liabilities, the analyst should note that large amounts of short-term bank debt may imply the inability of the firm to obtain financing on a long-term basis or that the firm has violated the terms of a long-term debt agreement, making the obligation callable. The application of SFAS 6 and SFAS 78 should provide adequate disclosures that assist the analyst in making informed judgements regarding the proper classification of the firm's debt.

However, some of the provisions of SFAS 6 and SFAS 78 are vague and may enable management to exercise some discretion in the classification of debt. For example, in applying the provisions of SFAS 6, management's "ability to refinance" and "demonstrating of the ability to refinance on a long-term basis" may be determined on a subjective basis. There can be a great deal of discretion on the part of management in determining if an agreement to refinance is "firm" and if the terms are "readily determinable". In this case, even if there is no actual refinancing during the post-balance sheet period, as long as there is an "agreement" to refinance there may be a reclassification of short-term to long-term debt. This improves the liquidity of the firm and may in fact prevent a technical default of another debt agreement containing a restrictive covenant based on working capital levels.

Similarly, a technical default of a long-term debt agreement would not result in reclassification to a current liability if management determines that under the provisions of SFAS 78, it is "probable" that the violation would be cured during the grace period. Although there should be disclosure of the rationale behind the decision not to reclassify the long-term obligation to short-term debt, the application of SFAS 78 still results in maintaining this debt as long-term, and prevents an adverse effect on the firm's liquidity position. Again, this could prevent violation of a liquidity based restrictive covenant in another debt agreement.

Accounting for Long-Term Debt

Accounting for bonds payable will be discussed in this section of the chapter in order to illustrate the analytical issues surrounding long-term debt. After presenting the basic principles of accounting for bond discounts and premiums and the interest rate method of amortization, the discussion moves to more complex issues such as early extinguishment of debt, in-substance defeasance and interest-rate swaps.

Basic Issues in Accounting for Bonds Payable. In all of the illustrations that follow it is assumed that each bond is a promissory note with a par or face value of $1,000 and with a fixed maturity date and a stated rate of interest. The bonds are sold in an issue through an underwriter or privately placed. For example, a $1,000,000 bond issue consists of 1,000, $1,000 par value bonds. Because there are multiple lenders, a contract between the corporation and the bondholders (represented by a trustee) must be drawn up to protect the bondholder/investor. The contract is called a bond indenture.

The bond indenture outlines the terms and provisions of the debt agreement.

The terms and provisions of the debt agreement include dividend restrictions, debt compliance provisions or restrictive covenants (e.g., maintenance of a certain level of working capital), manner of contract enforcement, the type of bonds, and the features associated with the bond. These features include whether the bonds are secured, serial bonds, registered, callable, redeemable or convertible.

Bonds can be issued at par, at a price above par (at a premium) or at a price below par (at a discount). In all cases, the bonds are priced to yield the market. That is, the issue price of the bonds will depend on the difference between the stated rate on the bonds (i.e., the nominal, cash, face or coupon rate) and the going market rate of interest. The nominal or face rate of interest is used in the determination of the coupon or cash interest. The semiannual cash interest is determined by multiplying the semiannual coupon rate of interest by the par value of the debt. The market rate is used to price the bonds. That is, the market rate is used to discount the future cash flows from the bond investment to determine the issue price of the bond.

The comparison of the coupon rate of interest with the market rate can result in three possible prices in relation to the par value of the bonds.

If the coupon rate is equal to the market rate, there is an equilibrium price which is equal to the par value of the bonds. The bonds can sell at their par value because, assuming that the rate of interest captures all pertinent factors such as risk, the investor is indifferent between the corporation's bond and any other bond investment in the market.

If the coupon rate is less than the market rate, the bonds will be issued at a price below par or at a discount. Since the investor can obtain a higher rate in the market, the supply of the corporation's bonds will exceed the demand and there will be downward price pressure. Prices fall until an equilibrium price is reached where the effective return for the investor and the effective cost of borrowing for the corporation is equal to the higher market rate.

Finally, if the coupon rate exceeds the market rate of interest, the bonds will sell at a price above par or at a premium. Since the investor obtains a greater interest rate than is available in the market, the demand for the corporation's bonds exceeds the supply and bids up the price. The upward price pressure continues until an equilibrium price is reached, where the effective return for the investor and the effective cost of borrowing for the corporation will equal the lower market rate.

It should be noted that the differences between the coupon rate of interest and the market rate are due to the time lag between the date the bond indenture is written, bonds are printed, etc., and the date the bonds are sold. Generally, the spread between the market rate and the coupon rate of interest is not as great as used in the following illustrations.

After issuance, the bonds are reported on the balance sheet at their carrying or book value. At any point in time, the carrying value of the bonds should be equal to the present value of the future cash flows related to the bond issue, discounted at the market rate of interest. From an accounting standpoint, the carrying value of the bonds is equal to the par value plus the balance of the premium (i.e., the unamortized premium), or net of the balance of the discount (i.e., the unamortized discount).

The following equation analysis presents the financial statement effects of bond issuance at par, at a premium and at a discount.

```
------------------------------------------|----------------------------------
              BALANCE SHEET               |       INCOME STATEMENT
------------------------------------------|----------------------------------
                                          |
                                          |
                        STOCKHOLDERS'     |  NET INCOME
ASSETS  =  LIABILITIES +    EQUITY        |  OR LOSS  =  REVENUES - EXPENSES
  |            |             |            |  |  |          |          |
  |            |             |            |  |  |          |          |
---------      |         --------------   |  |  |          |          |
  |     |      |         |            |   |  |  |          |          |
  |   NON-     |         |            |   |  |  |          |          |
  |   CASH     |       CAPITAL  +  RETAINED |NET INCOME    |          |
CASH + ASSETS = LIAB + STOCK      EARNINGS | OR LOSS  =  REVENUES - EXPENSES
----   ------ ------ ---------   --------- |---------   ----------  --------
                                      ^    |  |  |
                                      |    |  |  |
                                      |<---<---<-|
==================================================================================
 +Cash        +Bonds                      |
 (a)          Payable                     |
 (Debit)      a Par (a)                    |
              (Credit)                     |
==================================================================================
 +Cash        +Bonds                      |
 (b)          Payable                     |
 (Debit)      a Par (b)                    |
              (Credit)                     |
                                          |
              +Bond                        |
              Premium (b)                  |
              (Credit)                     |
==================================================================================
 +Cash        +Bonds                      |
 (c)          Payable                     |
 (Debit)      a Par (c)                    |
              (Credit)                     |
                                          |
              -Bond                        |
              Discount                     |
              (c)                          |
              (Debit)                      |
==================================================================================
```

(a) Entry to record the issuance of bonds at par.
(b) Entry to record the issuance of bonds at a premium.
(c) Entry to record the issuance of bonds at a discount.
==

It should be noted that the premium is an adjunct account to the bonds payable, and the bonds payable and the premium are usually reported in the aggregate. Conversely, the discount is a contra-liability account and is deducted from the par value of the debt. The bonds are usually reported net of the discount.

Illustrations of accounting for bonds issued at a discount and at a premium will be presented in the following section.

Illustration of Accounting for Bonds Sold at a Discount

In order to illustrate accounting for bonds issued at a discount, assume that on January 1, 1990, the Auto-Stop Corporation issued $10,000 of its $1,000 par value 8%, three-year bonds. Interest is payable semiannually each January 1st and July 1st. If the market rate of interest is 10%, the issue price of the bonds is determined as follows:

```
Semiannual coupon or cash interest = $10,000 x 8% x 1/2 = $400
                                                          =====

Total coupon interest = $400 x 6 = $2,400
                                   =======
```

To determine the issue price of the bonds, the future cash flows related to the bond are discounted at the semiannual market rate of interest so that the bonds will be priced to yield the market. In this case, the semiannual market rate of interest is 5% and should be discounted over six interest period

```
Cash Flows:

    Par value (an amount of $1):      $10,000 x  .746 = $ 7,460

    Interest (an ordinary annuity): $   400 x 5.076 =   2,030
                                                      ---------
        Selling price.................................. $ 9,490
        Par value.....................................  <10,000>
                                                      ---------
            Discount on bonds payable................ $    510
                                                      ========
```

Nature of the Discount. Economically, the discount represents additional interest for the corporation. In other words, the corporation borrows, and has the right to use $9,490 today, but must repay the full $10,000 at the maturity date. The reporting issue for the accountant is to determine when this additional cost of borrowing should be recognized in the financial statements.

The accountant gives recognition to this additional cost of borrowing by allocating or amortizing the discount over the life of the bond issue. There are two possible methods of amortization: the straight-line method and the effective interest-rate method. The effective interest-rate method is required by APB Opinion No. 21, "Interest on Receivables and Payables", unless the results obtained by using the

straight-line method are not materially different from the interest rate method.
Under either method, there are two primary effects of discount amortization:

1. Discount amortization increases the interest expense so that the corporation's effective cost of borrowing is brought up to the market rate of interest.

2. Discount amortization reduces the balance of the discount, and therefore,
    increases the carrying value of the bonds so that at maturity date, the carrying value of the bonds is equal to the par value.

The Straight-Line Method of Amortization. The straight-line method of amortization results in a constant amount of amortization each period. However, the
results are economically incorrect because the effective cost of borrowing fluctuates
from period to period. In the Auto-Stop Corporation illustration, the straight-line
amortization is computed as follows.

```
                           $510
Semi-annual amortization = --------- = $85 per semiannual interest period
                            6
```

The results for the first year (i.e., the first two interest periods) are presented
below.

```
Period                    Computations                          Cost of Borrowing
----------  ----------------------------------------------      ------------------

  1         ($400 + 85)/$9,490 = $485/$9,490          =            .0511 = 5.11%

  2         ($400 + 85)/($9,490 + 85) = $485/$9,575   =            .0506 = 5.06%
```

In each period the straight-line amortization results in a constant amount of
interest expense charged against income, $485 (i.e., the coupon interest of $400 plus
the $85 discount amortization). However, the effective cost of borrowing fluctuates
each interest period, a result that does not make economic sense. Therefore, the
straight-line method of amortization is not considered theoretically correct by
Opinion 21.

The Effective Interest Rate Method of Amortization. The effective interest-rate
method of amortization is considered theoretically correct and is the method required by Opinion 21, unless the effects of using the straight-line method are not
materially different. The effective interest rate method is considered theoretically
correct because the effective total interest is computed at a constant rate or constant cost of borrowing. This constant cost of borrowing is determined by multiplying the semiannual market rate of interest (which was used to establish the issue
price of the bonds) by the outstanding balance of the debt. Although the amount of
discount amortization varies each period, the rate of interest applied against the
outstanding balance of the debt is constant. The amount of the discount amortized

or allocated to each accounting period is the difference betweeen the effective total interest and the cash or coupon (nominal) interest. This amount is determined as follows.

```
Effective
Interest     = Semiannual market rate x Outstanding balance of the debt
Expense


Discount
Amortization = Effective interest expense - Cash (coupon) interest
```

The results of applying the effective interest-rate method are illustrated on the discount amortization table presented in Exhibit 3.2.

As noted in Exhibit 3.2, the discount amortization table constructed under the interest-rate method applies a constant rate of interest against the outstanding balance of the debt. The difference between the effective total interest of 5% and the cash or coupon interest of 4% is the discount amortization for the period. The effects of discount amortization are (a) to increase the effective cost of borrowing for the corporation to 5% semiannually or 10% annually, or to a total of $2,910, which is the sum of the coupon interest ($2,400) plus the discount ($510); and (b) to reduce the amount of the discount and to increase the carrying value of the bonds up to $10,000, the amount due at maturity.

In each accounting period, the effective interest expense is charged against the income statement, but only the coupon interest is reported on the cash flow statement. These effects can be seen in the following equation analysis.

EXHIBIT 3.2

Illustration: Discount Amortization Table Under the Effective Interest Rate Method

---

Period	4% Cash Interest	5% Effective Interest	Discount Amortization	Outstanding Balance of the Debt
(1)	(2)	(3) = 5% x (5)	(4) = (3) - (2)	(5) = Prior (5) + (4)
0	-	-	-	$ 9,490.00
1	$ 400	$ 474.50 *	$ 74.50 **	9,564.50 ***
2	400	478.23	78.23	9,642.73
3	400	482.14	82.14	9,724.87
4	400	486.24	86.24	9,811.11
5	400	490.56	90.56	9,901.67
6	400	498.33 (r)	98.33	10,000.00
Totals	$2,400	$2,910.00 (e)	$510.00	$ -0-

NOTES: * = $9,490 x 5% = $474.50.
        ** = $474.50 - 400.00 = $74.50.
        *** = $9,490.00 + 74.50 = $9,564.50.
        (r) = Rounding error = $3.25.
        (e) = Effective cost of borrowing can be determined as follows:

        Cash outflow (Principal + Interest = $10,000 + 2,400)...$12,400
        Cash inflow (Selling price)............................< 9,490>

        Effective cost of borrowing..........................$ 2,910
                                                               ========

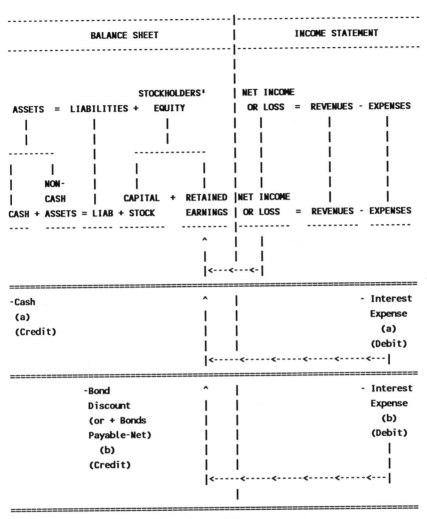

(a) Entry to record the semiannual cash interest payment.
(b) Entry to record the amortization of the discount (i.e., to increase the obligation and record the additional interest expense for the period).

Illustration of Accounting for Bonds Sold at a Premium

In order to illustrate accounting for bonds sold at a premium, assume that all information pertaining to the January 1, 1990 issuance of the Auto-Stop Corporation bonds is the same, except that the market rate of interest falls to 6% annually, or 3% semiannually. With the lower market rate of interest the issue price of the bonds would be determined by discounting the pertinent cash flows at 3% for six interest periods as follows.

```
Cash Flows:

    Par value (an amount of $1):      $10,000 x  .838 = $ 8,380

    Interest (an ordinary annuity):  $   400 x 5.417 =   2,167
                                                       ---------
        Selling price................................ $10,547
        Par value....................................  <10,000>
                                                       ---------
            Premium on bonds payable................. $    547
                                                       =========
```

Nature of the Premium. The premium represents "interest savings" for the corporation because it borrows and has the use of $10,547, but must only repay the creditor $10,000 at the maturity date.

Similar to the discount case, the premium or interest savings must be allocated or amortized to each interest period over the life of the bond issue.

The two effects of the premium amortization are to (a) reduce the interest expense so that the corporation's effective cost of borrowing is brought down to the market rate of interest, and (b) reduce the premium so that the carrying vaue of the bonds is brought down to the par value at the maturity date.

As in the case of the bond discount, the premium could be amortized by the straight-line method or the effective interest-rate method of amortization. As noted earlier, according to Opinion 21, the effective interest-rate method is required, unless the effects of using the straight-line method are not materially different. The theoretical superiority of the effective interest rate method relative to the straight-line method was explained and illustrated in the discussion of accounting for bonds sold at a discount and will not be repeated here.

The Effective Interest Rate Method of Amortization. Under the effective interest-rate method of amortization, the premium amortization is calculated in the same way as in the discount case. Specifically, the total effective interest for the period is determined by multiplying the semiannual market rate of interest by the outstanding balance of the debt. The amount of premium to amortize is the difference between the effective total interest and the cash or coupon interest for the period.

The premium amortization table under the effective interest rate method is presented in Exhibit 3.3.

As noted in Exhibit 3.3, the premium amortization table constructed under the interest rate method applies a constant rate of interest against the outstanding balance of the debt. The difference between the effective total interest at 3% and the cash or coupon interest of 4% is the premium amortization for the period. The effects of premium amortization are (a) to decrease the effective cost of borrowing for the corporation to 3% semiannually or 6% annually, or to a total of $1,853, which is the difference between the coupon interest ($2,400) and the premium ($547); and (b) to reduce the amount of the premium and to reduce the carrying value of the bonds down to $10,000, the amount due at maturity.

EXHIBIT 3.3

Illustration: Premium Amortization Table Under the Effective Interest Rate Method

---

Period (1)	4% Cash Interest (2)	3% Effective Interest (3) = 3% x (5)	Premium (s) Amortization (4) = (3) - (2)	Outstanding Balance of the Debt (5) = Prior (5) + (4)
0	-	-	-	$10,547.00
1	$ 400	$ 316.41 *	$ 83.59 **	10,463.41 ***
2	400	313.90	86.10	10,377.31
3	400	311.32	88.86	10,288.63
4	400	308.66	91.34	10,197.29
5	400	305.92	94.08	10,103.21
6	400	296.79 (r)	103.21	10,000.00
Totals	$2,400	$ 1,853.00 (e)	$547.00	$ -0-

NOTES:
    * = $10,547 x 3% = $316.41.
    ** = $316.41 - 400.00 = $83.59.
    *** = $10,547.00 - 83.59 = $10,463.41.
    (r) = Rounding error = $6.31.
    (e) = Effective cost of borrowing can be determined as follows:

        Cash outflow (Principal + Interest = $10,000 + 2,400)...$12,400
        Cash inflow (Selling price).............................<10,547>

        Effective cost of borrowing........................$ 1,853

    (s) = If the straight line method of amortization was used, the premium would be amortized $91.17 per interest period (i.e., $547.00 / 6 periods).

In each accounting period, the effective interest expense is charged against the income statement, but only the coupon interest is reported on the cash flow statement. These effects can be seen on the following equation analysis.

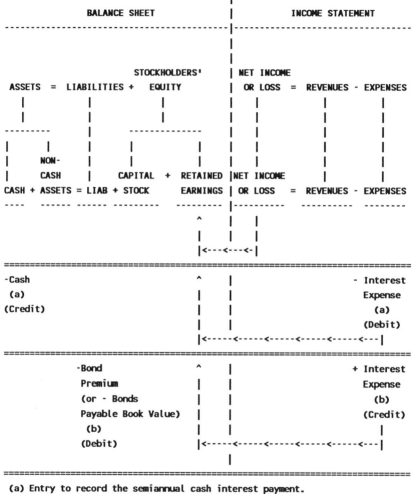

```
---------------------------------------------|---------------------------------
              BALANCE SHEET                   |       INCOME STATEMENT
---------------------------------------------|---------------------------------
                                              |
                                              |
                        STOCKHOLDERS'         | NET INCOME
ASSETS  =  LIABILITIES +   EQUITY             | OR LOSS  =  REVENUES - EXPENSES
  |          |             |                  |  |  |        |          |
  |          |             |                  |  |  |        |          |
--------     |          -------------         |  |  |        |          |
|     |      |          |           |         |  |  |        |          |
|  NON-      |          |           |         |  |  |        |          |
|  CASH      |       CAPITAL  +  RETAINED    |NET INCOME      |          |
CASH + ASSETS = LIAB + STOCK     EARNINGS    | OR LOSS  = REVENUES - EXPENSES
----   ------  ------  ---------   ---------  |----------   ----------  --------
                                        ^     |  |  |
                                        |     |  |  |
                                       |<---<---<-|
==============================================================================
-Cash                                   ^     |                  - Interest
 (a)                                    |     |                    Expense
(Credit)                                |     |                      (a)
                                        |     |                    (Debit)
                                       |<-----<-----<-----<-----<-----<---|
==============================================================================
            -Bond                       ^     |                  + Interest
            Premium                     |     |                    Expense
            (or - Bonds                 |     |                      (b)
            Payable Book Value)         |     |                    (Credit)
            (b)                         |     |                      |
            (Debit)                    |<-----<-----<-----<-----<-----<---|
                                              |
==============================================================================
(a) Entry to record the semiannual cash interest payment.
(b) Entry to record the amortization of the premium (i.e., to reduce the
    obligation and record the reduction of interest expense for the period).
==============================================================================
```

Bond Issue Costs

Bond issue costs include the costs of printing, and accounting, legal and underwriting fees. According to Opinion 21, these costs should be accounted for as a deferred charge on the asset side of the balance sheet, "unamortized bond issue costs". The deferred charge should be amortized to expense over the life of the bond issue. Although reported as a separate account on the asset side of the balance sheet, the balance of the unamortized bond issue costs is considered part of the carrying value of the bonds.

SPECIAL ISSUES RELATING TO CORPORATE DEBT

In accounting for corporate debt, several complex transactions can arise which either extinguish the debt or significantly modify the structure of the outstanding balance of the debt. Corporate debt can be retired by a call or an open market repurchase. The debt can also be removed from the balance sheet by a defeasance transaction. The structure of the debt can be modified by a restructuring agreement or an interest-rate swap. Some of these transactions pose formidable theoretical questions regarding proper accounting and reporting.

In this section of the chapter, the special issues related to accounting for corporate debt are examined. Specifically, this section presents the accounting and reporting standards for early extinguishment of debt, in-substance defeasance, interest rate swaps and troubled debt restructurings.

Early Extinguishment of Debt

According to APB Opinion No. 26, "Early Extinguishment of Debt", if debt is retired before maturity at the option of the issuing corporation, the transaction qualifies as an early extinguishment of debt. Transactions qualifying as an early extinguishment of debt include calling a bond issue, an open market purchase by the corporation, refinancing a bond issue and in-substance defeasance per paragraph 3 of SFAS 76, "Extinguishment of Debt". The gain or loss on any type of early extinguishment of debt is computed as follows.

```
Remaining carrying value of the debt extinguished........$ XXX
Less: The retirement price paid...........................  <XX>
                                                          -------
Gain (Loss) on early extinguishment of debt...........$ XXX
                                                          ======
```

That is, if the corporation pays less than the book value of the debt there is a gain and if the corporation pays more than the book value of the debt retired there is a loss.

According to paragraph 8 of SFAS 4, "Reporting Gains and Losses from Extinguishment of Debt", material gains or losses on early extinguishment of debt should be classified on the current income statement as an extraordinary item. The only exception to extraordinary treatment is set forth by SFAS 64, "Extinguishments of Debt Made to Satisfy Sinking Fund Requirements". According to SFAS 64, paragraph 4, if the gain or loss results from an early retirement needed to satisfy sinking fund requirements that must be met "within one year of the date of the extinguishment", it is considered ordinary income or loss.

Regardless of the classification for financial reporting purposes, the gain or loss from an early extinguishment of debt due to a call, open market purchase or a refinancing transaction is a taxable event. As will be discussed in the next section, an in-substance defeasance is not considered a transaction for tax purposes.

In order to illustrate the gain or loss computation for an early extinguishment of debt, consider the data applicable to the Auto-Stop Corporation presented in Exhibit 3.2. Assume that Auto-Stop decides to retire the debt at the end of the second year (i.e., the end of the fourth interest period) at a retirement price of $9,500. According to the amortization table, and assuming no deferred bond issue costs, the carrying value of the debt at the point of retirement is $9.811.11.

Based on the assumed retirement price, there would be a gain of $311.11 on the retirement (i.e., $9,811.11 - 9,500), and if material in amount the gain would be reported as an extraordinary item on the current income statement. Extraordinary items will be discussed in detail in chapter 8.

The financial statement effects of this transaction are presented in the following equation analysis.

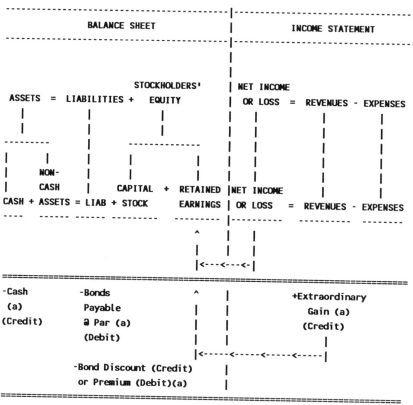

(a) Entry to record an early extinguishment of debt at a gain. Note that the carrying value of the debt retired must be removed from the accounts and the financial statements.

Sample disclosures for an early extinguishment of debt found in the 1987 financial statements of Sterling Software, Inc. are presented in Exhibit 3.4.

In-Substance Defeasance

FASB Statement No. 76, "Extinguishment of Debt", provides additional guidance regarding proper accounting and reporting of an early extinguishment of debt. SFAS 76 modifies Opinion 26 to include all extinguishments of debt, except debt conversions and troubled debt restructurings (to be discussed in a subsequent section of this chapter). By including all types of extinguishments in paragraph 16 of SFAS 76, the FASB broadened the scope of Opinion 26 to include any arrangement that relieves the debtor from primary liability for the debt with only a remote probability that the debtor would be responsible for future cash outflows relating to the obligation as guarantor of the debt. This increased scope enabled accountants to classify an in-substance defeasance transaction as an extinguishment of debt.

The defeasance transaction is highly complex, involving the theory underlying fund accounting and a great deal of legal and tax issues. The sections that follow present the principles of fund accounting, legal and tax considerations, the advantages and disadvantages of the transaction and the professional pronouncements relating to defeasance.

The Principles of Fund Accounting. An in-substance defeasance transaction utilizes the principles of fund or trust accounting. Under fund or trust accounting, a fund is created as a separate accounting entity and at times a separate legal entity. Fund accounting is found most often in government accounting and in accounting for not-for-profit entities. Although rarely used in corporate accounting, the principles of fund accounting are used extensively in accounting for pension plans.

The fund or trust is accounted for separately and is not combined with the other accounts, records and financial statements of the firm. For example, most corporate pension plans are established as separate trusts with their own management, financial statements and auditors. Transactions with the corporation and the pension fund are treated as if the pension fund is completely independent of the firm. The corporation may make cash contributions into the pension fund and record the pension expense and any pension obligation on its books. Although there are extensive pension disclosures made by the corporation, all of the assets, liabilities, revenues and expenses of the pension fund are not reported on the financial statements of the corporation. If the analyst requires additional information regarding the pension plan, the individual financial statements of the pension fund must be obtained.

In an in-substance defeasance transaction, the corporation applies the principles of fund accounting to an individual debt issue. That is, the corporation establishes the fund by placing the bonds in a trust. The trust is funded with government securities of similar maturity and in sufficient amounts to ensure that all interest payments will be made, and the debt can be paid at maturity. Because fund accounting is used, the debt is removed from the books of the corporation. One effect of this transaction is to improve debt statistics and fixed charge coverage ratios by "cleaning up" the firm's balance sheet and eliminating a portion of interest expense from the entity's income statement.

EXHIBIT 3.4

Sample Disclosure: Sterling Software, Inc.: Consolidated Statements of Income and Footnote Disclosure of an Early Extinguishment of Debt

---

STERLING SOFTWARE, INC.

CONSOLIDATED STATEMENTS OF INCOME

Years Ended September 30, 1987, 1986 and 1985
(in thousands, except per share information)

	1987	1986	1985
Revenues:			
Products	$ 97,084	$133,800	$44,318
Services	93,043	99,993	17,646
	190,127	233,793	61,964
Costs and expenses:			
Costs of sales:			
Products:			
Hardware	5,839	19,361	2,734
Other	16,060	23,973	6,866
Services	76,957	84,507	14,240
	98,856	127,841	23,840
Product development, maintenance and enhancement (Note 1)	13,043	20,789	7,442
Depreciation and amortization	11,277	11,664	4,162
Selling, general and administrative (Note 14)	51,754	51,942	19,582
	174,930	212,236	55,026
	15,197	21,557	6,938
Other income (expense):			
Interest expense	(10,076)	(14,514)	(2,255)
Investment income	6,425	3,746	1,144
Gains (losses) from business dispositions (Note 2)	(598)	3,750	
Other income, net	294	720	
	(3,955)	(6,298)	(1,111)
Income before provision for income taxes	11,242	15,259	5,827
Provision for income taxes (Note 9)	5,396	7,026	2,833
Income before extraordinary items	5,846	8,233	2,994
Extraordinary items — gain (loss) on early extinguishment of debt, net of applicable income taxes (Note 7)	360	(4,453)	
Net income	6,206	3,780	2,994
Preferred stock dividend requirements	(1,004)	(1,872)	(696)
Earnings available to common stockholders	$ 5,202	$ 1,908	$ 2,298

7. Long-term Notes Payable

Long-term notes payable consist of the following at September 30 (in thousands):

	1987	1986
8% Convertible Senior Subordinated Debentures Due 2001	$111,000	$115,000
Convertible Subordinated Debentures Due 1990	3,900	3,900
Other	240	323
	115,140	119,223
Less amounts due within one year	73	112
	$115,067	$119,111

136

Exhibit 3.4, continued

The 8% Convertible Senior Subordinated Debentures Due 2001 (the "Senior Debentures") were issued under an Indenture dated September 1, 1986, between the Company and the Trustee. The Senior Debentures are unsecured general obligations of the Company and mature on September 1, 2001. Interest is payable semiannually. The Senior Debentures are convertible at any time prior to maturity or redemption into shares of Common Stock of the Company at a conversion price of $21.60 per share, subject to adjustment under certain conditions.

The Senior Debentures are redeemable at any time, at the option of the Company, in whole or in part, on a pro rata basis at a premium of 108% which declines to 100% after September 1, 1996, together with accrued interest, except that no such redemption may be made on or prior to October 1, 1988, unless the closing price of the Company's Common Stock has been equal to at least 150% of the conversion price then in effect for any twenty trading days within thirty consecutive trading days prior to the date of the notice of redemption. Annual sinking fund payments commencing September 1, 1996, are calculated to retire 75% of the issue prior to maturity. The Company may deliver Senior Debentures in lieu of cash in making sinking fund payments.

The Senior Debentures will be subordinated to all Senior Indebtedness (as defined) of the Company. The Indenture does not restrict the incurrence of Senior Indebtedness or certain other indebtedness of the Company. In addition, the Senior Debentures will be effectively subordinated to all liabilities of the Company's subsidiaries. The terms of the Senior Debentures currently limit the Company's ability to pay dividends generally to 50% of net cumulative earnings since March 31, 1986, plus 100% of the consideration received from the issuances of capital stock from such date.

The net proceeds from the sale of the Senior Debentures were used to retire the outstanding principal balances of the Increasing Rate Senior Notes Due No Later Than 1990 and the 15.5% Senior Subordinated Notes Due 1993. The Company paid a premium in 1986 to effect the early retirement of the 15.5% Senior Subordinated Notes Due 1993 resulting in an extraordinary loss of $4,453,000, net of the applicable income tax benefit of $4,524,000.

During the third quarter of 1987, the Company purchased $4,000,000 face amount of the Senior Debentures in open market transactions resulting in an extraordinary gain of $360,000, net of applicable income taxes of $346,000.

Effective April 10, 1985, the Company issued $3,900,000 aggregate principal amount of Convertible Subordinated Debentures Due 1990 (the "Debentures") to certain officers and directors of the Company. The Debentures bear interest at prime (8¼% at September 30, 1987), payable annually. The Debentures will be convertible into 450,000 shares of Common Stock at prices of from $8.00 to $10.00 (averaging $8.67) per share. One-half of the Debentures are currently convertible and one-fourth will become convertible on each anniversary date until all Debentures are fully convertible. The conversion price is subject to certain adjustments to prevent dilution of the holders' conversion rights.

The aggregate principal payments on all notes payable, which are due in each of the next five years, are: 1988—$73,000; 1989—$89,000; 1990—$3,968,000; 1991—$10,000 , 1992—none; and $111,000,000 thereafter.

Source: Sterling Software, Inc. Form 10K for the Fiscal Year Ended September 30, 1987. Copyright, 1987, by Sterling Software, Inc. Reprinted with permission.

Legal and Tax Considerations. Legally, the term defeasance literally means "voiding an agreement". In-substance defeasance is an arrangement whereby an entity provides for the repayment of long-term debt at maturity by placing cash and government securities, approximately matching the maturities of the defeased debt, into an irrevocable trust. The irrevocable trust is created for the sole purpose of making interest and principal payments on the debt. The trustee could be a commercial bank or an investment bank and the trust is established at a fee.

Note that this transaction does not constitute an actual repayment of the debt. If the debt is public debt, the debt is still traded in the market. All of the specific restrictive covenants in the indenture of the defeased debt remain in force. Thus, the corporation must still be concerned with technical default of the defeased debt. Nonetheless, the defeasance itself could be used as a means of preventing technical default of other debt agreements.

If the debt is privately held, the bondholders may vote to allow the corporation to escape some of the restrictive covenants of the debt. With defeased public debt still traded in the market, the corporation continues to have the option to retire the debt in an open market purchase. If the corporation actually retires the debt, all of the trust assets would revert back to the corporation.

Although the trust is a separate accounting entity and the assets of the trust cannot be used by the corporation and the other corporate creditors do not have access to these assets, it is still not certain if the trust would survive intact in the event of bankruptcy of the corporation. That is, there is some question as to the degree of the separate legal existence of the trust.

Because the transaction is only a defeasance "in-substance", the transaction is not legally recognized by taxing jurisdictions. For tax purposes, the liability is still treated as outstanding debt and the trust assets are considered a new corporate investment. The trustee's fees and debt interest are tax deductible by the corporation. The interest revenue of the trust is taxable to the corporation in the year earned. However, the IRS has placed several restrictions on the tax benefits derived from the activities of the trust in a defeasance transaction:

1. After 7/18/84, the corporation cannot claim a net interest deduction if the coupon rate on the trust assets is less than the coupon rate on the defeased debt.

2. After 7/18/84, the corporation cannot take a net interest deduction when the interest expense incurred on a new debt series, whose proceeds were used to fund the trust assets, exceeds the interest revenue earned by the trust.

3. After 7/1/87, the capital gains benefits generated from purchasing the trust securities at a discount were eliminated.

It should be noted that state and local governments had used defeasance for quite some time. A significant difference between governmental defeasance and corporate in-substance defeasance is that state and local government defeasance is a legal defeasance and the governmental unit would escape all restrictive covenants contained in the indenture.

In-Substance Defeasance--The Exxon Case. In order to understand the potential magnitude of a defeasance transaction, the Exxon case will be examined.

In 1982, Exxon placed in trust six of its own 5.8% to 6.8% bond issues maturing in 2009 and totaling $515 million, and deposited cash which was used by the trust to purchase $313 million in government securities yielding 14% to service the principle and interest on the debt. Exxon removed the $515 million of bonds payable from its balance sheet and reported a gain of $202 million on its income statement. The gain increased earnings per share by $.15 per share. The gain was not taxable because there was no legal extinguishment of the debt.

Advantages and Disadvantages of Defeasance.[1] There are clear cosmetic benefits from the Exxon transaction: the balance sheet is "cleaned up" by removing significant amounts of debt, which could avoid technical default on another debt issue; and earnings per share increase without any tax consequences. Although debt/equity and fixed charge coverage ratios would improve, bond ratings on publicly traded debt issues would probably not be affected by the defeasance transaction.

As a substitute for an actual open market repurchase, the defeasance has several advantages. First, although the cost of riskless securities may exceed the open market purchase price, the gain on the open market purchase is taxable. Second, the defeasance is a "quicker" transaction and guarantees that all of the debt can be "extinguished" with a cost that is certain. In an open market purchase, it may take some time to have all of the bondholders dispose of their investments and there could be significant upward price pressure over the purchase period, making the final cost of the transaction uncertain. Because of the existence of call premiums, calling in the issue may be too expensive to implement.

The financial community has also recognized several disadvantages of the defeasance transaction. First, the gain on the defeasance does not provide any cash flow. That is, the increase in reported profits is purely cosmetic, not having any real effect on the value of the firm. Second, even after tax consequences, it may have actually been cheaper to purchase the debt in the open market. Third, the reported gain results from the defeasance transaction by removing old, low-interest cost debt with a smaller amount of cash or government securities. This benefit only exists in a period of rising interest rates. Therefore, if the firm requires additional financing in the near future, it would have to borrow at higher interest rates. In effect, the firm may be refinancing cheap debt by issuing new, high cost obligations. Finally, there could be an adverse reaction by common shareholders. Common stockholders may view the defeasance transaction with apprehension because of the "costless benefit" to bondholders: the debt is now backed by riskless securities, without additional cost to the bond investor. However, this benefit could be costly to the common shareholders; although reported earnings per share increase, there is no corresponding cash inflow. In fact, there is a significant cash outflow to fund the trust, which erodes the liquidity position of the firm and possibly affects its dividend paying ability. The potential adverse effect on the common stockholders could increase the cost of raising future equity capital.

Professional Standards Governing Defeasance. The accounting profession responded to the use of in-substance defeasance in November 1983 with the issuance of FASB Statement No. 76. SFAS 76 represents the profession's approval of the defeasance transaction.

Under the provisions of SFAS 76, in order to be considered an extinguishment of debt (i.e., removing the debt from the balance sheet and recording the gain or loss from early extinguishment), the following criteria must be met:

1. The debtor must place cash or risk-free securities, which includes instruments backed by the U.S. government, in an irrevocable trust which must be used solely for payment of interest and principal of the defeased debt.

2. The probability that the debtor will be required to make any future payments with respect to the debt must be remote.

3. The defeasance transaction must be disclosed in the footnotes to the financial statements and include "a general description of the transaction and the amount of the debt that is considered extinguished at the end of each accounting period, for as long as the debt remains outstanding".

4. Any gain or loss on the defeasance must be reported as an extraordinary item per SFAS 4.

It is also assumed that the assets held by the trustee will provide future cash flows which approximately match the timing of the required cash payments on the defeased debt.

The theory underlying SFAS 76 is found in SFAC 6, "Elements of Financial Statements". That is, the liability is removed from the balance sheet because it no longer meets the SFAC 6 definition of a liability: the defeased debt does not represent "a probable future sacrifice of economic resources from a current obligation of the entity to transfer assets or to provide services to other entities in the future as result of current or past transactions".

Finally, SFAS 76 only applies to existing debt. If a firm issues new debt and simultaneously sets up a trust with foreign government securities to take advantage of interest rate differentials in world markets, the transaction would be accounted for as an issuance of debt and an investment. This type of transaction is sometimes known as "instantaneous defeasance".

One month after the issuance of SFAS 76, the SEC sanctioned the use of in-substance defeasance transactions by the issuance of Financial Reporting Release (FRR) No. 15. FRR 15 provides for clarification and additional requirements such as independence of the trustee, only securities of the U.S. government can be considered riskless for purposes of establishing the trust, and the trust should be established such that neither the corporation nor its creditors should have the ability to claim or use the trust assets.

Sample disclosures of defeasance transactions are presented in Exhibit 3.5.

Interest Rate Swaps

Under an interest rate swap, the parties to the transaction agree to exchange interest payments. The obligation for the principal amount of the debt involved remains with the original debtor. The purpose of the swap transaction is to enable

EXHIBIT 3.5

Sample Disclosure: Exxon Corporation and PepsiCo, Inc.: Footnote Disclosure of an In-Substance Defeasance Transaction

----

Exxon Corporation:

In 1982, debt totaling $515 million was removed from the balance sheet through the creation of an irrevocable trust. The principal and interest of the funds deposited with the trustee will be sufficient to fund the scheduled principal and interest payment of these debt issues. During 1983, $51 million of these debt issues were retired, leaving a balance of $464 million at year-end 1984.

Source: Exxon Corporation 1984 Annual Report. Copyright, 1985, by The Exxon Corporation. Reprinted with permission.

PepsiCo Inc.

During 1984, PepsiCo issued $104 million of Deutsche mark denominated bearer bonds yielding 7-1/4 percent, due February 26, 1994. A major portion of the bond proceeds were used to purchase higher yielding notes of the West German Government that yield cash flows sufficient to meet the interest and principal payments of the bearer bonds. PepsiCo defeased the bonds by depositing the Deutsche mark denominated government notes in an irrevocable trust established for the sole purpose of servicing the bearer bonds. This defeasance resulted in a $1.7 million ($.02 per share) gain, after related expenses and taxes. The bearer bonds and promissory notes of the West German Government offset each other in the Consolidated Balance Sheet.

Source: PepsiCo, Inc. 1984 Annual Report. Copyright PepsiCo, Inc., 1985. Reproduced with permission.

the firms involved to minimize their individual interest costs and at the same time borrow using a desired type of loan, variable or fixed rate, by sharing their relative borrowing advantages. The swap partners are usually brought together by an intermediary, such as an investment bank or a commercial bank, for a commission or a fee. The fee charged can be collected by the intermediary through sharing in the net interest saved by the swap partners.

Interest Rate Swap Illustration. Exhibit 3.6 provides an illustration of a basic swap transaction. This illustration is taken from the May 1985 edition of the Coopers and Lybrand *Executive Alert*.[2] Although highly simplified, this example illustrates the fundamental mechanics of the swap transaction. The discussion of other, more complex swap arrangements is beyond the scope of this text.

An alternative treatment of the Coopers and Lybrand solution which places emphasis on the interest-rate savings, is presented below.

```
-------------------------------------------------------------------------
|          Company A              |           Company B                 |
|---------------------------------|-------------------------------------|
|Desired   : Variable 11% (Prime) |Desired    : Fixed 14%               |
|Can Borrow: Fixed 12%            |Can Borrow: Variable at Prime + 1% = |
|                                 |             12%                     |
|---------------------------------|-------------------------------------|
|               Swap Transaction                                        |
|---------------------------------|-------------------------------------|
|Borrows fixed...............<12.0%>|Borrows variable..............<12.0%>|
|                                 |                                     |
|Swap interest received.+12.5%<-------Swap interest paid.....<12.5%>    |
|                                 |                                     |
|Swap interest paid.....<11.0%>------->Swap interest received.+11.0%    |
|         -------                 |             ------                  |
|Net swap received...............1.5% |Net swap paid.................< 1.5%>|
|         -------                 |             -------                 |
|Net cost of borrowing.........<10.5%>|Net cost of borrowing........<13.5%>|
|         =======                 |             ========                |
|Interest savings...............+ 0.5% |Interest savings...............+ 0.5% |
|         =======                 |             =======                 |
|---------------------------------|-------------------------------------|
```

Note that Company A borrows at 12%, which is 1% more than originally desired, and Company B borrows at 12%, which is 2% less than originally planned. The net savings from the swap transaction is 1%, which is shared equally by the two firms. Actually, there may be some other sharing arrangement, and if a third party intermediary structured the deal, some of those interest savings would be paid to the third party in the form of commissions or fees.

In this illustration, Company B structures the deal so that it incurs a fixed rate of interest equal to 13.5%. This is achieved through the fixed swap payment from Company B to Company A of 12.5%. Fixed rate debt was preferred by Company B from the outset. On the other hand, Company A actually incurs variable rate debt by making the required swap payment to Company B equal to the prime rate. That

EXHIBIT 3.6

Illustration: Coopers and Lybrand Interest Rate Swap Example

How a Swap Can Save on Interest Costs

Company A, with a high credit rating, may be able to obtain fixed rate financing at 12% or floating rate financing at prime (assumed to be 11%). Company A prefers to borrow at a floating rate. Company B, with low credit rating, may have to pay 14% for fixed rate financing or prime+1% for floating rate financing. Company B wishes to borrow at a fixed rate.

Both companies can save on their interest costs by entering into an interest rate swap agreement in which Company A borrows at a *fixed* rate and swaps its fixed rate for the floating rate obligation of Company B, while Company B borrows at a *floating* rate and swaps its floating rate for the fixed rate obligation of Company A.

The interest rate swap allows both parties to reduce interest costs by letting them share the spread between their respective fixed borrowing costs. Company A's fixed borrowing rate is 2% below that of Company B's borrowing rate. Since Company B pays a 1% premium on floating rate debt, the 1% savings that remains is shared by the two parties.

This 1/2% savings for each company can be illustrated by comparing the interest costs of the two companies both with and without a hypothetical swap transaction:

	Without Swap		With Swap	
Company A (high credit)				
Principal borrowed	$10,000,000	(floating)	$10,000,000	(fixed)
Debt interest paid	$ 1,100,000	(prime 11%)	$ 1,200,000	(12%)
Swap interest paid	—		1,100,000	(prime)
Swap interest received	—		(1,250,000)	(12½%)
Net interest cost	$ 1,100,000	(prime)	$ 1,050,000	(prime-½%)
Nature of borrowing	Floating:	11%	Floating:	10½%
Company B (low credit)				
Principal borrowed	$10,000,000	(fixed)	$10,000,000	(floating)
Debt interest paid	$ 1,400,000	(14%)	$ 1,200,000	(prime+1%)
Swap interest paid	—		$ 1,250,000	(12½%)
Swap interest received	—		(1,100,000)	(prime)
Net interest cost	$ 1,400,000	(14%)	$ 1,350,000	(13½%)
Nature of borrowing	Fixed:	14%	Fixed:	13½%

Source: Coopers and Lybrand "Executive Alert Newsletter", May, 1985. Copyright, 1985, by Coopers and Lybrand (USA) Communications Department, 1251 Avenue of the Americas, New York, New York 10020. Reprinted with permission.

is, Company A is exposed to interest rate fluctuations, as originally desired. Therefore, if the prime goes up to 12%, Company B would now have to borrow at 13% (i.e., prime + 1%) and pay a net swap interest of 0.5% to Company A. Company B yields a constant savings of 0.5% over the original fixed rate of 14%. Company A also saves by borrowing fixed and paying the variable rate through the swap. If the prime goes up to 12%, Company A pays fixed at 12% but receives a net swap interest from Company B of 0.5%. The net interest cost for Company A is 11.5%. If Company A borrowed variable as originally desired, it must pay the prime rate of 12%. Thus, the swap transaction also results in a constant savings for Company A equal to 0.5% below prime. The 12% prime rate case is illustrated below.

```
-----------------------------------------------------------------
|            Company A             |            Company B          |
|----------------------------------|------------------------------|
|Desired   : Variable 12% (Prime)  |Desired   : Fixed 14%         |
|Can Borrow: Fixed 12%             |Can Borrow: Variable at Prime + 1% = |
|                                  |            13%               |
|----------------------------------|------------------------------|
|                    Swap Transaction                            |
|----------------------------------|------------------------------|
|Borrows fixed.................<12.0%>|Borrows variable..............<13.0%>|
|                                  |                              |
|Swap interest received.+12.5%<--------Swap interest paid.....<12.5%>     |
|                                  |                              |
|Swap interest paid.....<12.0%>------->Swap interest received.+12.0%       |
|            -------               |            -------           |
|Net swap received...............0.5% |Net swap paid.................< 0.5%>|
|            -------               |            -------           |
|Net cost of borrowing.........<11.5%|Net cost of borrowing........<13.5%>|
|            ========              |            ========          |
|Interest savings..............+ 0.5% |Interest savings..............+ 0.5% |
|            =======               |            ========          |
|----------------------------------|------------------------------|
```

Professional Standards on Swap Accounting. To date, the accounting profession has not prescribed special accounting treatment for the swap transaction. The interest expense reported on the income statement would be equal to the net interest cost (i.e., the debt service paid plus the swap interest paid less the swap interest received). Of course, full disclosure of the swap transaction should be provided, probably as part of the long-term debt footnote.

Recently, there has been serious criticism of the quality and usefulness of the interest-rate swap disclosures. Specifically, interest-rate swap disclosures have been inadequate in terms of reporting the possible credit risk (i.e., higher interest payments) that can result if the swap partner defaults on the transaction in addition to the usual risk from unfavorable interest-rate fluctuations. The risk for Company A if Company B defaults is the higher fixed rate debt at 12%. Of course, the intermediary can absorb most of the risk in exchange for a higher fee.

Interest-rate swaps and other financing and investing issues are now being considered in the FASB's Financial Instruments Project.

As part of the first phase of the FASB's Financial Instruments Disclosure Project, the FASB issued Statement No. 105, "Disclosure of Information about Financial Instruments with Off-Balance Sheet Risk and Financial Instruments with Concentrations of Credit Risk", in June 1990.

SFAS 105 requires the following disclosures effective for fiscal years ending after June 15, 1990.

All entities with financial instruments that have "off-balance sheet" risk should disclose:

1. Information about the face, contract or notional principal amount;

2. The nature and terms of the instruments;

3. The accounting loss that would occur if any party to the instrument failed completely to perform;

4. The company's policy for requiring collateral or other security and a description of the collateral held.

Subsequent project phases will consider disclosure of additional information about all financial instruments, including market values, and address recognition and measurement issues.[3]

Disclosure requirement number three would probably be applied to interest-rate swap transactions by disclosing the interest-rate risk exposure that would be caused by a default by one of the swap partners.

As part of the second phase of the FASB's long-term financial instruments project, the Board is proposing that all firms disclose the market value of all financial instruments, both assets and liabilities, if it is practical to estimate these values. If it is not practical to estimate market values, other disclosures would be required. The proposal is presently at the exposure draft stage. If approved, the exposure draft entitled "Disclosures About Market Value of Financial Instruments" would be effective for fiscal years ending after December 15, 1991.

Accounting for a Troubled Debt Restructuring

Accounting and reporting requirements for a troubled debt restructuring are set forth in FASB Statement No. 15, "Accounting by Debtors and Creditors for Troubled Debt Restructurings". Under SFAS 15, paragraph 2, a troubled debt restructuring is defined as a restructuring of a debt agreement of troubled debtors where, for economic and legal reasons relating to a debtor's financial difficulties, the creditor makes concessions to the debtor that it may not otherwise consider. That is, SFAS 15 does not apply to modifications of debt agreements made in response to changes in general economic conditions.

Basic Forms of Restructuring. According to SFAS 15, paragraph 5, there are two basic forms of restructuring:

1. Settlement of the debt at less than its recorded amount. In this type of restructuring, the debt agreement is terminated. The creditor's claim is satisfied by accepting either a transfer of assets from the debtor or a transfer of an interest in the equity of the debtor. Because concessions are being granted by the creditor, this is a "bargain settlement".

2. Continuation of the debt agreement with modified terms (i.e., "a modification"). In this case, the debt still continues to exist, but the creditor can make modifications to the terms of the original agreement which reduce the principal, reduce the interest rate, forgive accrued and unpaid interest, and extend the term. Any one or all of these modifications can be made to the original agreement.

Accounting for a troubled debt restructuring is relatively straightforward for a bargain settlement. However, accounting for a modification is highly controversial and has been criticized by the accounting and financial community for its inconsistent methodology. Accounting and reporting issues relating to a troubled debt restructuring are discussed in the next section.

Accounting for a Debt Restructuring--Bargain Settlement. When the debt restructuring is in the form of a bargain settlement, the asset or the equity transfer is accounted for at the fair value of the transfer.

Settlement by an Asset Transfer. If the debtor transfers noncash assets in full settlement of the obligation, the difference between the carrying value of the note on the date of the restructure and the fair market value of the assets transferred is an extraordinary gain (per SFAS 4) to the debtor and an ordinary loss to the creditor. The creditor can also charge the allowance for bad debts or a loan loss reserve for the amount of the loss, rather than recording the loss on the income statement. The debtor also records an ordinary gain or loss on the asset transfer, which is measured as the difference between the fair market value and the net book value of the assets transferred.

Illustration: Settlement by an Asset Transfer to the Creditor. In order to illustrate the effects of bargain settlement implemented with an asset transfer, assume that the Holly Corporation owes the King Trust Company $1,000,000, which represents the outstanding balance or carrying value of a five-year, 10% loan. Holly recently experienced financial difficulty and King agreed to settle the obligation by accepting a transfer of equipment with a fair value of $600,000 and a net book value to Holly of $500,000.

Based on the above information, King Trust Company would report a $400,000 ($1,000,000 - $600,000) ordinary loss or a $400,000 charge against its bad debt allowance. Holly Corporation would report an extraordinary gain of $400,000 on the restructure and an ordinary gain of $100,000 ($600,000 - 500,000) on the disposal of the equipment used in the asset transfer.

Settlement by a Transfer of an Equity Interest to the Creditor. If the bargain settlement is implemented through a transfer of an interest in the equity of the debtor, there is only an ordinary loss to the creditor and an extraordinary gain to the debtor on the restructure. There is no gain or loss recorded by the debtor on the transfer of the equity interest because this is nothing more than an issuance of new capital stock or a sale of treasury shares (to be discussed in a subsequent section of this chapter).

Illustration: Settlement by a Transfer of an Equity Interest to the Creditor. To illustrate a bargain settlement with a transfer of an equity interest, assume that instead of the asset transfer, the Holly Corporation now issues 20,000 shares of its $10 par value common stock to the King Trust Company. On the date of the transfer, the shares had a fair market value of $15 per share. The total value of the equity transferred to King is $300,000 (20,000 shares at $15 per share).

In this case, the King Trust would report an ordinary loss of $700,000 ($1,000,000 - 300,000) or reduce the bad debt allowance by the same amount. The Holly Corporation would record the issuance of the new shares of stock and the $700,000 extraordinary gain on the restructure.

Accounting for a Debt Restructuring--Modification. Accounting for a troubled debt restructuring that continues the debt agreement with modified terms is the most controversial area in SFAS 15. The controversy centers around the failure of SFAS 15 to recognize economic losses to creditors in certain situations.[4] In fact, under the terms of some debt modification agreements, no gain or loss is recorded on the transaction. Part of the reason for the failure to recognize economic losses to the creditor and the resulting asymmetrical accounting treatment (i.e., recognition of gain or loss on some modifications versus no gain or loss recognition on others) is the use of undiscounted future cash flows in the accounting computations.

The determination of whether to recognize the gain or loss on modification and the amount of gain or loss to be recognized is based on a comparison of the prerestructuring carrying amount of the debt with the undiscounted total future cash flows after modification (i.e., the postrestructuring nominal value). Issues relating to gain or loss recognition on modification are presented in the following sections.

Recognition of the Gain or Loss. If the prerestructuring carrying value is greater than the postrestructuring nominal value, then the gain or loss is recognized. There is an extraordinary gain to the debtor and an ordinary loss or a write-off to the bad debt allowance for the creditor. The gain or loss is measured by taking the difference between the prerestructuring carrying value of the debt and the total future undiscounted cash flows after modification.

The gain or loss actually reduces the prerestructuring carrying value of the debt so that it equals the total undiscounted future cash flows. Since the debtor will now repay less than it borrowed, the effective cost of borrowing is zero so that there is no interest expense or interest income recognized in future periods.

Nonrecognition of the Gain or Loss. Conversely, if the prerestructuring carrying value of the debt is less than the sum of the undiscounted future cash flows after modification (i.e., postrestructuring nominal value), then no gain or loss is recognized under SFAS 15 in the year of the restructure. Instead, the total carrying amounts of the debt and the receivable are unchanged, but any amounts of principal reduction and/or interest forgiven are reclassified by creating a "premium" account on the books of the debtor and a "discount" on the books of the creditor. The amount of the premium and discount is equal to the principal reduction and any accrued interest forgiven. As a result, the creditor reclassifies the amount of the principal reduction and interest forgiven out of notes and accrued interest receivable into the discount account. This discount is added to the balance of notes receivable in order to maintain a constant carrying value of the asset. The debtor reclassifies this same amount out of notes and accrued interest payable into the premium account. The premium account is added to the notes payable in order to maintain a constant carrying value of the debt. Thus, the total prerestructuring carrying value of the receivable and payable are unchanged by the reclassification adjustments.

The premium (discount) accounts are used rather than recognizing a gain (loss). A new effective interest rate must be determined and used in the amortization of the premium and discount. Because the new effective interest rate is less than the original effective cost of borrowing, the amortization of the premium and discount reduces the creditor's interest income and reduces the debtor's interest expense systematically over the remaining life of the debt. In substance, nonrecognition of the economic gain or loss defers the gain or loss and the subsequent amortization spreads the creditor's "loss" and the debtor's "gain" over the remaining life of the modified debt agreement.

By not using discounted cash flows in the computations for the debt modification, the FASB backed itself into a corner. If symmetrical accounting treatment was to be given to those cases where the prerestructuring carrying value of the debt was less than the total undiscounted future cash flows after modification, then the creditor would have a gain and the debtor would have a loss. But how could the creditor grant significant concessions to the debtor and still gain while the creditor suffers a loss? To avoid this problem and continue to use undiscounted cash flows, SFAS 15 adopted the asymmetrical accounting treatment and does not recognize gains and losses in the year of the modification if the prerestructuring carrying value is less than the total undiscounted future cash flows after the modification.

Illustration: Modification with Gain and Loss Recognition. In order to illustrate a continuation of the troubled debt with modified terms, assume that the King Trust Company now agrees to the following modifications of theHolly Corporation debt:

1. Reduction of the face amount of the debt from $1,000,000 to $600,000;

2. Forgiveness of $20,000 of accrued interest;

3. Reduction of the interest rate from 10% to 7%;

4. There is no extension of the maturity date so that the debt is still due in four years.

At the date of the restructure, the debt has a carrying value of $1,020,000 (i.e., $1,000,000 of principal plus $20,000 of accrued interest). The total future undiscounted cash flows amount to $768,000 (i.e., $600,000 plus 7% interest for four years at $42,000 per year). Because the prerestructuring carrying value of the debt ($1,020,000) exceeds the total future undiscounted cash flows after modification ($768,000), the gain and loss can be recognized. The amount of gain and loss is $252,000 ($1,020,000 - 768,000).

The creditor would recognize a loss or a write-off to the allowance for bad debts for $252,000. The creditor would also reduce its receivable from the debtor by $232,000 and write off the $20,000 of the accrued interest receivable. Because the effective cost of borrowing is now zero, all future "interest" payments are applied against the principal so that there is a balance of $600,000 at the maturity date. This last point can be summarized as follows.

```
Notes receivable:

    Original principal.....................$1,000,000

    Less: Adjustment on modification.......  <232,000>
                                          ------------

    Adjusted receivable balance............$  768,000
                                          ============
```

The note receivable will be paid off through the 7% "interest" payments of $42,000 per year for four years (or a total of $168,000), and the principal payment of $600,000 at maturity.

The debtor would record an extraordinary gain of $252,000 with a corresponding reduction of the note payable by $232,000 and a write-off of the accrued interest payable of $20,000.

A key criticism of SFAS 15 is its failure to recognize the economic loss on the modification.[5] By not using discounted cash flows in the computations, the resultant loss on the books of the creditor is severely understated. For example, if the creditor's required rate of return was still 10%, the discounted future cash flows after the modification for four years would be determined as follows.

```
$600,000 x .6830 ...............$409,800

$42,000 x 3.170 ................ 133,140
                              ---------
     Discounted cash flows.....$542,940
                              =========
```

In this case the economic loss to the creditor is $477,060 (i.e., $1,020,000 - 542,940).

By following SFAS 15, the creditor only reports a nominal loss of $252,000 and is not required to disclose the economic loss. The nominal loss understates the economic loss by almost 50% and could have a significant effect on the financial analysis of the creditor's financial statements.

Illustration: Modification with Nonrecognition of the Gain and Loss. In order to illustrate the provisions of SFAS 15 for a modification without gain or loss recognition, assume that King Trust Company modifies the Holly Corporation debt as follows:

1. Reduction of the face value of the debt from $1,000,000 to $900,000;

2. Forgiveness of $20,000 of accrued interest;

3. Reduction of the interest rate from 10% to 7%;

4. There is no extension of the maturity date so that the debt is still due in four years.

In this case the total future undiscounted cash flows amount to $1,152,000 (i.e., the principal of $900,000 plus the annual 7% interest of $63,000 for four years). Under the provisions of SFAS 15, no gain and loss can be recognized because the prerestructuring carrying value of the debt ($1,020,000) is less than the total future undiscounted cash flows after modification ($1,152,000).

To record the modification in this case, the creditor records a discount on notes receivable of $120,000. The amount of the discount is equal to the principal reduction of $100,000 and the forgiveness of the $20,000 of accrued interest. There is a corresponding reduction of the face value of the receivable for $100,000 and a $20,000 write-off of the accrued interest receivable. The debtor would record a premium on notes payable of $120,000 with a corresponding reduction of $100,000 of the outstanding debt and the accrued interest payable by $20,000.

In order to amortize the premium and discount, the new effective interest rate on the modified debt agreement must be determined. The new effective interest rate must be solved by interpolation. That is, the new effective interest rate is the rate that will equate the prerestructure carrying value of the debt to the present value of the future cash flows after modification. In this illustration, the new effective interest rate would be determined as follows:

$1,020,000   = $900,000 x (Factor for PV of $1, n = 4)

+ $63,000 x (Factor for PV of an Ordinary Annuity, n = 4)

The rate that solves the above equation is 3.3812%. The amortization table for the King Trust Company and the Holly Corporation is presented in Exhibit 3.7.

As noted in Exhibit 3.7, the amortization of the premium and discount brings the carrying value of the debt down to $900,000 by the maturity date. The cash interest payment is $63,000 per year, which is equal to the nominal interest rate of 7% multiplied by the modified principal of $900,000. The effective interest expense is determined by multiplying the carrying value of the debt at the beginning of each year by the new effective interest rate of 3.3812%. The difference between the cash interest payment and the effective interest expense is the amount of the amortization of the premium or discount. It is also the "principal paydown" or reduction of the prerestructuring carrying value. It should be noted that after modification and the reclassification adjustments, the prerestrucuring carrying value is still $1,020,000. However, it now consists of the new principal of $900,000 plus the premium or discount of $120,000. By amortizing the premium or discount to zero, the carrying value is reduced to $900,000 at the end of four years, and is paid off at maturity.

With each cash payment of $63,000 the debtor recognizes the effective interest expense and reduces the premium account by the difference between the cash paid and the effective interest. Similarly, with each cash payment of $63,000 the creditor recognizes the effective interest income and amortizes the discount by the

EXHIBIT 3.7

Illustration: Amortization Table After Modification of a Troubled Debt

---

Year	7% Cash Payment	3.3812% Effective Interest	Amortization of Premium and Discount	Pre-restructuring Carrying Value of the Debt **
(1)	(2) *	(3)=(5)x3.3812%	(4)=(2)-(3)	(5)=Prior(5)-(4)
0	-	-	-	$ 1,020,000
1	$ 63,000	$ 34,488	$ 28,512	991,488
2	63,000	33,524	29,476	962,012
3	63,000	32,528	30,472	931,540
4	63,000	31,460 ***	31,540	900,000
	$252,000	$132,000	$120,000	$ -0-

NOTES: * = The annual cash payment is equal to 7% x $900,000.
** = The prerestructuring carrying value of the debt does not change
by the modification. The modification results in certain
reclassifications so that the sum of the Note Receivable + Discount
and the Note Payable + Premium will both equal the prerestructuring carrying value of the debt (i.e., the principal +
accrued interest).
*** = Rounding error of $37.00.

difference between the cash payment and the effective interest income.

As was the case with gain and loss recognition, the application of SFAS 15 to the nonrecognition case fails to recognize the economic loss. If it is assumed that the creditor's required rate of return is still 10%, the discounted future cash flows would be determined as follows:

```
$900,000 x .6830 ...............$614,700

$ 63,000 x 3.170 ............... 199,710
                                ---------

    Discounted cash flows.....$814,410
                                ========
```

In this case the economic loss to the creditor would be $205,590 (i.e., $1,020,000 - 814,410). Under the provisions of SFAS 15, the economic loss would neither be recognized nor disclosed in the financial statements of the creditor.

Disclosure Requirements Under SFAS 15. Under SFAS 15, paragraph 25, the debtor is required to disclose the following information for troubled debt restructurings as of the date of each balance sheet:

1. A description of the terms of the debt modification agreement or the settlement;

2. The aggregate gain on the restructuring of debt, net of the related tax effects;

3. The aggregate gain on restructuring per share, net of tax;

4. The aggregate gain or loss on the transfer of assets recognized during the period;

5. Information regarding any contingent payments that are related to the restructured debt.

Creditors with outstanding receivables where the terms have been modified must disclose the following at the date of each balance sheet in accordance with SFAS 15, paragraph 40:

1. The balance of creditor's investment in the receivable;

2. The gross interest income that would have been recognized by the creditor if there was no debt restructuring;

3. The amount of interest income that was actually recorded and included in net income for the period;

4. The amount of any commitments to make additional loans to debtors that

have outstanding loans whose terms have been modified.

The Rationale Behind SFAS 15's Treatment of Modification. In SFAS 15, the FASB implies that the creditor's primary objective in modifying the terms of a debt agreement is to recover its initial investment. When the total future undiscounted cash flows exceed the prerestructuring carrying amount of the debt, the creditor's investment is recovered, or at least the creditor's position is unchanged, so that no gain or loss is recognized. SFAS 15 also views a modification as a nonreciprocal transfer, which is not considered a transaction. In addition, there is no change in the assets or liabilities of the parties to the modification. If a firm's net assets are unchanged, there is no gain or loss to be recognized.

This justification is clearly not theoretically sound. When the future cash flows are discounted, the position of the parties changes significantly and the creditor will not recover its initial investment. There is an economic loss that is not recognized on the books of the creditor. In addition, the provisions of SFAS 15 are inconsistent with the FASB's Conceptual Framework which specifically encourages the use of discounted cash flows as a means of asset and liability valuation. Similarly, Opinion 21 requires the use of a discounted cash flow methodology in accounting for long-term receivables and payables.

If the theoretical foundation and the methodology of SFAS 15 are unsound, the obvious question is, why was this standard approved and why is SFAS 15 still in effect? One answer to this question is that SFAS 15 obtained a great deal of support from the banking industry and other financial institutions. There was substantial agreement with the provisions of SFAS 15 that required accounting procedures which tended to minimize loss recognition in the year of a troubled debt restructuring, and spread that loss over the remaining term of the loan.

Other support for SFAS 15 is indicated by the fact that there is legislation that permits the use of FASB standards for troubled debt restructuring. For example, Section 402 of the Competitive Equality Banking Act of 1987 provides specific authorization of the use of SFAS 15 in accounting for a troubled debt restructuring.[6]

Regardless of the industry support for SFAS 15 and the legislative sanctions of its use, the standard is unsound in that it ignores economic reality, violates the theoretical foundation of accounting, and prescribes an approach for accounting for receivables and payables that is inconsistent with existing accounting principles. It is clear that the FASB should reconsider its standards of accounting for a troubled debt restructuring and develop standards of accounting and reporting which reflect the economic effects of the transaction and are consistent with the conceptual framework of accounting and other accounting principles.

Analysis of Pension Obligations

Employers can adopt two types of pension plans; defined contribution plans and defined benefit plans. Under a defined contribution plan, the employer's only responsibility is to make the periodic contributions to the pension plan as defined by benefit formula. Because the contributions are fixed (i.e., defined), the risk of loss from the assets accumulated by the fund are borne by the employee. In accounting for the defined contribution plan, the accountant simply charges the income statement for the amount of the defined contribution. If the contribution is less than the defined amount, a liability is recorded. Conversely, if the employer contributes more to the fund than required by the plan's contribution formula, a prepaid pension asset is recorded. In the case of a defined contribution plan, the only footnote disclosures required are a description of the plan, the employee group covered, the formula for determining the defined contribution and the nature and impact of significant events affecting financial statement comparability from period to period.

Under the defined benefit plan, the benefits to be received by the employee are determined by a formula which usually provides for pension benefits based on a particular salary level (e.g., the average of the employee's last three years of employment), and the number of years of service provided. Because the future benefits are defined, the risk of loss on the plan assets are borne by the employer. In addition, the employer must determine the magnitude of current funding requirements (i.e., contributions to the plan) in order to meet the mandatory pension benefit payments over the employee's retirement years. Because the employer's pension cost and obligation are dependent on future variables, the accounting and disclosure requirements for a defined benefit pension plan are more complex than for a defined contribution plan.

It should be noted that either a defined benefit or defined contribution plan can be "qualified" by the IRS for preferential tax treatment. Under a qualified plan, contributions made by the employer are tax deductible. In addition, plan earnings are not taxed. The employees are only taxed upon receipt of the pension benefits.

In the analysis of the pension information disclosed for a defined benefit pension plan in corporate financial statements, it is often difficult to determine the actual obligation for pension benefits. The reason for this difficulty is that the liability reported in the balance sheet by the accountant may be quite different from the actuarially determined obligation disclosed in the footnotes to the financial statements.

The accountant determines the pension liability or prepaid pension asset by implementation of FASB Statement No. 87, "Employers' Accounting for Pensions". SFAS 87 requires the use of some of the actuarial information, but the accountant's pension asset or obligation will not always equal the funded status of the plan. As noted in the section of this chapter dealing with in-substance defeasance, the pension plan is a separate legal and accounting entity. As a result, the pension plan may have its own management and a separate set of financial statements, audited by a different, independent CPA firm. In fact, accounting for the pension plan itself is covered by FASB Statement No. 35, "Accounting and Reporting by Defined Benefit Pension Plans". Due to the separation of the two entities (i.e., the employer and the defined benefit pension plan), one of the disclosure requirements of SFAS 87 is to provide a reconciliation of the net liability or asset as determined by the pension plan with the accountant's asset or obligation on the corporation's balance sheet.

The purpose of this section of the chapter is to provide a discussion of the determination of the pension asset or liability by the actuary, and compare it to the accountant's computation of the pension asset or obligation and the annual pension expense under a defined benefit plan. In addition, this section will illustrate the required reconciliation between the actuarially determined asset and liability and the accountant's pension asset or obligation.

The Actuarial Present Value of the Pension Obligation. The actuary determines the pension obligation by taking the present value of the future pension benefits to be distributed under the terms of the pension plan. The computation requires several assumptions as to employee base, salary levels, life expectancy, expected rates of return on plan assets and the expected discount rate at which the liability will ultimately be settled (i.e., the "settlement rate").

The actuarial present value of the benefit obligation is measured in three ways, based on the assumptions as to salary levels and whether or not the benefits are vested.

The salary level assumed will impact the future obligation because the defined pension benefits to be paid are usually determined by a formula that is based on salary levels and years of service. Vested benefits represent the pension benefits an employee is entitled to receive that are not contingent on further employment. Typically, there is a minimum service requirement that must be met before an employee can vest in the pension plan.

The different measures of the pension liability are discussed in the next section.

Different Measures of the Actuarial Pension Obligation. The three different measures of the pension obligation are the vested benefit obligation, the accumulated benefit obligation, and the projected benefit obligation.

The first measure of the pension obligation is the vested benefit obligation. The vested benefit obligation is determined by taking the present value of the future cash flows for the expected years of service by vested employees, using current salary levels in the benefit formula. The vested benefit obligation is the "most restrictive" pension liability for the corporation because these benefits are not dependent on additional years of service by the employee and are legally protected. The vested benefit obligation is protected by the Employee Retirement Income Security Act (ERISA) of 1974.

The general purpose of the ERISA legislation is to protect an employee's rights under pension plans. Specifically, ERISA requirements result in minimum funding amounts, guaranty of equal employee participation in the plan and protection of vested pension benefits. The Pension Benefit Guaranty Corporation (PBGC) was established by ERISA for the purpose of administering terminated plans. Upon termination of a plan, the PBGC can impose a lien against an employer's assets for the excess of vested benefit obligations over the fair value of the plan's assets. Although limited to 30% of the employer's net worth, the lien imposed by the PBGC takes priority over most creditor's claims. After settling the vested benefit obligation, any remaining plan assets may revert back to the corporation, subject to PBGC approval. Under ERISA requirements the corporation cannot obtain excess pension assets unless the original provisions of the plan specifically permit asset reversion. In addition, there could be excise tax penalties on plan termination.

Under the 1990 Budget Act, the excise tax on reversions of surplus pension plan assets is increased from 15% to 20% and the tax further increases to 50% unless a portion of the reverted assets are transferred to a replacement plan. Reversions in which the transferred assets are used to fund employee medical plans are exempt from the excise tax. The increased excise tax rate generally applies to all terminations after September 30, 1990. However, the excise tax will be held to a 20% maximum if the firm is in Chapter 7 bankruptcy liquidation, if 25% of the plan's excess assets are placed in a successor plan, and if at least 20% of the plan's surplus assets are used to increase participants' benefits. In addtion to the excise tax, the value of the reverted assets are subject to tax at ordinary income rates.

Due to the restrictive provisions of the ERISA legislation with respect to vested benefits, the excess of the vested benefit obligation over the fair value of the plan's assets is generally considered part of a firm's off-balance sheet debt in the analysis of financial statements. It should be noted that this off-balance sheet debt only arises in the event of plan termination and is not to be considered part of an employer's obligation as a going concern.

The next measure of the pension obligation is known as the accumulated benefit obligation. The accumulated benefit obligation is determined by taking the present value of the future pension benefits to be paid to all employees, vested and nonvested, computed by using the current salary levels in the benefit formula. The accumulated benefit obligation will be larger than the vested benefit obligation, and the difference between the two represents the obligation for unvested benefits. Because it is based on current salary levels and does not account for expected increases in salaries, the accumulated benefit obligation is considered by many to be an understatement of the pension obligation of the firm and is therefore the least conservative approach.

The final measure of the pension liability is called the projected benefit obligation. The projected benefit obligation is the largest pension obligation because it is determined by taking the present value of benefits to be paid to both vested and unvested employees, and by using expected future salary levels in the benefit formula. The projected benefit obligation is favored by the FASB for the accountant's computation of the pension expense and the resulting pension asset or obligation because it considers the most realistic situation facing the corporation: a commitment to make pension benefit payments based on a benefit formula using expected salary levels over current and future years of service, rather than simply applying the current salary level to all future years of service. The projected benefit method usually results in the largest and therefore the most conservative pension obligation.

The excess of the projected benefit obligation over the fair value of the plan's assets represents the employer's pension obligation on an ongoing (i.e., a going-concern) basis. It assumes a continuing plan with no changes in actuarial assumptions.

As will be illustrated below, the footnotes to the financial statements will provide the analyst with information that is sufficient to determine the funded status of the plan on an ongoing basis (i.e., the difference between the projected benefit obligation and the fair value of the plan's assets), and the funded status of the plan on a termination or liquidation basis (i.e., the difference between the vested benefit obligation and the fair value of the plan's assets).

Other Actuarial Considerations. The actuarial present value of the pension obligation, determined under any method, also considers all prior service costs, the actual gains and losses on pension assets and any gains or losses from changes in assumptions due to experience and additional information.

Prior or past service costs represent the cost of retroactive benefits for past service relating to an amendment or an initial adoption of a pension plan.

The actuarial gains or losses include the actual gains or losses on pension fund investments and adjustments to the pension obligation resulting from changes in actuarial assumptions. The actuary can revise assumptions such as those relating to life expectancy, rates of return on plan assets, expected salary levels and the settlement rate.

Accounting for Pension Obligations. The accountant's measurement of pension expense and the pension asset or obligation is based on the provisions of SFAS 87. According to SFAS 87, paragraph 20, the annual pension expense consists of six elements. These are:

1. Service or normal cost. The service cost component of the total pension expense is the actuarial present value of the formula benefits for services rendered by employees during the current period. Service cost is actually the change in the projected benefit obligation due to the change in the deferred pension benefit component. The total change in the projected benefit obligation would include increases for interest on the opening balance and decreases for benefit payments made during the year, in addition to the change in the deferred pension benefit. It should be noted that the service cost component is provided in the actuary's report.

2. Interest on the projected benefit obligation. Interest on the projected benefit obligation represents the change in the pension liability "due to the passage of time". It is computed by multiplying the settlement rate by the beginning balance of the projected benefit obligation.

3. The actual return on plan assets. The actual return on the plan assets is also provided by the actuary's report. SFAS 87, paragraph 30, requires the use of the expected return rather than the actual return on plan assets. The difference between the actual and the expected return, the "unexpected return", is included as an adjustment in the actuarial gain or loss recognition for the year. The gain or loss recognized is a separate component of the total pension expense. The expected return is computed by multiplying the expected rate of return on plan assets by the fair market value of the plan assets at the beginning of the year.[7]

4. Amortization of prior service costs. Unlike the actuary, the accountant does not recognize the full amount of the cost of retroactive benefits for past service in the year of an amendment or at the initial adoption of a plan. Instead, the total prior service should be amortized over the future service lives of the employees expected to receive benefits from the plan. The prior service cost is usually amortized by an accelerated method, similar to the sum of the years digits method, under the assumption that the employer is more likely to realize greater productivity from the labor force in the earlier years than in the later years.

5. Amortization of the transition amount. The transition amount resulted from adopting SFAS 87 and switching out of the old pension requirements of APB Opinion No. 8, "Accounting for the Cost of Pension Plans". The transition amount is the funded status of the plan at the date the firm adopts SFAS 87, where the funded status of the plan is the difference

between the projected benefit obligation and the fair market value of the plan assets. The transition amount could be a net asset, (unrecognized transition gain), or liability, (unrecognized transition loss), at the date of the change to SFAS 87. The amortization of the transition amount is usually done on a straight-line basis over the average remaining service lives of the employee base. The transition amortization could either increase or decrease the pension expense for the year, depending on the funded status of the plan at the date of the change in method. Regardless of the direction of the amortization, it is usually combined with the amortization of the prior service cost.

6. Actuarial gain or loss recognition. This component includes the adjustment to bring the actual return on plan assets up or down to the expected return (i.e., "the unexpected return"). In addition, the accountant may recognize a portion of the actuarial experience gain or loss. The objective of SFAS 87 with respect to experience gains or losses was to minimize or smooth the amount of gain or loss recognized in any one year. This was done in order to avoid wide fluctuations in the amount of pension expense charged against income which were caused by modifications in actuarial assumptions and estimates.

In order to accomplish the objective noted in 6 above, SFAS 87, paragraph 32, requires the use of the "Corridor Approach". The "corridor" is a materiality threshold for gain or loss recognition. The corridor is defined as 10% of the greater of the projected benefit obligation or the fair value of plan assets at the beginning of the year. If the beginning balance of the unrecognized net gain or loss (including the cumulative unexpected return as of the beginning of the period) exceeds the corridor, the excess is amortized over the average remaining service life of the employees, but only for the current year. This is known as the "minimum amortization". According to paragraph 33 of SFAS 87, another "systematic method of amortization" can be used. However, the method must be "applied consistently, applied similarly to both gains and losses and must be disclosed". In addition, the minimum amortization must be used in any year in which the "minimum amortization is greater (reduces the net balance more)" than the other systematic approach.

In each subsequent year, another corridor test must be performed and if the balance of the unrecognized net gain or loss is less than the corridor, the amortization is suspended and no part of the net gain or loss is recognized in that period.

The accountant's pension expense charged against current income is equal to the net result of combining these six components. Pension footnote disclosures generally report the first three components individually and aggregate the last three components into a single line item entitled "other components of pension expense".

The amount of the accountant's pension asset or liability reported on the balance sheet depends on the amount of the pension contribution or funding made during the period. The funding decision by the employer is dependent on current and future cash flow requirements as well as on the ERISA minimum funding requirements and the maximum tax deduction permitted by the IRS code.

If the amount of the pension contribution is equal to the pension expense, there is no pension asset or liability. If the contribution exceeds the pension expense, there is a prepaid pension asset and if the contribution is less than the pension expense, a pension obligation is recorded.

Finally, after the determination of the pension expense and the resulting pension asset or liability, SFAS 87, paragraph 36, requires a test for a "minimum liability". The minimum liability test becomes necessary because the use of the corridor approach could avoid or minimize recognition of large actuarial losses and the amortization of prior service costs could spread the effects of a significant plan amendment over several years, again minimizing the amount of pension cost recognized. Both of these effects could result in a significant understatement of the pension liability reported on the balance sheet.

In order to ensure that a reasonable amount of the pension obligation is reported in the current balance sheet, while maintaining pension expense measurement under the accrual basis of accounting and the matching principle, SFAS 87 requires that the firm report, at a minimum, a pension obligation equal to the unfunded accumulated benefit. The unfunded accumulated benefit is equal to the excess of the accumulated benefit obligation over the fair value of plan assets at year end. Because the accumulated benefit obligation is based on current rather than expected future salary levels, it is usually the minimum obligation. Note that there cannot be a "minimum asset".

The minimum liability is compared to the accountant's balance in the prepaid pension asset or the pension liability account. If there is a prepaid pension asset, an adjustment must be made which in effect removes the prepaid asset and records the minimum liability. This requires recording an additional pension obligation equal to the sum of the prepaid pension asset and the minimum liability. If there is an existing pension obligation and it exceeds the minimum liability, no adjustment is required. If the existing pension obligation is less than the minimum liability, an additional pension obligation must be recorded so that the total obligation is equal to the minimum liability.

In the adjustment for the minimum liability, an additional pension obligation is either created or adjusted. The other side of the entry would record an intangible asset, "deferred pension cost", but only to the extent of unamortized prior service costs, including the transition amount. If the amount of the minimum liability adjustment exceeds the balance of the unamortized prior service costs, the excess adjustment is recorded as a contra or negative stockholders' equity account, "net loss not recognized as pension expense" or "excess of additional pension liability over unamortized prior service cost". Neither the intangible asset nor the adjustment to total stockholders' equity are amortized to pension expense. The balances of these accounts are adjusted each year so that the sum of the intangible asset and the contra stockholders' equity account equal the balance in the additional pension liability. Note that the accrual-based pension expense is not affected by the measurement of the total pension obligation. In effect, the implementation of SFAS 87 results in a separate measurement and accounting for the pension expense and the pension asset or liability.

It is evident from the previous discussion that the accountant's pension obligation or prepaid asset could be significantly different from the economic value of the pension plan or the funded status of the plan as reported by the actuary. SFAS 87, paragraphs 54, 223 and 234, require substantial disclosures of the corporation's pension plans, which include a reconcilation of the funded status of the plan to the accountant's pension asset or obligation on the balance sheet. The following section presents a comprehensive illustration of pension accounting as prescribed by SFAS 87, including the footnote reconciliation and financial statement disclosures of the pension asset or liability.

Comprehensive Pension Illustration. The data for the illustration are contained in Exhibit 3.8. The information provided in Exhibit 3.8 includes balances at December 31, 1991 and 1992 and all assumptions required to implement SFAS 87.

The illustration will take a step-by-step approach which first builds the six components of the pension expense defined by SFAS 87, and determines the pension asset or liability. This includes the test for the minimum liability. Finally, the financial statement presentation of the pension accounts and the footnote reconciliation of the funded status and the accountant's pension obligation are presented.

1. Service cost. The 1992 service cost is provided by the actuary's report and is equal to $20,000. The current service cost increases the 1992 pension expense.

2. Interest on the projected benefit obligation. This is the interest on the beginning projected benefit obligation. In this illustration, the settlement rate is assumed to be 12 1/2% and the projected benefit obligation at December 31, 1991 (i.e., January 1, 1992) is equal to $331,250. The interest on the projected benefit obligation is $41,406 and increases the 1992 pension expense.

3. The actual return on plan assets. The actual return reported by the actuary is $27,500. This gain reduces the firm's current pension expense. Nonetheless, SFAS 87 requires the use of the expected return on plan assets. The expected return on plan assets is equal to the beginning balance of the plan assets at fair value multiplied by the expected rate of return. In this case, it is assumed that the expected return is also equal to 12 1/2% and the fair value of plan assets at December 31, 1991 is equal to $199,500. Therefore, the expected return was $24,937. The unexpected return is equal to a gain of $2,563 (i.e., $27,500 - 24,937). The actual gain must be adjusted to the expected gain by deducting $2,563 (or increasing pension expense) in the actuarial gain or loss component of pension expense below.

4. Amortization of prior service cost. This illustration assumes that the prior service costs are being amortized by the accelerated method. In 1992, the amortization rate is 55% or $22,000 (i.e., 55% x $40,000). The $20,000 amortization increases pension expense.

5. Amortization of the transition amount. This illustration assumes that there is no transition amount.

6. Actuarial gain or loss. This component of pension expense includes the adjustment of the actual return to the expected return. In this case, the adjustment was determined to be an addition to pension expense of $2,563.

EXHIBIT 3.8

Data for Pension Illustration

	December 31	
	1992	1991
Service cost.....................................	$ 20,000	
Settlement rate.................................	12.5%	
Expected rate of return on plan assets.........	12.5%	
Actual return on plan assets...................	$ 27,500	
Amortization of unrecognized prior service cost (55% of beginning balance)...........	$ 22,000	
Actual contributions (funding).................	$ 33,750	$ 30,000
Pension benefits paid..........................	$ 22,500	
Vested benefit obligation......................	$ 243,750	
Accumulated benefit obligation.................	$ 328,750	
Average remaining service life of employees....	20 years	
Projected benefit obligation...................		$ 331,250
Fair value of plan assets......................		$ 199,500
Unrecognized prior service costs...............		$ 40,000
Unrecognized net actuarial <gain> loss.........		$ 37,425
Pension expense................................		$ 52,075
Pension liability per financial statements.....		$ 54,345
Additional pension liability...................		$ 46,925
Deferred pension cost (intangible asset).......		$ 40,000
Net loss not recognized as pension expense (contra stockholders' equity account).......		$ 6,925
Transition amount..............................	NONE	NONE

The second part of this component of pension expense includes the potential amortization of unrecognized actuarial net gain or loss as of the beginning of the year. Determination of the net gain or loss recognized requires the application of the corridor approach.

The corridor is equal to 10% of the larger of the beginning projected benefit obligation or beginning the fair value of plan assets. In this case, the balance of the beginning projected benefit obligation ($331,250) exceeds the beginning fair value of plan assets ($199,500) so that the corridor is $33,125 (i.e., 10% x $331,250). The amount of net gain or loss to amortize is determined as follows:

```
Beginning unrecognized net loss...........$37,425

Less: Corridor.............................<33,125>
                                          ----------

        Excess net loss over corridor.....$ 4,300

Divided by the Average Remaining Service
Life..................................... 20 years
                                          ----------

1992 Amortization of unrecognized net
loss......................................$   215
                                          ==========
```

With all six components determined, the 1992 pension expense would be calculated as follows:

```
1992 Pension Expense:
----------------------

    Service cost..........................................$ 20,000

    Interest on the projected benefit obligation.........  41,406

    Actual return on plan assets......................... <27,500>

    Amortization of prior service cost...................  22,000

    Gain or loss recognition:
        Unexpected return on plan assets........$ 2,563
        Amortization of unrecognized net loss...    215
                                                -------- 2,778
                                                ----------
    1992 Pension expense.................................$ 58,684
                                                ==========
```

Assuming no changes in actuarial assumptions, the pension plan's account balances at December 31, 1992 would be determined as follows:

```
1992 Plan assets at fair value:
-------------------------------
      Balance, January 1, 1992.............................$ 199,500

      Add:  Actual return on plan assets....................  27,500

      Add:  1992 Contributions or funding...................  33,750

      Less: 1992 Pension benefits paid...................... < 22,500>
                                                             ----------
      Balance, December 31, 1992.........................$ 238,250
                                                             ==========
1992 Projected benefit obligation:
----------------------------------
      Balance, January 1, 1992.............................$ 331,250

      Add:  1992 Service cost...............................  20,000

      Add:  1992 Interest on projected benefit obligation...  41,406

      Less: 1992 Pension benefits paid...................... < 22,500>
                                                             ----------

      Balance, December 31, 1992...........................$ 370,156
                                                             ==========
```

Before the minimum liability test, the following corporate account balances are determined at December 31, 1992:

```
1992 Pension obligation:
------------------------
      Balance, January 1, 1992.............................$ 54,325

      Add:  1992 Pension expense accrual...................  58,684

      Less: 1992 Contribution or funding................... <33,750>
                                                             ----------

      Balance, December 31, 1992 before minimum
      liability test.........................................$ 79,259
                                                             ==========
```

1992 Unrecognized prior service cost:

      Balance, January 1, 1992.............................$ 40,000

      Less: 1992 amortization............................ <22,000>

      Balance, December 31, 1992.........................$ 18,000
                                         =========

1992 Unrecognized net loss:

      Balance, January 1, 1992.............................$ 37,325

      Less: Unexpected gain recognized...................... < 2,563>
      Amortization of unrecognized net loss.......... <   215>

      Balance, December 31, 1992...........................$ 34,647
                                         =========

With all of the necessary accounting information determined, the minimum liability test can be conducted as follows:

1992 Minimum liability test:

      Accumulated benefit obligation at December 31, 1992....$ 328,750

      Less: Fair value of plan assets at December 31, 1992....<238,250>

      Unfunded accumulated benefit (Minimum Liability).......$ 90,500

      Less: Pension obligation at December 31, 1992.......... < 79,259>

      Additional pension liability required..................$ 11,241

      Less: Unamortized prior service costs at December
           31, 1992... < 18,000>

      Required balance in the contra stockholders'
      equity account...$ - 0 -
                                         ==========

The results of the minimum liability test indicate that the additional liability required is $11,241. However, before adjustment, the additional liability account from prior years is already equal to $46,925. As a result, this account must be reduced by $35,864. Because the balance in the contra stockholders' equity account is no longer required, the entire balance of $6,925 is removed and the remaining adjustment of $28,759 (i.e., $35,864 - 6,925), reduces the intangible asset or deferred pension cost account. At this point, the intangible asset account is equal to the required additional liability. That is:

```
1992 Deferred pension cost (intangible asset):
-----------------------------------------------

Balance, January 1, 1992........................................$ 40,000

Less: Adjustment from minimum liability test............... <28,759>
                                                           ----------

Balance, December 31, 1992...................................$ 11,241
                                                           =========
```

Exhibit 3.9 presents the disclosure of pension information on the financial statements. On the December 31, 1992 balance sheet, the intangible asset, deferred pension cost, is included with the noncurrent assets. Because the intangible asset does not exceed the balance of the unrecognized prior service costs, it is exactly equal to the additional pension obligation required by the minimum liability test, and precludes the use of the contra stockholders' equity account. The accrued pension liability account is equal to the sum of the accountant's pension accrual plus the additional pension obligation. The classification of this liability is usually long term due to the discretionary nature of the pension contributions made by management.

The income statement for the year ended December 31, 1992 would report the pension expense for the year.

The cash flow statement would report a reconciling item in the operating cash flows section adding back to accrual basis net income that portion of the pension charge on the income statement that was not paid in cash. In a separate schedule or in a footnote, the company would be required to disclose the noncash changes in the deferred pension cost and the contra stockholders' equity accounts due to the minimum liability adjustment.

The footnote disclosures required under SFAS 87 are presented in Exhibit 3.10. The first section of the footnote presents the components of pension expense. As indicated earlier, the disclosure generally provides the first three components: service cost, interest on the projected benefit obligation, and the actual return on plan assets, and aggregates the remaining components in a single line item, "not other components of pension expense".

The remaining sections of the pension footnote include information relating to the funded status of the plan and the reconciliation of the funded status of the plan to the accountant's measure of the pension liability. The accountant's pension

EXHIBIT 3.9

Illustration: Financial Statement Presentation of Pension Information

---

Balance Sheet at December 31, 1992:

| Noncurrent Assets | Liabilities |

Deferred pension cost......$11,241   Accrued pension obligation....$90,500

NOTE: The accrued pension obligation is the sum of the pension liability of
$79,259 and the additional pension liability of $11,241 required
to meet the minimum liability.

===

Income Statement for the year ended December 31, 1992:

Operating Expenses:

Pension expense..........................$58,684

===

Cash Flow Statement for the year ended December 31, 1992:

Cash flows generated from operating activities:

Adjustments to reconcile net income to cash
flows provided by operating activities:

Add back:

Unfunded portion of current pension expense
($58,684 - 33,750).............................$24,934

Noncash financing and investing activities:

The $28,759 decrease in the noncurrent intangible asset, deferred pension
cost, and the $6,925 write-off of the contra stockholders' equity account, net
loss not recognized as pension expense, were caused by the minimum liability
adjustment which reduced the additional pension obligation by $35,684.

===
----

obligation, even after the minimum liability adjustment, is usually less than the projected benefit obligation in excess of the plan assets because of the accountant's failure to recognize the full impact of prior service costs and actuarial gains or losses.

Analysis of the Pension Obligation. Although most critics agree that SFAS 87 represents a significant improvement over the previous pension reporting standards, credit and financial analysts should be aware of the limitations of the accountant's pension measures. In fact, the analyst would probably find the pension footnote the most important information for decision making.

The pension footnote provides valuable information regarding the funded status of the plan. In Exhibit 3.10, the analyst should consider the magnitude of the three measures of the pension obligation:

1. The excess of the vested benefit obligation over the fair value of plan assets (i.e., $5,500 = $243,750 - $238,250). This amount represents the employer's obligation or funded status on a termination basis and is generally considered the analytical measure of the firm's off-balance sheet debt related to its pension plans.

2. The excess of the projected benefit obligation over the fair value of the plan assets (i.e., $131,906). This is the employer's obligation or funded status on a going-concern basis.

3. The accountant's liability on the balance sheet (i.e., $90,500). This is the obligation determined by GAAP in accordance with the matching principle and the accrual basis of accounting. In this illustration, the obligation reported on the balance sheet is also equal to the minimum liability. The minimum liability is also the unfunded accumulated benefit (i.e., the excess of the accumulated benefit obligation over the fair value of the plan assets).

The 1987 pension footnote for Cooper Industries is presented in Exhibit 3.11. In the disclosure of the funded status of the defined benefit pension plans, the plans are segregated into those plans with accumulated benefits in excess of plan assets, or "underfunded plans", and those plans that are in an excess asset position, or "overfunded plans". The existence of underfunded plans provides the analyst with information regarding the magnitude of the potential obligation. Of particular interest is the most restrictive portion relating to the vested benefit obligation. For example, in 1986 Cooper Industries reported underfunded vested benefits of $6,364 (i.e., $123,207 - 116,843), which is considered the extent of the off-balance sheet financing related to the firm's pension plans. Similarly, the existence of an overfunded plan may provide important information because if the plan is terminated, settled or curtailed, the net pension assets in excess of the vested benefit obligation could revert back to the corporation, subject to the excise tax penalties discussed earlier. In merger and acquisition activity, the net pension assets may represent a significant unrecorded economic resource to the acquiring company. In addition, the gains from settlement of a pension plan with or without asset reversion are immediately recognized in the financial statements under the provisions of FASB Statement No. 88, "Employers' Accounting for Settlements and Curtailments of

EXHIBIT 3.10

Illustration: SFAS 87 Pension Footnote Disclosure

Pension Footnote in the 1992 Financial Statements:

Pension cost for 1992 for the Company's significant defined benefit pension plans includes the following components:

```
Service cost benefits earned during the year..............$20,000
Interest on projected benefit obligations................. 41,406
Actual return on plan assets.............................<27,500>
Net other components of pension cost...................... 24,778
                                                          ---------
     Net pension cost.....................................$58,684
                                                          =======
```

The plan's status at December 31, 1992, was as follows:

Plans in Which Accumulated Benefit Obligations Exceed Plan Assets
Actuarial Present Value of Benefit Obligations:

```
     Vested benefits....................................$<243,750>
     Nonvested benefits................................. <85,000>
                                                         ----------
     Accumulated benefit obligation....................$<328,750>
     Less: Plan assets at fair value................... 238,250
                                                         ----------
     Accumulated benefit obligation in excess of
     plan assets.......................................$ <90,500>
                                                         ==========
```

===

```
Projected benefit obligation...........................$ <370,156>
Less: Plan assets at fair value........................ 238,250
                                                        -----------
Projected benefit obligations in excess of plan
assets (funded status)................................$ <131,906>
<Add> Deduct:
Unrecognized prior service costs......................   18,000
Unrecognized net actuarial loss.......................   34,647
                                                        -----------
Accrued pension liability.............................$ <79,259>
Additional pension liability..........................  <11,241>
                                                        -----------
Total accrued pension obligation......................$ <90,500>
                                                        ==========
```

EXHIBIT 3.11

Sample Disclosure: Cooper Industries, Inc.: SFAS 87 Footnote Disclosure for Defined Benefit Pension Plans

----

In 1986, the Company adopted Statement of Financial Accounting Standards (SFAS) No. 87—Employers' Accounting for Pensions with respect to the determination of domestic pension expense. The effect of this change was not material.

The Company and its subsidiaries have numerous pension, savings and/or profit sharing plans covering substantially all United States employees and, in foreign locations, pension and similar arrangements in accordance with local custom. Pension expense amounted to $11,700,000 in 1987 ($7,900,000 in 1986 and $7,800,000 in 1985) including $7,100,000 ($5,900,000 in 1986 and $4,700,000 in 1985) with respect to contributions (generally set forth in labor agreements) made to United States defined contribution plans in which various groups of domestic hourly employees participate.

	Components of Domestic Defined Benefit Plan Pension Expense	
	Year Ended December 31,	
	1987	1986
	(000 omitted)	
Service cost—benefits earned during the period	$ 16,959	$ 18,984
Interest cost on projected benefit obligation	55,823	51,732
Actual return on assets	(51,596)	(73,624)
Net amortization and deferral	(18,484)	3,143
Net pension cost	$ 2,702	$ 235

	Funded Status of Domestic Defined Benefit Plans			
	Plans With Assets in Excess of Accumulated Benefits		Plans With Accumulated Benefits in Excess of Assets	
	December 31,		December 31,	
	1987	1986	1987	1986
	(000 omitted)			
Actuarial present value of:				
Vested benefit obligation	$ (477,783)	$ (396,076)	$ (57,925)	$ (123,207)
Accumulated benefit obligation	$ (611,445)	$ (524,521)	$ (61,802)	$ (132,260)
Projected benefit obligation	$ (627,374)	$ (541,521)	$ (61,802)	$ (132,260)
Plan assets at fair value	679,652	614,560	57,179	116,843
Projected benefit obligation				
(in excess of) or less than plan assets	52,278	73,039	(4,623)	(15,417)
Unrecognized net (gain) loss	21,771	10,047	(1,931)	3,105
Unrecognized net (asset) obligation				
from adoption date	(75,744)	(87,290)	5,845	9,557
Adjustment required to recognize				
minimum liability	—	—	(6,844)	(18,215)
(Pension liability) at end of year	$ (1,695)	$ (4,204)	$ (7,553)	$ (20,970)

Exhibit 3.11, continued

	Computational Assumptions			
	Net Pension Cost		Projected Benefit Obligation	
	1987	1986	1987	1986
Discount rate	8%	8½%	8½%	8%
Rate of increase in compensation levels	5½	6	6	5½
Expected long-term rate of return on assets	9	9½	—	—
Benefit basis:				
Salaried plans – earnings during career				
Hourly plans – dollar unit multiplied				
by years of service				

The $6,844,000 liability for pension plans with accumulated benefits in excess of assets has been recorded in the Company's consolidated financial position as a long-term liability with an offsetting intangible asset. The assets of the various domestic pension plans are maintained in various trusts and consist primarily of equity and fixed income securities.

In years prior to 1986, the Company's policy was to fund all amounts expensed with respect to domestic pension plans. As a result of the adoption of SFAS No. 87, starting in 1986 expensing and funding are different. The Company's policy is to fund normal cost plus an amortization of past service costs and actuarial gains and losses over periods ranging from 15 to 30 years.

The actuarially computed value of the Company's Canadian plans at December 31, 1987, reflect vested benefits of $17,596,000 ($11,700,000 for 1986), nonvested benefits of $1,147,000 ($700,000 for 1986) and plan assets of $32,544,000 ($21,700,000 for 1986). The actuarially computed value of vested benefits and plan assets has not been determined for the Company's pension and similar plans in countries other than the United States and Canada, although the amounts are not believed to be significant.

In addition to pension plans, most of the Company's employees are covered by savings plans, and certain domestic employees of the acquired McGraw-Edison operations are covered by profit sharing plans. The expense related to the various profit sharing and savings plans amounted to $18,950,000 in 1987 ($15,000,000 in 1986 and $8,300,000 in 1985). During 1987, 53,000 (85,000 in 1986) shares of Common stock were issued under the stock ownership plan. Contributions to the employee stock ownership plan did not affect net income, because the Company receives a U.S. Federal income tax credit equal to the market value of the stock contributed.

Defined Benefit Pension Plans and for Termination Benefits". Settlements without asset reversion include the purchase of nonparticipating annuity contracts. Specifically, in the settlement of an overfunded pension plan without asset reversion, there can be a full or partial settlement of the projected benefit obligation by purchasing an annuity contract from an insurance company. A common type of annuity contract used in a settlement is a single premium, fixed payment, nonparticipating buy-out for retired employees. All pension benefits are now paid by the insurance company to the retirees. The employer is completely relieved from all future obligations under the pension plan. Under the provisions of SFAS 88, the gain on settlement of the overfunded plan is recognized immediately in the employer's income statement. The gain recognized is primarily made up of the unamortized transition asset and any unrecognized actuarial gains. For example, if Cooper Industries in Exhibit 3.11 settled its overfunded plan at December 31, 1986 without asset reversion, the net deferred gain of $77,243 (i.e., $87,290 - 10,047), would be recognized in the 1986 income statement. The majority of this gain results from the unrecognized transition amount of $87,290. The difference between the recognized gain of $77,243 and the elimination of the accrued pension liability of $4,204 would be recorded as a prepaid pension asset. Note that the settlement of an existing projected benefit obligation by purchasing an annutiy contract does not terminate the plan. Thus, the prepaid pension asset can be applied against future pension obligations arising from the continued participation in the plan by active employees. Because the plan is not terminated and there is no asset reversion, there are no tax consequences for the employer. Similar to an in-substance defeasance transaction, the company improves reported net income and earnings per share without any tax implications, but without any real cash inflows to the firm. As a result, settlements without asset reversion simply represent a vehicle by which a firm can accelerate income statement recognition of transition assets and actuarial gains.

The pension footnote in Exhibit 3.11 also includes a comparison or reconciliation of the funded status of the plan with the accountant's pension asset or obligation at the end of the year. As noted earlier, this comparison indicates the extent of the accountant's understatement of the pension obligation.

Finally, the sample pension disclosures include the actuarial or computational assumptions used in the determination of the pension information. The analyst can use this information to assess the propriety of the assumptions used and to determine the effect on the financial statements from changes in actuarial assumptions. If material, the effects of changes in actuarial assumptions on net income and earnings per share, net of tax, are also disclosed in the pension footnote.

Accounting for Postretirement Benefits. The FASB recently issued Statement No. 106, "Employers' Accounting for Postretirement Benefits Other than Pensions". Postretirement benefits include the costs of providing health care benefits to retirees. The new standard of accounting, which will become effective in 1993, will require firms to accrue estimated costs of providing postretirement benefits on the income statement and record the related obligation on the balance sheet.

Prior to the new FASB standard, companies were accounting for postretirement benefits on a cash basis (i.e., the cost of providing health care benefits were charged to expense only when paid). The FASB objected to the use of the cash basis because it significantly understated the firm's future obligations (i.e., off-balance sheet obligations).

Preliminary estimates made by the *New York Times* indicate that the new standard will reduce the income of the largest 1,000 companies a total of $227 billion. When General Mills voluntarily adopted the accrual basis of accounting for postretirment benefits in 1989, health care expenses charged against income doubled to more than $10.5 million.

Redeemable Preferred Stock

Redeemable preférred stock is preferred stock that provides for a fixed number of shares to be redeemed, at the option of the shareholder at specified maturity dates. The redemption feature makes these preferred shares more like debt than equity because of the mandatory requirement to disburse corporate resources at fixed maturity dates.

FASB Statement No. 47, "Disclosure of Long-Term Obligations", paragraph 10, only requires the disclosure of redeemable preferred stock in the footnotes to the financial statements. The footnote disclosure should include the following:

1. The maturities of the redeemable preferred stock and any sinking fund requirements for each of the next five years;

2. The dollar amounts of the mandatory redemption requirements for each of the next five years.

The SFAS disclosures are similar to those found in the long-term debt footnote.

The Securities and Exchange Commission takes a much stronger position in Financial Reporting Release (FRR) No. 1, Section 211, (originally Accounting Series Release [ASR] No. 268). In addition to the SFAS 47 footnote disclosures, the SEC specifically prohibits the inclusion of redeemable preferred stock in the stockholders' equity section of the balance sheet. Instead, the SEC requires three separate financial statement categories or captions:

1. Redeemable preferred stock, which is to be reported after long-term debt, but before stockholders' equity (i.e., in "accounting limbo");

2. Nonredeemable preferred stock, which is to be reported within the stockholders' equity section of the balance sheet;

3. Common stock, which is also to be reported in the stockholders' equity section of the balance sheet.

A general argument against the SEC's position on the disclosure of redeemable preferred stock is that the dividends declared on this class of stock are not reclassified as interest on the income statement. In other words, in order to be consistent, if the SEC considers redeemable preferred stock to be debt, then dividends on redeemable preferred stock should be classified as interest expense. Nonetheless, dividends on redeemable preferred stock are not to be treated as interest and continue to be distributions of retained earnings and should not enter into the determination of net income or loss for the period.

Sample disclosures for redeemable preferred stock for Ashland Oil, Inc., and Subsidiaries are presented in Exhibit 3.1.

ANALYSIS OF STOCKHOLDERS' EQUITY

A brief discussion of the stockholders' equity section of the balance sheet is presented in this section. Stockholders' equity represents the residual claims against the assets of the firm, after the superior claims of corporate creditors have been satisfied. Stockholders' equity is also known as the net assets or the book value of the firm.

Objectives of Accounting for Stockholders' Equity

Due to the large absentee ownership of most publicly held corporations, the major objectives of accounting for stockholders' equity are primarily concerned with disclosing the elements of stockholders' equity by source and to indicate the terms and conditions of other security agreements that affect the residual rights of the common shareholder. Specifically, these objectives are:

1. To classify the elements of stockholders' equity by source. The stockholders' equity section of the balance sheet can be classified into two major sources: contributed or paid-in capital and retained earnings. Contributed or paid-in capital includes the amounts paid in by common and preferred shareholders. Retained earnings represent the historical record of earnings that have not been distributed as dividends.

    The amounts paid in or contributed by shareholders are usually segregated between the amounts received as par value, the arbitrary face value of a share of capital stock registered with the state of incorporation, and any amounts received in excess of par value. It should be noted that shares can also be registered as no-par stock. However, a no-par stock can be assigned a stated value by resolution of the board of directors. If the stock has a stated value, the amounts contributed that relate to the stated value are reported separately from amounts received in excess of stated value. In substance, the accounting and reporting of no-par stock with a stated value is the same as accounting for par value stock.

2. To disclose the rights of various classes of stock.

3. To disclose any restrictions on dividend distributions.

4. To disclose the terms of securities that can potentially dilute the interest of the common shareholder. Potentially dilutive securities include convertible and redeemable securities, stock rights, stock options and other contingent

share arrangements.

These objectives and other issues relating to the stockholders' equity section of the balance sheet will be discussed in the sections that follow.

Classes of Capital Stock

The objectives noted above are primarily concerned with providing the common shareholder, the residual equity class, with information regarding dilution of their interest, claims of senior securities and any restrictions on receiving dividends.

These disclosures are important for the common shareholder due to the fact that the residual equity class is usually only entitled to two primary rights: the right to vote and a preemptive right. The preemptive right gives the common shareholder the right to maintain a proportionate interest in the corporation in the event additional shares are issued.

The preferred shareholder may or may not have the right to vote. Nonetheless, preferred stock has important preferences over common stock with respect to dividends and assets in liquidation.

Preferred dividends are paid as a fixed dollar amount or a fixed percentage of par value. If dividends are declared by the board of directors, preferred dividends must be paid before common dividends. However, if dividends are not declared (i.e., passed) by the board of directors, the preferred shareholder has no right to receive dividends, even if the preferred shares are cumulative. If the preferred shares are cumulative, it means that if dividends are not declared by the board of directors in any given year, the dividends "accumulate". The accumulated back dividends are known as "dividends in arrears". Dividends in arrears are not an actual obligation because they must only be paid if and when another dividend is declared by the board of directors. As a result, dividends in arrears are treated by the accountant in a manner that is similar to accounting for a contingent liability. Due to the contingency related to dividends in arrears, they must be disclosed in the footnotes to the financial statements. The disclosure of dividends in arrears is important for a potential investor in common stock because, upon declaration, all of the dividends in arrears must be paid first before the common shareholder can receive any dividend distributions.

In the event of liquidation, the preferred shareholders have the right to share in the assets of the corporation, after the creditors' claims have been satisfied, but before the common shareholder is entitled to any distribution. In some cases, the preferred stock carries a liquidation value, which consists of par value plus a premium over par, in the event of liquidation. This liquidation value must be disclosed either parenthetically on the face of the balance sheet or in the footnotes to the financial statements. Exhibit 3.1 provides an illustration of a liquidation value for the redeemable preferred stock of Ashland Oil.

In addition to dividend and liquidation preferences, the preferred stock can also carry other rights, features or characteristics. As noted earlier, the preferred stock can be redeemable. Additionally, the preferred shares can be convertible into common stock or participate with the common shareholder in dividend distributions. The latter class of preferred equity is called participating preferred stock. Participating preferred stock will receive the fixed preferred dividend, plus it has the additional right to share in the remaining dividend distribution on the same basis as common stock.

Due to the fixed dividend characteristics and the existence of redeemable preferred stock, many analysts and bond rating agencies treat preferred stock in a manner similar to debt in several financial ratios. For example, frequently used preferred stock ratios include:

1. Preferred stock as a percentage of long-term debt and stockholders' equity, including minority interests. The sum of long-term debt, stockholders' equity and minority interest is also known as book capitalization.

2. Preferred stock and long-term debt as a percentage of book capitalization.

3. Interest coverage ratio, including preferred dividends. This ratio is usually computed as the ratio of earnings before interest and taxes divided by interest expense plus preferred dividends.

Regardless of the debt characteristics of preferred stock and the SEC's classification of redeemable preferred stock on the balance sheet, preferred stock is still legally equity. Therefore, preferred dividends are not an expense of the corporation and are not tax deductible.

Issuance of Capital Stock

In general, capital stock (i.e., common or preferred) can be issued for cash or through subscriptions. There are no analytical issues with respect to the sale of stock for cash. The total proceeds must be segregated between the par or stated value and the amounts in excess of par or stated value. If the shares are no-par stock, the total proceeds are allocated only to the capital stock account.

Capital Stock Issued Through Subscriptions. A subscription is a contract between the corporation and the potential shareholder (i.e., the subscriber), where the corporation agrees to issue a fixed number of shares, at a fixed price and at a specified date in the future. The transaction results in a receivable from the subscriber and a special stockholders' equity account, "unissued capital stock subscribed", at par. Any amounts received over par are classified as additional paid-in capital (APIC). When the subscription is paid in full, the subscriptions receivable is removed from the balance sheet. There is also a reclassification out of unissued capital stock subscribed, at par, into capital stock, at par.

There has recently been some question as to the nature of the stock subscription receivable. Because the stock subscription receivable is not legally enforceable in many states, collectibility is highly uncertain and the asset value of the receivable is questionable. Therefore, the SEC has ruled that the stock subscription cannot be reported as an asset (unless the receivable has been collected during the post-balance sheet period), and must be shown as a negative or a contra-equity account in the stockholders' equity section of the balance sheet. At times, no entry is made at the time the subscription is signed due to the offset of the contra-equity account (i.e., the subscriptions receivable), and the sum of the unissued capital stock account and the additional paid-in capital in the stockholders' equity section. Nonetheless, the transaction must be fully disclosed in the footnotes to the financial statements due to potential dilution of existing shareholders' interests, if the contingent shares relating to the subscription are issued.

The following equation analysis illustrates the flow of accounting entries relating to the stock subscription.

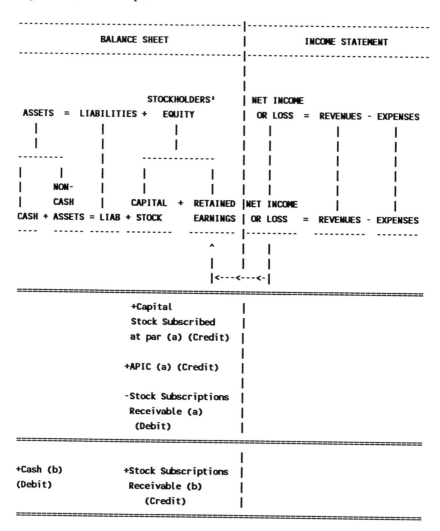

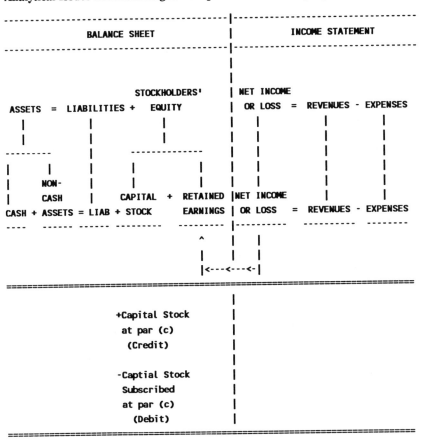

(a) Entry to record the subscription contracts. Note that the unissued capital stock subscribed account is at par and amounts over par are classified as additional paid-in capital (APIC). The stock subscriptions receivable is a negative or a contra-stockholders' equity account.

(b) Entry to record the collection of the receivable. The effect of this transaction is to increase cash and to reduce the subscription receivable (which increases stockholders' equity).

(c) Entry to record the issuance of the capital stock upon full payment of the subscriptions receivable.

Other Sources of Contributed Capital

In addition to issuance of common and preferred shares, the contributed capital section of stockholders' equity can also be changed by stock dividends and treasury stock transactions.

Accounting for Stock Dividends. There are two primary types of dividends: cash dividends and stock dividends. Regardless of the type of dividend, all dividends represent a distribution or a reduction of retained earnings. There are exceptions, such as dividend distributions from contributed capital (capital surplus), allowed in many states. In fact, one reason for the establishment of a stated value on no-par stock may be to create capital surplus as a potential source of dividend distributions.

A stock dividend may be declared to avoid passing the annual or quarterly dividend, while at the same time preserving corporate assets. From the accounting standpoint, the stock dividend results in a simple reclassification within the stockholders' equity section of the balance sheet, which transfers retained earnings into contributed capital (i.e., capital stock at par and additional paid in capital, if any). This interequity transfer is said to be a "capitalization of retained earnings".

The stock dividend has no effect on total assets, total liabilities and total stockholders' equity. Because there is no obligation to distribute corporate assets, the stock dividend is not a legal liability of the corporation, even if declared by the board of directors.

On the surface, the stock dividend does not seem to pose any significant analytical or accounting questions. However, the primary issue facing the accountant is the valuation of the stock dividend. The accountant must determine the value distributed to the shareholder or what amount of retained earnings should be capitalized. The amount of retained earnings to transfer to contributed capital depends on whether the dividend is classified as a large or a small stock dividend.

According to accounting theory, if the number of shares to be distributed in the stock dividend is approximately 25% of the previously outstanding shares, and unless there is evidence to the contrary, the accountant assumes that a dividend of this magnitude would not have a material adverse effect on the market price of the stock when the additional shares are distributed. Therefore, the dividend should be valued (i.e., retained earnings should be capitalized) at the market price of the stock at the date of declaration of the stock dividend. It is assumed that this is the value that the shareholder can receive if the additional shares are sold and converted into cash.

Conversely, if the stock dividend is over 25% of the previously outstanding shares, and unless there is evidence to the contrary, the accountant assumes that a dividend of this size would materially reduce the market price of the stock when the additional shares are distributed. As a result, the actual value given to the shareholder is unknown. However, the dividend cannot be valued below minimum legal capital, which is the par value of the stock.

It should be noted that a large stock dividend is sometimes accounted for as a stock split. This is particularly true if the stock does not have a par or stated value. If accounted for as a stock split, the firm could either increase the number of shares and reduce the par value proportionately, or reclassify the appropriate amount of the stock dividend out of additional paid-in capital (capital surplus) and into capital stock.

Accounting for Treasury Stock Transactions. Treasury stock is the corporation's own stock that is authorized, issued and previously outstanding. The shares are reacquired by the corporation for a specific purpose such as stock option, stock bonus or employee stock option plans (ESOPs); to be used to exchange for the voting shares of another corporation in a merger and acquisition; or to support the market price of the stock.

The treasury stock acquisition is not an asset or an investment of the corporation. Under the cost method, treasury stock is treated as a negative equity or a contra-stockholders' equity account. It is measured at its cost to the corporation and is reported as a reduction of total stockholders' equity. Because the treasury shares are no longer outstanding, they are not effective shares in that the shares cannot vote and cannot receive dividends.

An important question arises on the disposition of the treasury shares. If the treasury shares are sold or reissued in exchange for value (e.g., executive compensation) in excess of cost, the "gain" is recorded as additional paid-in capital from treasury stock transactions. The "gain" cannot be reported on the income statement.

If the treasury shares are sold or reissued in exchange for value below cost, there is a "loss" on the transaction. The "loss" is not to be reported on the current income statement. Instead, the "loss" is first used to reduce any additional paid-in capital from previous treasury stock transactions, if any. If the additional paid-in capital from treasury stock transactions is reduced to zero, the remainder of the "loss" is used to reduce retained earnings. The reduction of retained earnings is actually an "in-substance dividend distribution".

To understand this last point, assume that the purchase and the reissuance of the treasury shares were both cash transactions, and if the shares are reissued below cost, the stockholders hold the same number of shares but now have a cash distribution from the corporation. Hence, the reduction of retained earnings or the dividend treatment of the excess loss. In fact, many states restrict dividend distributions to the extent of the cost of treasury shares held by the corporation.

The Retained Earnings Section

In addition to the net income or loss for the period and dividend declarations, retained earnings will be affected by prior period adjustments and appropriations of retained earnings.

Prior Period Adjustments. Prior period adjustments are defined by FASB Statement No. 16, "Prior Period Adjustments". According to SFAS 16, paragraph 11, all items of profit and loss should be reported in the current income statement, except for the following:

1. Corrections of errors made in previously issued financial statements. Errors include mathematical mistakes, estimates not made in good faith, misapplication of GAAP, changing from a method that was not GAAP to a method that is GAAP, and failure to record an accural or deferral adjustment.

2. Realization of income tax benefits arising from preacquisition net operating loss carryforwards of purchased subsidiaries.

According to SFAS 16, these two events and only these two events are considered prior period adjustments. This means that there is little or no judgement involved in the determination of a prior period adjustment.

Once identified, a prior period adjustment must be reported as an adjustment to opening retained earnings, net of tax.

Appropriations of Retained Earnings. An appropriation of retained earnings is a disclosure device which indicates the reasons why dividends are not paid or were less than expected. Simply stated, the appropriation is a disclosure of dividend restrictions.

There are three types of appropriations:

1. Voluntary or discretionary. These appropriations are at the discretion of the board of directors and include appropriations for plant expansion or self-insurance.

2. Legal or statutory. As indicated earlier, certain states require a restriction on dividend distributions equal to the cost of treasury stock held by the corporation.

3. Contractual. Restrictive covenants in debt agreements may place limitations on dividend distributions.

There are two accounting alternatives for an appropriation of retained earnings. The first, and most common, is a footnote disclosure. The second type of disclosure requires a reclassification of retained earnings into two categories: free and unappropriated retained earnings and retained earnings appropriated. This does not change the total of retained earnings but simply makes the disclosure of the appropriation on the face of the balance sheet.

Regardless of the accounting approach used, it should never be assumed by the reader of the financial statements that there is a fund of cash or other economic resources available to satisfy the purpose for which the appropriation is established. The appropriation is simply a disclosure of a restriction or limitation on dividend distributions.

Other Adjustments to Total Stockholders' Equity

With the issuance of the AICPA's Objectives of Financial Statements in 1973[8] and the establishment of the FASB's Conceptual Framework in 1978,[9] there has been an attempt on the part of the accounting profession to develop accounting standards which result in reporting an accrual basis net income that is more closely correlated with the underlying cash flows of the firm. As a result, recent accounting standards have established a position that if an event does not have a high probability of cash realization in the short term, it should not be reported as an element of profit or loss on the income statement. Instead, a cumulative valuation adjustment account ("a reserve account") is created as an adjustment to total stockholders' equity. The cumulative valuation adjustment accounts include:

1. Net loss not recognized as pension expense (discussed earlier in this chapter);

2. Unrealized losses on the long-term portfolio of marketable equity securi-

ties (discussed in chapter 2);

3. Foreign currency translation gain or loss. According to paragraph 13 of FASB Statement No. 52, "Foreign Currency Translation", this is the gain or loss resulting from currency fluctuations when translating the financial statements of a foreign subsidiary into the United States dollar. These gains or losses could only be realized in cash by liquidating the subsidiary and should not be reported in the income statement. Rather, the cumulative foreign currency adjustments are reported as an element of stockholders' equity. Exhibit 3.12 provides an illustration of the cumulative valuation adjustment account for foreign currency transaction gain or loss for Squibb Corporation and Subsidiaries.

Finally, it should be noted that if there are numerous and complex changes in the stockholders' equity section during the year, a separate statement of stockholders' equity may be prepared and presented with the three basic financial statements or as a supplementary schedule. A supplementary footnote disclosure of a statement of stockholders' equity for Minnesota Mining and Manufacturing Company and Consolidated Subsidiaries (i.e., 3M Company) is presented in Exhibit 3.13.

EXHIBIT 3.12

Sample Disclosure: Squibb Corporation and Consolidated Subsidiaries: Balance Sheet Disclosure of Foreign Currency Valuation Adjustments

----

Consolidated Balance Sheet

Squibb Corporation and Subsidiaries
December 31, 1984, 1983 and 1982
(Dollar amounts in thousands)

	1984	1983	1982
Assets			
Current Assets:			
Cash and time deposits	$ 288,609	$ 195,377	$ 133,482
Marketable investments, at cost	3,559	10,455	2,039
Receivables, net	445,479	418,918	433,933
Inventories	401,085	353,723	371,413
Prepaid expenses	25,595	32,110	28,124
Deferred taxes on income	59,666	52,971	56,468
Total current assets	1,223,993	1,063,554	1,025,459
Investments and Long-Term Receivables	180,967	230,273	316,012
Property, Plant and Equipment, net	617,724	564,613	511,821
Other Assets	111,427	87,325	76,420
	$2,134,111	$1,945,765	$1,929,712
Liabilities and Shareholders' Equity			
Current Liabilities:			
Current installments of long-term debt	$ 101,547	$ 1,074	$ 11,586
Notes payable	67,959	53,389	50,831
Accounts payable and accrued expenses	330,614	311,055	317,416
Taxes on income	40,605	86,363	61,839
Total current liabilities	540,725	451,881	441,672
Long-Term Debt	200,023	204,427	336,314
Deferred Taxes on Income	17,432	17,743	16,768
Other Liabilities	47,491	40,333	39,139
Shareholders' Equity:			
Common stock, par value $1.00 per share:			
Authorized 100,000,000 shares; issued 53,429,927 shares (52,996,066 in 1983 and 51,472,063 in 1982)	53,430	52,996	51,472
Additional paid-in capital	240,031	228,145	171,151
Retained earnings	1,176,217	1,057,778	955,396
Cumulative foreign currency adjustments	(141,027)	(107,367)	(82,126)
	1,328,651	1,231,552	1,095,893
Less cost of 15,319 shares of stock held in treasury (14,486 in 1983 and 12,071 in 1982)	211	171	74
Total shareholders' equity	1,328,440	1,231,381	1,095,819
	$2,134,111	$1,945,765	$1,929,712

Source: Squibb Corporation and Subsidiaries 1984 Annual Report. Copyright, 1985, by Bristol-Myers Squibb Company. Reprinted with permission.

182

EXHIBIT 3.13

Sample Disclosure: 3M Company: Supplementary Footnote Disclosure of a Statement of Stockholders' Equity

---

Stockholders' Equity
Common stock. without par value, of 150.000.000 shares is authorized. with 118.004.132 shares issued in 1986, 1985 and 1984. Treasury stock of 3.737.751 shares at December 31. 1986.

3.431.845 shares in 1985 and 1.705.767 shares in 1984 is reported at cost. Preferred stock of 10.000.000 shares. without par value, is authorized but unissued.

(Dollars in millions)	Common Stock	Reinvested Earnings	Treasury Stock	Cumulative Translation	Total
Balance. December 31. 1983	$296	$3.819	$ (62)	$(355)	$3.698
Net income		733			733
Dividends paid ($3.40 per share)		(398)			(398)
Reacquired stock (1.855.044 shares)			(144)		(144)
Issuances pursuant to employee stock and benefit plans (792.961 shares)		(10)	65		55
Acquisition of businesses in exchange for stock*		(5)	10		5
Translation adjustments				(135)	(135)
Balance. December 31. 1984	$296	$4.139	$(131)	$(490)	$3.814
Net income		664			664
Dividends paid ($3.50 per share)		(403)			(403)
Reacquired stock (2.753.290 shares)			(218)		(218)
Issuances pursuant to employee stock and benefit plans (1.021.081 shares)		(10)	83		73
Acquisition of businesses in exchange for stock*		(1)	1		—
Translation adjustments				78	78
Balance. December 31. 1985	$296	$4.389	$(265)	$(412)	$4.008
Net income		779			779
Dividends paid ($3.60 per share)		(412)			(412)
Reacquired stock (1.891.693 shares)			(199)		(199)
Issuances pursuant to employee and director stock and benefit plans (1.580.354 shares)		(22)	151		129
Acquisition of businesses in exchange for stock*		—	—		—
Translation adjustments				158	158
Balance. December 31. 1986	$296	$4.734	$(313)	$(254)	$4.463

*Common stock issued related to acquisitions totaled 5.433 shares in 1986. 6.131 shares in 1985 and 55.730 shares in 1984. Common stock issued in conversion of subsidiary preference stock related to a prior acquisition totaled 69.697 shares in 1984.

Source: 3M Company 1986 Annual Report. Copyright, 1987, by The 3M Company. Reprinted with permission.

183

NOTES

1. Michael Blumstein, "Pros and Cons of Defeasance," The Wall Street Journal (January 12, 1984), D8-D9.

2. Coopers and Lybrand, Executive Alert (New York: Coopers and Lybrand (USA) Communications Department, May 1985), 12-15.

3. "Statement on Financial Instruments Disclosures," News Report, The Journal of Accountancy (June, 1990), 19-20.

4. David B. Praiser, "Financial Reporting Implications of Troubled Debt," The CPA Journal (February, 1989), 32-39.

5. Ibid.

6. Senate Banking, Housing and Urban Affairs Committee, Competitive Equality Banking Act of 1987, 100th Cong., 1st sess., 1987, S.790.

7. The term "fair market value" will be used throughout this section to represent the market valuation of the pension plan's assets. However, SFAS 87, paragraph 30, states that the "market related asset value" should be used in the required pension computations. The market related asset value may be determined by taking the ending fair market value for some plan assets or a five year moving average for other plan assets. When a method is selected, it should be applied consistently for each asset type and from year to year.

8. Objectives of Financial Statements (New York: AICPA, October 1973).

9. Statement of Financial Concepts No. 1, Objectives of Financial Reporting by Business Enterprises (Stamford, CT: FASB, November, 1978).

CASE 3.1. J.C. Penney Company, Inc.: Accounting for Long-Term Debt[1]

J.C. Penney is a major retailer, with stores in all 50 states and Puerto Rico. The major portion of the Company's business consists of providing merchandise and services to consumers through retail outlets and catalog operations. The Company primarily markets clothing, furnishings and accessories for the home.

Source: J. C. Penney Company, Inc. Annual Report for the Fiscal Year Ended January 28, 1989. Copyright, 1989, by J. C. Penney Company, Inc. Reprinted with permission.

REQUIRED: Study the April 1981 announcement of the new debt issues for J.C. Penney on May 1, 1981 and the long-term debt footnote disclosures for the year ended January 28, 1989.

1. Determine the market rate or yield on the zero coupon notes. Be certain that your answer is reasonable when compared to the yield disclosed in the current maturities of long-term debt footnote.

2. Prepare an amortization table for the zero coupon bonds and verify that current maturity of the zero coupon note is $194 million at January 28, 1989. Note that the footnote indicates that this is the balance for fiscal 1988, but this is actually for the year ended January 28, 1989.

3. Determine the market rate or yield for the 6% debentures. Be certain that your answer is reasonable when compared to the yields disclosed in the long term debt footnote.

In all requirements assume that all debt was issued on May 1, 1981 and that interest is payable semiannually.

NEW ISSUES   April, 1981

$400,000,000

J.C. Penney Company, Inc.

$200,000,000
Zero Coupon Notes Due 1989
Price 33.247%
plus accrued amortization of original issue discount from May 1, 1981

$200,000,000
6% Debentures Due 2006
Price 42.063%
plus accrued interest from May 1, 1981

---

*Copies of each Prospectus may be obtained from any of the several underwriters,
including the undersigned, only in States in which such underwriters are qualified
to act as dealers in securities and in which the Prospectus may legally be distributed.*

The First Boston Corporation

Goldman, Sachs & Co.		Merrill Lynch White Weld Capital Markets Group
		Merrill Lynch, Pierce, Fenner & Smith Incorporated
Bache Halsey Stuart Shields	Bear, Stearns & Co.	Blyth Eastman Paine Webber
Incorporated		Incorporated
Dillon, Read & Co. Inc.	Donaldson, Lufkin & Jenrette	Drexel Burnham Lambert
	Securities Corporation	Incorporated
E. F. Hutton & Company Inc.	Kidder, Peabody & Co.	Lazard Frères & Co.
	Incorporated	
Lehman Brothers Kuhn Loeb		L. F. Rothschild, Unterberg, Towbin
Incorporated		
Shearson Loeb Rhoades Inc.		Smith Barney, Harris Upham & Co.
		Incorporated
Warburg Paribas Becker	Wertheim & Co., Inc.	Dean Witter Reynolds Inc.
A. G. Becker		

Source: Copyright, 1981, by J. C. Penney Company, Inc. Reprinted with
permission.

Liabilities and Stockholders' Equity

Accounts payable and accrued expenses (In millions)	1988	1987	1986
Trade payables	$ 646	$ 525	$ 555
Accrued salaries, vacations, profit-sharing, and bonuses	348	401	394
Taxes, including income taxes	300	244	216
Worker's compensation and public liability insurance	95	65	74
Dividend payable	62	51	46
Other	215	309*	204
Total	$1,666	$1,595	$1,489

Includes provision for relocation of corporate headquarters.

Short term debt (In millions)	1988	1987	1986
Commercial paper	$ 663	$ 831	$ 407
Master notes and other	93	124	190
Short term debt	$ 756	$ 955	$ 597
Average borrowings	$1,194	$ 889	$ 955
Peak outstanding	$1,553	$1,922	$1,257
Average interest rates	7.6%	6.7%	6.7%

Current maturities of long term debt (In millions)	1988	1987	1986
Bank loan, variable rate, due April, 1989	$ 50	$ —	$ —
Zero coupon note, due 1989, $200 at maturity, yields 14.25%	194	—	—
Sinking fund debentures called for redemption, weighted average rate of 11.5%, with maturities of 2010 to 2015	—	—	274
Other	—	—	210
Total	$244	$ —	$484

Long term debt (In millions)	1988	1987	1986
Original issue discount			
Zero coupon notes and 6% debentures, due 1992 to 1994 and 2006, $700 at maturity, yields 13.5% to 15.1%, effective rates 12.5% to 13.0%	$ 355	$ 488	$ 436
Debentures and notes			
5.375% to 8.875%, due 1991 to 1998	397	414	429
9% to 9.75%, due 1995 to 2016	1,023	831	656
10.2% to 11.875%, due 1990 to 1994	224	239	471
12.125% to 13.75%, due 1991 to 1993	143	295	295
Other	53	128	144
	2,195	2,395	2,431
Present value of commitments under capital leases	201	213	224
Guaranteed LESOP notes, 8.17%, due 1998*	668	—	—
Long term debt	$3,064	$2,608	$2,655
Average interest rates	10.6%	10.9%	11.1%

Source: J. C. Penney Company, Inc. Annual Report for the Fiscal Year Ended January 28, 1989. Copyright, 1989, by J. C. Penney Company, Inc. Reprinted with permission.

Changes in long term debt (In millions)	1988	1987	1986
Increases			
9% to 11% sinking fund debentures, due 2015 to 2016	$ —	$ —	$ 350
8.375% to 10.875% notes, due 1990 to 1998	200	202	247
Amortization of original issue discount	60	52	46
Guaranteed LESOP notes, 8.17%, due 1998*	700	—	—
	960	254	643
Decreases			
Retirements from debt restructure program			
Open market purchases, weighted average rate of 12% with maturities of 1990 to 2015	—	—	562
Sinking fund debentures called for redemption, weighted average rate of 11.5% with maturities of 2010 to 2015	—	—	274
10.75% and 11.875% notes, due 1990, called in 1987	—	219	—
Other transfers to current maturities of long term debt	244	—	185
13.625% and 13.750% notes, due 1991 and 1999, called in 1988	152	—	—
Other, including LESOP amortization	108	82	66
	504	301	1,087
Net increase (decrease) in long term debt	$456	$ (47)	$ (444)

*For further discussion, see LESOP on page 20.

Maturities of long term debt (In millions)	Long term debt	Capital leases
1989	$ 288	$ 24
1990	137	24
1991	192	24
1992	294	24
1993	111	24
1994 to 1998	1,213	94
Thereafter	556	84
Total	$2,791	298
Less future interest and executory expenses		97
Present value		$201

Other liabilities (In millions)	1988	1987	1986
Life insurance operation, principally policy and claims reserves ...	$ 298	$299	$256
Casualty insurance operation, principally claims reserves	201	198	224
Bank operation, principally customer deposits	488	290	89
Real estate development operation	115	105	89
Total	$1,102	$892	$658

Source: J. C. Penney Company, Inc. Annual Report for the Fiscal Year Ended January 28, 1989. Copyright, 1989, by J. C. Penney Company, Inc. Reprinted with permission.

NOTES

1. This case is an extension of a case originally published in Glenn M. Pfeiffer and Robert M. Bowen, Financial Accounting: A Casebook (Englewood Cliffs, NJ: Prentice-Hall, 1985), 94-95.

Part II

An Analysis of Critical Issues
in Corporate Financial Reporting

4

Accounting for Income Taxes

INTRODUCTION

By definition, accounting for income taxes involves reporting the tax consequences of a firm's transactions on its financial statements, accounted for under the accrual basis and prepared in accordance with GAAP. The traditional purpose of accounting for income taxes under APB Opinion No. 11, "Accounting for Income Taxes", was to properly match costs with revenues. That is, the accountant was to determine and report an amount of income tax expense that was matched with accounting income. Accounting income was assumed to be based on the accountant's principles of revenue and expense recognition, and therefore may not be related to accounting techniques used on the firm's federal, state and local income tax returns.

More recently, with the issuance of FASB Statement No. 96, "Accounting for Income Taxes", accountants have become more concerned with the proper measurement of the liability (asset) for taxes to be paid (reduced) currently and in the future resulting from current economic events and transactions reflected on the firm's financial statements. Nonetheless, with the firm's financial statements tied to the accrual basis accounting and prepared in accordance with GAAP, the determination of income tax expense is still based on accounting income and not the taxable income found on the firm's tax returns.

This chapter first examines the basics of accounting for income taxes as originally required by Opinion 11, and still in effect under SFAS 96. Then, the basic accounting for income taxes is extended to include an in-depth analysis of the complex provisions of SFAS 96. It should be noted that SFAS 96 was originally made effective for fiscal years beginning after December 15, 1988 (i.e., calendar 1989). However, due to the complexity and cost of compliance with the provisions of this pronouncement, the effective date of SFAS 96 has been suspended until calendar 1992 under the provisions of FASB Statement No. 103, "Accounting for Income Taxes--Deferral of the Effective Date of FASB Statement No. 96. Recently, the FASB voted 5 to 2 to explore a proposal to revise SFAS 96.

INTERPERIOD TAX ALLOCATION

It is evident from the introduction to this chapter that there will usually be differences between the accountant's measurement of income tax expense on the firm's income statement and the actual amount of income taxes due and payable to the various taxing jurisdictions per the firm's income tax returns. The reason for the differences between income tax expense per the income statement and the income taxes payable per the tax return is that different principles of accounting measurement are used on the income statement and on the tax return. These differences are known as book-tax differences.

As noted in chapter 1, different methods of accounting for financial statement purposes and tax reporting arise in response to the differences in the objectives of financial and tax accounting. The main objective of tax accounting is to raise revenue. The primary objective of financial reporting is to provide information needed to make rational economic decisions. In satisfying the primary objective of financial reporting, accountants will strictly adhere to the matching principle. Under the matching principle, the income tax expense reported on the income statement must be recognized in the period in which the related accounting income is realized. Simply stated, this means that the income tax expense must be allocated to the periods in which the related accounting income is earned, regardless of the amount of tax actually due and payable to the federal, state, local and even foreign governments. This allocation of tax expense to the related periods of benefit is known as interperiod tax allocation.

The application of interperiod tax allocation is the reason why the income tax expense on the income statement is based on book or pretax accounting income and the income taxes payable on the balance sheet (and the ultimate cash outflow for taxes) is based on taxable income on the tax returns. As implied above, due to the use of different methods of accounting, income tax expense and income taxes payable are rarely equal. The difference between the income tax expense on the income statement and the current income taxes payable on the balance sheet is known as the deferred income tax liability (asset) on the balance sheet. To illustrate, consider the following simple diagram.

```
            Income Statement                    Tax Return
                (Book)                            (Tax)
             Based on GAAP                  Based on the IRS Code
---------------------------------    ----------------------------------


Pretax accounting income....$XXX     Taxable income...........$XXX

x Tax rate.................. x r      x Tax rate............... x r
            ------                               ------

Income tax expense on the            Income taxes payable on
income statement.............$XXX     the balance sheet........$XXX
                             =====                            =====
                          ^                               ^
                          |     Deferred income taxes on the     |
                          |            balance sheet             |
                          |-------------------------------------|
```

Although the income tax expense per books would not actually be determined by multiplying a tax rate against pretax accounting income, the above diagram does serve to illustrate the fact that, assuming the same tax rates are used, the only factor causing deferred taxes is the book-tax difference in accounting methods. The actual approach used to determine the income tax expense per book will depend on the type of book-tax difference. The types of book-tax differences will be discussed in the next section of this chapter. The following equation analysis illustrates the financial statement effects of recording the income tax provision for the period, assuming the existence of a deferred tax liability.

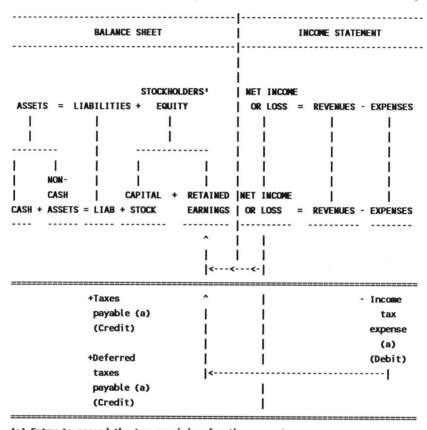

As noted above, the tax expense reduces reported net income and a liability for income taxes is recorded. Part of that liability is currently payable and the balance deferred and allocated to future accounting periods when these amounts will become payable.

BOOK-TAX DIFFERENCES AND ACCOUNTING FOR DEFERRED INCOME TAXES

In accounting for income taxes, accountants have identified two types of book-tax differences. These are:

1. Permanent differences;

2. Temporary (Timing) differences.

Permanent and temporary book-tax differences and their implications for deferred income tax accounting will be discussed in the following sections.

Permanent Differences

Permanent differences represent items of revenue and expense that will be reported on the firm's tax return but never on its financial statements, or events that will be reported on the firm's financial statements but never on its income tax returns. The permanent differences represent differences between book and taxable income that never "reverse" or will never have an equivalent effect on the future income reported on either the books or the tax returns. Because the differences between income tax expense and income taxes payable are permanent, these differences cannot be deferred to future accounting periods. In other words, the principles of deferred tax accounting do not apply to permanent differences.

Examples of Permanent Differences. Some of the more common permanent book-tax differences include:

1. Amortization of goodwill. Goodwill amortization is an expense for financial reporting, but is not tax deductible.

2. Interest received on tax-free securities. Interest is an item of revenue for financial reporting purposes, regardless of its source. However, interest on tax-free securities is not taxable.

3. Deduction for the cost of officer's life insurance. This cost is deducted as an expense for financial reporting purposes, but is not tax deductible.

4. Percentage (statutory) depletion of a natural resource in excess of cost. Statutory depletion is a tax deduction, but depletion in excess of cost is not permitted for financial reporting under GAAP.

An Illustration of Permanent Differences. As noted above, permanent differences never reverse, and as a result, are not deferred. If the analysis of the tax accounts indicate that the firm only has permanent book-tax differences, the accountant simply sets the income tax expense on the income statement equal to the income tax liability obtained from the firm's income tax returns. In substance, the accountant ignores permanent differences in accounting for income taxes.

To illustrate, assume a firm reports a pretax accounting income of $10,000. Included within the accounting income is $2,000 of tax exempt interest. If the assumed income tax rate is 40%, the firm's condensed federal income tax return would appear as follows.

Federal Income Tax Return:

```
Pretax accounting income per books...............$10,000

Less: Tax-exempt interest........................< 2,000>
                                                 --------
Taxable income per tax return (IRS)..............$ 8,000

           Income tax rate....................... x 40%
                                                 ---------

      Income taxes payable.......................$ 3,200
                                                 ========
```

In this illustration, the income tax expense would be set equal to the $3,200 of income taxes payable reported on the balance sheet. Therefore, if there are only permanent differences, there are no deferred income taxes and the principles of interperiod tax allocation do not apply. When the firm has both permanent and temporary book-tax differences, the analysis becomes more complex. The effects of temporary book-tax differences are discussed in the following section.

Temporary (Timing) Differences

Temporary or timing differences represent items of revenue and expense that are recognized for financial reporting purposes in a different period from when these same events are recognized on the firm's income tax returns. Because the revenues and expenses will ultimately be reported for both book and tax purposes, the differences between pretax accounting income and taxable income are only temporary and will eventually reverse. That is, at the end of the life of a particular transaction, the differences caused by the timing of revenue or expense recognition will fully offset, and additional taxes will be due and payable or a reduction of taxes will be realized. Because the ultimate reversal of the effects of the transaction will result in either future taxable amounts or future deductible amounts, the tax consequences of the reversal should be deferred and recognized on the current period's balance sheet.

Examples of Temporary Differences. Common examples of temporary differences include the following:

1. Installment sales. In general, installment sales are accounted for under the accrual basis for financial reporting and accounted for under the cash basis (installment method) for tax purposes. Under these circumstances, the entire amount of the sale would be recognized as revenue for financial reporting, but only an amount of the gross profit in proportion to the cash collected would be recognized as income on the tax return. Therefore, income tax expense is based on the full amount of the sale, while the tax liability is based on income recognized in proportion to the amount of cash received. Because the tax expense exceeds the income taxes payable, a

deferred tax liability would be recorded. The deferred liability would be due and payable to the government as taxable income is reported in proportion to the balance of the cash collected (i.e., as reversal takes place).

2. Depreciation. In practice, the straight-line method is generally used for financial reporting while an accelerated method is used on the firm's income tax return (e.g., the Federal Modified Accelerated Cost Recovery System [MACRS]). Because tax depreciation is higher in the earlier years of the asset's useful life, tax deductions are accelerated and less tax is paid. However, the tax expense per books is based on a lower depreciation charge so that the income tax expense on the income statement is greater than the income taxes payable on the balance sheet. The difference is reported as a deferred income tax liability on the current balance sheet. The deferred liability is due and payable in the later years of the asset's useful life when the depreciation differences reverse and the higher tax deductions are lost.

3. Advance collections for subscriptions. If a publisher collects subscriptions in advance, the cash receipt is not recognized as income for financial reporting until the books, magazines, etc., are delivered to the subscriber. However, if the firm uses the cash basis for tax purposes, the entire amount of the cash received would be included in taxable income in the year of the advance collection. As a result, more taxes are paid today than the income tax expense reported on the income statement by the accountant. Within the SFAS 96 limitations on asset recognition (to be discussed), the excess of income taxes paid over the income tax expense reported on the income statement may be reported as a deferred tax asset on the balance sheet. The deferred tax asset represents a prepaid tax in the current period, which will be realized in the future when reversal takes place. In this case, when the books, magazines, etc., are actually delivered to the subscriber, accounting income is recognized but there is no taxable income during the periods of delivery because income was already recognized in the year of the advance collection. This is the point of reversal, and the benefits of the prepaid taxes are realized in the form of lower income taxes payable than the income tax expense reported for financial reporting purposes.

Computation of Income Tax Expense with Both Permanent and Temporary Book-Tax Differences. When both temporary and permanent differences exist, the accountant does not calculate income tax expense by multiplying pretax accounting income on the income statement by the applicable tax rate. In practice, the income tax expense should be calculated as follows.

```
Income taxes payable (from the tax returns)................$XXX

Add: The deferred tax expense (which is also known as the
     deferred tax provision. This amount is equal to the
     temporary book-tax differences multiplied by
     the tax rate)............................................ XX
                                                             -----
Income tax expense............................................$XXX
                                                             =====
```

This approach simplifies the computation of income tax expense because it restricts the accountant's work to an analysis of temporary book-tax differences and does not require any consideration of permanent differences. Of course, in the simple case where there are only temporary differences, the income tax expense could be computed by multiplying pretax accounting income by the tax rate.

It should be noted that the effective tax rate, reported in the footnotes to the financial statements, is determined only after the calculation of the income tax expense as above and does not enter into the determination of the income tax expense. Therefore, the effective tax rate is still only based on financial accounting numbers. As a result, there will usually be differences between the accounting effective tax rate and the federal statutory tax rate.

The effective tax rate is determined as follows:

$$\text{Effective tax rate} = \frac{\text{Income tax expense}}{\text{Pretax accounting income}}$$

As will be discussed, a disclosure of a reconciliation between the effective tax rate and the federal statutory tax rate is required under SFAS 96, paragraph 28.

THE FASB STATEMENT NO. 96 APPROACH

Thus far, there seems to be few differences between the requirements of Opinion 11 and SFAS 96. The primary difference, however, is that the focus of the new pronouncement is on proper asset and liability recognition and valuation.

According to SFAS 96, paragraph 14, a deferred tax liability results from expected taxes to be paid in the future resulting from the reversal of current period temporary book-tax differences. The amount of the reversals are also known as "future taxable amounts". A deferred tax asset results from expected tax reductions to be received in the future resulting from the reversal of current period temporary book-tax differences. Here, the amount of the reversals are also known as "future deductible amounts".

A fundamental concept underlying the provisions of SFAS 96 is found in paragraph 15. According to SFAS 96, asset recognition is generally not supported when its value is contingent on future events. This restriction on asset recognition has its foundation in conservatism. Therefore, under SFAS 96, recognition of the deferred tax asset is limited and is only permitted when there are future taxable amounts to offset the future deductible amounts on which the deferred tax asset is based. In other words, the income needed to give future deductible amounts asset value cannot be anticipated. However, income can be anticipated only if it is in the form of future taxable amounts realized on the reversal of temporary book-tax differences. This limitation makes the recognition and valuation of the deferred tax asset quite complex and realizable only under highly restrictive conditions.

In the following sections, basic illustrations of the deferred tax liability and the deferred tax asset are presented. The discussion will be extended in subsequent sections by presentation of the requirements of the liability method and the net operating loss provisions of SFAS 96.

Basic Deferred Tax Liability Illustration

In the simple case there will be no differences in accounting for the deferred tax liability under Opinion 11 and SFAS 96. However, a difference could arise in the event of changes in the tax rate. SFAS 96 requires the use of the liability method, which accounts for future tax rate changes, while Opinion 11 requires the use of the deferred method, which uses the current tax rate and does not consider changes in the future tax rate.

In the basic illustrations of the deferred tax liability, it is assumed that the income tax rate is constant over time. As a result, the differences between the liability method and the deferred method will not be relevant here.

To illustrate the basics of accounting for the deferred tax liability, consider a firm that uses the straight-line method of depreciation for financial reporting and the MACRS for income tax purposes. Exhibit 4.1 presents an illustration of accounting for the deferred tax liability where there is only one temporary difference resulting from depreciation. Exhibit 4.2 complicates the first case scenario by including a permanent difference, tax exempt interest income.

As noted in Exhibit 4.1, for the first two years of the asset's life the depreciation deduction for tax purposes exceeds the depreciation expense per books. Because less tax is paid today than the expense on the income statement, there is a future liability for additional taxes when reversal takes place. In the accounting periods ending in 1986 and 1987, the provision for the future liability is recorded as a deferred tax liability. In this case, the originating differences will result in future taxable amounts in 1988 through 1991, the reversal period. It should be noted that the term *originating difference* simply refers to the original direction for recording the difference in the deferred tax account (i.e., as an asset or a liability). The reversing differences represent the realization of the tax reduction or additional payments when the direction of the deferred tax account changes.

The illustration in Exhibit 4.1 represents a simple case where there are no permanent differences and no tax rate changes. Without permanent differences, the income tax expense is simply the tax rate multiplied by the pretax accounting income per books. The tax liability on the balance sheet is the amount due per the tax returns. The deferred tax provision, or the change in the deferred tax account for the year, is the difference between the income tax expense on the income state-

EXHIBIT 4.1

Illustration: Deferred Tax Liability Without Permanent Differences

	1986 Book	1986 Tax	1987 Book	1987 Tax	1988 Book	1988 Tax	1989 Book	1989 Tax	1990 Book	1990 Tax	1991 Book	1991 Tax
Income before tax and depreciation	$40,000	$40,000	$65,000	$65,000	$50,000	$50,000	$60,000	$60,000	$80,000	$80,000	$60,000	$60,000
Less: Depreciation	< 4,000>	< 8,000>	< 8,000>	<12,800>	< 8,000>	< 7,680>	< 8,000>	< 4,608>	< 8,000>	< 4,608>	< 4,000>	< 2,304>
Income before tax	$36,000	$32,000	$57,000	$52,200	$42,000	$42,320	$52,000	$55,392	$72,000	$75,392	$56,000	$57,696
Tax at 40%	$14,400	$12,800	$22,800	$20,880	$16,800	$16,928	$20,800	$22,157	$28,800	$30,157	$22,400	$23,078
Deferred tax expense or provision	$1,600		$1,920		< $128>		<$1,357>		<$1,357>		< $678>	
Cumulative deferred tax payable	$1,600		$3,520		$3,392		$2,035		$678		$0	

Depreciation Information:

Machinery cost = $40,000
Books: 5 year property using straight-line depreciation.
Tax : 5 year property using Federal MACRS.
For both books and tax, there is 1/2 depreciation in the first and last years.

Book Depreciation = $40,000/5 years = $8,000 per year.

Tax Depreciation:

Year	MACRS %	Depreciation Computation
1	20.00%	20.00% x $40,000 = $ 8,000
2	32.00%	32.00% x $40,000 = 12,800
3	19.20%	19.20% x $40,000 = 7,680
4	11.52%	11.52% x $40,000 = 4,608
5	11.52%	11.52% x $40,000 = 4,608
6	5.76%	5.76% x $40,000 = 2,304

Temporary Book-Tax Differences:

Year	MACRS	S/L	Difference	Deferred Tax at 40%
1	$ 8,000	$ 4,000	$4,000	$1,600
2	12,800	8,000	4,800	1,920
3	7,680	8,000	<320>	<128>
4	4,608	8,000	<3,392>	<1,357>
5	4,608	8,000	<3,392>	<1,357>
6	2,304	4,000	<1,696>	<678>
Totals	$40,000	$40,000	-0-	-0-

Note 1: From 1986 to 1987 there are "originating" differences and and from 1988 to 1991 there are "reversing" differences.

Note 2: The determination of income tax expense should actually be made by adding income taxes payable to the deferred tax expense. In this case, the same result is obtained by multiplying income before tax by the tax rate. However, this approach is only valid if there are no permanent differences.

ment and the income taxes payable on the balance sheet. The cumulative deferred taxes payable account is the balance of the deferred tax liability on the balance sheet. Of course, the income tax expense could also be determined by adding the deferred tax provision for the year to the current income taxes payable.

Over the asset's useful life the same total depreciation has been deducted, $40,000, and at the end of the asset's life the deferred tax account is zero as full reversal takes place.

The illustration in Exhibit 4.2 considers the effects of permanent differences on accounting for income taxes. In practice, the accountant does not have to address the impact of permanent differences directly. As noted in Exhibit 4.2, permanent differences are excluded on the tax return. The accountant will usually be given the bottom line income taxes payable from the preparer of the tax returns. As a result, the accountant only needs to analyze the temporary book-tax differences.

In the illustration presented in Exhibit 4.2, the income tax expense can only be determined by adding the deferred tax expense for the period to the income tax liability obtained from the tax returns. With the existence of permanent differences, the income tax expense on the income statement and the income taxes payable on the balance sheet are different from these same amounts derived without permanent differences in Exhibit 4.1. However, the deferred tax account is constant in both illustrations. There should be no differences in the deferred tax account because this account is only based on temporary book-tax differences. This illustrates a point made earlier: permanent differences are not relevant to deferred tax accounting.

Basic Deferred Tax Asset Illustration

As noted earlier, the recognition of the deferred tax asset has been severely restricted by the provisions of SFAS 96. In the following basic illustration, only one of the SFAS 96 limitations will be discussed: the recognition of the deferred tax asset is recognized only up to the point that future deductible amounts will equal future taxable amounts upon reversal. The second and more complex limitation on recognition of the deferred tax asset is based on the net operating loss provisions. This will be discussed later in this chapter.

For the present illustration, assume that Lloyd's, Inc. a conglomerate company, reports an income tax liability of $100,000 each year based on a 40% tax rate. Upon analysis of the firm's 1990 temporary book-tax differences, the following transactions are discovered.

1. There is an $80,000 balance in the deferred advertising expense account. This amount was deducted in full in 1990 on the income tax return under the cash basis. However, it was deferred or capitalized as a prepaid asset under the accrual basis on the financial statements in 1990 and will be deducted in full in 1991 when the expected benefits of the advertising on sales are realized. Therefore, a future taxable amount will be created in 1991 when reversal takes place and a deferred tax liability must be provided for in 1990.

EXHIBIT 4.2

Illustration: Deferred Tax Liability With Permanent Differences

	1986 Book	1986 Tax	1987 Book	1987 Tax	1988 Book	1988 Tax	1989 Book	1989 Tax	1990 Book	1990 Tax	1991 Book	1991 Tax
Income before tax and depreciation......	$40,000	$40,000	$65,000	$65,000	$50,000	$50,000	$60,000	$60,000	$80,000	$80,000	$60,000	$60,000
Less: Depreciation......	<4,000>	<8,000>	<8,000>	<12,800>	<8,000>	<7,680>	<8,000>	<4,608>	<8,000>	<4,608>	<4,000>	<2,304>
Less: Tax Exempt Interest......		<5,000>		<7,000>		<10,000>		<11,000>		<15,000>		<10,000>
Income before tax......	$36,000	$27,000	$57,000	$45,200	$42,000	$32,320	$52,000	$44,392	$72,000	$60,392	$56,000	$47,696
Taxes Payable at 40% on the Balance Sheet....		$10,800		$18,080		$12,928		$17,757		$24,157		$19,078
Add: Deferred tax expense or provision......	1,600		1,920			<128>		<1,357>		<1,357>		<678>
Income Tax Expense on the Income Statement.....	$12,400		$20,000		$12,800		$16,400		$22,800		$18,400	
Cumulative deferred tax payable......	$1,600		$3,520		$3,392		$2,035		$678		$0	

Depreciation Information:

Machinery cost = $40,000
Books: 5 year property using straight-line depreciation.
Tax: 5 year property using Federal MACRS.
For both books and tax, there is 1/2 depreciation in the first and last years.

Book Depreciation = $40,000/5 years = $8,000 per year.

Tax Depreciation:

Year	MACRS %	Depreciation Computation
1	20.00%	20.00% x $40,000 = $8,000
2	32.00%	32.00% x $40,000 = $12,800
3	19.20%	19.20% x $40,000 = $7,680
4	11.52%	11.52% x $40,000 = $4,608
5	11.52%	11.52% x $40,000 = $4,608
6	5.76%	5.76% x $40,000 = $2,304

Temporary Book-Tax Differences:

Year	MACRS	S/L	Difference	Deferred Tax at 40%
1	$8,000	$4,000	$4,000	$1,600
2	12,800	8,000	4,800	1,920
3	7,680	8,000	<320>	<128>
4	4,608	8,000	<3,392>	<1,357>
5	4,608	8,000	<3,392>	<1,357>
6	2,304	4,000	<1,696>	<678>
Totals	$40,000	$40,000	-0-	-0-

Note 1: From 1986 to 1987 there are "originating" differences and from 1988 to 1991 there are "reversing" differences.

2. There was an advance collection of $60,000 for book subscriptions. The firm recognized the full amount in 1990 as income on the tax return under the cash basis. Under the accrual basis, the initial collection in 1990 is recorded as a liability for future delivery of goods on the balance sheet. When the books are delivered and revenues earned in 1991, the firm will recognize the income. Therefore, a future deductible amount will be created upon reversal in 1991 and a deferred tax asset may be provided for in 1990, subject to the SFAS 96 limitations.

To determine the extent of recognition of the deferred tax asset, a schedule of future taxable and deductible amounts by expected reversal date should be prepared at December 31, 1990.

1990 Schedule of Taxable and Deductible Amounts

Reversal Expected in 1991

Deferred Advertising (Future Taxable Amount)..........$80,000

Advance Collections (Future Deductible Amount)........<60,000>

Net Taxable Amount.............................$20,000
                                              =======

The deferred tax asset can be recognized in full in this case because the future deductible amounts are fully offset by the future taxable amounts. This assumes that reversal takes place during the same accounting period for both temporary differences and that the net operating loss provisions do not apply.

Computation of the 1990 Income Tax Expense

Income taxes payable per tax returns (given)..........$100,000

Add: Deferred tax liability (40% x $80,000)........ 32,000

Deduct: Deferred tax asset (40% x $60,000).............< 24,000>

Income tax expense.............................$108,000
                                              =========

If the taxes payable and the temporary book-tax differences were related to the same taxing jurisdiction, and because they are both current accounts (i.e., reversal within one year from the balance sheet date), they could be offset and a net deferred tax liability of $8,000 (i.e., $32,000 - 24,000) could be reported on the company's 1990 balance sheet. The principles of balance sheet classification, the right to offset the asset and the liability and the SFAS 96 scheduling requirements will be discussed more fully in subsequent sections of this chapter.

The provisions of SFAS 96 would permit asset recognition under the circumstances described in this illustration because there will be future income or taxable amounts that are reasonably assured which give value to the future tax deductions. The future deductible amounts only have asset value to the firm if they can be used, and the deductions can only be used if there is future taxable income. Due to conservatism, accountants generally do not anticipate future income and do not recognize assets contingent on future earnings. However, in the case of future taxable amounts, there is a reasonable degree of certainty that reversal will take place and the future service potential of the asset will be fully realized. In other words, without considering the net operating loss provisions, the deferred tax asset can only be recognized to the extent of the deferred tax liability. For example, if the facts in the previous illustration were reversed (i.e., deferred advertising was equal to $60,000 and advance collections were equal to $80,000), the following information would be analyzed at December 31, 1990.

```
1990 Schedule of Taxable and Deductible Amounts
-------------------------------------------------


                                        Reversal Expected in 1991
                                        -------------------------
    Deferred Advertising (Future Taxable Amount)..........$60,000

    Advance Collections (Future Deductible Amount)........<80,000>
                                                          --------

        Net Deductible Amount.............................$<20,000>
                                                          ========
```

Assuming that the net operating loss provisions do not apply, the net deductible amount cannot be used in the deferred tax computations because it results from an excess future deductible amount over future taxable amounts. Simply stated, the future tax deductions have no asset value if there is no future taxable income against which these deductions can be used. Therefore, the deferred tax asset is limited to the tax rate multiplied by $60,000 or $24,000. This is exactly equal to the deferred tax liability. In this case the income tax expense would be set equal to the income taxes payable per the tax returns.

```
Computation of the 1990 Income Tax Expense
---------------------------------------------


Income taxes payable per tax returns (given)..........$100,000

Add:    Deferred tax liability (40% x $60,000)........  24,000

Deduct: Deferred tax asset (40% x $60,000 limit)......< 24,000>
                                                        -----------


    Income tax expense..............................$100,000
                                                    =========
```

Case 4.1 at the end of this chapter will also consider the basics of accounting for the deferred tax asset and deferred tax liability.

EXTENSIONS OF THE BASIC ACCOUNTING FOR DEFERRED TAXES

The basic accounting for deferred income taxes as prescribed by Opinion 11 was made more complex by the issuance of SFAS 96. The two major extensions of deferred tax accounting under SFAS 96 are the use of the liability method and the application of the net operating loss provisions in the recognition of the deferred tax asset.

The Liability Method

SFAS 96 requires that the liability method be used in accounting for the deferred tax account. This method replaces the deferred method which was required under Opinion 11.

The liability method consists of two major changes in the accounting for the deferred tax account:

1. The use of future tax rates;

2. The adjustment of the balance of the deferred tax account in the year in which tax rate changes have been enacted into law.

Future Tax Rates. The liability method requires that deferred income taxes should be recorded at the amounts at which they will be recovered or settled when the underlying temporary differences reverse. This would require the use of the future tax rate that will be in effect at the reversal date. Nevertheless, SFAS 96, paragraph 20, went on to require that tax rates other than the current rate may be used only when the future tax rates have been enacted into law. Even if it is probable that the tax law will change, if the change has not yet been enacted into law, the current tax rate must be used in all calculations.

For example, if Congress passes a new tax act which phases in the provisions of the new law over several years, the deferred tax account must be computed by multiplying the temporary book-tax difference by the future tax rate expected in the year in which the underlying temporary differences reverse. However, if the tax act has not been enacted into law by Congress, the current tax rate must be used.

Revision of Future Tax Rates. When a change in the tax rate has been enacted into law, its effect on the deferred income tax and the related tax expense must be recognized immediately. SFAS 96, paragraph 20, requires that "the effect shall be included in income from continuing operations for the period that includes the enactment date".

To illustrate the application of the liability method when there has been a change in the tax law, consider a firm in 1987 that expects future taxable amounts of $300,000 reversing in equal amounts of $100,000 each in 1989, 1990 and 1991. It is assumed that no other temporary book-tax differences originate over this three-year period. At December 31, 1987, the current tax rate is 50% and there have been no changes in the tax rate enacted into law. Therefore, the deferred tax liability account at December 31, 1987, was recorded at $150,000 (i.e., $300,000 x 50%).

Assume that at December 31, 1988, a new tax law is enacted by Congress reducing the firm's tax rate to 40% effective January 1, 1990. Under the liability method, the deferred tax account must be adjusted in the year in which the tax rate change is enacted into law. Therefore, at December 31, 1988, the deferred tax liability account should be reduced to $130,000 as follows:

	1989	1990	1991	Total
Taxable amounts (reversals in)	$100,000	$100,000	$100,000	
Tax rate	x 50%	x 40%	x 40%	
Deferred tax liability	$ 50,000	$ 40,000	$ 40,000	$130,000

To adjust the deferred tax liability at December 31, 1988, the deferred tax liability account is reduced by $20,000, (i.e., $150,000 - 130,000) and there is a corresponding reduction of the income tax expense on the income statement. This will increase reported income from continuing operations and earnings per share for 1988.

The potential increase in reported earnings resulting from the application of the provisions of SFAS 96 has been a concern of many credit and financial analysts and discussed often in the financial press. For example, the Tax Reform Act (TRA) of 1986 reduced the top corporate tax rate from 46% to 34% effective 1988. Many firms elected early adoption of SFAS 96 and reported large, one-time gains in income. These one-time gains do not provide an increase in current cash flows and result in reduced comparability of the financial statements for the analyst.

Balance Sheet Classification of Deferred Income Taxes

The deferred tax liability and the deferred tax asset (within the limitations to be discussed) can be classified as either current or long-term. The classification depends on the expected reversal date. If the reversal is expected within one year from the balance sheet, the deferred tax liability or asset is classified as current. Otherwise, the deferred tax account should be classified as noncurrent.

The cumulative balance in the deferred tax account is the result of many temporary book-tax differences. Some of these differences will give rise to deferred tax liabilities and others will result in deferred tax assets. Similarly, some differences within each group will be current and others will be classified as noncurrent. At the end of the accounting period, the accountant must analyze the composition of the deferred tax account and classify each reversal of a book-tax difference as either current or long-term. The accountant must then determine the extent of the net deferred tax liability or net deferred tax asset. The accountant can derive a net liability or a net asset as long as the right to offset exists. The right to offset exists only if the amounts are payable and receivable from the same taxing jurisdiction. If netting is appropriate, the end result will be a net current liability or asset and a net noncurrent liability or asset. For example, assume that a firm has two book-tax differences in 1991. The first relates to advance collections for subscriptions. The subscriptions were recognized as income for tax purposes when collected but will be reported as income on the financial statements under the accrual basis only when earned, that is, when the books are delivered. It is assumed that the books will be delivered and reversal of the future deductible amounts will take place in 1992 for $20,000 and 1993 for $35,000.

The second book-tax difference relates to excess tax depreciation under the MACRS method. The excess of MACRS over straight-line depreciation results in future taxable amounts of $100,000 in 1992 and $225,000 in 1993. Given this information, the accountant prepares the following schedule to determine the proper classification of the deferred tax account on the 1991 balance sheet:

For the Balance Sheet at 12/31/91

Book-tax difference	Reversals in 1992 Current	1993 Noncurrent
Advance collection of subscriptions (accounted for under the accrual basis for books and the cash basis for tax)................................	<$ 20,000>	<$ 35,000>
Straight-line depreciation for books and the MACRS depreciation for tax......	$ 100,000	$ 225,000
Net future taxable amounts.........	$ 80,000	$ 190,000
Assumed tax rate....................	x 40%	x 40%
Net deferred tax liability.........	$ 32,000	$ 76,000

On the 12/31/91 balance sheet, $32,000 is classified as a current liability and the $76,000 is classified as a long-term liability.

The Net Operating Loss (NOL)

A net operating loss (NOL) is simply a net loss for income tax purposes. That is, tax deductions exceed taxable revenues. As in the case of deferred tax accounting in general, the NOL is treated differently for income tax purposes than for financial accounting and reporting (i.e., GAAP).

Tax Law. According to the provisions of the IRS code, a firm reporting an NOL (within the limitations to be discussed below) can elect one of two tax options:

1. The NOL carryback/carryforward option. Under this option, a firm can carryback the NOL for three years and claim a refund for taxes previously paid in those years, but it must be carried back to the earliest year first. Any remaining or unused portion of the NOL can be carried forward, in chronological order, for a period of 15 years to offset future taxable income. Any unused portion of the NOL remaining after the 15-year period expires.

2. The NOL carryforward option. Under the second available option, the firm can elect to only carryforward the NOL for a period of 15 years to offset

future taxable income. Again, after the 15-year period has passed, the unused portion of the NOL is considered expired.

Once an option is elected, it is irrevocable.

Limitation on the NOL Carryforward Benefits. Prior to the TRA of 1986, one of the most valuable assets acquired in many mergers and acquisitions was a significant amount of unused, preacquisition NOLs of the acquired company. However, under the 1986 TRA the use of preacquisition NOLs is subject to certain limitations. One of the most significant limitations is described in the following paragraphs.

After a change in ownership of more than 50% of the value of the stock in a loss corporation, over a three-year period and no matter how the change is effected (i.e., merger, acquisition, etc.), the future taxable income available for offset by the preacquisition NOL is limited to the following annual amount:

```
Annual limit on NOL benefit    Long-term tax      Value of the NOL
    realization              =  exempt rate    x   corporation's equity
```

The long-term tax exempt rate to be used in this computation is the highest T-bill rate reported over the three months immediately before the acquisition. The value of the NOL corporation's equity is to be measured by the fair market value (usually the acquisition price) of the equity interests before the ownership change. This valuation will usually be modified to reflect IRS upward adjustments to items such as asset bases. This annual limitation is known as the "Section 382 limitation".

In addition to the Section 382 limitation, there are other provisions of the IRS code that must be satisfied in order to maximize realization of NOL carryforward benefits of the acquired firm. For example, NOL carryforwards are disallowed unless the loss corporation satisfies the continuity of business enterprise rule that applies to tax-free reorganizations for the two year period following the ownership change. There are many other, more complex restrictions on the NOL realization that are beyond the scope of this text.

Illustration of the NOL Tax Provisions. The following diagram provides the data for the NOL illustration. As indicated by the diagram, there is an NOL in 1993 amounting to $190,000. The hypothetical NOL corporation reported an aggregate taxable income of $165,000 from 1990 through 1992. Thus the NOL can be carried back for the three years and refunds can be claimed for the taxes paid on the $165,000 of taxable income, and the $25,000 balance of the NOL can be carried forward up to a period of 15 years. In this illustration, sufficient taxable income is reported in 1994 and 1995 so that the carryforward is fully utilized within the two-year period.

In this illustration, the flow of the NOL would be charted as follows:

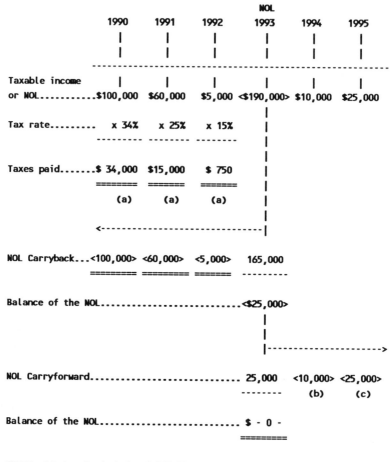

```
                                          NOL
                1990      1991      1992      1993      1994      1995
                 |         |         |         |         |         |
                 |         |         |         |         |         |
                -------------------------------------------------------------
Taxable income   |         |         |         |         |         |
or NOL..........$100,000  $60,000   $5,000 <$190,000> $10,000   $25,000
                                                       |
Tax rate.........  x 34%    x 25%    x 15%             |
                 ---------  --------  --------         |
                                                       |
Taxes paid.......$ 34,000  $15,000   $ 750            |
                 ========  =======   ======           |
                    (a)      (a)       (a)             |
                                                       |
                 <--------------------------------------|

NOL Carryback...<100,000> <60,000>  <5,000>   165,000
                ========  ========  ======    ---------

Balance of the NOL..............................<$25,000>
                                                    |
                                                    |
                                                    |--------------------->

NOL Carryforward...............................  25,000   <10,000> <25,000>
                                                 --------    (b)      (c)

Balance of the NOL.............................. $ - 0 -
                                                 ========
```

NOTES: (a) A refund claim of $49,750 (i.e., $34,000 + 15,000 + 750) is
           applied for in 1993, the year of the loss.
       (b) There would be no taxes due in 1994 because the available NOL
           carryforward fully offsets taxable income.
       (c) There would be $1,500 taxes due in 1995. The tax liability
           would be computed as follows:

```
Taxable income...........$25,000

Less: NOL carryforward...<15,000>
                         --------

Taxable income after the
application of available
NOL carryforwards........$10,000

Tax rate.................. x 15%
                         ---------

Tax liability............$ 1,500
                         ========
```

Accounting for the NOL Under SFAS 96

Accounting for the NOL could result in realization of tax benefits in a different period than when recognized for income tax purposes. The extent of the inconsistency between financial accounting and tax reporting depends on whether the accountant is dealing with an NOL carryback or an NOL carryforward.

Accounting for the NOL Carryback. In the case of an NOL carryback, the NOL gives rise to a refund that is both measureable and currently realizable. As a result, accountants are certain as to the refund and recognize the NOL benefits on the financial statements in the year of the loss. In this case, financial accounting is consistent with treatment of the NOL on the income tax return.

The accountant's recognition of the NOL carryback benefits in the year of the loss results in creating a short-term receivable for the tax refund claim and increasing ordinary income or reducing the loss on the income statement in the year of the NOL. The equation analysis of this transaction is presented below.

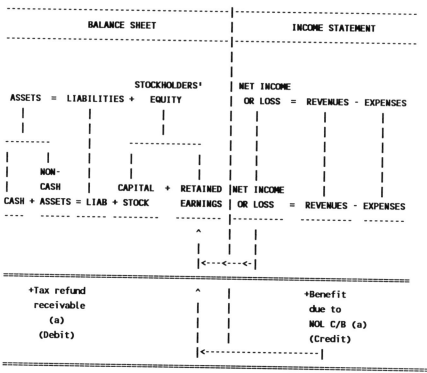

(a) Entry to record the refund receivable due to the NOL carryback.
This entry is made in the year of the loss.

Accounting for the NOL Carryforward. The realization of the future tax benefits from an NOL carryforward is dependent on future taxable income and is uncertain. Therefore, the accounting issue surrounding the NOL carryforward is when to recognize the tax benefits from the NOL carryforward on the financial statements: in the year the income is actually earned, or in the year of the loss.

This issue can be very problematic for the accountant because a basic premise of SFAS 96 is that future income should not be considered in the measurement and valuation of an asset. Therefore, recognition of the NOL carryforward benefits are usually only recognized in the year in which the related income is actually earned. However, SFAS 96 does provide for an exception to this general rule and under certain conditions will allow recognition of the future NOL carryforward benefits in the year of the loss. Nonetheless, if there is recognition of the NOL carryforward benefits in the year of the loss, an asset cannot be recognized under any circumstances.

Accounting for the NOL carryforward benefits in the year in which income is earned and in the year of the loss is presented in the following sections.

Recognition of the NOL Carryforward Benefit in the Year in Which Income is Earned. When recognition of the NOL carryforward benefit is deferred until the year in which income is actually earned, it implies that in the year of the loss, the accountant determines that the ultimate realization of the NOL tax benefit is not reasonably assured. Because the recognition of the NOL carryforward benefit will not be made until income is earned, there are no accounting entries in the year of the loss. In the year of actual income, a reduction of income tax expense and taxes payable is recorded. This is illustrated in the following equation analysis.

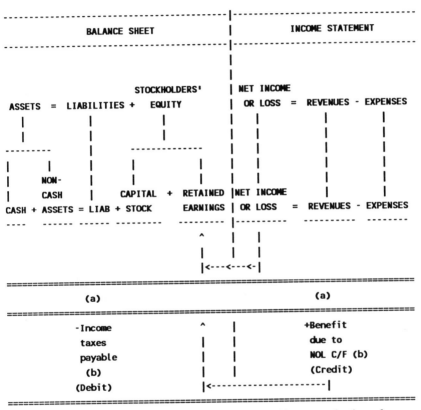

(a) If the NOL carryforward benefits are not reasonably assured, there is no accounting recognition in the year of the loss.

(b) In the year in which income is earned, the realization of the NOL carryforward benefits reduce the taxes payable for both book and tax purposes. In this case, GAAP and tax accounting provide consistent results. This adjusting entry is usually made after recording the current year's tax provision (i.e., income tax expense, income taxes payable and the deferred tax provision, if any).

Recognition of the NOL Carryforward Benefit in the Year of the Loss. The NOL carryforward benefits can be recognized in the year of the loss when the accountant determines that the future realization of these benefits is reasonably assured. However, according to SFAS 96, the NOL carryforward benefits can be recognized in the year of the loss only when there are net taxable amounts that will reverse and become part of taxable income over the carryforward period. As discussed earlier, taxable amounts result from the reversal of current period book-tax temporary differences that increase the deferred tax liability. For example, in the deferred tax liability illustrations presented in Exhibits 4.1 and 4.2, in the years in which the excess tax depreciation reversed, valuable tax deductions were lost and lost tax deductions increased taxable income (i.e., they become taxable amounts).

The existence of the reversals and the creation of future taxable amounts are sufficient to provide the accountant with reasonable assurance that the NOL carry-forward benefits will be realized. Under these circumstances, SFAS 96 permits recognition of the future NOL carryforward benefits in the year of the loss. However, if any NOL carryforward benefits are recognized in the year of the loss, the benefits can only be used to reduce the deferred tax liability related to the reversal of the taxable amounts over the carryforward period. The other side of the accountant's entry would increase ordinary income or reduce the loss on the income statement in the year of the loss. Because realization is dependent on future income, an asset or receivable cannot be created.

The recognition of the NOL carryforward in the year of the loss is outlined in the following equation analysis.

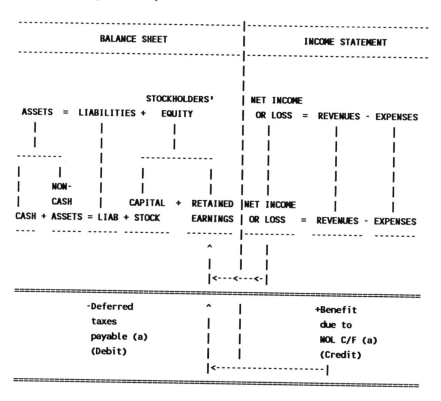

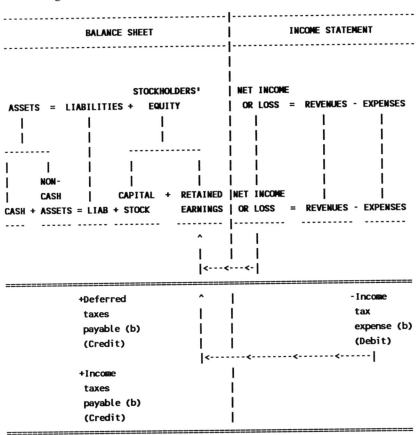

(a) Entry to record the NOL carryforward benefits in the year of the loss.
(b) Entry to record the income tax provision in the year in which income is
    earned, given prior recognition of the NOL carryforward benefits. This
    illustration assumes that the NOL realization in the year in which income
    is earned is not sufficient to fully offset taxable income. If the NOL
    fully offsets the taxable income there would be no taxes payable and the
    income tax expense would equal the deferred tax expense for the year.
    The increase in the deferred tax account fully offsets the reduction of
    this account in the year of the loss when the NOL carryforward benefits
    were recognized.

Regardless of the accounting treatment of the NOL carryforward benefits in
the year of the loss, the amounts of the future NOL carryfoward benefits are usually
disclosed in the footnotes to the financial statements. The footnote includes the
amounts and expected reversal dates of the NOL carryforward benefits, computed
on both the accrual basis and a tax basis.

THE SCHEDULING REQUIREMENTS OF SFAS 96 AND THE EFFECTS OF SCHEDULING ON THE RECOGNITION OF THE DEFERRED TAX ASSET

One of the most complex requirements of SFAS 96 is the use of "scheduling" in the computation of the deferred tax account. Specifically, when calculating the amount of the deferred taxes, "hypothetical income tax returns" are prepared for each future year covering the expected reversal period of the current, temporary book-tax differences. In other words, the only taxable income and tax deductions to be included in the hypothetical tax returns are the reversals of temporary book-tax differences. The current balance of deferred tax liabilities will result in future taxable amounts (i.e., taxable income) upon reversal, and the transactions that could be recorded as deferred tax assets will result in future deductible amounts (i.e., tax deductions) when reversal takes place.

The need for scheduling arises under SFAS 96 primarily due to the use of the liability method and the restrictions on recognition of the deferred tax asset. Under the liability method, tax rate changes must be implemented currently and must be applied to each year depending on expected reversal date. This point was illustrated earlier in the discussion of the liability method.

The second reason for scheduling is its usefulness in determining if the deferred tax asset should be recognized. As noted several times in this chapter, SFAS 96 places significant restrictions on the recognition of the deferred tax asset. Realization of the value of a deferred tax asset is dependent on future tax deductibility of the item upon reversal. That is, realization is dependent on the existence of future taxable income, which is needed in order to utilize the tax deduction. Simply stated, the future tax deduction has no asset value to the entity unless it can be used to offset future taxable income and thereby reduce the firm's cash outflow for taxes. Because future taxable income is uncertain, SFAS 96 generally prohibits the recognition of the deferred tax asset. However, there are two exceptions to this general rule.

The first exception was presented earlier in the basic deferred tax asset illustration. The deferred tax asset could only be recognized to the extent of the deferred tax liability. In the simple case, a net deferred tax asset is not permitted. The second exception allows a net deferred tax asset to be recognized by applying the NOL carryback and carryforward rules.

As in the case of the recognizing of the NOL carryforward benefits in the year of the loss, if there are reversals of temporary book-tax differences from the deferred tax liability in the future, the accountant concludes that there are future taxable amounts or taxable income available for offset and that these amounts are reasonably assured. The same theory is applied to the recognition of the deferred tax asset. The deferred tax asset gives rise to future deductible amounts. Any "net deductions" or excess future deductible amounts over future taxable amounts scheduled in any one reversal period are treated as an NOL. This hypothetical NOL is treated as an actual NOL and is therefore carried back three years on the schedule to offset previously reported income (taxable amounts), and any balance is carried forward for 15 years on the schedule to offset future income (taxable amounts). The amount of the NOL utilized to offset the taxable amounts in the current and future periods is multiplied by the appropriate income tax rate to determine the amount of the deferred tax asset to be recognized, and is reported on the current balance sheet. Again, the justification for asset recognition is the existence of future taxable amounts which provide evidence that realization of the deferred tax asset's benefits are reasonably assured.

Illustration of Scheduling

In order to illustrate the scheduling requirements of SFAS 96, assume a firm has only two temporary book-tax differences. The first book-tax difference results from excess MACRS tax depreciation over book depreciation. The depreciation book-tax difference amounts to $800 and will reverse over the next four years. The second book-tax difference results from an accrual of a warranty expense in the current year to provide for the future cost of customer service under the company's warranty program. The accrual results in deducting a warranty expense on the financial statements the year of the sale, but will not be recognized for tax purposes until the warranty services are actually provided. The firm expects to satisfy the provisions of the warranty program two years hence. If the pretax accounting income per books was $400 in the current year, the hypothetical tax returns prepared under the SFAS 96 scheduling requirements in 1990 would appear as follows.

	Current Year	Schedule by Expected Reversal Date			
	1990	1991	1992	1993	1994
Pretax accounting income....	$ 400				
Temporary book-tax differences:					
Excess MACRS depreciation over straight-line.........	<800>	100	100	200	400 (a)
Warranty accrual per books, cash basis for tax..........	3,000		<3,000> (b)		
Taxable income or loss......	$2,600	$100	<2,900>NOL	$200	$400
NOL carryback and carryforward option...........	<2,600>	<100>	2,900	<200>	-
Balance......................	$ -0-	$ -0-	$ -0-	$ -0-	$400

Carryback 3 years | Carryforward 15 years

<--------------------|-------------------->

```
Notes: (a) Future taxable amounts.
       (b) Future deductible amounts.
========================================================================
```

In this illustration, there are taxable amounts that can be offset against the future deductible amounts when the NOL rules are applied. Because the future taxable amounts are sufficient to offset the future deductible amounts, the deferred tax asset can be fully recognized. This assumes that there is only one taxing jurisdiction so that the right to offset exists. Given the data in this illustration and assuming a 34% tax rate, the 1990 provision for income taxes would be determined as follows:

```
Income Tax Return:

    Income taxes payable..................$2,600 x 34% = $  884
                                                          =====
Financial Statements:

    1990 Balance Sheet:
                                                  Classification
                                          -----------------------
                                          Current    Noncurrent
                                          --------   ----------

    Deferred tax asset...........<$3,000> x 34% =               <$1,020>
    Deferred tax liability.......   700  x 34% =                   238
    Deferred tax liability.......  $100  x 34% =      $34
                                                    --------   --------
    Current deferred tax liability...................$34
                                                    =====
    Net noncurrent deferred tax asset........................<$  782>
                                                             =========
```

The net deferred tax asset would be classified as a noncurrent asset on the 1990 balance sheet because reversal is expeced in 1992 which is more than one year from the balance sheet date. The liability is considered current for the $100 reversal that is expected to occur within one year from the balance sheet date and is noncurrent for the $700 reversal taking place in more than one year from the balance sheet date.

```
    1990 Income Statement:

    Deferred tax expense or provision
        for 1990 ($<782> + 34).............................<$  748>
    Add: Income taxes payable per tax return.................   884
                                                            -------
    Income tax expense....................................... $  136
                                                             ======
```

If scheduling was not used, as in the case of the basic illustration of the deferred tax asset, and the NOL carryover provisions were not applied, the deductible amounts that could be recognized would be limited to the extent of future taxable amounts of $100, reversing in 1992 with the future deductible amounts. Assuming reversal during the same future accounting period, there would be an offset of the deferred tax liability, but the excess deductible amounts could not be recognized and a net deferred tax asset could not be recorded. Thus, the deferred tax provision for the year would be $238 (i.e., $700 x .34), and the income tax expense would be set equal to $1,122, which is the sum of the income taxes payable on the tax return, $884 and the deferred tax provision of $238.

THE ALTERNATIVE MINIMUM TAX (AMT)

The TRA of 1986 initiated a new, more restrictive version of the Alternative Minimum Tax (AMT), which for the first time considers the effects of accounting income. Under the 1986 AMT provisions, a corporation determines its regular tax liability based on existing tax law and by taking advantage of all available tax preferences, credits and book-tax differences discussed throughout this chapter. Next, the corporation would be required to determine its AMT. The AMT basically consists of recalculating taxable income by "giving back" some of these tax preferences and book-tax differences, i.e., the book income adjustment). This revised taxable income or "AMT income" (AMTI) is taxed at a rate of 20%. This is the AMT. The corporation is required to pay the greater of the regular tax or the AMT.

In 1990, the AMT provisions of the IRS Code were revised to include the computation of the Adjusted Current Earnings Adjustment (ACE) in lieu of the book income adjustment or the "Untaxed Accounting Profits Adjustment". The prior book income adjustment required an add-back to AMTI equal to 50% of all book tax differences, other than specific tax preferences such as tax-free interest. Unlike the adjustment to AMTI for untaxed accounting profits, the new ACE adjustment is not strictly based on financial statement income. Rather, ACE is intended to approach a measure of economic income by making a series of adjustments to book income. Under both the 1986 and the 1990 AMT provisions, the AMT applies to AMTI over $40,000. This is known as the AMT exemption. However, this $40,000 exemption is reduced by 25 cents for each dollar that AMT income exceeds $150,000. Thus, the $40,000 exemption is completely unavailable when the AMT income exceeds $310,000 (i.e., [$310,000 - 150,000] x $.25 = $40,000).

In the revised computation of the adjusted or AMT income (AMTI), the corporation is required to "give back" all of the specific tax preference items as defined by the IRS (see sample list below), and 75% of the excess of ACE over the preadjusted AMTI. This "75% add-back" is known as the ACE adjustment. Where, the preadjusted AMTI consists of AMT income before AMT NOLs and the ACE adjustment.

In determining AMTI, the regular NOL deduction must be replaced with the AMT NOL deduction. To calculate the AMT NOL deduction, the regular NOL must be adjusted in the same way that taxable income is adjusted in arriving at

AMTI, and the regular NOL must be reduced by adding back any tax preference items. The AMT NOL deduction cannot exceed 90% of AMTI before the NOL deduction.

It should be noted that unlike the 1986 book income adjustment, the new ACE adjustment could be positive or negative. Negative ACE adjustments can be offset against the sum of all prior years' positive ACE adjustments. However, if there are no prior positive ACE adjustments, or if these prior period positive ACE adjustments are not sufficient to offset the negative ACE adjustment, the excess negative ACE adjustment is lost and cannot be carried forward.

The specific tax preferences identified by the IRS include the most advantageous book-tax differences, such as

1. Excess tax depreciation. The excess tax depreciation is defined as the excess MACRS depreciation over an alternative depreciation measured by using 150% declining balance for personal property and 40-year straight-line for real property;

2. Tax exempt interest on certain municipal bonds (e.g., bonds used to finance mass transit or waste disposal plants);

3. The excess of percentage of completion income (books) over the completed contract income (tax) reported for construction projects;

4. Excess intangible drilling costs deducted on the tax return over the amounts capitalized for financial reporting purposes (book);

5. Percentage (tax or statutory) depletion in excess of cost.

The ACE adjustment includes numerous add-backs and deductions. For example the firm is allowed to deduct "ACE depreciation", but must add back the depreciation deducted for tax purposes. ACE depreciation is computed by using an acceptable tax method, using either the ACRS or MACRS tables, depending on when the asset was placed into service. Other ACE adjustment items include:

1. ADD   : Proceeds on officers' life insurance.

2. ADD   : All other tax exempt interest not included in AMTI (i.e., tax exempt interest not specifically identified as a tax prefence item).

3. ADD   : The increase in the cash surrender value of officers' life insurance.

4. ADD   : An increase in the LIFO Reserve (i.e., the excess of FIFO or Average Cost over LIFO).

5. DEDUCT: A decrease in the LIFO Reserve.

The last two items listed above are considered to be part of a class of adjustments known as "accounting method items". It should be noted that the above list of adjustments made in the ACE computation is not intended to be all inclusive. There are other ACE adjustment items involving tax issues that go beyond the scope of this book.

Foreign tax credits are available to the corporation to reduce the final AMT, but are limited to 90% of the minimum tax. Other incentive tax credits can be used (e.g., research and development tax credits), but only to the extent of 25% of the AMT. Unused tax credits can be carried back and forward without time limit.

Basic AMT Illustration

The following schedule presents a condensed tax return, an income statement and a summary of the book-tax differences for the Sullivan Group:

	Taxable Income	Pretax Accounting Income	Book-Tax Differences
Revenue...........	$4,000,000	$7,000,000	$3,000,000 Tax-free interest
Cost of sales.....	<1,000,000>	< 500,000>	500,000 Inventory unit cost composition
Depreciation......	<2,600,000>	<2,000,000>	600,000 Excess MACRS Depr.
Net income........	$ 400,000	$4,500,000	$4,100,000

Other Information:

- The ACE depreciation allowed, based on when the asset was placed into service, amounted to $2,100,000.

- The increase in the LIFO Reserve for the year was $300,000.

- $2,000,000 of the tax-free interest was earned on investments in mass trasnsit bonds.

- There are no NOL deductions available to the company.

Regular Tax

Taxable income.........$ 400,000
Tax rate (assumed).....   x 40%

Regular tax liability..$ 160,000
                      ===========

The AMT Computation

```
Regular taxable income...........$  400,000

Add:  100% of specific tax preferences
      -Tax-free interest on mass
       transit bonds............... 2,000,000
      -Excess tax (MACRS)
       depreciation................   600,000
                                    -----------
      AMTI before AMT NOLs and the
      ACE adjustment...................$3,000,000
                                    ===========
```

ACE Adjustment Computation and the Final AMT

```
Preadjustment AMTI (above).......$3,000,000

Add:  Depreciation deducted for AMTI... 2,000,000
Less: ACE Depreciation allowed.........<2,100,000>

      Add-Backs:

      -Increase in the LIFO Reserve....   300,000
      -Other tax-free interest......... 1,000,000
                                       -----------
      Adjusted Current Earnings (ACE)..$4,200,000
Less: Preadjustment AMTI (above).......<3,000,000>
                                       -----------
      Excess ACE over AMTI.............$1,200,000
      Inclusion rate...................   x 75%
                                       -----------
      The ACE Adjustment................$  900,000
                                       ===========

      Preadjustment AMTI (above).......$3,000,000
      ACE adjustment (above)...........   900,000
                                       -----------
      Adjusted AMTI....................$3,900,000

      AMT tax rate......................    x 20%
                                       -----------
      AMT.............................$  780,000
                                       ===========
```

The $40,000 exemption is not available to the firm because AMT income exceeds $310,000. There are also no foreign tax credits or incentive tax credits assumed to be available to reduce the AMT liability.

In this illustration, the Sullivan Group would be required to pay the AMT of $780,000 because it is greater than the regular tax liability of $160,000. However, any AMT in excess of an adjusted tax liability (to be discussed) results in a minimum tax credit that can be carried forward indefinitely until used to offset future regular corporate tax in excess of the AMT. The AMT credit cannot be carried back nor can it be used to offset any future AMT liability.

The AMT credit for any year is the difference between the AMT computed according to statute and the tax determined by considering only percentage depletion, tax-free interest and appreciated property charitable contributions. The resulting difference is called the *adjusted net minimum tax*. Under this definition of the adjusted net minimum tax, only the AMT relating to timing differences is permitted as a tax credit. Assuming that the AMT liability in the previous illustration, computed without timing differences, is $675,000, the AMT credit to be carried forward is equal to $105,000 (i.e., $780,000 - 675,000).

It should be noted that in applying the principles of deferred tax accounting and the provisions of SFAS 96, both the AMT and the AMT tax credits must be considered in the determination of income taxes payable, income tax expense, and the deferred tax provision in the current year and in satisfying the scheduling requirements. In addition, in meeting the scheduling requirements, the NOL carryback-carryforward rules must be applied.

OTHER ISSUES IN ACCOUNTING FOR TAXES

Disclosure Requirements

SFAS 96, paragraph 27, requires that the significant components of income tax expense reported on the income statement should be disclosed. This disclosure includes:

1. The "current income tax expense" or tax reduction;

2. The"deferred tax expense or benefit, exclusive of (5) below";

3. The amount of tax credits taken, if any;

4. Realization of NOL carryforward benefits;

5. Adjustments to the deferred tax account resulting from changes in the tax law or changes in the tax rate.

In addition, SFAS 96, paragraph 28, requires a reconciliation of the income tax expense from continuing operations as reported on the income statement with the amount of the tax expense that would have resulted from the application of the federal statutory tax rate to the pretax accounting income from continuing operations.

The last disclosure requirement is similar to the SEC's disclosure guidelines for income tax disclosures for public companies. Specifically, the SEC requires a reconciliation between the reported income tax expense or the effective tax rate and the amount that would result from applying the federal statutory rate to pretax accounting income. In addition, the SEC guidelines require the disclosure of the following:

1. The significant components of the deferred tax expense for the current year;

2. The current and the deferred components that comprise the total income tax expense. These components must also be classified by taxing jurisdictions: Federal, State, Local and Foreign.

A sample of the SEC's disclosure requirements for Mentor Corporation in its 1988 annual report is presented in Exhibit 4.3.

Tax Planning Strategies

The provisions of SFAS 96, paragraphs 17 through 19, allow a firm to assume the application of a qualified tax planning strategy in determining if and when temporary book-tax differences reverse. According to SFAS 96, paragraph 19, in order to be utilized, a tax planning strategy must meet both of the following criteria.

1. The strategy must be "prudent and feasible" and it must be under management's "discretion and control". "Management must have both the ability and the intent" to use the strategy to reduce taxes.

2. "The strategy cannot involve a significant cost to the enterprise."For example, a qualified tax planning strategy would not include making significant pension contributions to accelerate tax deductions where such a large disbursement would impair the liquidity position of the firm.

Qualified tax strategies include the acceleration of reversal of deferred tax liabilities to create taxable amounts or income, so as to utilize an NOL carryforward near expiration. For example, income on installment sales is generally not taxable until collected. The firm could plan to accelerate cash collection and the recognition of taxable income by a transfer (discount) of the installment sale receivable with recourse. This transaction would be accounted for as a sale for tax purposes and the taxable income recognized could be used to realize the NOL carryforward benefits. Assuming that this strategy meets both of the SFAS 96 criteria, the accountant could include this tax planning strategy in the scheduling and the determination of the deferred tax asset or liability.

ANALYTICAL ISSUES RELATED TO ACCOUNTING FOR INCOME TAXES

The analysis of the deferred tax account has traditionally been a subject of

EXHIBIT 4.3

Sample Disclosure: Mentor Corporation: Income Statement and Balance Sheet Presentation of Income Taxes and the SFAS 96 Footnote Disclosure

----

Consolidated Statements of Income

	Year Ended March 31.		
	1988	1987	1986
	(in thousands, except per share data)		
Net sales	$39,651	$32,808	$28,042
Costs and expenses:			
Cost of sales	15,096	13,668	13,307
Selling, general and administrative	14,556	11,298	8,941
Research and development	1,381	904	808
	31,033	25,000	23,140
Operating income	8,618	6,038	5,700
Interest income	1,499	305	200
Interest expense	(1,384)	(71)	(205)
Other income	369	740	—
Gain on sale of assets	1,012	—	—
Income before income taxes	10,114	7,012	5,731
Income taxes	3,716	3,664	2,500
Net income	$ 6,398	$ 4,248	$ 3,171
Net income per share	$ .57	$ .37	$ .20

Exhibit 4.3, continued

Consolidated Statements of Financial Position

	March 31	
	1988	*1987*
	(dollars in thousands)	
Assets		
Current assets:		
Cash and equivalents	$ 4,809	$ 918
Marketable securities	26,903	6,572
Accounts receivable, net of allowance for doubtful accounts of $131 in 1988 and $184 in 1987	7,098	6,144
Inventories	5,865	5,585
Other	391	448
Total current assets	45,066	19,007
Property and equipment:		
Land	1,662	1,580
Buildings	6,904	6,335
Equipment	9,145	8,456
	17,711	16,380
Less accumulated depreciation	4,838	3,085
	12,873	12,095
Other assets:		
Patents, licenses, trademarks and bond issuance costs, net of accumulated amortization of $1,724 in 1988 and $1,225 in 1987	4,274	3,005
Goodwill, net of accumulated amortization of $108 in 1988 and $75 in 1987	1,037	1,060
Other assets	2,161	—
	7,472	4,704
	$65,411	$37,126

	1988	*1987*
Liabilities and shareholders' equity		
Current liabilities:		
Accounts payable	$ 1,229	$ 1,241
Accrued compensation	721	883
Income taxes payable	(169)	407
Interest payable	1,259	—
Dividends payable	434	458
Accrued royalties	325	200
Other accrued liabilities	1,341	823
Current portion of long-term debt	41	41
Total current liabilities	5,181	4,173
Deferred income taxes	1,135	830
Long-term debt	27,231	574
Shareholders' equity:		
Common shares, $.10 par value:		
Authorized — 20,000,000 shares;		
Issued and outstanding — 10,861,414 shares in 1988; 11,462,414 shares in 1987	1,086	1,146
Capital in excess of par value	13,969	18,205
Retained earnings	16,809	12,198
	31,864	31,549
	$65,411	$37,126

Exhibit 4.3, continued

Note G Income Taxes

	Year Ended March 31,		
	1988	*1987* *(in thousands)*	*1986*
Income tax expense consists of:			
Current	$3,401	$3,020	$2,335
Deferred	315	44	225
	$3,716	$3,004	$2,500
Deferred income tax expense consists of:			
Excess of tax over book depreciation	$ 329	$ 301	$ 308
Installment sale for tax purposes	(194)	—	—
Financial statement expenses not currently deductible for tax	164	(160)	(122)
Other	16	(91)	30
	$ 315	$ 44	$ 225

The reconciliation of the federal statutory rate to the Company's effective rate is as follows:

	Year Ended March 31,		
	1988	*1987*	*1986*
Federal statutory rate	37.0%	46.0%	46.0%
Increase (decrease) resulting from:			
State tax, net of federal tax benefit	3.7	3.5	3.1
Capital gains rates	(.2)	(.6)	(.9)
Non-taxable interest and dividends	(3.1)	(1.5)	(1.0)
Research and development credit	(.8)	(.8)	(1.0)
Investment credit and other	.1	(.3)	(1.5)
	36.7%	46.3%	44.7%

Investment tax credit was $83,000 in 1986. In October 1987, the United States Congress enacted legislation which, among other things, repealed the investment tax credit, therefore, no investment tax credit was available in fiscal 1988 or 1987.

The Company has made tax payments of $3,820,000, $3,600,000 and $4,143,000 in the fiscal years 1988, 1987 and 1986, respectively.

On December 30, 1987, the Financial Accounting Standards Board issued Statement of Financial Accounting Standards No. 96, "Accounting for Income Taxes." The Company is required to adopt the new method of accounting for income taxes no later than fiscal 1990. The Company has not decided whether it will implement the Statement early or restate any periods. However, the adoption of Statement 96 is not expected to have an adverse impact on the Company's financial position.

---

great concern for the credit and financial analyst. Under Opinion 11, most analysts believed that the long-term deferred tax liability was not a true obligation of the firm. Because the emphasis of the previous tax accounting standards was on matching the tax expense with the revenue reported on the income statement, the valuation and the reversal of the temporary book-tax differences underlying the deferred tax liability was in doubt. In fact, many believed that reversal was so far out into the future that the present value of the obligation was zero. Similarly, the deferred tax asset was viewed as an economic resource with questionable value.

As noted throughout this chapter, a primary objective of SFAS 96 was to properly value the deferred tax liability and the asset. Under SFAS 96 the use of the liability method is required. The liability method values the deferred tax account at the tax rate expected to be in effect when the underlying book-tax temporary differences reverse. The use of scheduling severely restricts deferred tax asset recognition. If and when a deferred tax asset is recognized, there is reasonable assurance that the asset value will be realized in the future.

With the required use of the liability method and scheduling, the analyst may place more reliance on the valuation of the deferred tax liability and asset. In addition, the SFAS 96 classification of the deferred tax account based on expected reversal date also provides more reliable information regarding the current or long-term nature of the deferred tax account. For example, if the deferred tax liability is classified as current under SFAS 96, the analyst can be reasonably assured that there will be cash outflow for payment of the deferred taxes within twelve months from the balance sheet date.

Nonetheless, the implementation of SFAS 96 cannot prevent managerial actions taken that avoid or delay the effects of reversal. Expansion of the firm's capital expenditure base, switching depreciation methods for tax purposes, or changing any alternative accounting method can slow down or prevent reversal from taking place. As a result, the long-term deferred tax liability would continue to increase and again would not be considered a true obligation in the sense of requiring a future cash drain on the firm.

Proper use of the income tax disclosure could assist the analyst in assessing the potential reversals of book-tax temporary differences and the extent of the obligation to be paid in the short run. For example, in Exhibit 4.3, the footnote section entitled "Deferred income tax consists of:" contains the amount of deferred taxes generated by various temporary book-tax differences. This information could be used to determine the trend of a particular book-tax difference. Usually the most significant book-tax temporary difference is the excess tax depreciation. In Exhibit 4.3 there is an increasing trend in excess tax depreciation. This trend can be seen more clearly by dividing the deferred tax expense by the effective tax rate to determine the amount of the excess tax depreciation. In this case there would be a significant increase in 1988 which is determined as follows.

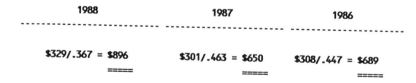

1988	1987	1986
$329/.367 = $896	$301/.463 = $650	$308/.447 = $689

The significant increase in tax depreciation was probably due to an increase in capital expenditures made in 1988. The expansion of plant and equipment would provide increased originating differences (i.e., future tax deductions), which should delay or more than offset the reversal of temporary book-tax differences and avoid any additional tax payments relating to the deferred tax account in the short term.

Finally, a review of the tax footnote may reveal information regarding the amount and expiration dates of NOL carryforward tax benefits. Realization of the NOL carryforward benefits will result in positive cash flows to the firm in the future and represents a valuable economic resource of the firm, even if it is not recorded as a receivable in the asset section of the balance sheet.

CASE 4.1. EMERY AIR FREIGHT: BASIC ANALYSIS OF DEFERRED INCOME
TAXES

Emery Air Freight markets its services under the names of Emery and Emery
Worldwide. It is the oldest overnight air courier and air cargo transportation system
in the United States. The Company maintains 168 offices, 56 of which are outside
the United States in 29 countries and territories. Agents act in the Company's
behalf in another 40 countries.

The Company uses its own ground and air transportation system that currently
includes almost 2,000 vehicles and more than 70 aircraft, with a total nighlty airlift
capacity in excess of two and a half million pounds.

Source: Emery Air Freight Corporation 1984 Annual Report. Copyright, 1985, by
Consolidated Freightways, Inc. Reprinted with permission.

REQUIRED: Study Emery's financial statements and the footnote information
relating to the Company's income taxes.

1. Verify the Company's reported effective tax rate for 1982-1984 found in
    Note 6--Income Taxes.

2. How much did the Company pay (in cash) for income taxes in 1984?

3. The Company's 1984 Statement of Changes in Financial Position (now the
    Statement of Cash Flows) indicates that the net deferred tax provision for
    the year is equal to $2,028,000. Using the liability section of the Company's
    Balance Sheet and the information provided in Note 2--Other Current
    Assets, determine the composition of the change in the net deferred tax
    provision for the year. Be certain to indicate the impact on the 1984 bal-
    ance of the deferred tax asset and the deferred tax liability.

4. Approximate the amount of depreciation and amortization the Company
    deducted for tax purposes.

5. Using the components of the deferred tax provision found in Note 6--
    Income Taxes, indicate what inferences can be made regarding the firm's
    future cash flows with respect to income taxes.

Emery Air Freight Corporation
CONSOLIDATED STATEMENT OF INCOME

	For the Years Ended December 31,		
	1984	1983	1982
	(amounts in thousands except per share amounts)		
Revenue:			
Air Cargo	**$800,533**	$677,270	$595,415
Other Services	**17,256**	13,392	12,064
	817,789	690,662	607,479
Operating Expenses:			
Air Cargo:			
Air transportation and sorting facility	**344,664**	281,095	254,347
Terminal and ground handling	**227,582**	202,382	185,397
Sales and marketing	**77,067**	70,966	58,527
Other operating, general and administrative	**89,526**	70,926	70,422
	738,839	625,369	568,693
Other Services	**14,655**	10,335	10,029
	753,494	635,704	578,722
Operating Income	**64,295**	54,958	28,757
Interest Expense	**8,578**	12,619	19,290
Other Income, net	**751**	3,173	4,611
Income before Income Taxes	**56,468**	45,512	14,078
Income Taxes	**24,583**	20,526	3,872
Net Income	**$ 31,885**	$ 24,986	$ 10,206
Weighted Average Common Shares Outstanding	**18,799**	17,178	15,724
Net Income Per Share	**$ 1.70**	$ 1.45	$ .65

See accompanying notes to consolidated financial statements.

Emery Air Freight Corporation
CONSOLIDATED BALANCE SHEET

Assets	December 31, 1984	1983
Current Assets:	(dollars in thousands)	
Cash and short-term investments, at cost which approximates market	$ 12,478	$ 4,831
Accounts receivable, less allowance of $3,488 in 1984 and $2,409 in 1983	111,538	97,345
Estimated income tax refunds receivable	18,377	16,700
Other current assets	33,470	13,771
Total Current Assets	175,863	132,647
Property and Equipment, at cost:		
Aircraft	85,061	88,854
Facilities held under capital leases	75,503	50,328
Equipment	48,058	37,529
Leasehold improvements	11,221	10,039
Land and buildings	9,996	8,220
	229,839	194,970
Accumulated depreciation and amortization	(64,360)	(49,975)
	165,479	144,995
Marketable Securities Held for Investment, at lower of cost or market	11,129	11,734
Restricted Construction Funds	16,732	23,195
Other Assets, net of amortization	10,307	10,233
Total Assets	$379,510	$322,804

See accompanying notes to consolidated financial statements.

Source: Emery Air Freight Corporation 1984 Annual Report. Copyright, 1985, by Consolidated Freightways, Inc. Reprinted with permission.

Liabilities and Stockholders' Equity	December 31, 1984	1983
Current Liabilities:	(dollars in thousands)	
Accounts payable and accrued expenses	**$ 86,214**	$ 68,074
Short-term debt	**—**	20,000
Accrued vacation and salaries	**7,617**	6,435
Obligations under capital leases	**604**	562
Income taxes payable	**11,668**	3,897
Total Current Liabilities	**106,103**	98,968
Long-Term Debt	**5,000**	30,000
Obligations under Capital Leases, less current portion	**72,380**	57,864
Deferred Income Taxes	**21,395**	17,496
Unearned Income and Other Non-Current Liabilities	**7,105**	—
Commitments and Contingent Liabilities (Notes 3 and 9)	**—**	—
Stockholders' Equity:		
Common Stock — $.20 par value:		
Authorized — 30,000,000 shares		
Issued — 19,045,847 shares in 1984 and 17,788,281 in 1983	**3,809**	3,558
Amount in excess of par value	**62,429**	36,483
Retained earnings	**103,336**	81,047
Net unrealized (loss) on marketable equity securities	**(595)**	(600)
Foreign currency translation adjustment	**(1,413)**	(744)
	167,566	119,744
Treasury stock, at cost, 2,103 shares in 1984 and 66,536 shares in 1983	**(39)**	(1,268)
Stockholders' Equity	**167,527**	118,476
Total Liabilities and Stockholders' Equity	**$379,510**	$322,804

Source: Emery Air Freight Corporation 1984 Annual Report. Copyright, 1985, by Consolidated Freightways, Inc. Reprinted with permission.

Emery Air Freight Corporation
CONSOLIDATED STATEMENT OF CHANGES IN FINANCIAL POSITION

	For the Years Ended December 31.		
	1984	1983	1982
Funds Were Provided from:	(dollars in thousands)		
Operations:			
Net income	**$ 31,885**	$ 24,986	$ 10,206
Non-cash charges to income:			
Depreciation and amortization	**23,901**	18,624	15,693
Deferred income taxes	**2,028**	5,892	5,249
Funds provided from operations	**57,814**	49,502	31,148
Working capital —'sources (uses):			
(Increase) decrease in current assets,			
including accounts receivable	**(33,698)**	(40,296)	10,444
Increase (decrease) in current liabilities,			
primarily accounts payable and accrued			
expenses	**26,970**	23,959	(8,988)
Net funds provided from operations	**51,086**	33,165	32,604
Financing transactions:			
Net proceeds from issuance of common stock	**22,980**	23,227	—
(Repayment of) proceeds from short-term debt	**(20,000)**	2,500	17,500
Repayment of long-term debt	**(25,000)**	(35,000)	(5,000)
Disposition of aircraft	**14,739**	—	—
Increase in unearned income and other non-current			
liabilities	**7,105**	—	—
Obligations under capital leases:			
Issuance of Daily Adjustable Special Facilities			
Refunding Revenue Bonds	**65,000**	—	—
Refinancing of Special Facilities Revenue Bonds	**(51,541)**	—	—
Other	**1,057**	(228)	(1,992)
Decrease (increase) in restricted construction funds	**6,463**	(2,811)	(664)
Stock plan transactions and other	**3,777**	3,596	1,241
Net funds from (used by) financing	**24,580**	(8,716)	11,085
	75,666	24,449	43,689
Funds Were Required for:			
Additions to property and equipment, net of retirements	**57,469**	15,165	31,217
Cash dividends paid on common stock	**9,431**	8,565	11,768
Increase in other assets, net of amortization, and			
marketable securities held for investment	**1,119**	589	8,541
	68,019	24,319	51,526
Net Increase (Decrease) in Cash and Short-Term			
Investments	**7,647**	130	(7,837)
Balance, beginning of period	**4,831**	4,701	12,538
Balance, end of period	**$ 12,478**	$ 4,831	$ 4,701

See accompanying notes to consolidated financial statements.

Source: Emery Air Freight Corporation 1984 Annual Report. Copyright, 1985, by Consolidated Freightways, Inc. Reprinted with permission.

Note 1 — Summary of Significant Accounting Policies:

Income taxes — The company provides deferred income taxes on all significant timing differences between financial statement pre-tax income and taxable income. The deferred tax on these differences pertains principally to depreciable plant and equipment. Investment tax credits, relating to purchases of equipment, are accounted for under the flow-through method. Investment tax credits, relating to leveraged leasing activities of the company's finance subsidiary, are deferred and amortized over the lives of the related leases.

Note 2 — Other Current Assets:

The components of other current assets were as follows:

	(amounts in thousands)	
	December 31,	
	1984	1983
Deposits on equipment	$21,240	$ 5,892
Deferred income taxes	4,575	2,704
Fuel, spare parts, and supplies	2,070	2,520
Other current assets	5,585	2,655
	$33,470	$13,771

Note 6 — Income Taxes:

The components of pre-tax income were as follows:

	(amounts in thousands)		
	Years Ended December 31,		
	1984	1983	1982
Domestic Operations	$39,120	$39,300	$14,966
International Operations	25,926	18,831	18,402
Interest Expense	(8,578)	(12,619)	(19,290)
	$56,468	$45,512	$14,078

The components of the provision for income taxes were as follows:

	(amounts in thousands)		
	Years Ended December 31,		
	1984	1983	1982
Current:			
Federal	$13,532	$ 9,778	$(5,009)
Foreign	6,081	2,912	2,730
State and local	2,942	1,944	902
	22,555	14,634	(1,377)
Deferred:			
Federal	2,028	5,892	5,249
	$24,583	$20,526	$ 3,872

The components of the deferred income tax provision were as follows:

	(amounts in thousands)		
	Years Ended December 31,		
	1984	1983	1982
Accelerated depreciation for tax purposes	$ 5,375	$ 6,335	$ 6,442
Deferred costs and credits	(3,865)	2,295	1,018
Utilization of tax credits	1,969	(3,341)	(2,487)
Other	(1,451)	603	276
	$ 2,028	$ 5,892	$ 5,249

Total income tax expense is less than the amount which would be provided by applying the statutory U.S. federal income tax rate to pre-tax income for the following reasons:

	1984	1983	1982
U.S. federal income tax statutory rate	46.0%	46.0%	46.0%
State income taxes, net of federal income tax benefit	2.7	2.3	3.4
Investment tax credits	(6.1)	(3.6)	(16.2)
ESOP credits	(.3)	(.4)	(7.7)
Other	1.2	.8	2.0
	43.5%	45.1%	27.5%

A significant amount of foreign source income is derived from the company's overseas branches and is subject to U.S. federal income taxes. Taxes paid by overseas branches to foreign countries are utilized as foreign tax credits against the U.S. federal income tax liability.

For U.S. federal income tax purposes, the company has $3.9 million of foreign tax credit carryforwards available to offset future years' U.S. federal income tax liabilities ($1.4 million expires in 1987, $2.3 million expires in 1988, and $.2 million expires in 1989). For financial reporting purposes, such amounts have been applied against deferred income taxes.

5

An Analysis of
Intercorporate Investments

LONG TERM INVESTMENTS IN EQUITY SECURITIES: AN INTRODUCTION

In accounting for intercorporate investments in equity securities, the accounting method used depends on the percentage of voting stock held by the investor company and its implied control over the investee company. Implied or economic control is inferred from the percentage ownership of voting stock, as well as from other information regarding the relationship between the investor and investee companies.

The following table summarizes the general percentage rules regarding the implied levels of control over the investee company and the related method to use in accounting for investments in equity securities.

```
===================================================================

General Guidelines:
------------------

Percent of Voting Stock Held----->Implied Control----->Accounting Method
---------------------------       -----------------    -----------------------

     1 - 19%                      No economic          Cost or lower of cost
                                  control              or market (LCM) (SFAS
                                                       12)
----------------------------------------------------------------------

     20 - 50%                     Economic             Equity method (APB
                                  control              Opinion No. 18)

----------------------------------------------------------------------

     50 - 100%                    Legal                Consolidation Accounting
                                  control              (APB Opinion Nos. 16 and
                                                       17 and SFAS 94)
===================================================================
```

It should be emphasized that these are only general guidelines. With the exception of a majority owned subsidiary, all information must be considered when determining the extent of economic control exercised by the investee company. In FASB Interpretation No. 35, "Criteria for Applying the Equity Method of Accounting for Investments in Common Stock", and APB Opinion No. 18, "The Equity Method of Accounting for Investments in Common Stock", several illustrations are provided which indicate the areas in which judgement is required in determining the appropriate accounting method to use. For example, if an investor corporation holds 25% of the voting stock of the investee corporation, but was rejected membership on the investee's board of directors, it may indicate that the investor does not exercise considerable economic control over the investee company. In this case, the equity method of accounting may not be appropriate. Conversely, if the investor corporation holds only 15% of the voting stock of the investee company, but has membership on the investee's board of directors, is a major supplier or customer of the investee company, or exchanges management with the investee, it may provide evidence that the investor has the ability to exercise economic control over the investee company and that the equity method should be used, regardless of the percentage of voting stock held. Thus, the use of the equity method is based on the ability of the investor to "control" the investee company. With less than a majority ownership, control must be determined by considering all factors and not by simply utilizing the general guidelines based on the percent of voting stock held. The details of applying the equity method of accounting are discussed in the following section.

THE EQUITY METHOD OF ACCOUNTING FOR INTERCORPORATE INVESTMENTS

When economic control is indicated by the level of voting stock held by the investor company and all other available information does not contradict the percentage guidelines, according to Opinion 18 the accountant would conclude that the investor corporation has the ability to exercise "significant influence and control" over the financing, operating and investing activities of the investee company. Due to this influence and control, the investment is to be accounted for as an "unconsolidated subsidiary".

In applying the requirements of Opinion 18, the investor's (i.e., "parents") long-term investment account on the balance sheet is carried at the percentage ownership multiplied by the common book value of the investee (i.e., "subsidiary") company. The carrying value of the investment is originally recorded at cost and is subsequently adjusted for the investor's share of changes in the common book value of the investee's stockholders' equity. The book value of the investee's common stockholders' equity is increased by net income and is reduced by a net loss and dividend distributions. In addition, new share issuances would increase the book value of the investee but the investor would acquire its proportion of the new issue by exercising its preemptive rights.

In other words, whatever affects the book value of the investee's common stockholders' equity must be reflected proportionately in the carrying value of the investor's investment account. It should be noted that in determining the percentage ownership for the evaluation of economic control and applying the general guidelines, both voting common and voting preferred, if any, are included in the percentage. However, for determination of the investor's recognition of its share of the change in the investee's stockholders' equity, only the percentage of the voting common stock is used.

In the recognition of the investor's share of investee net income or net loss, intercompany transactions are eliminated as if the investee company was consolidated. In addition, any dividends for cumulative preferred stock of the investee company must be eliminated from the net income or loss available for computing the investor's share.

The investor's share of investee net income or loss must be classified in a manner consistent with the investee's classification. Usually, the investor's share of investee earnings or losses are disclosed as a single amount (i.e., "a one line consolidation") in the income statement, except for the investor's share of extraordinary items and prior period adjustments which must be shown separately in the investor's income statement.

If the investor pays more than the book value of the investee company's net assets, the excess is "goodwill" and is usually recorded in a separate account entitled "excess cost over the net assets acquired". According to APB Opinion No. 17, "Intangible Assets", the excess cost over the underlying equity in the investee's net assets would be amortized by systematic charges against income, over a maximum of 40 years.

Due to the judgement that is occasionally involved in determining the appropriate accounting treatment for a long-term investment in common stock, it is interesting to compare the effects of the cost (or LCM) method and the equity method. The following table summarizes the main points of the previous discussion by listing the differences in accounting for an intercorporate investment under the cost and equity methods.

```
=====================================================================
Cost versus the Equity Method of Accounting for Intercorporate Investments
- - - - - - - - - - - - - - - - - - - - - - - - - - - - - - - - - - - - - - - -

      Cost Method (LCM)          |          Equity Method
- - - - - - - - - - - - - - - - - - - - - - - - - - - - - - - - - - - - - - - -
                                 |
1. The investment is originally recorded | 1. The investment is originally
   at cost and is carried at cost or LCM  |    recorded at cost, but is
   until sold or permanently written down |    adjusted to reflect changes in
   to market.                             |    the net assets of the investee
                                          |    company (see 2 and 3 below).
                                          |
- - - - - - - - - - - - - - - - - - - - - - - - - - - - - - - - - - - - - - - -
                                          |
2. Cash dividends are recorded as         | 2. Cash dividends are recorded as a
   investment or dividend income. An      |    return of investment and thereby
   exception can exist if the amount of   |    reduce the investment account.
   dividends received or accrued are in   |
   excess of the investor's cumulative    |
   share of investee net income. In this  |
   case, the cash dividend is recorded as |
```

Cost Method (LCM)	Equity Method
a return of investment and thereby reduces the investment account.	
3. Investor proportionate share of investee net income or net loss is not recognized.	3. The carrying value of the investment account is increased or decreased by the investor's proportionate share of investee net income or net loss, which is recognized in the investor's income statement.
4. Stock dividends only require a memo of the increased number of shares held and the reduced cost per share.	4. Same as under the cost method.
5. Goodwill is not recognized.	5. The excess of cost over the amount of the underlying equity in the net assets of the investee is recorded as goodwill and is amortized against income over a maximum period of 40 years.
6. The gain or loss on the disposal of the investment is computed as the difference between the net selling price and the cost of the investment.	6. The gain or loss on the disposal of the investment is computed as the difference between carrying of the investment (including any unamortized balance of goodwill) and the net selling price.

In the case of a "permanent and significant decline" in the market value of an investment, valued at either cost or equity, there must be a write-down to market. This write-down is accounted for as a realized loss, without the use of the allowance account as under LCM accouting, and subsequent recoveries are not permitted.

Finally, the valuation under the equity method is based on the book value of the investee company and therefore should not be considered the equivalent of the market value of the stock.

The following equation analysis illustrates the financial statement effects of the cost and equity methods of accounting. For simplicity, it is assumed that there is no goodwill on the acquisition and that there are no income tax provisions made for the equity income. The tax considerations under the equity method will be discussed in a subsequent section of this chapter.

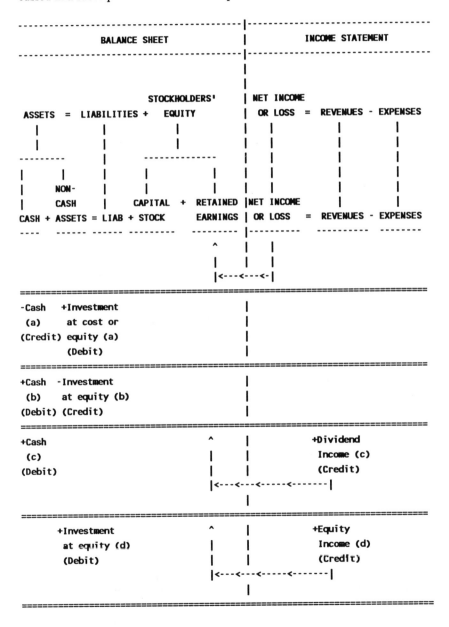

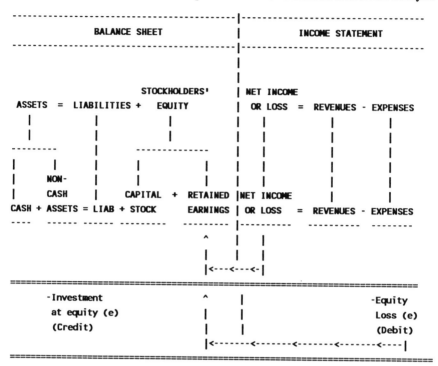

(a) Entry to record the initial investment under either the equity or cost
    method.
(b) Entry to record the receipt of a cash dividend under the equity method.
(c) Entry to record the receipt of a cash dividend under the cost method.
(d) Entry to record the investor's share of investee net income under the
    equity method. No entry is required under the cost method.
(e) Entry to record the investor's share of investee net loss under the equity
    method. No entry is required under the cost method.

The equation analysis illustrates an important difference between the cost and
equity methods. Under the cost method, there is a positive correlation between the
recognition of income from the investment and the underlying cash flows. When
cash dividends are received (or accrued), income is recognized on the investor's
income statement. One exception to income recognition for cash dividends under
the cost method is when dividends received (or accrued) are in excess of the investor's cumulative share of investee net income. In this case, the excess dividends
received (or accrued) would be reported as a reduction of the investment account
carried at cost (i.e., a return of investment). In other words, dividends received (or
accrued) out of investee accumulated earnings prior to the date of acquisition are
recorded as a return of investment under the cost method.   Conversely, when cash
dividends are received on an equity investment, the carrying value of the investment
is reduced and there is no recognition of income. However, when the proportionate
equity income or loss is recognized on the investor's income statement, there is no

cash flow. Therefore, the accountant will make adjustments to accrual basis net income for undistributed equity earnings on the statement of cash flows for an entity using the equity method.

Even with adjustments on the cash flow statement, the analyst should realize that, regardless of the accounting method used, the cash flows from the investment are identical for each accounting period and over the life of the investment. These points will be illustrated in the following example.

Illustration: Cost versus Equity Valuation

The example presented in Exhibit 5.1 provides a numerical illustration of accounting for an intercorporate investment accounted for under both the cost and equity methods. In reviewing this illustration, the reader should compare the effects on reported income and earnings per share with the cash flow consequences of each transaction. In addition, note that over the life of the investment cash flows are identical under both methods for each accounting period; cash flows are identical for both methods over the life of the investment; and the total accrual basis income from the investment measured under both methods will be identical over the life of the investment. Therefore, only the timing of accrual-based income recognition will vary from period to period when comparing the cost and equity methods of accounting.

Disclosures Under the Equity Method

According to Opinion 18, investments accounted for under the equity method should include the following disclosures:

1. The name of the investment and the percentage of voting stock held.

2. The investor's accounting policies used in implementing the reporting requirements for the equity investment (e.g., if the investee's financial reporting period does not coincide with the investor's, the investor should use the most recent available financial statements of the investee, and the time lag should be consistent from period to period).

3. The difference between the carrying value of the investment and the underlying net assets of the investee company (i.e., goodwill). The amortization policy with respect to this differential must be disclosed.

4. If significant, the investor must disclose the assets, liabilities and the results of operations of an equity investment in a footnote or in a separate statement. This disclosure typically takes the form of condensed financial statements of the investee company or aggregate financial statements for all investee company investments carried under the equity method.

5. If significant, the impact on the investor of any convertible securities of the

EXHIBIT 5.1

Illustration: Cost versus the Equity Method of Accounting

Assume an investor acquires a 30% share of the Investee Company on January 1, 1988, paying book value. Therefore, there is no goodwill to record and subsequently amortize.

	12/31/88 Investee Net Income = $200,000 No Dividends	12/31/89 Investee Net Loss = $100,000 No Dividends	12/31/90 Investee Breakeven Dividends = $50,000
1/1/88 Acquisition			

Investee Net Assets:

Capital				
Stock.......$100,000	$100,000	$100,000	$100,000
R/E......... 300,000	500,000	400,000	350,000
Net Assets..$400,000	$600,000	$500,000	$450,000

Investor Valuation at Equity: Assumes that 30% results in economic control.

Balance Sheet:
Investment

at 30%......$120,000	$180,000	$150,000	$135,000

Income Statement Effect:

N/A	$60,000 Income = $200,000 x 30%.	<$30,000> Loss = <$100,000> x 30%.	-0-

Cash Flow Effect:

<$120,000>	-0-	-0-	$ 15,000

246

Investor Valuation at Cost: Assumes that 30% does not result in economic control.

1/1/88 Acquisition	12/31/88 Investee Net Income = $200,000 No Dividends	12/31/89 Investee Net Loss = $100,000 No Dividends	12/31/90 Investee Breakeven Dividends = $50,000
Balance Sheet: Investment at 30%......$120,000	$120,000	$120,000	$120,000
	========	========	========
Income Statement Effect: N/A	-0-	-0-	$ 15,000
	========	========	========
Cash Flow Effect: <$120,000>	-0-	-0-	$ 15,000
	========	========	========

Assume that on January 1, 1991, the investor sells the entire investment for $250,000. The gain or loss on disposal under the two valuation methods is presented below.

	At Equity	At Cost
Selling price.............	$ 250,000	$ 250,000
Less: Carrying value............	<135,000>	<120,000>
Gain on sale..............	$ 115,000	$ 130,000
	=========	=========
Cash flow.................	$ 250,000	$ 250,000
	=========	=========

The following table summarizes the income recognized over the life of the investment.

	At Equity	At Cost
Investee income, 1988.....	$ 60,000	$ -0-
Investee loss, 1989.......	<30,000>	-0-
Dividend income, 1990.....	-0-	15,000
Gain on sale, 1991........	115,000	130,000
Total income on investment................	$145,000	= $145,000
	=======	========

---

investee company.

6. An explanation is required if the equity method is not used for an investment of 20% or more, or if the equity method is used for an investment of less than 20%. The name of the investee companies for these situations must also be disclosed.

Financial statement presentation of the investment account on the balance sheet, equity earnings on the income statement and the footnote disclosures for the equity investments of Xerox Corporation are presented in Exhibit 5.2.

Special Considerations Under the Equity Method

Provision for Income Taxes. In theory, using the equity method for financial reporting and the cost method for income tax returns results in a temporary book-tax difference. Because subsidiary earnings are not taxable to the parent until distributed as dividends, the undistributed equity earnings represent a temporary difference, which reverses when the earnings are ultimately remitted by the subsidiary to the parent company. According to APB Opinion No. 23, "Accounting for Income Taxes: Special Areas", and maintained by SFAS 96, a tax provision should be made for the undistributed earnings of a subsidiary, either consolidated or carried at equity. The tax provision should be based on the assumption that the undistributed earnings will be remitted to the parent or investor company in the current period.

In practice, however, a tax provision is usually not provided for undistributed equity earnings. Opinion 23 provided for "indefinite reversal exceptions" for which deferred taxes do not have to be provided. The indefinite reversal exceptions were also maintained by SFAS 96. Specifically, deferred income taxes do not have to be provided for temporary book-tax differences subject to indefinite reversal, if certain criteria are met. The most common types of temporary differences meeting these criteria are the undistributed equity earnings of subsidiaries and corporate joint ventures. Under the indefinite reversal exceptions, deferred taxes do not have to be provided for undistributed equity earnings if the company can provide evidence that it plans to permanently reinvest these undistributed earnings or that they will be distributed to the parent in a tax free liquidation. Given this flexibility, the decision to provide income taxes for undistributed earnings may be left to the discretion of management. Nonetheless, SFAS 96, paragraph 25, has significantly expanded the disclosure requirements about the indefinite reversal exceptions.

The expanded disclosures for amounts subject to indefinite reversal include the amount of undistributed earnings for which no income taxes have been provided, the cumulative amount of the temporary differences, the unrecognized deferred tax liability for each indefinite reversal exception, and the types of events that may result in these items becoming taxable.

Theoretically, the fact that deferred income taxes are not provided on the temporary book-tax differences relating to undistributed equity earnings would imply that "partial income tax allocation" was used. However, the impact of not providing income taxes on these items is usually included as a permanent difference in the reconciliation of the federal statutory income tax rate with the firm's effective

EXHIBIT 5.2

Sample Disclosure: Xerox Corporation: Balance Sheets, Statements of Income and Footnotes Relating to Investments Carried at Equity

---

Consolidated Balance Sheets

Xerox Corporation

Assets (In millions)	December 31	1985	1984
Current Assets			
Cash and bank time deposits		$ 221.5	$ 168.0
Marketable securities, at the lower of cost or market		45.1	58.9
Trade receivables (less allowance for doubtful receivables: 1985-$62.7; 1984-$84.6)		1,257.4	1,337.7
Accrued revenues		616.7	614.5
Inventories		1,469.8	1,300.0
Other current assets		290.0	260.1
Total current assets		3,900.5	3,739.2
Trade Receivables Due after One Year		209.5	267.4
Rental Equipment and Related Inventories, net		1,237.1	1,519.5
Land, Buildings and Equipment, net		1,422.6	1,391.8
Investment in Xerox Financial Services, Inc., at equity		2,121.3	2,175.1
Other Investments, at equity		478.2	252.9
Deferred Income Taxes		176.4	—
Other Assets		271.1	191.2
Total Assets		$9,816.7	$9,537.1

Liabilities and Shareholders' Equity

		1985	1984
Current Liabilities			
Notes payable and current portion of long-term debt		$ 402.9	$ 654.7
Accounts payable		390.3	310.5
Salaries, profit sharing and other accruals		911.9	916.9
Income taxes		129.5	136.1
Unearned income		205.4	211.7
Other current liabilities		175.3	221.2
Total current liabilities		2,215.3	2,451.1
Long-Term Debt		1,582.6	1,614.3
Due to Xerox Financial Services, Inc.		256.1	78.0
Other Noncurrent Liabilities		355.4	260.8
Deferred Income Taxes and Investment Tax Credits		74.0	149.0
Outside Shareholders' Interests in Equity of Subsidiaries		505.1	440.9
$5.45 Cumulative Preferred Stock		442.0	442.0
Common and Class B Shareholders' Equity			
Common and Class B stock and additional paid-in capital		892.7	871.0
Retained earnings		3,897.9	3,759.4
Net unrealized appreciation of equity investments		78.3	17.3
Cumulative translation adjustments		(476.4)	(536.8)
Class B stock receivables and deferrals		(6.3)	(9.9)
Total common and Class B shareholders' equity		4,386.2	4,101.0
Total Liabilities and Shareholders' Equity		$9,816.7	$9,537.1

The accompanying notes are an integral part of the consolidated financial statements.

Exhibit 5.2, continued

Consolidated Statements of Income

Xerox Corporation

(In millions, except per share data) Year Ended December 31	1985	1984	1983
Income			
Sales	$4,372.3	$3,935.9	$3,391.9
Rentals	2,595.1	2,986.8	3,286.9
Service	1,764.7	1,504.6	1,267.2
Equity in income from continuing operations of unconsolidated companies			
Xerox Financial Services, Inc.	76.1	73.5	196.8
Other	40.4	29.1	26.5
Other income	105.9	116.0	116.0
Total	8,954.5	8,645.9	8,285.3
Costs and Other Deductions			
Cost of sales	2,126.4	2,003.2	1,744.1
Cost of rentals	1,458.7	1,547.9	1,627.0
Cost of service	871.5	707.7	589.7
Research and development expenses	603.1	561.4	535.6
Selling, administrative and general expenses	3,019.5	2,986.5	2,849.1
Interest expense	230.0	260.5	189.9
Other, net	36.7	12.5	75.0
Income taxes	164.9	144.0	143.6
Outside shareholders' interests	63.2	70.4	64.0
Total	8,574.0	8,294.1	7,818.0
Income from Continuing Operations	380.5	351.8	467.3
Discontinued Operations	94.8	(61.3)	(.9)
Net Income	$ 475.3	$ 290.5	$ 456.4
Income (Loss) per Common Share			
Continuing operations	$3.46	$3.17	$4.43
Discontinued operations	.98	(.64)	(.01)
Net Income per Common Share	$4.44	$2.53	$4.42
Average Common Shares Outstanding	96.2	95.7	94.9
Dividends on Preferred Stock	$48.2	$48.2	$46.8

The accompanying notes are an integral part of the consolidated financial statements.

Exhibit 5.2, continued

Foreign Currency Translation

An analysis of the changes in cumulative translation adjustments for each of the years in the three-year period ended December 31, 1985 follows:

(In millions)	1985	1984	1983
Cumulative translation adjustments at beginning of year	$(536.8)	$(402.0)	$(335.0)
Translation adjustments and intercompany foreign currency transactions	108.6	(209.0)	(103.2)
Outside shareholders' interests	(48.2)	74.2	36.2
Cumulative translation adjustments at end of year	$(476.4)	$(536.8)	$(402.0)

Net aggregate foreign currency exchange losses of $34.5 million, $20.2 million and $11.0 million in 1985, 1984 and 1983, respectively, are included in other, net in the consolidated statements of income.

Working Capital

The increase (decrease) in other working capital included in the consolidated statements of changes in financial position consists of:

(In millions)	1985	1984	1983
Other current assets	$118.5	$ 3.0	$ (75.8)
Accounts payable	(93.6)	(26.1)	(28.0)
Salaries, profit sharing and other accruals	(26.0)	34.3	(9.7)
Income taxes	5.2	48.3	(5.8)
Unearned income	6.3	(43.5)	(43.8)
Other current liabilities	32.8	(104.3)	(53.5)
Increase (decrease) in other working capital	$ 43.2	$ (88.3)	$(216.6)

Inventories

Inventories are carried at the lower of average cost or market and consist of:

(In millions)	1985	1984
Finished products	$1,092.8	$ 970.8
Work in process	146.2	124.4
Raw materials and supplies	230.8	204.8
Total inventories	$1,469.8	$1,300.0

Rental Equipment and Related Inventories

The cost of rental equipment and related inventories and accumulated depreciation follow:

(In millions)	1985	1984
Rental equipment and related inventories	$3,401.5	$3,798.5
Less accumulated depreciation	2,164.4	2,279.0
Rental equipment and related inventories, net	$1,237.1	$1,519.5

Rental equipment is depreciated over estimated useful lives, generally two to seven years.

Land, Buildings and Equipment

The cost of land, buildings and equipment and related accumulated depreciation follow:

(In millions)	Estimated Useful Lives (years)	1985	1984
Land		$ 65.9	$ 61.7
Buildings and building equipment	20 to 50	593.5	598.4
Leasehold improvements	Term of lease	221.4	208.3
Plant machinery	4 to 12	947.6	876.4
Office furniture and equipment	3 to 10	867.5	741.8
Other	3 to 20	129.2	198.3
Construction in progress		104.8	93.7
Total		2,929.9	2,778.6
Less accumulated depreciation		1,507.3	1,386.8
Land, buildings and equipment, net		$1,422.6	$1,391.8

The cost of assets under capital leases included above, principally buildings and office furniture and equipment, amounted to $113.3 million and $128.9 million at December 31, 1985 and 1984, respectively; related accumulated depreciation amounted to $54.9 million and $56.3 million at December 31, 1985 and 1984, respectively.

In December 1985 the Company transferred title to its International Center for Training and Management Development (XICTMD) in Leesburg, Virginia to certain of C&F's insurance subsidiaries for the purpose of increasing their statutory capital. Concurrent with this transfer, Xerox leased back XICTMD for a period of 25 years. In addition, Xerox will manage the facility and pay all operating expenses. Accordingly, the related net book value of XICTMD, approximately $30 million, continues to be included in land, buildings and equipment, net. The appraised fair market value of the property was approximately $165 million at the date of transfer. Neither the Company nor C&F recognized any gain or asset revaluation for financial reporting purposes.

Investment in Xerox Financial Services, Inc., at equity

During 1985, the Company established a new subsidiary—Xerox Financial Services, Inc. (XFSI), a holding company, and transferred to XFSI its investments in its wholly-owned domestic financial services subsidiaries, Crum and Forster, Inc. (C&F), Xerox Credit Corporation (XCC) and Van Kampen Merritt Inc. (VKM). The Company's direct and indirect investments in its XFSI companies are accounted for by the equity method and consist of the following at December 31, 1985 and 1984:

(In millions)	1985	1984
Crum and Forster, Inc.	$1,551.0	$1,666.7
Xerox Credit Corporation	385.9	337.8
Van Kampen Merritt Inc.	186.2	170.6
Xerox Financial Services, Inc.	(1.8)	—
Total	$2,121.3	$2,175.1

251

Exhibit 5.2, continued

Differences between these amounts and the underlying net assets as shown in the consolidated financial statements of the individual subsidiaries are caused by certain capital transactions directly between XFSI and the other financial services subsidiaries.

The income (loss) of the XFSI companies included in Equity in Income from Continuing Operations of Unconsolidated Companies in the Company's consolidated statements of income, for the years ended December 31, 1985, 1984 and 1983 follows:

(In millions)	1985	1984	1983
Crum and Forster, Inc.	$(15.7)	$(4.7)	$144.8
Xerox Credit Corporation	68.1	57.7	52.0
Van Kampen Merritt Inc.	25.6	20.5	—
Xerox Financial Services, Inc.	(1.9)	—	—
Total	$ 76.1	$73.5	$196.8

The following consolidated financial data of XFSI have been summarized from the audited financial statements of the individual subsidiaries. As more fully discussed under Discontinued Operations, during 1985 the Company announced plans to discontinue the operations of the Industrial Indemnity Financial Corporation unit (IIFC) of C&F and, accordingly, the data for 1984 and 1983 have been restated to exclude IIFC's financial position and results of operations from the captions shown. Insurance premiums earned and other revenues of IIFC were $30.4 million for the nine-month period ended September 30, 1985, $28.0 million in 1984 and $16.5 million in 1983.

(In millions)	1985	1984	1983
Summary of Operations			
Income			
Insurance premiums earned	$2,168.9	$2,073.7	$1,812.5
Investment and other income	455.7	402.2	352.9
Finance and investment banking income	379.7	317.6	213.5
Total income	3,004.3	2,793.5	2,378.9
Losses and expenses			
Losses and loss expenses	2,035.2	1,861.3	1,401.2
L.W. Biegler special charge for losses and loss expenses	125.0	—	—
Other insurance operating expenses	673.4	729.8	597.4
Interest expense	171.4	151.7	137.0
Administrative and general expenses	196.8	147.0	79.5
Total losses and expenses	3,201.8	2,889.8	2,215.1
Operating income (loss) from continuing operations before income taxes	(197.5)	(96.3)	163.8
Income (taxes) benefits	177.2	129.8	(2.9)
Operating income (loss)	(20.3)	33.5	160.9
Realized capital gains of C&F, net of income taxes	96.4	40.0	35.9
Income from continuing operations	76.1	73.5	196.8
Discontinued operations	(111.3)	(5.8)	.3
Net income (loss)	$ (35.2)	$ 67.7	$ 197.1

(In millions)	1985	1984
Balance Sheets		
Assets		
Investments and cash	$4,429.4	$3,720.5
Finance receivables, net	1,985.7	1,753.2
Premiums and other receivables	1,208.0	916.5
Due from Xerox Corporation, net	302.9	232.8
Other assets	537.4	352.7
Excess of cost over fair value of net assets acquired	1,004.1	1,033.9
Total assets	$9,467.5	$8,009.6
Liabilities and Shareholder's Equity		
Unearned premiums and unpaid losses and loss expenses	$4,223.2	$3,458.3
Notes payable	1,382.4	1,231.4
Accounts payable and accrued liabilities	1,170.1	812.8
Net liabilities of discontinued IIFC operations	212.2	52.3
Deferred income taxes	358.3	279.7
Shareholder's equity	2,121.3	2,175.1
Total liabilities and shareholder's equity	$9,467.5	$8,009.6

During 1985 and 1984 the XFSI subsidiaries paid an aggregate of $80 million and $35 million, respectively, in dividends to the Company.

C&F, an insurance holding company, was acquired by the Company in a merger which became effective as of January 1, 1983. The purchase was paid for in cash or at the option of C&F's former shareholders, with a combination of common and preferred stock. The merger was accounted for as a purchase. The total purchase price of $1,615.9 million exceeded the fair net assets of C&F by approximately $943 million and this excess has been recorded on C&F's balance sheet.

C&F writes, through its subsidiaries, property-casualty insurance throughout the United States and Canada. C&F's insurance subsidiaries are restricted by insurance laws as to the amount of dividends they may pay without the approval of regulatory authorities. There are additional restrictions with regard to the amount of loans and advances that these subsidiaries may make to C&F. These restrictions indirectly limit the payment of dividends and the making of loans and advances by C&F, through XFSI, to the Company. The amount of restricted net assets of C&F's insurance subsidiaries at December 31, 1985 approximated $1.2 billion.

In September 1985, C&F incurred a one time pre-tax charge of $125 million in connection with reserve strengthening at its L.W. Biegler unit. This charge reduced the Company's after-tax earnings by $67.5 million or $.70 per share.

Effective May 31, 1985, C&F terminated its defined benefit pension plan (the "Plan"). Participants in the Plan became fully vested upon its termination for benefits accumulated through December 31, 1985. The Trustee of the Plan purchased annuity contracts which provide for the payment of the accumulated benefits to all participants. The excess of Plan assets over accumulated benefits of approximately $99.2 million will be refunded to C&F. The excess Plan assets and balance sheet accruals resulted in a termination gain of approximately $108.2 million. The termination gain will be amortized to income over a ten-year period beginning in 1985. Such amortization increased the Company's 1985 net income by $5.4 million or $.06 per share. A new defined benefit pension plan was established to be effective January 1, 1986.

Exhibit 5.2, continued

During 1985 the Company made a $200 million interest bearing cash advance to XFSI. XFSI used such proceeds to make a capital contribution to C&F which replenished the capital that had been depleted by the L.W. Biegler and IIFC charges.

C&F's portfolio of equity investments is carried at fair market value. The net unrealized appreciation on this portfolio, less applicable income taxes, was added to the Company's investment in C&F and to common and Class B shareholders' equity.

XCC is engaged principally in financing accounts receivable arising out of equipment sales by the Company and is also engaged in the business of financing leases for third parties. Receivables were sold by the Company to XCC during the years ended December 31, 1985, 1984 and 1983 for $699.3 million, $709.6 million and $591.9 million, respectively.

The operating agreement between the Company and XCC specifies that XCC shall retain an allowance for losses on receivables purchased from the Company at an amount which is intended to protect against future losses on the portfolio. The amount of the allowance is determined principally on the basis of past collection experience and the Company will fund any additional allowance required.

In addition, the terms of a support agreement with XCC provide that the Company will make income maintenance payments, to the extent necessary, so that XCC's earnings, before fixed charges, income taxes and extraordinary items, shall not be less than one and one-quarter times XCC's fixed charges. No income maintenance payments have been required. The support agreement also requires that the Company retain 100% ownership of XCC's voting capital stock.

VKM, an investment banking firm which specializes in packaging insured long-term tax exempt municipal unit investment trusts and in organizing and managing mutual funds, was acquired by the company in an acquisition which was effective as of January 1, 1984. The purchase price was $150 million and consisted of a combination of cash and thirty-year notes. The purchase agreement also provides for an additional contingent payment of $35 million based on VKM's cumulative earnings through 1986. The acquisition was accounted for as a purchase. The purchase price exceeded the fair value of the net assets of VKM by approximately $99 million at the date of the acquisition and this excess has been recorded on VKM's balance sheet.

The amounts due from Xerox Corporation primarily relate to C&F's tax benefits that are included or expected to be included in the Company's consolidated U.S. tax return, net of the Company's $200 million advance to XFSI.

Other Investments, at equity

Other investments, at equity consist of the following at December 31, 1985 and 1984:

(In millions)	1985	1984
Fuji Xerox Co., Ltd.	$264.5	$206.9
Xerox Canada Finance Inc.	139.2	—
Rank Xerox Finance Companies	28.5	1.8
Xerox Real Estate Companies	21.4	22.4
Other investments	24.6	21.8
Total	$478.2	$252.9

Rank Xerox Limited (RXL) owns 50% of the outstanding stock of Fuji Xerox Co., Ltd. (Fuji Xerox), a corporate joint venture. Fuji Xerox is located in the Far East and operates principally in the reprographics business.

Xerox Canada Finance Inc. (XCFI) was incorporated in December, 1984 and is wholly owned by the Company's Canadian subsidiary, Xerox Canada Inc. (XCI). XCFI is engaged principally in financing accounts receivable arising out of equipment sales by XCI and is also engaged in the business of financing leases for third parties. On January 1, 1985, XCI transferred substantially all of its investment in sales-type leases and notes receivable relating to service contracts to XCFI. The amount of such transfer, net of related deferred income taxes, was $181.8 million of which $148.3 million was contributed to XCFI's capital. Trade receivables amounting to $242.5 million also were sold to XCFI from XCI during 1985.

As of December 31, 1985 the Company, through RXL, organized eight international credit companies. These companies are referred to as the Rank Xerox Finance Companies (RXFIN). The purpose of RXFIN is to finance the Rank Xerox Companies' sales of Xerox equipment in a manner similar to the financing activities of XCC and XCFI. Sales-type leases, net of related deferred taxes, and trade receivables transferred by RXL to RXFIN were $38.6 million in 1985.

The Company has sold certain land at fair market value to its domestic real estate subsidiary, Xerox Realty Corporation (XRC). All gains on such land sales are deferred and will be included in consolidated income only as the land is sold to non-affiliated parties.

Other investments carried at equity primarily consist of the Company's investment in Delphax Systems, a manufacturer of non-impact printers.

The condensed financial data set forth below have been summarized from the audited financial statements of Fuji Xerox for each of the years ended October 20, 1985, 1984 and 1983 and as of October 20, 1985 and 1984, combined with the financial statements of other investments carried at equity for their respective fiscal years.

(In millions)	1985	1984	1983
Summary of Operations			
Total operating revenues	$1,596.9	$1,342.6	$1,117.1
Costs and expenses	1,433.0	1,194.4	992.9
Income before income taxes	163.9	148.2	124.2
Income taxes	93.9	87.9	69.6
Net income	$ 70.0	$ 60.3	$ 54.6

(In millions)	1985	1984
Balance Sheets		
Assets		
Current assets	$1,042.4	$ 672.4
Rental equipment and other assets	1,222.2	568.7
Total assets	$2,264.6	$1,241.1
Liabilities and Shareholders' Equity		
Current liabilities	$ 930.9	$ 608.5
Advances from Xerox Corporation	200.8	6.1
Long-term debt	150.6	46.4
Other noncurrent liabilities	234.6	146.3
Shareholders' equity	747.7	433.8
Total liabilities and shareholders' equity	$2,264.6	$1,241.1

Source: Xerox Corporation 1985 Annual Report. Copyright, 1986, by the Xerox Corporation. Reprinted with permission.

tax rate. As noted earlier, this reconciliation is included within the income tax disclosures required under SFAS 96.

Changing Methods. With changing ownership of the voting stock of the investee company, the investor will alter the extent of its economic control over the operating, financing, and investing activities of the subsidiary company. Therefore, the investor can gain economic control by a piecemeal acquisition of the voting shares of the investee or the investor can relinquish control through disposal of part of its equity investment.

At the time an existing investment qualifies for the use of the equity method, the investor must adopt the equity method by retroactive application. The retroactive adjustment involves applying the equity method in the current and all prior periods for which the investment was held. The carrying value of the investment must be increased for all current and prior net income reported by the subsidiary and reduced for all prior dividend distributions and net losses of the investee. The current year's equity income or loss must be reported on the investor's income statement. Finally, retained earnings must be adjusted for the net effect of all prior years' equity earnings, losses and dividends.

If an existing investment no longer qualifies for use of the equity method, the application of the equity method must be discontinued. At the date of discontinuance of the equity method, the equity-based carrying value of the investment becomes its "cost". The new "cost" is to be carried at cost or LCM and therefore all future dividend distributions are generally accounted for as dividend income.

Negative Carrying Value Under the Equity Method. According to Opinion 18, if there are excessive losses on an equity investment, the basis of the investment is generally not reduced below zero. At this point, the use of the equity method is usually suspended unless the investor's loss is not limited to the original investment. For example, if the investor has guaranteed the debt of the investee or is committed to provide continued financial support, losses can exceed the cost of the original investment. Under these circumstances, continued losses can be recognized and a negative carrying value of the investment is permissible. The investor may also continue the equity method and recognize additional losses (i.e., carry a negative equity investment), if future profitable operations of the investee are reasonably assured.

In those cases where the investor suspends the use of the equity method, the investor should resume the use of the equity method only when the investee company subsequently reports net income and that income exceeds the investor's share of any cumulative net losses not recognized during the period the cost method was used.

Majority-Owned Nonhomogeneous Subsidiaries. The financial statement and footnote disclosures for the equity method presented in Exhibit 5.2 includes 100% (majority) owned, unconsolidated subsidiary companies accounted for by the equity method.

Under APB Opinion No. 16, "Business Combinations" (to be discussed), certain subsidiaries, even if 100% owned, were not consolidated. The reason for not consolidating certain majority-owned subsidiaries was that these firms were operating in industries that were not compatible with the operations of the parent. These unconsolidated subsidiaries were primarily captive finance companies or other firms operating in the financial services industry. These firms include credit corporations, insurance companies, investment banks and commercial banks. The operations of a firm in the financial services industry were not considered to be compatible with an industrial or a manufacturing business.

When the majority-owned, nonhomogeneous subsidiaries are excluded from the consolidated financial statements, financial and credit analysts must compute financial ratios and other statistics from the consolidated financial statements and are therefore unable to utilize all available information regarding the combined entity. The only way in which the analyst could include financial information relating to the finance subsidiaries would be to incorporate the equity method footnote disclosures into the analysis. If the footnote information is not used, significant amounts of long-term debt are kept "off-balance sheet".

As a result of this off-balance sheet financing and other problems, the FASB amended Opinion 16 in 1987 by issuing FASB Statement No. 94, "Consolidation of All Majority-Owned Subsidiaries", which required the consolidation of all majority-owned subsidiaries, regardless of the nature of their business operations.

The provisions of SFAS 94 became effective in 1988. Because SFAS 94 has only been in effect for a short period of time, data relating to the impact of this standard are not readily available. However, some proforma statistics have been prepared. Exhibit 5.3 provides the debt/equity ratios for 15 transportation equipment manufacturers computed using the financial statements as reported and recomputed on a proforma basis as if SFAS 94 was applied. For some firms, the consolidation of the finance subsidiaries significantly increases their debt/equity ratios.

Although implementation of the provisions of SFAS 94 will provide the analyst with more useful information, a different problem is created. With the implementation of SFAS 94, the restated financial information will not be comparable with prior years. Not only will the total amount of long-term debt and other accounts be higher with the addition of the balances from the finance subsidiaries, new financial statement line items will be added to the balance sheet, income statement and the statement of cash flows. These new line items may represent the effect of transactions and specialized accounting techniques peculiar to firms operating in the financial services and other industries. As a result the accountant and the analyst may no longer be able to "specialize" in certain industries. Due to the conglomerate nature of most corporations, the accountant and the analyst may now be forced to deal with many unfamiliar transactions and accounting practices specific to a particular industry, which were avoided in the past when the finance subsidiaries were kept "off-balance sheet". These problems are illustrated in Exhibit 5.4. It presents the transition period financial statements of General Electric Company and Consolidated Subsidiaries (as required under SFAS 94), General Electric Company (GE) (as would have been reported under prior standards), and General Electric Financial Services (GEFS) (which was previously unconsolidated and summarized in the aggregate within the equity basis footnote). Case 5.1 at the end of this chapter illustrates the proforma consolidation of the finance subsidiaries of the Xerox Corporation which were presented in Exhibit 5.2.

EXHIBIT 5.3

Illustration: Proforma Effects of Consolidation of Nonhomogeneous Subsidiaries

DEBT/EQUITY RATIOS OF "TRANSPORTATION EQUIPMENT MANUFACTURERS"—1982

Company Name	Debt/Equity As Reported	Debt/Equity Pro Forma	Percentage Increase*
Lockheed	4.8316	5.3236	10.18%
Ford Motor Co.	2.6162	4.9496	89.19
United Technologies	1.6253	1.8127	11.53
Allen Group	1.5582	2.0980	34.65
Eaton	1.5529	1.6478	6.11
Bangor Punta	1.4782	2.2063	49.26
Rockwell International	1.3461	1.4191	5.42
General Motors	1.2638	3.4117	169.96
General Dynamics	1.2234	1.5866	29.68
A.O. Smith	1.1706	1.7962	53.44
Dana	.9478	1.9091	101.44
Borg-Warner	.8139	2.6177	221.62
Cessna Aircraft	.7384	2.0859	182.49
Textron	.7355	1.0399	41.40
Ex-Cell-O	.6774	.7035	3.86

*Calculated as: $\dfrac{\text{Pro Forma Ratio - As Reported Ratio}}{\text{As Reported Ratio}}$

Source: Rosanne M. Mohr, "Unconsolidated Finance Subsidiaries: Characteristics and Debt/Equity Effects," Accounting Horizons, (March, 1988).
Copyright, 1988, by the American Accounting Association. Reprinted with permission.

Sample Disclosure: General Electric Company: Transitional Statement of Financial Position in the Year of Adoption of SFAS 94

Statement of Financial Position

At December 31 (In millions)	General Electric Company and consolidated affiliates 1988	1987	GE 1988	1987	GEFS 1988	1987
Assets						
Cash (note 12)	$ 2,187	$ 2,543	$ 1,554	$ 1,834	$ 633	$ 709
Marketable securities carried at cost (note 13)	5,779	5,353	349	858	5,430	4,495
Marketable securities carried at market (note 14)	5,089	4,000	—	—	5,089	4,000
Securities purchased under agreements to resell	13,811	12,889	—	—	13,811	12,889
Current receivables (note 15)	6,780	6,745	7,110	6,782	—	—
Inventories (note 16)	6,486	6,265	6,486	6,265	—	—
GEFS financing receivables (investment in time sales, loans and financing leases) — net (note 17)	35,832	27,839	—	—	35,939	27,931
Other GEFS receivables (note 18)	4,699	4,458	—	—	4,806	4,641
Property, plant and equipment (including equipment leased to others) — net (note 19)	13,611	12,973	9,360	9,255	4,251	3,718
Investment in GEFS	—	—	4,819	3,980	—	—
Intangible assets (note 20)	8,552	5,748	6,984	4,430	1,568	1,318
All other assets (note 21)	8,039	6,601	4,621	4,896	3,418	1,705
Total assets	$110,865	$ 95,414	$ 41,283	$ 38,300	$ 74,945	$ 61,406
Liabilities and equity						
Short-term borrowings (note 22)	$ 30,422	$ 23,873	$ 1,861	$ 1,110	$ 28,731	$ 22,848
Accounts payable (note 23)	6,004	5,728	2,136	2,615	4,132	3,329
Securities sold under agreements to repurchase	13,864	13,187	—	—	13,864	13,187
Securities sold but not yet purchased, at market (note 24)	2,088	1,407	—	—	2,088	1,407
Progress collections and price adjustments accrued	3,504	3,760	3,504	3,760	—	—
Dividends payable	369	319	369	319	—	—
All other GE current costs and expenses accrued (note 25)	5,549	4,867	5,549	4,867	—	—
Long-term borrowings (note 26)	15,082	12,517	4,330	4,491	10,862	8,037
Reserves of insurance affiliates	4,177	3,549	—	—	4,177	3,549
All other liabilities (note 27)	6,986	6,325	5,481	5,088	1,505	1,237
Deferred income taxes	3,373	3,100	(641)	(620)	4,014	3,720
Total liabilities	91,418	78,632	22,589	21,630	69,373	57,314
Minority interest in equity of consolidated affiliates (note 28)	981	502	228	190	753	112
Common stock (926,564,000 shares issued)	584	584	584	584	1	1
Other capital	823	878	823	878	1,379	1,328
Retained earnings	17,950	15,878	17,950	15,878	3,439	2,651
Less common stock held in treasury	(891)	(860)	(891)	(860)	—	—
Total share owners' equity (notes 29 and 30)	18,466	16,480	18,466	16,480	4,819	3,980
Total liabilities and equity	$110,865	$ 95,414	$ 41,283	$ 38,300	$ 74,945	$ 61,406
Commitments and contingent liabilities (note 31)						

Source: General Electric Company 1988 Annual Report. Copyright, 1989, by The General Electric Company. Reprinted with permission.

BUSINESS COMBINATIONS

This section presents the accounting and analytical issues relating to mergers and acquisitions and consolidated financial statements. The accounting and reporting standards relating to business combinations are set forth in Opinions 16 and 17 and in SFAS 94. After a brief introduction to consolidated financial statements, the accounting issues relating to a "purchase" and a "pooling of interests" will be discussed.

Consolidated Financial Statements

The purpose of consolidated financial statements is to reflect the economic activities of an entity under common control, regardless of the separate legal existence of the individual subsidiaries. The consolidated financial statements are said to present the "economic substance over the legal form of the separate businesses".

The basic principles of consolidation accounting relating to the balance sheet and income statement are presented below. It should be noted that in most cases, the component entities maintain their own accounting records and separate financial statements, and are only combined on a consolidating spreadsheet at the end of the period when consolidated statements are prepared.

The Consolidated Balance Sheet. In the preparation of the consolidated balance sheet, the accountant combines the asset, liability, and stockholders' equity accounts, but eliminates all transactions that are not objective or "arms-length". Common consolidating elimination entries on the balance sheet include:

1. The elimination of all intercompany receivables and payables;

2. The elimination of intercompany profit in inventory purchased by or from the parent company at marked-up transfer prices;

3. The elimination of the parent's investment account against the stockholders' equity of the subsidiary. If there is less than 100% ownership, the difference between the total subsidiary stockholders' equity and the parent's investment represents the minority interest.

The minority interest reflects the outside shareholders' interest in the net assets of a subsidiary included in the consolidation. The valuation procedures for the minority interest are the same as those used in accounting for a long-term investment under the equity method. Initially, the minority interest is set up at the minority interest's percentage share of the net assets of the subsidiary. The minority interest account is increased by its share of the subsidiary's net income and is reduced by the minority interest's share of the subsidiary's net losses and dividend distributions.

It should be noted that even if the parent company owns less than 100% of the voting stock of a particular subsidiary, 100% of that subsidiary's assets and liabilities would be included in the consolidated balance sheet because the parent company has use and control over the subsidiary's productive resources and usually assumes the obligations of the subsidiary company. Although legally equity, the minority interest is generally presented between the liabilities and stockholders' equity section of the balance sheet (i.e., "accounting limbo"). One reason for this classification of the minority interest is that the parent controls all of the economic resources of the subsidiary but owns less than 100%. In this sense, the parent has a "stewardship" obligation to the minority shareholders and the minority interest account is reported immediately after long-term debt on the consolidated balance sheet. Other factors, such as a priority claim of the minority shareholders against the net assets of the subsidiary in the event of liquidation, may provide additional justification for the "liability" classification of the minority interest, or at least supports the exclusion of the minority interest from the stockholders' equity section of the consolidated balance sheet. The financial statement presentation of the minority interest of General Electric Company is presented in Exhibit 5.5.

After all of the adjustments and eliminations are made, the consolidated balance sheet should only reflect events and transactions between the consolidated entity and the "outside world" (i.e., all parties outside of the consolidated group).

The Consolidated Income Statement. In the preparation of the consolidated income statement, the accountant combines the revenues and expenses of the parent and its subsidiary companies, but eliminates all intercompany transactions. Common elimination entries for intercompany transactions include:

1. The elimination of all intercompany sales;

2. The elimination of all intercompany purchases;

3. The elimination of intercompany interest income and interest expense on intercompany receivables and payables;

4. The deduction (addition) of the minority interest's share of consolidated income (loss) as an operating expense (revenue) on the consolidated income statement. In addition, the minority share of income (loss) is added back to (deducted from) accrual basis net income in the reconciliation of net income to cash flows from operating activities on the statement of cash flows.

Exhibit 5.6 presents the minority interest share of consolidated net income on the income statement.

After all adjustments and eliminations are made, the consolidated income statement should only reflect events and transactions between the consolidated group and the "outside world" (i.e., parties outside of the consolidated group).

Special Issues in Consolidated Financial Statements

Reasons for Not Consolidating Subsidiaries. After the issuance of SFAS 94, there are only two reasons for not consolidating:

1. There is less than a controlling interest;

EXHIBIT 5.5

Sample Disclosure: General Electric Company: Minority Interest in the
Statement of Financial Position

Statement of Financial Position

General Electric Company and consolidated affiliates

At December 31 (In millions)	1983	1982
Assets		
Cash (note 8)	$ 1,828	$ 2,194
Marketable securities (note 8)	677	393
Current receivables (note 9)	5,249	4,740
Inventories (note 10)	3,158	3,029
Current assets	10,912	10,356
Property, plant and equipment — net (note 11)	7,697	7,308
Investments (note 12)	2,945	2,287
Other assets (note 13)	1,734	1,664
Total assets	$23,288	$21,615
Liabilities and equity		
Short-term borrowings (note 14)	$ 1,016	$ 1,037
Accounts payable (note 15)	1,993	1,744
Progress collections and price adjustments accrued	2,551	2,443
Dividends payable	228	193
Taxes accrued	685	585
Other costs and expenses accrued (note 16)	2,215	2,151
Current liabilities	8,688	8,153
Long-term borrowings (note 17)	915	1,015
Other liabilities	2,247	2,084
Total liabilities	11,850	11,252
Minority interest in equity of consolidated affiliates	168	165
Common stock	579	579
Other capital	657	676
Retained earnings	10,317	9,145
Less common stock held in treasury	(283)	(202)
Total share owners' equity (notes 18 and 19)	11,270	10,198
Total liabilities and equity	$23,288	$21,615
Commitments and contingent liabilities (note 20)		

Source: General Electric Company 1983 Annual Report. Copyright, 1984, by The
General Electric Company. Reprinted with permission.

EXHIBIT 5.6

Sample Disclosure: General Electric Company: Minority Interest in the Statement of Earnings

----

Statement of Earnings

General Electric Company and consolidated affiliates

For the years ended December 31 (In millions)	1983	1982	1981
Sales of products and services to customers	$26,797	$26,500	$27,240
Operating costs			
Cost of goods sold	18,701	18,605	19,476
Selling, general and administrative expense	4,463	4,506	4,435
Depreciation, depletion and amortization	1,084	984	882
Operating costs (notes 2 and 3)	24,248	24,095	24,793
Operating margin	2,549	2,405	2,447
Other income (note 4)	884	692	614
Interest and other financial charges (note 5)	(370)	(344)	(401)
Earnings before business restructurings, income taxes and minority interest	3,063	2,753	2,660
Business restructuring activities (note 6):			
Gains from sales of assets	117	—	—
Provisions for plant rationalizations and business exits	(147)	—	—
Earnings before income taxes and minority interest	3,033	2,753	2,660
Provision for income taxes (note 7)	(975)	(900)	(962)
Minority interest in earnings of consolidated affiliates	(34)	(36)	(46)
Net earnings	$ 2,024	$ 1,817	$ 1,652
Net earnings per share (in dollars)	$ 4.45	$ 4.00	$ 3.63
Dividends declared per share (in dollars)	$1.875	$1.675	$1.575
Operating margin as a percentage of sales	9.5%	9.1%	9.0%
Net earnings as a percentage of sales	7.6%	6.9%	6.1%

Per-share amounts have been adjusted for the 2-for-1 stock split in April 1983.

Source: General Electric Company 1983 Annual Report. Copyright, 1984, by The General Electric Company. Reprinted with permission.

2. There is material uncertainty as to the realization of subsidiary income. For example, there could be government-imposed restrictions on the remittance of earnings to the parent from a foreign subsidiary.

Accounting for Taxes on Undistributed Subsidiary Earnings. As noted in the section of this chapter discussing the equity method, subsidiary income is not taxable to the parent until distributed as dividends. Nonetheless, Opinion 23 and SFAS 96 require that a provision for taxes be made for undistributed subsidiary earnings because the accountant assumes that all undistributed earnings will ultimately be transferred to the parent. The "indefinite reversal exceptions to providing for income taxes on the undistributed subsidiary earnings involve cases where it is evident that a subsidiary will permanently reinvest its earnings or will remit these earnings to the parent in a tax free liquidation".

Debt on the Consolidated Balance Sheet. The consolidated debt reported on the balance sheet does not legally represent a claim against the total assets of the consolidated group, but only against the individual subsidiary incurring the obligation. Therefore, a creditor cannot adequately assess the risk involved with a particular outstanding loan unless the individual subsidiary financial statements are obtained and analyzed. However, if the parent company specifically guarantees the obligations of the subsidiary, there is additional security for the lender. In addition, even if the debt is not specifically guaranteed by the parent company, and although not legally bound to do so, the parent company is likely to cover the subsidiary's debt so as to maintain its own credit standing and reputation in the financial community.

Methods of Accounting for Business Combinations

There are two GAAP methods of accounting for business combinations as prescribed by Opinion 16. These are the Purchase Method and Pooling of Interests Method. The purchase method is a fair market basis of consolidation while the pooling of interests method is a book value (historical cost) approach to accounting for business combinations. These two methods are discussed in detail in the following sections.

The Purchase Method. Prior to World War II, the purchase method was the only approach used to account for business combinations. The theory underlying the purchase method implies that there is a dominant company in the transaction and that this dominant party "acquires", "takes over", "buys out" or "purchases" the other company.

Because this is a "purchase", the transaction must be accounted for at the fair market value of the subsidiary on the date of the acquisition. This means that all of the historical cost based assets and liabilities (i.e., the net assets) of the subsidiary must be revalued to reflect their fair market values. After the revaluation of the net assets by the parent company, any excess cost paid over the fair value of the net assets acquired is allocated to the intangible asset, goodwill.

In the year a business combination accounted for under the purchase method is consummated, a consolidated balance sheet is prepared as of the year end. However, a consolidated income statement can only be prepared from the date of the

acquisition because this is the only date at which the fair market values were determined. Nonetheless, footnotes to the financial statements must provide proforma
income information which reflects the net income or loss (or on a per share basis)
for the combined entity for the entire year, as if the entities were consolidated from
the beginning of the fiscal year.

After World War II, the purchase method began to come under serious criticism by the business community. The purchase method was viewed as having several cosmetic accounting disadvantages. These disadvantages include:

1. Since many of the subsidiary's assets may have be to written up to fair
   market value, charges for depreciation, depletion and amortization would
   increase and thereby reduce reported income. In addition, if the assets with
   increased carrying values (i.e., a "stepped-up basis") are disposed of, the
   gain on the sale would be reduced and the loss on disposal or the cost of
   goods sold for inventory would be increased. Again, the income of the
   consolidated entity would be reduced. Of course, these arguments assume
   that there are write-ups to fair market value due to the tendency of historical cost to undervalue assets. However, it is possible that assets could have
   been overstated and write-downs to fair market value would be required. If
   write-downs were required, income could actually increase, making the
   purchase method advantageous from a cosmetic accounting standpoint.

2. Goodwill was recorded on the consolidated balance sheet. The recognition
   of goodwill was seen as problematic in two ways. First, if the goodwill was
   amortized, income was reduced without income tax benefit because goodwill is not tax deductible. However, pre-1970 goodwill was not subject to
   amortization. With the issuance of Opinion 17 in 1970, all intangible assets,
   including goodwill, are subject to amortization.

   The second problem with goodwill recognition was the dubious value of
   the asset. Credit and financial analysts may not consider goodwill as an
   asset of real economic value, and of course, goodwill has no collateral
   value.

The general conclusion from these criticisms is that the purchase method is an
income reducing accounting alternative. For these and other reasons, the pooling of
interests method was created.

The Pooling of Interests Method. The first pooling was attempted in 1947 in the
merger of Celanese Corporation and Tubize Rayon Corporation. In filing for this
business combination with the SEC, the theory underlying a pooling of interests was
developed.

Instead of the acquisition of one company by another dominant firm, there was
to be a merging of two shareholder groups or a continuity of ownership interests
that would share in the future risks and opportunities of the pooled resources.

Originally it was assumed, among other things, that:

1. The two corporations would exchange voting stock and that ownership
   would be continuing;

2. The two combining entities would be approximately the same size;

3. Management personnel would continue to run the operations of the pooled entity.

Due to the fact that there was no takeover or acquisition, and that "nothing changed after the merger", the assets and liabilities (i.e., the net assets) of the combining companies could be brought together at historical cost or book values.

With the net assets combined at historical cost, the pooling of interests method was viewed as having several cosmetic accounting advantages over the purchase method. These advantages include:

1. The net assets are carried at historical cost. As a result, goodwill is not recognized and is not subsequently amortized against income.

2. Because assets are not written up to fair market value, there would be no increases in depreciation, depletion and amortization. In addition, if the assets were subsequently disposed of, gains on the sale would be inflated on disposal or the cost of sales for inventory would be reduced due to the probable undervaluation of the historical cost-based assets. This automatic income increasing effect resulting from a pooling is sometimes known as "instant earnings".

For these and other reasons, the pooling interests method is generally viewed as an income increasing accounting alternative.

Based on the theory underlying the pooling of interests method, the combined entity is accounted for as if the individual companies had always been merged. As a result, in the year of the pooling, a consolidated income statement can be prepared for the entire year, regardless of the date of the merger. Of course, the consolidated balance sheet is presented for the year then ended.

In the early history of the pooling of interests method, the most important issue facing the accountant was the determination of when pooling treatment was appropriate. It was clear that a pooling of interests and a purchase should not be considered alternative accounting methods. The accounting profession responded with several pronouncements regarding accounting for business combinations. These pronoucements are discussed in the next section.

Professional Pronouncements Regarding Business Combinations

The first pronouncement covering mergers and acquisitions was Accounting Research Bulletin No. 51, "Consolidated Financial Statements", issued in 1959. The early requirements for accounting for a business combination provided vague criteria and led to a deterioration of the underlying theory of a pooling of interests in practice. For example, in several cases nonvoting shares were exchanged by one of the combining companies, but the transaction was still accounted for as a pooling of interests. Due to the abusive practices that developed under Bulletin 51, the APB issued Opinion 16 in 1970.

Under Opinion 16, pooling and purchase accounting are not considered to be alternative accounting methods. In order to be accounted for as a pooling of interests, the business combination must meet all 12 Opinion 16 criteria. If any one of the 12 criteria is not met, the business combination must be accounted for as a purchase. It should be noted that if the combination meets all 12 of the Opinion 16 criteria it must be accounted for as a pooling of interests.

The 12 Opinion 16 Criteria for a Pooling of Interests

The criteria for a pooling of interests are classified into three groups:

A. The attributes of the combining companies;

B. The manner of combining interests;

C. The absence of planned transactions.

These criteria are listed and discussed in the following sections.

A. *The Attributes of the Combining Companies.*

1. Each of the combining companies should be autonomous and not have operated as a subsidiary or division of another company within two years before the plan of combination is initiated;

2. Each of the combining companies must be independent of each other. This means that no combining company or group of combining companies can hold as an intercompany investment more that 10% of the outstanding voting common stock of any other company.

   COMMENT: To qualify for a pooling of interests, the individual firms must be independent and cannot be "controlled" by one or the other firm. Prior control indicates the existence of a dominant party and therefore evidence of a purchase. This would violate the concept of combining common interests. If one of the firms was a subsidiary of another corporation, the merger would involve a major shift in ownership interests and again violate the concept of continuity of ownership interests.

B. *The Manner of Combining Interests.*

1. The combination should be effected in a single transaction or completed in accordance with a specific plan within one year after the plan of combination is initiated;

2. The combination should involve the issuance of voting common stock only in exchange for "substantially all" of the voting common stock

interest of the company being combined. "Substantially all" means at least 90% of the voting common stock of the company being combined. (This is consistent with the 10% independence requirement in A2 above).

COMMENT: Limiting the time period in which the combination must be completed prohibits long-term, piecemeal acquisitions which could result in major changes in ownership interests over time. The requirement to effect the combination by using only newly issued voting common stock prevents the use of treasury stock for more than 10% of the transaction. The use of treasury stock would involve cash payments to some of the former stockholders, which "buys out" this group, and therefore violates the concept of continuity of ownership interests.

3. None of the combining companies should change the equity interest of their voting common stock in contemplation of effecting the combination. For example, a major retirement of voting common shares would violate this criterion.

4. Each of the combining companies may reacquire shares of voting common stock only for purposes other than business combinations, and no company may reacquire more than a normal number of shares between the dates the plan of combination is initiated and consummated.

5. The ratio of the interest of an individual common stockholder to those of other common stockholders in a combining company should remain the same as a result of the exchange of stock to effect the combination. This condition assures that no common stockholder is denied his or her potential share of voting common stock interest in the combined corporation.

6. The stockholders of the resulting combined corporation cannot be deprived of, nor restricted in, their ability to exercise their voting rights on common stock of the combined company.

7. The combination must be resolved at the date the plan is consummated, and there must be no contingent arrangements for the issuance of additional securities or other consideration.

COMMENT: Criteria B3 through B7 were all designed to prevent any unusual changes in the voting rights of the common shares and to maintain the continuity of the existing ownership interests. The restriction on the use of treasury stock to effect the combination was discussed in criteria B2 above.

C. *The Absence of Planned Transactions*.

1. The combined corporation should not agree directly or indirectly to retire or reacquire any of the common stock issued to effect the

combination. This would negate the exchange of voting shares and would require a cash distribution to a particular shareholder group, which is the equivalent of a purchase.

2. The combined corporation cannot enter into other financial arrangements for the benefit of the former stockholders of a combining company, such as a guarantee of loans secured by the stock issued in the combination. This financial arrangement may require the payment of cash in the future (i.e., the loan payments), which would negate the exchange of equity securities, and therefore the combination would not qualify for pooling of interests treatment. Any arrangement resulting in preferential treatment of a group of shareholders would give differential rights and again violate the concept of a pooling.

3. The combined corporation may not intend to dispose of a significant part of the assets of the combining companies within two years after the combination. Some disposal of assets may be effected within the two-year period provided that the disposals would have been made in the ordinary course of the business of the formerly separate companies or if the disposals were made to eliminate duplicate facilities or excess capacity.

COMMENT: The last criterion was required so as to prevent reporting "instant earnings" from sale of undervalued assets acquired in the combination.

Relevance of the Provisions of Opinion 16. In reviewing the 12 Opinion 16 criteria for a pooling of interests, it is evident that each requirement was designed to prevent a specific managerial practice that was frequently used prior to the issuance of Opinion 16 to circumvent the theory of a pooling.

In recent years, there has been growing criticism of the criteria of Opinion 16, and many have suggested that this pronouncement be reviewed by the FASB, which should consider whether to revise the accounting standards for business combinations or to determine if a pooling of interests should continue to be permitted.[1]

The relevance of Opinion 16 has become questionable due to the fact that recently, the SEC has been ruling on pooling treatment on a case by case basis. For example, the SEC has ruled that if there are securities issued by merger candidates that possess "essentially the same characteristics as common stock", these securities must also be exchanged for common stock in order to qualify for a pooling of interests treatment.[2] Because there are no codified standards in this regard, the exact accounting treatment of a proposed merger may not be known with certainty and may no longer be based solely on the 12 criteria of Opinion 16. Therefore, "the Chief Accountant's Office of the SEC has become the de facto standard-setter for pooling of interests accounting."[3]

With the SEC ruling on a case-by-case basis, with the increased complexity of the capital structures of today's corporation, and the variety of securities used to effect a business combination, there is a great deal of uncertainty regarding the ultimate accounting treatment of a proposed merger and acquisition.

Tax Considerations. For tax purposes, nontaxable exchanges require the acquisition of voting common stock in exchange for the voting common stock of the other combining company. As a result, most nontaxable exchanges are accounted for as a pooling of interests. However, the exchange of voting shares is only one of the 12 requirements to be met in order to use the pooling of interests method. Therefore, if voting shares are exchanged, but one of the other Opinion 16 criteria is violated, the transaction would be accounted for as a purchase for book purposes and a nontaxable exchange for tax purposes. In addition, the requirements for a nontaxable exchange are not fully compatible with the accounting requirements for a pooling of interests. As a result, a pooling of interests can be classified as a taxable exchange for tax purposes.

The tax provisions relating to business combinations and reorganizations are extremely complex and go well beyond the scope of this work.

Accounting for Goodwill. As noted earlier, after the issuance of Opinion 17 in 1970, all intangibles, including goodwill, are subject to amortization. An intangible is to be amortized over its economic life or legal life, whichever is shorter, not to exceed 40 years. The straight-line method should be used, unless some other systematic method of amortization is shown to be preferable under the circumstances.

Goodwill is only recognized if the combination is accounted for under the purchase method. Goodwill is commonly called "the excess of purchase cost over the fair market value of the net assets acquired".

Negative Goodwill. In the event of an undervalued stock market, the acquiring firm could make a "bargain purchase" of a subidiary company selling for less than its book value. From the accounting standpoint, a bargain purchase occurs when the purchase cost is less than the fair market value of the net assets acquired. In this case, the excess of the fair market value of the net assets acquired over the purchase cost is known as "negative goodwill".

According to Opinion 16, when the purchase transaction results in negative goodwill, the accountant should follow a two-step approach.

1. The fair market values assigned to the noncurrent assets acquired, except for long-term investments in marketable securities, should be reduced by an allocation of the negative goodwill on a pro-rata basis, based on the relative fair market values of the noncurrent assets.

2. If the allocation reduces the noncurrent assets (except long-term investments in marketable securities) to zero, the remaining negative goodwill can be recorded as a long-term deferred credit or deferred revenue account, to be amortized to income by the straight-line method over the expected period of benefit, not to exceed 40 years.

It should be noted that both the write-down of the noncurrent assets and the amortization of the negative goodwill will increase the reported income of the combined entity because write-down of noncurrent assets will reduce or eliminate charges for depreciation, depletion and amortization. As is the case for any systematic write-off, these incremental income effects will not provide any additional cash flows.

Illustration of the Purchase and the Pooling of Interests Methods

Exhibit 5.7 presents an illustration of accounting for a business combination at the date of acquisition. Case A accounts for the transaction as a pooling of interests and Case B accounts for the transaction as a purchase.

In Case A it is assumed that the Buy Company issues 80,000 shares of its $1 par value common stock in exchange for all of the 10,000, $1 par value common shares of the Sell Company (i.e., there was an eight to one exhange ratio based on the market price of the shares of respective companies). If it is also assumed that the transaction meets all of the requirements for a pooling of interests, the consolidating adjustments and eliminations merely consist of eliminating the investment account recorded on the books of the Buy Company against the net assets of the Sell Company. In this case, after elimination of the $10,000 Sell Company common stock at par, the total par value of the new shares issued (i.e., the carrying value of the parent's investment) exceeds the total par value of the shares acquired by $70,000. The required adjustment first reduces the Sell Company's $40,000 of additional paid-in capital to zero. The $30,000 excess par value is then used to reduce the additional paid-in capital of the Buy Company to $50,000, the amount which is carried to the consolidated balance sheet. If the additional paid in capital of the Buy Company was reduced to zero, then the retained earnings of the Sell Company would be reduced. If reduced to zero, the retained earnings of the Buy Company would have to be reduced as well.

If the scenario assumed in this case was reversed so that the total par value of the newly issued shares (and the carrying value of the investment)of the Buy Company was less than the total par value of the Sell Company shares acquired, additional paid-in capital would be created in the consolidation. Retained earnings should not be created in any case.

In the pooling of interests, after the elimination of the parent's investment account against the consolidated stockholders' equity section, all of the remaining accounts are carried to the consolidated balance sheet at historical cost or book values. Because the economic resources of the two entities are pooled, the consolidated total assets are exactly equal to the sum of the book value of the assets of the individual entities before the combination (i.e., $400,000 = $300,000 + 100,000).

In Case B of Exhibit 5.7 it is assumed that the Buy Company pays $150,000 to acquire all of the voting common stock of the Sell Company. Due to the use of cash, this business combination must be accounted for as a purchase. The case also assumes that the assets of the Sell Company are undervalued by $40,000. Given the assumptions made in this case, goodwill on the acquisition is determined as follows.

EXHIBIT 5.7

Illustration: Pooling of Interests versus the Purchase Method of Accounting

----

Case A: Pooling of Interests - The Buy Company issues 80,000 shares of $1 par value common stock to acquire 100% of the common stock of the Sell Company.

Consolidating Balance Sheet (Date of acquisition):

	Buy Company at cost	Sell Company at cost	Eliminations and Adjustments	Consolidated at cost
Investment in Sell.	$ 80,000	$ -0-	(a) -80,000	$ -0-
Other Assets.......	300,000	100,000	-0-	400,000
Total Assets.......	$380,000	$100,000	-80,000	$400,000
Liabilities........	$ 50,000	$ 20,000		$ 70,000
Stockholders' Equity:				
Preferred stock.....	$ 20,000	$ -		$ 20,000
Common stock ($1 par)	110,000	10,000	(a) -10,000	110,000
Additional paid-in				
capital........	80,000	40,000	(a) -70,000	50,000
Retained earnings...	120,000	30,000		150,000
Total Stockholders'				
Equity.............	$330,000	$ 80,000	-80,000	$330,000
Total Liabilities & Stockholders'				
Equity.............	$300,000	$100,000	-0-	$400,000

(a) Entry to eliminate the parent's investment against the Sell Company stock and additional paid-in capital

===

Exhibit 5.7, continued

Case B: Purchase Method - The Buy Company pays $150,000 to acquire 100% of the common stock of the Sell Company. It is assumed that the assets of Sell Company were undervalued by $40,000.

Consolidating Balance Sheet (Date of acquisition):

	Buy Company at cost	Sell Company at cost	Eliminations and Adjustments	Consolidated at cost
Investment in Sell.	$150,000	$ -0-	(b) -150,000	$ -0-
Other Assets.......	150,000	100,000	(a) + 40,000	290,000
Goodwill	-	-	(a) + 30,000	30,000
Total Assets.......	$300,000	$100,000	- 80,000	$320,000
Liabilities........	$ 50,000	$ 20,000		$ 70,000
Stockholders' Equity:				
Preferred stock.....	$20,000	$ -		$ 20,000
Common stock ($1 par)	30,000	10,000	(b) - 10,000	30,000
Additional paid-in capital.......	80,000	40,000	(b) - 40,000	80,000
Retained earnings..	120,000	30,000	(a) + 70,000 (b) -100,000	120,000
Total Stockholders' Equity.............	$250,000	$ 80,000	- 80,000	$250,000
Total Liabilities & Stockholders' Equity.............	$300,000	$100,000	- 80,000	$320,000

(a) Entry to write-up the Sell Company's assets to fair market value and to record goodwill

(b) Entry to eliminate the Buy Company's investment account (or cash) against the stockholders' equity of the Sell Company

===

```
Purchase price (cost)............................$150,000

Book value (historical cost) of the net asset
acquired........................................... <80,000>
                                                   ----------

Excess of purchase cost over book value..........$ 70,000

Excess specifically identified with undervalued
assets (write-up of net assets to fair market
value)............................................ <40,000>
                                                   ----------

Unidentified excess allocated to goodwill (the
excess purchase cost over the fair market value
of the net assets acquired).......................$ 30,000
                                                   ==========
```

On the date of acquisition, two elimination entries are made. The first entry writes up the Sell Company's assets to fair market value and records the goodwill in consolidation. The assets (e.g., land) are increased by $40,000 and the goodwill of $30,000 is created in consolidation. The total write-up of $70,000 is actually a "gain" and flows through the retained earnings of the Sell Company in consolidation. At this point the retained earnings of the Sell Company are equal to $100,000 (i.e., $30,000 + 70,000).

The second entry eliminates the Buy Company's investment account against the total stockholders' equity of the Sell Company at fair market value (i.e., $150,000 = $10,000 [common stock at par] + 40,000 [additional paid in capital] + 100,000 [retained earnings adjusted for the write-up to fair market value in consolidation]).

The consolidated balance sheet presents the assets, liabilities and stockholders' equity of the Buy Company at historical cost plus the assets and liabilities of the Sell Company at fair market value, including goodwill. Note that the consolidated stockholders' equity only includes the stockholders' equity of the Buy Company. The Sell Company's stockholders' equity of $80,000 is completely eliminated in consolidation under the purchase method.

The size of the consolidated entity is $320,000, which is equal to the assets of the Buy Company at historical cost, net of the purchase price of the investment or $150,000 (i.e., $300,000 - 150,000), plus the $170,000 of assets of the Sell Company stated at fair market value.

The difference between the consolidated total assets (i.e., firm size) determined under a pooling ($400,000) and a purchase ($320,000) is due to the elimination of the $80,000 of total stockholders' equity of the Sell Company at historical cost.

Purchase and pooling of interests accounting is also discussed in Case 5.2 at the end of this chapter.

Other Issues in Business Combinations

Push Down Accounting. The concept of push down accounting is related to the purchase method of accounting. Although not widely used in practice, the SEC has required the use of push down accounting in those cases where there has been a significant change in ownership of the acquired company, and where the separate financial statements of the subsidiary are presented. A significant change in the ownership of the acquired company has been limited to a 100% change. To date, the FASB has not responded to the push down issue and the SEC has not extended its requirements to cases where less than 100% of the subsidiary is acquired.

Under push down theory, whenever there is a significant change in the ownership of the voting common stock of a company, the economic effect of the change should be reflected in the financial statements of that company. Essentially, push down accounting requires that the fair market values of the net assets of the subsidiary acquired in a purchase, including goodwill, be reflected (i.e., "pushed down") on the financial statements of the subsidiary. As mentioned earlier, if push down accounting is not used, the only place where the revaluation of the subsidiary's net assets occurs is on the consolidating spreadsheet.

When push down accounting is used, the balance sheet for the subsidiary reflects the fair market value of its assets and liabilities, and the income statement reports a net income or loss determined by utilizing the revalued amounts of depreciation, depletion, amortization and cost of goods sold.

If the principles of push down accounting were applied to the financial statements of Sell Company in Case B of Exhibit 5.7, its balance sheet would appear as follows.

```
                          Sell Company
                          Balance Sheet
                         (Push Down Basis)
-------------------------------------------------------------------
Assets:
--------


Assets................................................$140,000
Goodwill..............................................  30,000
                                                      ---------


      Total assets...................................$170,000
                                                      ========


Liabilities:
-----------


Liabilities...........................................$ 20,000


Stockholders' Equity:
--------------------


Common stock...........................$ 10,000
Additional paid in capital............  40,000
Retained earnings.....................  100,000 (a)
                                        ----------


      Total stockholders' equity...................... 150,000
                                                      ----------


      Total liabilities and stockholders' equity......$170,000
                                                      ========
-------------------------------------------------------------------


(a) The total retained earnings is comprised of the original balance of
    $30,000 plus the gain, or $70,000, on the write-up of the company's
    assets to fair market value.
```

Disclosure Requirements. The disclosure requirements for a business combination accounted for under the purchase and pooling of interests methods will vary due to the differences in the underlying theory of the two methods. The disclosure requirements for a purchase and a pooling of interests are presented separately in the following sections.

Disclosures Under the Purchase Method. In the period in which a business combination occurs and is accounted for under the purchase method, the following disclosures are required by Opinion 16:

1. The name of the company acquired, a brief description of the transaction and the total cost of the acquisition;

2. A statement that the purchase method of accounting was used;

3. The period for which the results of operations were combined on the income statement. As noted earlier, the period begins as of the date of acquisition;

4. The amount of and the amortization policy for goodwill;

5. Information relating to any contingent payments, options or other commitments.

In addition, the following supplementary proforma disclosures must be made in the year of acquisition:

1. The results of operations for the current period as if the acquisition took place as of the beginning of the period;

2. The proforma results of operations should also be provided for all years presented in comparative financial statements, as of the beginning of the first comparative period.

FASB Statement No. 79, "Elimination of Certain Disclosures for Business Combinations by Nonpublic Enterprises", issued in 1984, suspends the requirements for disclosures of proforma income information for nonpublic companies.

Disclosures Under the Pooling of Interests Method. In the year in which a business combination accounted for under the pooling of interests method occurs, the following disclosures required by Opinion 16 should be provided in the footnotes to the consolidated financial statements:

1. A description of the companies combined in the pooling;

2. A statement that the pooling of interests method of accounting was used;

3. A description and the amount of shares of voting stock issued to effect the combination;

4. The details of the results of operations for each of the combining companies prior to the date of combination that are included in the consolidated net income;

5. A description of the nature of the adjustments in net assets of the combin-

ing companies to adopt the same accounting methods;

6. If any of the combining companies changed their fiscal year due to the combination, disclosure should be made of any changes in stockholders' equity that were excluded from the reported results of operations;

7. The revenues and the results of operations previously reported by the acquiring company should be reconciled with the amounts now reported in the consolidated financial statements;

8. A plan of combination that has been initiated but not consummated as of the date of the financial statements should be included in the disclosure. Any effects of the plan of the combined operations and any expected changes should be disclosed.

NOTES

1. Richard Dieter, "Is Now the Time to Revisit Accounting for Business Combinations," The CPA Journal (July, 1989), 44-48.

2. Ibid.

3. Ibid.

CASE 5.1. XEROX CORPORATION: CONSOLIDATION OF FINANCE SUBSIDIARIES

Xerox Corporation is in the business equipment and financial services businesses worldwide, with about 36% of its revenues generated outside the United States. The Company's business equipment segment consists of the development, manufacture, marketing and maintenance of xerographic copiers and duplicators. It also includes the marketing of toner, paper and other supplies. The financial services segment consists of Xerox Credit Corporation, Crum and Foster, Inc., a property and liability insurance holding company, and Van Kampen Merritt, Inc., an investment banking firm.

Source: Xerox Corporation 1984 Annual Report. Copyright, 1985, by The Xerox Corporation. Reprinted with permission.

In October 1987, the Financial Accounting Standards Board issued Statement No. 94, "Consolidation of All Majority-Owned Subsidiaries", dealing with the equity method and consolidations. In this statement, the FASB requires the consolidation of all majority-owned subsidiaries. Prior to SFAS 94, financial service subsidiaries would not be consolidated under the theory that these companies were not "compatible" with manufacturing operations, etc. Therefore, the major effect of this pronouncement is the required inclusion of these "nonhomogeneous" subsidiaries in the firm's consolidated financial statements.

REQUIRED: Study the following information relating to Xerox Corporation's equity investments in financial services and other consolidated subsidiaries.

1. Prepare a schedule which reconciles the 1984 stockholders' equity of the finance subsidiaries with the "Investment in Financial Services Businesses at Equity" account in the noncurrent asset section of the Company's balance sheet.

2. Prepare a consolidating workpaper to consolidate the Balance Sheet of Xerox Corporation with its financial service and other subsidiaries for 1984. For purposes of this consolidation:

    a. Assume that the Company owns 58% of all other investments at equity that are not 100% owned;

    b. Assume that the year ends and accounting methods of all companies involved are comparable;

    c. Eliminate the subsidiaries equity against the Company's carrying value of the investments;

    d. Eliminate the intercompany payables and receivables against the Company's current assets and current liabilities.

3. Using the proforma consolidated statements, compute the following financial ratios:

a. Debt/Equity ratio;

b. Debt ratio;

c. Working capital (current) ratio.

Compare these statistics with the same ratios computed from the Xerox Corporation's financial statements as reported. Comment on the significance of the changes when the equity investments are consolidated on a proforma basis.

Xerox Corporation

Consolidated Statements of Income

(In millions, except per share data) Year Ended December 31	1984	1983	1982
Income			
Sales	**$4,282.4**	$3,695.1	$3,288.5
Rentals	**3,004.6**	3,305.6	3,973.9
Service	**1,504.6**	1,267.2	995.2
Equity in net income of financial services businesses	**67.7**	197.1	39.4
Other income	**142.9**	141.5	161.9
Total	**9,002.2**	8,606.5	8,458.9
Costs and Other Deductions			
Cost of sales	**2,080.9**	1,816.6	1,575.3
Cost of rentals	**1,556.9**	1,635.7	1,739.4
Cost of service	**707.7**	589.7	473.7
Research and development expenses	**561.4**	535.6	547.5
Selling, administrative and general expenses	**3,208.5**	3,046.5	3,125.2
Interest expense	**260.6**	190.4	153.3
Other, net	**12.1**	73.9	268.4
Income taxes	**168.1**	163.1	143.2
Outside shareholders' interests	**70.4**	64.0	76.0
Total	**8,626.6**	8,115.5	8,102.0
Income from Continuing Operations	**375.6**	491.0	356.9
Discontinued Operations	**(85.1)**	(24.6)	66.8
Net Income	**$ 290.5**	$ 466.4	$ 423.7
Income (Loss) per Common Share			
Continuing operations	**$3.42**	$4.68	$4.21
Discontinued operations	**(.89)**	(.26)	.79
Net Income per Common Share	**$2.53**	$4.42	$5.00
Average Common Shares Outstanding	**95.7**	94.9	84.7
Dividends on Preferred Stock	**$48.2**	$46.8	—

The accompanying notes are an integral part of the consolidated financial statements.

Source: Xerox Corporation 1984 Annual Report. Copyright, 1985, by The Xerox Corporation. Reprinted with permission.

Xerox Corporation

Consolidated Balance Sheets

Assets (In millions)	December 31	1984	198
Current Assets			
Cash and bank time deposits		$ **168.0**	$ 326.
Marketable securities, at the lower of cost or market		**58.9**	45.
Trade receivables (less allowance for doubtful receivables: 1984-$84.6; 1983-$79.4)		**1,337.7**	1,367
Accrued revenues		**614.5**	454.
Inventories		**1,300.0**	1,284.
Other current assets		**260.1**	176.
Total current assets		**3,739.2**	3,654.
Trade Receivables Due after One Year		**267.4**	274.
Rental Equipment and Related Inventories, net		**1,519.5**	1,528.
Land, Buildings and Equipment, net		**1,391.8**	1,469.
Investment in Financial Services Businesses, at equity		**2,175.1**	2,016.
Other Investments, at equity		**252.9**	203.
Other Assets		**191.2**	149.
Total Assets		**$9,537.1**	$9,296.

The accompanying notes are an integral part of the consolidated financial statements.

Source: Xerox Corporation 1984 Annual Report. Copyright, 1985, by The Xerox Corporation. Reprinted with permission.

Liabilities and Shareholders' Equity (In millions)	December 31	1984	1983
Current Liabilities			
Notes payable and current portion of long-term debt		$ 654.7	$ 542.6
Accounts payable		310.5	308.8
Salaries, profit sharing and other accruals		916.9	960.3
Income taxes		136.1	209.2
Unearned income		211.7	168.2
Other current liabilities		221.2	116.9
Total current liabilities		2,451.1	2,306.0
Long-Term Debt		1,614.3	1,460.9
Other Noncurrent Liabilities		338.8	204.4
Deferred Income Taxes		54.4	121.9
Deferred Investment Tax Credits		94.6	100.9
Outside Shareholders' Interests in Equity of Subsidiaries		440.9	438.4
$5.45 Cumulative Preferred Stock		442.0	442.0
Common and Class B Shareholders' Equity			
Common and Class B stock		95.9	95.1
Additional paid-in capital		775.1	695.3
Retained earnings		3,759.4	3,804.3
Net unrealized appreciation of equity investments		17.3	40.0
Cumulative translation adjustments		(536.8)	(402.0)
Class B stock receivables and deferrals		(9.9)	(10.3)
Total common and Class B shareholders' equity		4,101.0	4,222.4
Total Liabilities and Shareholders' Equity		$9,537.1	$9,296.9

Source: Xerox Corporation 1984 Annual Report. Copyright, 1985, by The Xerox
Corporation. Reprinted with permission.

Inventories

Inventories are carried at the lower of average cost or market and consist of:

(In millions)	1984	1983
Finished products	$ 970.8	$ 904.9
Work in process	124.4	171.2
Raw materials and supplies	204.8	208.7
Total inventories	$1,300.0	$1,284.8

Rental Equipment and Related Inventories

The cost of rental equipment and related inventories and accumulated depreciation follow:

(In millions)	1984	1983
Rental equipment and related inventories	$3,798.5	$3,987.0
Less accumulated depreciation	2,279.0	2,458.5
Rental equipment and related inventories, net	$1,519.5	$1,528.5

Rental equipment is depreciated over estimated useful lives, generally three to seven years.

Land, Buildings and Equipment

The cost of land, buildings and equipment and related accumulated depreciation follow:

(In millions)	Estimated Useful Lives (years)	1984	1983
Land		$ 61.7	$ 59.6
Buildings and building equipment	20 to 50	598.4	600.4
Leasehold improvements	Term of lease	208.3	207.5
Plant machinery	4 to 12	876.4	889.4
Office furniture and equipment	3 to 10	741.8	716.2
Other	3 to 20	198.3	199.4
Construction in progress		93.7	105.3
Total		2,778.6	2,777.8
Less accumulated depreciation		1,386.8	1,308.0
Land, buildings and equipment, net		$1,391.8	$1,469.8

The cost of assets under capital leases included above, principally buildings and office furniture and equipment, amounted to $128.9 million and $127.7 million at December 31, 1984 and 1983, respectively; related accumulated depreciation amounted to $56.3 million and $54.3 million at December 31, 1984 and 1983, respectively.

Investment in Financial Services Businesses, at equity

The Company's investment in financial services businesses which includes Crum and Forster, Inc. (C&F), Xerox Credit Corporation (XCC) and Van Kampen Merritt Inc. (VKM) is carried at equity, as shown in the consolidated financial statements of the individual subsidiaries, and consists of the following at December 31, 1984 and 1983:

(In millions)	1984	1983
Crum and Forster, Inc.	$1,666.7	$1,736.8
Xerox Credit Corporation	337.8	280.1
Van Kampen Merritt Inc.	170.6	—
Total	$2,175.1	$2,016.9

The net income (loss) of the individual subsidiaries, included in equity in net income of financial services businesses in the Company's consolidated statements of income, for the years ended December 31, 1984, 1983 and 1982 follows:

(In millions)	1984	1983	1982
Crum and Forster, Inc.	$(10.5)	$145.1	$ —
Xerox Credit Corporation	57.7	52.0	39.4
Van Kampen Merritt Inc.	20.5	—	—
Total	$ 67.7	$197.1	$39.4

The following combined financial data of the Xerox Financial Services Businesses have been summarized from the audited financial statements of the individual subsidiaries:

(In millions)	1984	1983	1982
Summary of Operations			
Income			
Insurance premiums earned	$2,099.4	$1,826.8	$ —
Investment and other income	403.6	355.1	4.7
Finance and investment banking income	314.1	213.5	173.2
Total income	2,817.1	2,395.4	177.9
Losses and Expenses			
Losses and loss expenses	1,883.0	1,410.2	—
Other insurance operating expenses	745.8	604.3	—
Interest expense	151.7	137.0	108.6
Administrative and general expenses	143.7	79.5	12.4
Total losses and expenses	2,924.2	2,231.0	121.0
Operating income (loss) before income taxes	(107.1)	164.4	56.9
Income (taxes) benefits	134.8	(3.2)	(17.5)
Operating income	27.7	161.2	39.4
Realized capital gains of C&F, net of income taxes	40.0	35.9	—
Net income	$ 67.7	$ 197.1	$ 39.4

Source: Xerox Corporation 1984 Annual Report. Copyright, 1985, by The Xerox Corporation. Reprinted with permission.

(In millions)	1984	1983
Balance Sheets		
Assets		
Investments and cash	$3,721.0	$3,382.7
Finance receivables, net	1,753.2	1,437.0
Premiums and other receivables	925.9	733.5
Due from Xerox Corporation, net	234.0	94.5
Other assets	375.7	297.4
Excess of cost over fair value of net assets acquired	1,033.9	927.8
Total assets	$8,043.7	$6,872.9
Liabilities and Shareholder's Equity		
Unearned premiums and unpaid losses and loss expenses	$3,533.9	$3,185.1
Notes payable	1,231.4	1,033.6
Accounts payable and accrued liabilities	823.6	406.6
Deferred income taxes	279.7	230.7
Shareholder's equity	2,175.1	2,016.9
Total liabilities and shareholder's equity	$8,043.7	$6,872.9

C&F is an insurance holding company which, through its subsidiaries, writes all types of property-liability insurance throughout the United States and Canada. C&F paid $35 million and $70 million in dividends to the Company in 1984 and 1983, respectively. C&F's insurance subsidiaries are restricted by insurance laws as to the amount of dividends they may pay without the approval of regulatory authorities. There are no additional restrictions with regard to the amount of loans and advances that these subsidiaries may make to C&F. These restrictions indirectly limit the payment of dividends and the making of loans and advances by C&F to the Company. The amount of restricted net assets of C&F's consolidated subsidiaries at December 31, 1984 approximated $970 million.

C&F's portfolio of equity investments is carried at fair market value. The net unrealized appreciation on this portfolio, less applicable income taxes, was added to the Company's investment in C&F and to common and Class B shareholders' equity.

XCC is engaged principally in financing accounts receivable arising out of equipment sales by the Company and is also engaged in the business of financing leases for third parties. Receivables were sold by the Company to XCC during the years ended December 31, 1984, 1983 and 1982 for $709.6 million, $591.9 million and $436.4 million, respectively.

The operating agreement between the Company and XCC specifies that XCC shall retain an allowance for losses on receivables purchased from the Company at an amount which is intended to protect against future losses on the portfolio. The amount of the allowance is determined principally on the basis of past collection experience and the Company will fund any additional allowance required.

In addition, the terms of a support agreement with XCC provide that the Company will make income maintenance payments, to the extent necessary, so that XCC's earnings shall not be less than one and one-quarter times XCC's fixed

charges. No income maintenance payments were required in 1984, 1983 or 1982. The support agreement also requires that the Company retain 100% ownership of XCC's voting capital stock.

VKM is an investment banking firm which specializes in packaging insured long-term tax exempt municipal unit investment trusts.

The amounts due from Xerox Corporation primarily relate to the financial services businesses' tax benefits that are included in the Company's consolidated U.S. tax return.

Other Investments, at equity
Other investments, at equity consist of the following at December 31, 1984 and 1983:

(In millions)	1984	1983
Fuji Xerox Co., Ltd.	$206.9	$192.8
Other	46.0	10.4
Total	$252.9	$203.2

Rank Xerox Limited owns 50% of the outstanding stock of Fuji Xerox Co., Ltd. (Fuji Xerox), a corporate joint venture. Fuji Xerox is located in the Far East and operates principally in the reprographics business. Other investments carried at equity primarily consist of the Company's real estate businesses and its 1984 investment in Delphax Systems, a manufacturer of non-impact printers. The condensed financial data set forth below have been summarized from the audited financial statements of Fuji Xerox for each of the years ended October 20, 1984, 1983 and 1982 and as of October 20, 1984 and 1983, combined with the financial statements of other investments carried at equity for their respective fiscal years.

(In millions)	1984	1983	1982
Summary of Operations			
Total operating revenues	$1,342.6	$1,117.1	$1,034.9
Costs and expenses	1,194.4	992.9	921.6
Income before income taxes	148.2	124.2	113.3
Income taxes	87.9	69.6	68.2
Net income	$ 60.3	$ 54.6	$ 45.1

(In millions)	1984	1983
Balance Sheets		
Assets		
Current assets	$ 672.4	$ 559.3
Rental equipment and other assets	568.7	539.1
Total assets	$1,241.1	$1,098.4
Liabilities and Shareholders' Equity		
Current liabilities	$ 608.5	$ 546.2
Advances from Xerox Corporation	6.1	6.4
Long-term debt	46.4	25.0
Other noncurrent liabilities	146.3	120.0
Shareholders' equity	433.8	400.8
Total liabilities and shareholders' equity	$1,241.1	$1,098.4

Other income in the consolidated statements of income includes Rank Xerox Limited's share of Fuji Xerox' net income ($31.6 million in 1984, $27.7 million in 1983 and $23.8 million in 1982), and the results of operations of the other investments carried at equity.

CASE 5.2. McCORMICK AND COMPANY, INC.: PURCHASE VERSUS
POOLING OF INTERESTS

McCormick and Company, Inc. is a diversified specialty food company and
worldwide leader in the marketing, manufacturing, and distribution of seasoning,
flavoring and food products to the food industry-retail outlets, food service and food
processors. A packaging group markets and manufactures plastic bottles and tubes
for food, personal care and other industries. Real estate is another significant
business.

Source: McCormick and Company, Inc. 1984 Annual Report. Copyright, 1985, by
The McCormick Company Inc. Reprinted with permission.

REQUIRED: Footnote 11--Acquisition, indicates that in June 1984 the
Company acquired Paterson Jenks, plc. The purchase method was used to account
for the acquisition. Study the Statement of Income and Retained Earnings and
Footnote 11.

1. Explain the purchase method of accounting and discuss the pooling of
   interests method of accounting. Include a comparison of these methods in
   terms of:

   a. Asset valuation;

   b. Reporting the results of operations for 1983--1984;

   c. Differences in cash flows;

   d. The impact on future years' net income or loss.

2. Did the acquisition of Paterson Jenks have a significant effect on the consolidated revenues, net income and earnings per share of McCormick?

3. From an accounting standpoint, why was McCormick required to use the
   purchase method to account for the Paterson Jenks acquisition?

Income and Retained Earnings

	Year ended November 30		
	1984	1983	1982
	(Dollars in thousands except per-share data)		
Net sales	**$788,359**	$743,154	$717,678
Cost of goods sold	**503,046**	464,275	449,744
Gross profit	**285,313**	278,879	267,934
Selling, general and administrative expense	**220,152**	212,154	207,920
Profit from operations	**65,161**	66,725	60,014
Other income			
Royalties	**1,228**	1,044	1,588
Interest	**1,071**	651	1,525
Miscellaneous	**3**	499	597
	2,302	2,194	3,710
	67,463	68,919	63,724
Other expenses			
Interest	**13,047**	10,932	12,490
Miscellaneous	**2,795**	5,881	3,584
	15,842	16,813	16,074
Income before income taxes	**51,621**	52,106	47,650
Provision for income taxes (Note 6)	**24,830**	25,744	22,760
Income from consolidated operations	**26,791**	26,362	24,890
Share of income of unconsolidated subsidiary and affiliates (Note 9)	**27,805**	13,751	79
Net income	**54,596**	40,113	24,969
Retained earnings, beginning of year	**158,621**	129,525	114,357
	213,217	169,638	139,326
Reductions in retained earnings			
Dividends declared			
Preferred stock—$5.00 per share	**14**	21	15
Common stock (voting and non-voting) per share, 1984—$1.13; 1983—$.88; 1982—$.79	**13,979**	10,996	9,786
Excess cost of treasury shares issued for employee stock option plans	**233**		
	14,226	11,017	9,801
Retained earnings, end of year	**$198,991**	$158,621	$129,525
Earnings per common share	**$ 4.40**	$ 3.22	$ 2.02

Source: The Seagram Company Ltd., Report for the twelve months ended January
31, 1987. Copyright, 1987, by the Seagram Company Ltd. Reprinted with
permission.

11. Acquisition: In June 1984, the Company acquired Paterson Jenks plc, a publicly held consumer products company in the United Kingdom, for a total cost of $54,500,000 in cash and notes to shareholders of Paterson Jenks. The acquisition has been accounted for using the purchase accounting method and, accordingly, the results of operations of the business acquired is included in the statements of income from the date of acquisition. The excess of the cost of purchase over the fair value of net assets acquired amounted to $43,100,000 and is being amortized using the straight line method over 40 years.

The following unaudited pro forma consolidated results of operations assume the acquisition occurred at the beginning of each period presented. This pro forma data has been prepared for comparative purposes only and does not purport to be indicative of the results of operations which would have actually resulted had the combination been in effect for the periods indicated or which may result in the future.

| | Year ended November 30 | |
	1984	1983
	(Dollars in thousands except per-share data)	
Net sales	**$825,195**	$791,206
Net income	**54,467**	40,011
Earnings per common share	**$4.39**	$3.21

Source: McCormick and Company, Inc. 1984 Annual Report. Copyright, 1985, by The McCormick Company, Inc. Reprinted with permission.

6

Computing Earnings Per Share

INTRODUCTION

Earnings per share (EPS) is a measure of operating performance used widely in credit and investment analysis. The EPS disclosure is probably the single most important financial statistic used in assessing the effectiveness of the management team in utilizing the economic resources entrusted to it by the common shareholders.

EPS is also used in the mechanistic valuation of common equity securities through the use of the price-earnings (P/E) multiple, and in the evaluation of the firm's ability to make dividend distributions to its common shareholders.

Due to the importance and extensive use of the EPS figure, the accountant provides the analyst with all required EPS information. The presentation of EPS on the face of the income statement is probably the only key financial ratio provided directly by the accountant. In all other cases, the analyst is required to use the information provided in the financial statements to compute financial ratios and other key statistics. Nevertheless, the EPS disclosure is subject to the same limitations of accrual basis accounting as all other financial information provided by the accountant in the annual report.

The EPS disclosure was first made mandatory in 1969 with the issuance of APB Opinion No. 15, "Earnings per Share". Due to the cost and complexity of the EPS computation, the FASB subsequently suspended all EPS requirements for nonpublic companies in 1978 with the issuance of FASB Statement No. 21, "Suspension of the Reporting of Earnings per Share and Segment Information by Nonpublic Enterprises".

Although the mandatory EPS information is provided on the face of the income statement, the analyst should still be familiar with the complexities of the EPS computation for purposes of making projections of EPS and for preparing proforma financial statements. For instance, an analyst may wish to determine the effect on reported EPS from additional debt financing versus equity financing. Similarly, the analyst may need a proforma calculation of EPS in order to assess the impact of a proposed merger on the reported EPS of the combined entity.

The purpose of this chapter is to present the reporting requirements of Opinion 15 and to demonstrate the details of the EPS computation. In addtion, several analytical issues related to the EPS disclosure will be discussed.

BASIC CONCEPTS IN COMPUTING EPS

The Basic or Unadjusted EPS

In its simplest form, the basic or unadjusted EPS is computed as follows:

$$EPS = \frac{\text{Net Income} - \text{Preferred Dividend Requirements}}{\text{Weighted Average Number of Common Shares Outstanding}}$$

The basic EPS figure is generally considered inadequate because it may be overstated if there are potentially dilutive securities outstanding such as stock options or convertible securities. As will be discussed throughout this chapter, the basic EPS ratio will be modified and adjusted by the accountant to reflect the possible future impact of potentially dilutive securities outstanding. Thus, the accountant assumes a conservative position with respect to EPS in that the lower or diluted EPS figure, based on hypothetical events, is preferred to the actual, but potentially overstated, basic EPS amount.

Preferred Dividend Requirements. In the EPS computation, preferred dividend requirements represent the claims of senior equity securities. These claims include dividends declared on noncumulative preferred stock and undeclared dividends on cumulative preferred stock for the current period. Any dividends in arrears on cumulative preferred stock relating to prior periods are not deducted from net income because these dividend requirements have already been reflected in prior periods' EPS computations. As noted in chapter 3, dividends in arrears on cumulative preferred stock must be disclosed in the footnotes to the financial statements due to their overall effect on future distributions to current and potential common shareholders. Because all preferred dividend requirements are deducted from the net income for the period, the numerator of the EPS ratio is known as *net income available to common.*

The Weighted Average Number of Common Shares Outstanding

The weighted average number of common shares in the basic EPS computation should only include outstanding shares. As discussed in chapter 3, outstanding shares represent shares issued less treasury shares.

The weighted average can be computed by weighting on a monthly or daily basis. Although more complex, the daily weighting provides the more accurate computation. Nonetheless, when share activity is not extensive, monthly weighting provides sufficient accuracy and will be assumed throughout this chapter.

When computing the monthly weighted average, the weights used in the computation are the number of months from the date of the transaction to the date of the EPS computation. The following example provides an illustration of a basic weighted average computation.

Basic Weighted Average Number of Shares: No Stock Dividends or Stock Splits. To illustrate the basic computation of the weighted average number of common shares outstanding, without stock dividends, stock splits or reverse splits, assume that the Herman Corporation begins the current year with 10,000 common shares outstanding. Additional shares of 5,000 and 6,000 were issued through sales on May 1 and October 1, respectively. In addition, the firm reacquired 1,000 shares of treasury stock on July 1. Given this information, the weighted average number of common shares is computed as follows:

Date	Transaction and Number of Shares		% or Fraction of Year Outstanding	Shares X %
1/1	Balance	10,000	12/12	10,000
5/1	Issue	5,000	8/12	3,333
7/1	T/Stk	<1,000>	6/12	<500>
10/1	Issue	6,000	3/12	1,500
			Weighted Average......	14,333

Weighted Average Number of Shares: With Stock Dividends or Stock Splits. A fundamental concept underlying the EPS computation is the "if-converted" assumption. Under the if converted assumption, the accountant assumes that all actual stock dividends, stock splits or reverse splits occurred as of the beginning of the year, regardless of the actual month of the dividend or split. This is another conservative assumption because if it is assumed that events that reduce EPS occur at the beginning of the year, they would receive a full 12-month (or 360 day) weight and would therefore be more dilutive and result in an even greater reduction of EPS.

It should be noted that treasury stock transactions should be included in the weighted average computation only at the exact date of the acquisition. The rationale behind the special treatment for splits and dividends is that these transactions do not involve corporate resources and therefore could be declared only at year end to avoid any dilution of the current year's EPS. The acquisition of treasury shares, although causing an increase in EPS, could involve substantial cash outflows. As a result, there could be a significant cost to achieve a cosmetic increase in EPS. In addition, it would be in management's best interests to acquire treasury shares earlier in the accounting period so as to maximize the increase in EPS with the fewest number of shares reacquired.

In applying the if-converted assumption to actual stock dividends and stock splits occurring during the period, an adjustment is needed in the weighted average computation in order to give retroactive application to the additional shares as if the event took place at the beginning of the period.

The above illustration is now modified to include a stock dividend. Assume that the Herman Corporation begins the year with 10,000 common shares outstanding. An additional 5,000 and 1,000 shares are issued on May 1 and November 1, respectively. In addition, a 10% stock dividend is declared and distributed on July 1. Given the revised assumptions, the weighted average number of common shares outstanding are computed as follows:

Date	Transaction and Number of Shares	% or Fraction of Year Outstanding	Shares X %
1/1	Balance 10,000	12/12	10,000
5/1	Issue 5,000	8/12	3,333
		Subtotal Before Dividend...........13,333	
7/1	Retroactive Application of 10% Stock Dividend..X 1.10		
		Subtotal After Dividend............14,666	
11/1	Issue 1,000	2/12	167
		Weighted Average.........14,833	

The Effect of Mergers and Acquisitions on EPS. The computation of net income available to common and the weighted average number of common shares becomes more complex with the introduction of merger and acquisition activity. The actual procedural modifications are dependent on the method used to account for the business combination. The two methods of accounting for a business combination, the purchase method and the pooling of interests method, were discussed in chapter 5.

If the business combination is accounted for as a pooling of interests, net income is combined for the full year, as if the individual entities were always under common control. Similarly, the number of shares issued to effect the combination are included as of the beginning of the year (i.e., given a full weight) in the EPS computation. This retroactive treatment for both income and common shares is consistent with the philosophy of a pooling: two stockholder groups merging all resources to carry on future operations as equal participants in the combined entity.

On the other hand, if the combination is accounted for under the purchase method, net income is combined and the number of shares issued in the purchase are included in the EPS calculation only as of the date of acquisition. As noted in chapter 5, proforma income and EPS information can be disclosed in a footnote, as if the combination took place as of the beginning of the year. However, there are no retroactive adjustments in a purchase due to the theory underlying the transaction: there is an acquisition or takeover of one entity by another. All items of financial position and the results of operations are stated at the fair market value as of the date of acquisition, and only proforma income information can be provided prior to that date.

SIMPLE AND COMPLEX CAPITAL STRUCTURES

The need for and the extent of the adjustments to the basic EPS ratio will depend on whether the firm is considered to have a simple or complex capital structure. The type of capital structure is defined by the provisions of Opinion 15. These provisions are discussed in the sections that follow.

Simple Capital Structure

A firm is considered to have a simple capital structure if it issues only common and preferred stock, without any potentially dilutive securities or contingent share arrangements. In the case of a simple capital structure, only a basic or unadjusted EPS is required. This is known as the single presentation.

Complex Capital Structure

A firm is considered to have a complex capital structure if it issues both common and preferred stock, and potentially dilutive securities and contingent share arrangements. Potentially dilutive securities include options and warrants (which include unpaid stock subscriptions and deferred compensation stock purchase agreements) and convertible securities.

A complex capital structure generally results in the so-called dual presentation. The dual presentation of EPS consists of primary EPS and fully diluted EPS. The components of the dual presentation will be discussed in detail throughout the remainder of this chapter.

The Three-Percent Materiality Test. The dual presentation is required only if dilution is considered to be material. Dilution of EPS is considered to be material if the three-percent materiality test is met. The three-percent test states that if the potential dilution (using fully diluted EPS) of the unadjusted EPS figure is less than three-percent, then dilution is not considered material and the firm should be treated as if it has a simple capital structure. Thus, only the single presentation of unadjusted EPS is required.

In practice, the implementation of the three-percent test involves the following simple computation:

```
If Fully Diluted EPS  < or =  (97% x Unadjusted EPS),
Then dilution is considered material and the Dual Presentation
is required.
```

The Dual Presentation

As indicated in the previous section, if the firm is considered to have a complex capital structure and dilution is determined to be material by the three-percent test, the dual presentation is required. The dual presentation consists of reporting both primary EPS and fully diluted EPS on the face of the income statement.

Primary EPS. Primary EPS adjusts the basic EPS by including the effects of the common stock equivalents (CSEs) within the basic computation. CSEs are securities that are not common stock but, based on the terms and conditions under which they were issued, give the holder the right to become a common stockholder.

CSEs always consist of options and warrants which include other potentially dilutive securities such as unpaid stock subscriptions and deferred compensation stock purchase agreements. In addition, participating securities and two-class common stocks can also be considered CSEs if these securities share in the earnings of the corporation on substantially the same basis as the common stockholder. For example, fully participating preferred stock may be considered a CSE, but all of the terms of the security must be considered in the final determination.

Convertible securities such as convertible debt and convertible preferred stock are considered to be CSEs if the two-thirds Yield Test is met.

The two-thirds yield test, as modified under FASB Statement Nos. 55 and 85,[1] states that a convertible security is considered a CSE, if at the time of issuance and based on its market price, its effective yield is less than two-thirds of the then-current average Aa corporate bond rate.

If the convertible security meets this test, the security is considered to be a CSE because the investor would not be willing to accept the significantly lower return unless the common stock characteristics were made available.

Implementation Issues for the Yield Test. Several points should be noted in the implementation of the two-thirds yield test. First, the use of the effective yield under SFAS 85 captures the effects of low yield or even zero coupon bonds. Prior to SFAS 85, the cash yield was used. If the cash yield was still used in practice, all zero coupon convertible bonds would always meet the two-thirds test.

Second, the use of the average Aa corporate bond rate was required under SFAS 55. For convertible securities sold outside the United States, the comparable foreign yield should be used in the yield test. Prior to SFAS 55, the then-current prime bank rate of interest was used in the two-thirds yield test. The FASB decided to modify the yield test in SFAS 55 because in the years following the issuance of Opinion 15, the prime rate of interest had become more volatile. This volatility resulted in several disadvantages in using the prime rate that outweighed the original justification for it: practicability, simplicity and ready availability.

Third, the status of convertible security as a CSE is generally determined at the time of issuance and is not subsequently modified. However, there are certain exceptions made when there are future issuances of the same security with identical terms. For example, assume that a convertible security issued in 1986 is not a CSE according to a yield test conducted at that time. If the same security with identical terms is issued in 1990 and is classified as a CSE, then the original 1986 security is also considered a CSE. However, prior periods EPS are not restated to reflect the change in status of the original issuance. Finally, assume that in 1994 the same security is issued with identical terms, but if the yield test is conducted at that time, it would not be a CSE. Nonetheless, because the 1990 issuance passed the yield test, then the 1994 issuance is also classified as a CSE at the time of its issuance.

When including options, warrants and convertible securities meeting the two-thirds test in the primary EPS computation, the accountant is considering potentially dilutive securities with probable conversion into common shares. Due to the reasonable probability of conversion into common stock, primary EPS is considered to be the most realistic dilution of the basic EPS figure.

Finally, the assumed conversion of convertible debt and preferred stock will not only increase the denominator of the EPS ratio with the inclusion of the additional shares issued on the assumed conversions, but the numerator is also increased. Net income available to common is increased by the avoidance of the after-tax interest expense on the debt converted and by the add back of the preferred dividends no longer required on the assumed conversion of the convertible preferred stock.

Fully Diluted EPS. Fully diluted EPS assumes that all securities that have the right to become common stock will be exercised or converted, unless the effect of the assumed conversion or exercise would increase EPS or would be antidilutive. That is, fully diluted EPS includes the weighted average number of common shares adjusted for the effects of common stock equivalents included in primary EPS, and all other convertible securities not meeting the two-thirds yield test.

As in the case of primary EPS, the assumptions used in fully diluted EPS require adjustments to income available to common for after-tax interest and preferred dividend savings on the assumed debt and preferred stock conversions. The denominator is also increased for the additional shares issued on the assumed conversions.

Fully diluted EPS represents the maximum potential dilution of the basic EPS figure. It is the worst case scenario in the sense that, even if the assumed conversion is not highly probable, a security is still included in the computation. Therefore, fully diluted EPS is the least probable of the EPS disclosures.

Fully diluted EPS should not exceed primary EPS. The two EPS figures could possibly be identical only in the event that all dilutive securities are classified as CSEs.

The implementation of the incremental effects of moving from the unadjusted EPS to fully diluted EPS is illustrated in Exhibit 6.1.

The "If-Converted" Assumption Revisited

The requirement of a dual presentation for a firm with a complex capital structure expands the scope of the if-converted assumption. With both primary and fully diluted EPS, the if-converted assumption requires that:

1. All hypothetical conversions take place at the beginning of the year if the security was outstanding for a full year. If the security was issued during the year, the conversion is assumed to take place at the date of issuance (i.e, the point at which the contingency arises). If there was an actual conversion or exercise during the year, the additional shares of common

EXHIBIT 6.1

Adjustments to Basic EPS: Unadjusted to Primary to Fully Diluted

----

Basic (Unadjusted) EPS	Primary EPS	Fully Diluted EPS

NUMERATOR:

Net Income - Preferred Dividend Requirements ---->	+ Adjustments for After-Tax Interest ---> and Dividend Savings on Conversion of CSEs and by application of the Treasury Stock Method.	+ Adjustments for After-Tax Interest and Dividend Savings on Conversion of all other dilutive securities and by the application of the Treasury Stock Method.

DENOMINATOR:

Weighted Average Number of Common Shares Outstanding ---->	+ Additional Shares ----> Issued on the Assumed Conversion of CSEs as adjusted by the application of the Treasury Stock Method.	+ Additional Shares Issued on the Assumed Conversion of all other dilutive securities as adjusted by the the application of the Treasury Stock Method.

stock would be included at the appropriate point in the weighted average computation. However, for fully diluted EPS, when shares are issued upon conversion or exercise during the year, they are to be given retroactive treatment and included in the computation as if the conversion or exercise took place at the beginning of the year.

2. The after-tax interest expense on convertible debt and preferred dividends on convertible preferred stock are avoided for the periods of time indicated by the if-converted assumptions made in (1) above. As a result, net income available to common is increased by the add-back of after-tax interest expense and the elimination of the preferred dividends.

3. In order to be included in the EPS computations, the exercise and conversion options must be exercisable within five years from the balance sheet date for primary EPS and within ten years of the balance sheet date for fully diluted EPS.

4. If there is more than one conversion rate available on a convertible security at different points in time, the accountant should use the earliest conversion date for primary EPS and the most advantageous rate (i.e., resulting in the largest number of shares issued) for fully diluted EPS.

Some of the requirements of the if-converted assumption as well as the other provisions of Opinion 15 are illustrated below.

Basic EPS Illustration. The General Standards Corporation began 1992 with 800,000 common shares outstanding. On August 1, 1992, the company issued an additional 300,000 shares. The company also has $20,000,000 of 6% convertible bonds, convertible into 500,000 shares of common stock. None of the bonds were converted in 1992. The bonds were issued several years ago at par on a date when the average Aa corporate bond rate was 12%. If the company's net income after tax was $8,500,000 and the tax rate was equal to 46%, determine primary and fully diluted EPS.

Solution. The first step in the solution is to determine the basic or unadjusted EPS. This, in turn, requires the computation of the weighted average number of common shares outstanding.

```
Weighted Average Number of Shares = 800,000 + (5/12 x 300,000) = 925,000
```

Given the weighted average number of shares outstanding, the unadjusted or basic EPS is computed as follows:

```
                    Net Income - Preferred Dividend Requirements
Unadjusted EPS =    -------------------------------------------- =
                    Weighted Average Number of Common Shares
```

$$\text{Unadjusted EPS} = \frac{\$8,500,000}{925,000} = \$9.19/\text{share}$$

The dual presentation is required if fully diluted EPS is less than or equal to $8.91/share (i.e., 97% x $9.19).

With the existence of potentially dilutive securities in this case, a dual presentation may be required. In this example, the only potentially dilutive security is the convertible debt. Based on the yield test, the convertible debt is a CSE (i.e., 6% < (2/3 x 12%) = 6% < 8%). If its effects on EPS are dilutive, the convertible debt must be included in the determination of both primary and fully diluted EPS.

In this illustration, primary and fully diluted EPS will be identical because the only dilutive security is a CSE. Primary (and fully diluted) EPS would be computed as follows:

$$\text{Primary EPS} = \frac{\text{Net Income - Preferred Dividend Requirements + After Tax Interest Savings on Convertible Debt}}{\text{Weighted Average Number of Common Shares + Shares Issued on Conversion of Debt}}$$

$$\text{Primary EPS} = \frac{\$8,500,000 + [(1 - .46) \times \$1,200,000]}{925,000 + 500,000} = \frac{\$9,148,000}{1,425,000}$$

$$\text{Primary EPS} = \$6.42/\text{share}$$

In this case, the dual presentation is required because dilution is material (i.e., $6.42 < $8.91). On the income statement, a single line item, "Primary and Fully Diluted Earnings Per Share.....$6.42", would be presented immediately following net income for the period.

THE TREASURY STOCK METHOD FOR THE ASSUMED EXERCISE OF OPTIONS AND WARRANTS

When dealing with the assumed exercise of options and warrants, the accountant faces the additional problem of deciding how the corporation would utilize the hypothetical proceeds from the assumed exercise of these securities. Under the provisions of Opinion 15, the treasury stock method is used to account for the hypothetical proceeds received on the assumed conversion of options and warrants. There are cases, however, where a warrant agreement or debt indenture contains provisions that require the tendering of debt, usually at face amount, or other securities of the issuer in payment for all or part of the exercise price. The terms of some debt securities issued with stock warrants may also require that the proceeds of the exercise of the warrants be used to retire the debt. In the event that these types of agreements exist, the if-converted assumption requires that the exercise of the options is assumed as of the beginning of the year, and at this same point in time, the proceeds are first used to retire the related debt or are used to satisfy a purpose specifically stated in a warrant or debt agreement. Any excess proceeds are accounted for under the treasury stock method as outlined in the paragraphs that follow.

The Treasury Stock Method

Under the treasury stock method, the accountant makes the following assumptions with respect to the use of the hypothetical proceeds received on the assumed exercise of options and warrants:

1. The hypothetical proceeds from the exercise that are not restricted as to use, are first used to purchase treasury stock, but only up to 20% of the previously outstanding shares. Of course the option must be "in the money" to assume exercise. That is, the exercise price must be less than or equal to the market price. Not only is this a realistic condition (because an investor would not exercise if it was less expensive to purchase the securities in the open market), but the fact that the exercise price is less than the market price of the stock results in incremental shares. With the lower proceeds on exercise and the higher market price, the firm can buy back fewer treasury shares than it issues on the assumed exercise. If the exercise price was greater than the market price of the stock, the firm would be able to reacquire more shares than issued on the assumed exercise and the weighted average number of shares would decrease. This would result in an increase in EPS or antidilution, which is not permitted under the provisions of Opinion 15.

In order to operationalize the requirement for incremental shares, Opinion 15 states that a three-month criterion be satisfied. Specifically, the three month criterion states that the exercise of options and warrants may not be assumed unless the market price of the stock is above the exercise price of the option or warrant for substantially all of three consecutive months before year end. Substantially all is defined as 11 of the last 13 weeks of the year.

If the three-month criterion is met, the accountant can assume exercise of outstanding options and warrants. In all subsequent computations the accountant must use: (i) the average for the period market price in primary EPS, and (ii) the closing or year end market price for fully diluted EPS if the closing price is higher than the average for the year market price. The use of the higher market price in the fully diluted computation reduces the assumed number of treasury shares that can be repurchased. This results in an increased number of incremental shares on the assumed exercise of options and warrants and thereby reduces EPS or maximizes dilution.

There are actually two restrictions in the implementation of the treasury stock method. The first is the 20% rule as noted above. The second is a limitation based on the magnitude of the hypothetical proceeds and the market price used for the assumed reacquisition of treasury shares. This additional limitation can be determined as follows:

Maximum Number of Shares That Can Be Purchased	=	Hypothetical Proceeds ----------------------- Market Price per Share

The maximum number that can be purchased could be less than 20% of the previously outstanding shares. In this case, the maximum number of shares is limited by the magnitude of the proceeds and the market price of the common stock. Only if the maximum number of shares that can be purchased as determined by the above ratio is greater than 20% of the previously outstanding shares does the 20% limitation apply.

2. After the hypothetical proceeds received on the exercise of options and warrants have been used to purchase treasury stock up to the limits discussed above, any excess hypothetical proceeds are assumed to be used in the following order: (i) to retire short-term debt (this requires the addition of the after-tax interest savings to net income available to common); (ii) to retire long-term debt (this also requires the addition of the after-tax interest savings to income available to common); and (iii) to purchase government securities or commercial paper (this requires the addition of the after tax interest revenue to net income available to common).

The net effect of applying these assumptions are considered and are only incorporated into the EPS computation if the net effect is dilutive.

The following example illustrates the application of the treasury stock method in the EPS computation.

EPS Illustration: The Treasury Stock Method. Assume that the Woody Corporation earned an after-tax net income of $15,000,000 for fiscal 1992. The firm's tax rate was equal to 46%. The weighted average number of shares was equal to 8,000,000 shares, which was also equal to the number of outstanding shares at year end.

The average for the year market price for Woody's common stock was $70 per share while the year-end closing price was $72 per share. Woody had outstanding options outstanding to acquire 2,000,000 shares of common stock at an exercise price of $60/share. The exercise price was below the market price of the stock for the entire year.

The firm had $6,000,000 of 9% convertible debt outstanding which was convertible into 160,000 shares of common stock. The convertible debt was considered a CSE through the application of the two-thirds yield test. In addition, the firm had $5,000,000 of 12% convertible debt outstanding that was convertible into 50,000 shares of common stock. Based on the two-thirds yield test, the 12% convertible debt does not qualify as a CSE. Woody also had $10,000,000 of 10% nonconvertible debt outstanding.

Based on this information, you are asked to compute both primary and fully diluted EPS.

Solution. The first step in any EPS computation is the determination of the unadjusted EPS for the period.

$$\text{Unadjusted EPS} = \frac{\text{Net Income - Preferred Dividend Requirements}}{\text{Weighted Average Number of Common Shares}}$$

$$\text{Unadjusted EPS} = \frac{\$15,000,000}{8,000,000} = \$1.88/\text{share}.$$

The threshold for requiring the dual presentation under the three-percent materiality test is that fully diluted EPS must be less than or equal to $1.82/share (i.e., 97% x $1.88).

In the computation of primary and fully diluted EPS, the treasury stock method must be applied to the assumed exercise of the stock options. In this case the hypothetical proceeds are equal to $120,000,000 (i.e., 2,000,000 x $60/share). The hypothetical proceeds must first be applied to the acquisition of treasury shares, subject to the two limitations described earlier.

The first limitation is based on the magnitude of the hypothetical proceeds and the share price used to reacquire the treasury shares. For primary EPS the average for the period market price must be used. For the Woody Corporation, the average market price of its common stock is $70/share. Based on this market price, the firm can repurchase 1,714,286 shares (i.e., $120,000,000/$70). However, based on the second limitation, the 20% rule, the maximum number of treasury shares that can be acquired is 1,600,000 (i.e., 8,000,000 x 20%). The incremental shares and the excess procceds available to retire long-term debt are determined below:

	Amount	Number of Shares
Hypothetical Proceeds...............	$120,000,000	2,000,000
Purchase of Treasury Shares ($70 x 1,600,000)..............	<112,000,000>	<1,600,000>
Excess Proceeds to Reduce Debt......	$ 8,000,000	
Incremental Shares..................		400,000
Interest Rate......................	x 10%	
Pretax Interest Savings.............	$ 800,000	

```
After-Tax Interest Savings
    ($800,000 x (1 - .46)).........  $     432,000
                                        ===============
```

Because the convertible debt is considered a CSE, there are additional shares assumed to be issued on conversion (i.e., 160,000 shares) and after-tax interest savings of $291,600 (i.e., $6,000,000 x 9% x [1 - .46]). Based on the information in this case, primary EPS is computed as follows:

```
                   Net Income - Preferred Divided Requirements + After-Tax
                   Interest on Debt Retired + After-Tax Interest Savings
                                  on Convertible Debt
Primary EPS  =  ----------------------------------------------------------
                   Weighted Average Number of Shares + Incremental Shares
                   from the Treasury Stock Method + Shares Issued on
                                  Conversion of Debt


                   $15,000,000 + 432,000 + 291,600     $15,723,600
Primary EPS  =  ------------------------------------ = -----------
                   8,000,000 + 400,000 + 160,000        8,560,000


Primary EPS  =  $1.84/share
```

The computation of fully diluted EPS assumes the same hypothetical proceeds as in the primary EPS case (i.e., $120,000,000); however, the limitations on the treasury share repurchase are modified due to the use of the closing market price in fully diluted EPS. Because the closing price is greater than the average for the year price, it must be used in the fully diluted computation. For fully diluted EPS, the maximum number of shares that can be reacquired from the option proceeds is now 1,666,667 shares (i.e., $120,000,000/$72). Nonetheless, the 20% limitation is the controlling factor and the maximum number of assumed treasury shares that can be purchased is the same as for primary EPS (i.e., 1,600,000 shares). Determination of the incremental shares and the excess proceeds to be used to retire debt is presented below.

	Amount	Number of Shares
Hypothetical Proceeds...............	$120,000,000	2,000,000
Purchase of Treasury Shares ($72 x 1,600,000)..............	<115,200,000>	<1,600,000>
Excess Proceeds to Reduce Debt......	$ 4,800,000	
Incremental Shares..................		400,000
Interest Rate.......................	x 10%	
Pretax Interest Savings.............	$ 480,000	
After-Tax Interest Savings ($480,000 x (1 - .46))..........	$ 259,200	

As noted in the computation of primary EPS, the 9% convertible debt is considered a CSE, and there are 160,000 additional shares assumed to be issued on conversion and after-tax interest savings of $291,600 (i.e., $6,000,000 x 9% x [1 - .46]). The 12% convertible debt was not a CSE and normally would be excluded from primary but would be included in the determination of fully diluted EPS. However, for fully diluted EPS in this case, the inclusion of the 12% convertible debt would individually be antidilutive, and would also be antidilutive in the aggregate. Specifically, including the convertible debt in the fully diluted computation would individually increase EPS by $6.48 (i.e.,($5,000,000 x 12% x [1 - .46])/50,000 shares), and increase fully diluted EPS in the aggregate to $1.84/share. As will be illustrated below, without including the effects of the 12% convertible debt, fully diluted EPS is only $1.82/share. Due to the antidilutive effect of the 12% convertible debt, it cannot be included in the computation of fully diluted EPS presented below.

$$\text{Fully Diluted EPS} = \frac{\text{Net Income - Preferred Dividend Requirements + After-Tax Interest on Debt Retired + After-Tax Interest Savings on Convertible Debt}}{\text{Weighted Average Number of Shares + Incremental Shares from the Treasury Stock Method + Shares Issued on Convertible Debt}}$$

$$\text{Fully Diluted EPS} = \frac{\$15,000,000 + 259,200 + 291,600}{8,000,000 + 400,000 + 160,000} = \frac{\$15,550,800}{8,560,000}$$

Fully Diluted EPS = $1.82/share

The three-percent materiality test is met and the dual presentation is required because fully diluted EPS is equal to the materiality threshold of $1.82 as computed earlier.

OTHER ISSUES IN REPORTING EPS

Contingent Share Arrangements

As noted earlier, the firm may have contingent share arrangements such as stock subscriptions in addition to outstanding options and warrants. If contingent shares are issuable with the mere passage of time, and there are no other conditions to be met or no other restrictions on issuance, the shares must be considered as CSEs in the computation of both primary and fully diluted EPS.

Similarly, if the issuance of the shares is contingent on reaching some specified level of earnings or an earnings increase, and that earnings level is met, then the additional shares must be included in the computation of both primary and fully diluted EPS. However, if the conditional level of earnings is not met, the additional shares are only considered outstanding for fully diluted EPS. In this case, the net income available for common must be increased to the conditional earnings level.

If the contingency expires, the additional shares would not be included in the current computation of EPS and the EPS disclosures reported for all prior periods presented must be restated to reflect the expiration of the contingency. If the contingency is dependent on the market price of stock, in whole or in part, the year-end market price of the stock will determine the number of shares included as CSEs. However, fluctuations in the market price will require retroactive restatement of prior period's EPS, if comparative financial statements are presented.

Disclosure Requirements

The extent of disclosures required under Opinion 15 is dependent on the firm's capital structure. Several of these disclosures have been discussed in previous sections of this chapter, but are repeated here for convenience. The primary disclosure requirements for EPS are presented in the following paragraphs.

First, EPS must be reported on the face of the income statement immediately below the net income for the period. In order to provide more useful information, the total EPS figures (both primary and fully diluted if applicable) must be disaggregated into EPS from each component of net income, such as from continuing operations, discontinued operations, extraordinary items, and the cumulative effect from the change in accounting principle.

Second, the footnotes to the financial statements should include the following information:

1. A summary statement of all applicable rights and privileges of the various classes of equityholder. These rights include dividends and liquidation preferences, participation rights, call options including call prices and dates, and any conversion options, including conversion prices and dates.

2. The details of the computation of primary and fully diluted EPS. These details should include the amount of the weighted average number of common shares used in both primary and fully diluted EPS and a description of the securities classified as CSEs, the assumptions used and information relating to the number of shares issued on conversion or exercise.

3. Information relating to post-balance sheet or subsequent events effecting EPS such as the impact of conversions or exercises of options, etc., and stock dividends, stock splits or reverse splits occurring after the date of the financial statements but before the financial statements are issued.

4. The effects of any restatement of prior periods' EPS presented in the comparative financial statements.

5. The impact of any recapitalization occurring during the accounting period. For example, if the firm retires debt through the issuance of common stock during the period, a footnote should include the effect of this transaction on EPS as if the recapitalization took place at the beginning of the year.

Sample EPS disclosures for the Goodyear Tire and Rubber Company are presented in Exhibit 6.2.

ANALYTICAL ISSUES IN THE EPS COMPUTATION

The complexities of the EPS computation could pose many formidable analytical problems for the analyst. These problems include the complexities of the mechanical EPS computation itself, the implementation and consistency of the assumptions used and the extent and diversity of the disclosures provided by the accountant. These issues are discussed in the paragraphs that follow.

To begin with, because of its dependence on the net income figure, the EPS computation is subject to all the same limitations of accrual basis accounting discussed throughout this text. The resulting EPS disclosures will only be as reliable as the accrual basis net income determined by the accountant. The analytical problems associated with EPS are compounded by the extensive use of assumptions and use of arbitrary percentage guidelines such as the 20% rule and the two-thirds yield test. In addition, a great deal of the accountant's EPS computation is dependent on internal information used to implement the assumptions of Opinion 15. Due to the complexities involved in the computation and the heavy reliance on internal information, it is generally impossible for the analyst to verify or recompute the account-

EXHIBIT 6.2

Sample Disclosure: Goodyear Tire and Rubber Company and Subsidiaries: Consolidated Statement of Income, Per Share Presentation and EPS Footnote

Consolidated Statement of Income
The Goodyear Tire & Rubber Company and Subsidiaries

(Dollars in millions, except per share)	Year Ended December 31,		
	1987	1986	1985
Net Sales	$ 9,905.2	$9,040.0	$8,341.1
Other Income	179.9	121.0	114.2
	10,085.1	9,161.0	8,455.3
Cost and Expenses:			
Cost of goods sold	7,374.6	6,941.5	6,550.4
Selling, administrative and general expense	1,634.9	1,596.6	1,380.9
Interest and amortization of debt discount and expense	282.5	121.9	101.5
Unusual items	(135.0)	10.1	21.3
Foreign currency exchange	38.9	19.1	33.8
Minority interest in net income of subsidiaries	16.8	9.6	6.6
	9,212.7	8,698.8	8,094.5
Income from continuing operations before income taxes	872.4	462.2	360.8
United States and foreign taxes on income	358.5	245.4	133.7
Income from continuing operations	513.9	216.8	227.1
Discontinued operations	257.0	(92.7)	185.3
Net Income	$ 770.9	$ 124.1	$ 412.4
Per Share of Common Stock:			
Income from continuing operations	$ 8.49	$2.02	$2.11
Discontinued operations	4.24	(.86)	1.73
Net Income	$12.73	$1.16	$3.84

Net Income Per Share	Net income per share has been computed based on the average number of common shares outstanding, including for this purpose only those treasury shares allocated for distribution under the incentive profit sharing plan; and for 1987, 1986 and 1985 was 60,564,981, 107,092,197 and 107,369,517, respectively.

ant's EPS disclosure. Case 6.1 presented at the end of this chapter is designed to illustrate some of the problems faced by the analyst in reconstructing the EPS disclosure.

Not only are the assumptions of Opinion 15 difficult to implement, in many cases they may seem inconsistent. For example, if a security does not qualify as a CSE in the year of issuance because the two-thirds yield test is not met, but if a similar security is a CSE at some future date, the original security is reclassified as a CSE. However, a security would not be reclassified as a CSE to reflect changing market conditions. This limitation may prove to be highly unrealistic in those situations where the market actually reacts to the security as a CSE, but this same security is excluded from the EPS computation.

Finally, the analyst must utilize all available disclosures, including the president's letter and management's discussion and analysis, in the assessment of the quality of the EPS disclosure. A change in EPS can be due to a variety of factors such as an increase in net income, a reduction in the number of common shares outstanding, a reduction in the number of other potentially dilutive securities, or an expiration of contingent share arrangements. A cosmetic improvement of EPS resulting from a large treasury stock repurchase is of lower quality than if the EPS increase was due to a significant increase in profitability.

Use of the EPS Computation in Credit and Financial Analysis: Proforma Financial Information

Understanding the detailed requirements of Opinion 15 can be an invaluable resource for the credit and financial analyst in the preparation of proforma financial information. Proforma information can be used in determining the financial statement effects of a proposed merger or raising additional capital. The following discussion provides an illustration of how the EPS figure is used in the assessment of financing alternatives.

Evaluation of Financing Alternatives: Proforma EPS Computations. In order to illustrate the use of EPS in assessing alternative means of financing, consider a firm that wishes to raise $18,000,000 in additional capital in 1992. The firm presently has 5,000,000 shares of common stock outstanding without preferred shares and no potentially dilutive securities outstanding. The projected after-tax earnings for 1992 are equal to $8,000,000. The expected income tax rate is 46%.

The firm is willing to consider four mutually exclusive financing alternatives. These are:

1. Issue an additional 1,500,000 shares of common stock at a time when the market price is expected to be $12/share.

2. Issue $18,000,000 of 14%, $1,000 par value nonconvertible debentures. This will result in an after-tax interest charge of $1,360,800 (i.e., $18,000,000 x 14% x [1 - .46]).

3. Issue $18,000,000 of 11%, $1,000 par value convertible bonds. Each of the 18,000 bonds issued is convertible into 50 shares of the firm's common

stock or a maximum of 900,000 shares if all bonds convert. During the periods that the debt is not converted, it will result in an after-tax interest charge of $1,069,200 (i.e., $18,000,000 x 11% x [1 - .46]). At the target issue date, the expected average Aa corporate bond rate is 15%. Therefore, the convertible debt does not qualify as a common stock equivalent (i.e., 11% > [2/3 x 15%]). As a result, if its effects are dilutive, the convertible debt will only be included in fully diluted EPS.

4. Issue $18,000,000 of $100 par value, $9 nonconvertible, noncumulative preferred stock. The dividend requirement for the 180,000 preferred shares is $1,620,000 (i.e., $9.00 x 180,000).

Without the additional financing, the proforma unadjusted EPS for 1992 would be determined as follows:

$$\text{Proforma Unadjusted EPS} = \frac{\$8,000,000}{5,000,000} = \$1.60/\text{share}$$

The following computations would be made for each of the four financing alternatives. With the exception of the convertible debt, all financing alternatives would still result in a single presentation of EPS. The resulting proforma EPS disclosures are presented below.

Common Stock:

$$\text{Proforma Unadjusted EPS} = \frac{\$8,000,000}{5,000,000 + 1,500,000} = \$1.23/\text{share}$$

Nonconvertible Debentures:

$$\text{Proforma Unadjusted EPS} = \frac{\$8,000,000 - 1,360,800}{5,000,000} = \$1.33/\text{share}$$

Convertible Bonds:

$$\text{Proforma Primary EPS} = \frac{\$8,000,000 - 1,069,200}{5,000,000} = \$1.39/\text{share}$$

$$\text{Proforma Fully Diluted EPS} = \frac{\$8,000,000}{5,000,000 + 900,000} = \$1.36/\text{share}$$

Preferred Stock:

$$\text{Proforma Unadjusted EPS} = \frac{\$8,000,000 - 1,620,000}{5,000,000} = \$1.28/\text{share}$$

If only the cosmetic effect on reported EPS is considered, the best alternative in this illustration is to issue the convertible debt because it has the least dilutive effect on EPS. Of course, other factors must be considered in the financing decision, particularly future cash flows and the ability to meet required debt service payments or dividend distributions.

NOTES

1. FASB Statement No. 55, "Determining Whether a Convertible Security is a Common Stock Equivalent", changed the rate to be used in the "two-thirds test" from the prime rate to the average corporate Aa bond yield in 1982. FASB Statement No. 85, "Yield Test for Determining Whether a Convertible Security is a Common Stock Equivalent", issued in 1985, changed the security yield to be used in the "two-thirds test" from the cash yield to the security's effective yield in order to accommodate low and zero coupon bonds issued at deep discounts.

CASE 6.1. THE SEAGRAM COMPANY LIMITED: EARNINGS PER SHARE--RECONSTRUCTING THE OPINION 15 EARNINGS PER SHARE DISCLOSURE FROM ANNUAL REPORT INFORMATION

The Seagram Company Limited is a leading producer and marketer of distilled spirits and wines, with affiliates in 27 countries.

REQUIRED: Carefully study the Consolidated Statement of Income, Consolidated Balance Sheet, Note 3--Credit Arrangements and Long-Term Indebtedness, and Note 5--Common Shares and Earnings Per Share.

1. Assuming the year end stock price was $67/share and the average for the year price was $40/share, recompute the company's primary earnings per share for 1987.

2. Using the same assumptions as to stock price, recompute the company's fully diluted earnings per share for 1987.

3. Why is full dilution considered material? In other words, why is the dual presentation required under Opinion 15?

NOTE: ROUNDING ERRORS OR ERRORS DUE TO LACK OF INTERNAL INFORMATION COULD RESULT IN DIFFERENCES OF A FEW CENTS PER SHARE.

Consolidated Statement of Income

(U.S. dollars in thousands, except per share amounts)

The Seagram Company Ltd
(Incorporated under the Canada Business Corporations Act
and Subsidiary Companies)

	Twelve Months Ended January 31,		
	1987	1986	1985
Sales and other income	$3,344,820	$2,970,669	$2,821,245
Cost of goods	2,189,628	1,940,993	1,834,233
	1,155,192	1,029,676	987,012
Selling, general and administrative expenses	927,360	815,021	741,399
Restructuring costs	35,000	—	—
Operating Income	192,832	214,655	245,613
Interest expense	84,294	82,013	88,054
Income before income taxes	108,538	132,642	157,559
Provision for income taxes	5,715	33,417	43,742
Income from spirits and wine operations	102,823	99,225	113,817
Interest expense related to share repurchase, after income taxes	(2,513)	(6,683)	(12,845)
Dividend income from E.I. du Pont de Nemours and Company, after income taxes	154,091	150,838	141,294
Equity in unremitted earnings of E.I. du Pont de Nemours and Company	169,057	75,694	141,352
Net Income	$ 423,458	$ 319,074	$ 383,618
Earnings per share data:			
Income from operations and dividends	$2.67	$2.63	$2.67
Equity in unremitted earnings of E.I. du Pont de Nemours and Company	1.78	.81	1.55
Net Income—primary	$4.45	$3.44	$4.22
—fully diluted	$4.30	$3.34	$4.05

Source: McCormick and Company, Inc. 1984 Annual Report. Copyright, 1985, by
The McCormick Company, Inc. Reprinted with permission.

Consolidated
Balance Sheet
(U.S. dollars in thousands)

Assets	January 31,	
	1987	1986
Current Assets		
Cash and short-term investments at cost, which approximates market	$ 593,590	$ 386,466
Receivables	590,155	508,383
Inventories	1,250,029	1,250,165
Prepaid expenses	48,110	36,095
Wine company assets held for sale	220,000	—
Total current assets	2,701,884	2,181,109
Common Stock of E.I. du Pont de Nemours and Company	3,329,727	3,150,611
Note Receivable from Sun Company, Inc.	51,000	67,500
Property, Plant and Equipment, at cost	842,593	917,551
Accumulated depreciation	(343,634)	(346,023)
	498,959	571,528
Investments and Advances—spirits and wine companies	76,686	49,330
Sundry Assets, including excess of cost over net assets of companies acquired	228,206	202,079
	$6,886,462	$6,222,157

Source: The Seagram Company Ltd., Report for the twelve months ended January 31, 1987. Copyright, 1987, by the Seagram Company Ltd. Reprinted with permission.

The Seagram Company Ltd.
Incorporated under the Canada Business Corporations Act
and Subsidiary Companies

	January 31,	
Liabilities and Shareholders' Equity	1987	1986
Current Liabilities		
Short-term borrowings	$ 460,410	$ 233,838
United States excise taxes	61,047	86,370
Payables and accrued liabilities	450,780	404,283
Income and other taxes	57,637	77,040
Indebtedness payable within one year	72,420	141,952
Total current liabilities	1,102,294	943,483
Long-Term Indebtedness	911,764	803,601
Deferred Income Taxes and Other Credits	882,040	918,959
Minority Interest	34,804	34,133
Shareholders' Equity		
Shares without par value		
1987—95,494,856 shares; 1986—95,145,420 shares	257,368	222,426
Share purchase warrants	27,679	27,691
Cumulative currency translation adjustments	(228,456)	(311,874)
Retained earnings	3,898,969	3,583,738
Total shareholders' equity	3,955,560	3,521,981
	$6,886,462	$6,222,157

Approved by the Board: Edgar M. Bronfman, Director, and C.E. Medland, Director.

Source: The Seagram Company Ltd., Report for the twelve months ended January
31, 1987. Copyright, 1987, by the Seagram Company Ltd. Reprinted with
permission.

Note 3: Credit Arrangements and Long-Term Indebtedness

Short-term borrowings at January 31, 1987 comprised bank borrowings of $131,420,000 and commercial paper of $328,990,000, bearing interest at prime or equivalent rates, respectively. The Company's unused lines of credit at January 31, 1987, a portion of which supports outstanding commercial paper, totaled $767,023,000.

Long-term indebtedness comprised:

	January 31,	
	1987	1986
	(thousands)	
11³/₈% Guaranteed Notes, due November 1, 1986	—	$125,000
Eurodollar Notes, due November 25, 1988 through August 16, 1994; interest at 7.9% on average (8.5% in 1986)	$107,816	107,816
12% Promissory Notes, due February 1, 1989	—	5,000
12³/₄% Eurodollar Notes, due October 1, 1989	—	99,738
7⁵/₈% Debentures, due December 15, 1991	11,761	12,157
7% Eurodollar Subordinated Debentures, due May 15, 1993	109,399	101,699
12¹/₄% Guaranteed Bonds, due November 23, 1994	50,969	32,568
10⁷/₈% Debentures, due June 1, 1995	29,595	31,073
10% Eurodollar Bonds, due June 27, 1995	100,000	100,000
8¹/₂% Eurodollar Bonds, due April 15, 1996	100,000	—
12% Promissory Notes, due July 15, 1996	41,000	52,800
Liquid Yield Option Notes, due March 5, 2006	96,658	118,870
12³/₄% Debentures, due October 31, 2012 (£50,000,000)	75,368	70,312
6% Swiss Franc Bonds, due September 30, 2085 (Sfr. 250,000,000)	162,028	—
Sundry	99,590	88,520
	984,184	945,553
Less: Indebtedness payable within one year	72,420	141,952
	$911,764	$803,601

In May 1983, the Company issued $125 million 7% Eurodollar Subordinated Debentures due May 15, 1993, with detachable share purchase warrants which expire September 15, 1988. Detachable warrants issued with debentures are accounted for as paid-in capital. Accordingly, based on the relative fair values of the debentures and warrants, $27.7 million of the $125 million offering was allocated to the share purchase warrants and included in shareholders' equity. Note 5 provides additional information.

In November 1984, for consideration of $5.5 million Joseph E. Seagram & Sons, Inc. (JES), the principal United States subsidiary, issued 125,000 debt warrants entitling holders to purchase at par $125 million 12¹/₄% Guaranteed Bonds due November 23, 1994; the warrants expire November 23, 1989. At January 31, 1987, 3,705 of the warrants were exercisable.

In August 1985, JES issued $575 million face amount of Liquid Yield Option Notes (LYONs), which are zero coupon notes with no interest payments due until maturity on March 5, 2006. The LYONs were offered at $200 for each $1,000 face amount note; accordingly, gross proceeds from the issue totaled $115 million. The LYONs are convertible at the option of the holders into the Company's common shares at a conversion rate of 4.61 shares for each $1,000 face amount. Note 5 provides additional information.

The Company has guaranteed the LYONs on a subordinated basis and unconditionally guaranteed the 12¹/₄% Bonds due 1994. Summarized financial information for JES and its subsidiaries is presented below:

	Twelve Months Ended January 31,		
	1987	1986	1985
	(thousands)		
Sales and other income	$2,777,905	$2,485,854	$2,333,741
Cost of goods	1,911,043	1,719,428	1,637,712
Net income	337,649	246,958	314,166

	January 31,	
	1987	1986
	(thousands)	
Current assets	$2,288,606	$1,833,163
Noncurrent assets	4,012,817	3,907,026
	$6,301,423	$5,740,189
Current liabilities	$1,055,121	$ 825,840
Noncurrent liabilities	1,516,125	1,564,376
Shareholder's equity	3,730,177	3,349,973
	$6,301,423	$5,740,189

In November 1981, the Company repurchased 15 million of its common shares for $300 million; interest expense on the borrowings to finance the repurchase, less income tax benefits of $2.1 million, $5.7 million and $10.9 million in the twelve-month periods ended January 31, 1987, 1986 and 1985, respectively, has been shown separately in the Consolidated Statement of Income to obtain comparability among the periods presented.

Interest expense on long-term indebtedness was $68.2 million, $70.1 million and $68.7 million in the twelve months ended January 31, 1987, 1986 and 1985, respectively. Annual repayments and redemptions for the five years subsequent to January 31, 1987 are: 1988—$72.4 million; 1989—$76.8 million; 1990—$32.6 million; 1991—$11.3 million; 1992—$46.9 million.

Note 5: Common Shares and Earnings Per Share

The Company is authorized to issue an unlimited number of common shares without nominal or par value. At January 31, 1987, the Company had outstanding warrants to purchase 3,498,500 common shares at $37 per share and JES had outstanding LYONs convertible into 1,992,801 of the Company's common shares (see Note 3). Earnings per share were based on the weighted average number of shares outstanding in the twelve-month periods ended January 31: 1987—95,112,193; 1986—92,624,843; 1985—90,896,522.

Source: The Seagram Company Ltd., Report for the twelve months ended January 31, 1987. Copyright, 1987, by the Seagram Company Ltd. Reprinted with permission.

7

Accounting for Leases

INTRODUCTION

Over the last three decades, leasing has become a major means of financing the acquisition of capital assets. Along with the extensive volume of lease transactions came the increasing concern over the proper accounting treatment and subsequent financial analysis of the lease. As will be discussed throughout this chapter, the most significant analytical problems result from the choice of accounting method used to reflect the lease transaction on the financial statements of the lessee.

Regardless of the method of accounting for lease contract, title to the equipment generally does not pass to the lessee. A noncancelable commitment may or may not be created under the terms of the lease agreement. Nonetheless, the economic substance of the transaction and management's intention may render the lease agreement an equivalent to financing the acquisition of plant assets through the issuance of long-term debt.

The purpose of this chapter is to present the theoretical foundation, the mechanical procedures and the required disclosures in accounting for leases under FASB Statement No. 13, "Accounting for Leases". In addition, an analysis of the lease transaction is presented which attempts to provide a framework that enables the credit and financial analyst to determine the economic substance of the lease contract and to assess the impact of the extent of the lessee's off-balance sheet financing.

ACCOUNTING FOR LEASES: THE THEORY UNDERLYING SFAS 13

Regardless of the legal form of the transaction, a noncancelable lease commitment that transfers substantially all of the risks and rewards of ownership to the lessee should be recorded as an acquisition of a capital asset and the incurrence of a long-term obligation. According to SFAS 13, paragraph 5(f), the term noncancelable literally means noncancelable or that the lease is cancelable due to the "occurrence of some remote contingency; permission of the lessor; the lessee entering into another lease agreement with the lessor", or cancellation that would require payment of such a substantial penalty that lease termination is highly unlikely.

In other words, a noncancelable lease agreement that provides the lessee with all of the economic benefits and risks of ownership or use and control of a productive asset over substantially all of its useful life should be reflected on the financial statements as "in substance" a purchase of a fixed asset and the incurrence of a long-term obligation. Even if the lease contract does not transfer legal title from the lessor to the lessee, the accountant should recognize the economic substance of the transaction. In those cases where the lease agreement is recorded by the lessee as an asset acquisition financed by long-term debt, the contract is classified as a capital or finance lease and is accounted for under the capitalization or finance method. If the lease is also classified as a finance lease on the books of the lessor, the capitalization method is used and a long-term receivable and a sale is recorded.

If the lease agreement does not transfer the economic benefits and risks of ownership to the lessee, the lease is classified as a simple operating lease, which is accounted for under the so-called operating method. Under the operating method the lessee only records the rent expense each period and does not record a plant asset or long-term liability. Similarly, the lessor only records rental income without giving any recogintion to a receivable and a sale. Thus, under the operating method the accountant views the lease as a simple executory contract.

The provisions of SFAS 13 set forth the standards for determining the economic substance of the transaction and the type of lease to be recorded for both the lessor and the lessee. Although the accounting issues for both the lessor and lessee will be discussed, the key analytical issues are concerned with the proper lease classification and the potential off-balance sheet financing for the lessee.

Lessee Accounting: Criteria for Use of the Capitalization Method

The primary accounting issue for the lessee is the determination of the proper classification of the agreement, either, capital or operating lease. That is, the key lease reporting issue asks the question, How does the accountant determine if the economic substance of the agreement is such that it represents a purchase of equipment financed by long-term debt?

Under the provisions of SFAS 13, paragraph 7, the accountant should classify the agreement as a capital lease on the books of the lessee if, at the inception of the lease, any one of the following four criteria are met:

1. "The lease transfers ownership of the property to the lessee at the end of the lease term."

    For purposes of implementation of SFAS 13, the lease term is defined in paragraph 5(f) as the initial, noncancelable term plus any bargain renewal options. A bargain renewal option is an option which enables the lessee to extend or renew the lease contract at a rental payment that is substantially below the expected fair rental value at the renewal date. In addition, the lease term may also include renewal options such that failure to renew the lease would result in a penalty of such magnitude that, at the inception of the lease, renewal seems certain; the lessor has the option to renew or extend the lease; and there are ordinary renewal periods prior to the bargain renewal option term. In any case, the lease term cannot be considered to "extend beyond the date upon which any bargain purchase (defined below) option becomes exercisable".

2. "The lease contains a bargain purchase option." A bargain purchase option is an option enabling the lessee to acquire the property at a price which is substantially below the expected fair market value of the property at the date the option becomes exercisable.

In both of the first two SFAS 13 criteria, there is the implication that the lease payments allow the lessee to build up equity in the property. With a significant amount of equity created by the lease payments, either ownership is transferred automatically upon termination or by making a nominal final payment to obtain legal title.

3. "The lease term (as defined above) is greater than or equal to 75% of the estimated economic life of the property." This criterion is sometimes called the seventy-five-percent rule or seventy-five-percent test.

The rationale behind the seventy-five-percent test is based on the lessee's use and control of the property. That is, if the lessee has the ability to exercise exclusive use and control of the property over substantially all of the property's economic life, the lease agreement is in substance the acquisition of the asset.

4. "The present value of the minimum lease payments is greater than or equal to 90% of the fair market value of the property at the inception of the lease." This criterion is also known as the ninety-percent rule or ninety-percent test.

The inception of the lease occurs at the point where all of the lease terms are fixed and there are no parts of the agreement to be determined.

Minimum lease payments are the "pure lease payments" exclusive of the executory costs. Executory costs include charges for maintenance, insurance and taxes.

The rationale behind the ninety-percent test is based on the fact that the fair market value of the property is equal to today's cash price. Meeting the ninety-percent test implies that if the present value of the future cash outflows relating to the lease contract are greater than or equal to 90% of today's cash price, the lessee is virtually indifferent between the lease and the cash acquisition. This type of reasoning treats the lease as an equivalent to a long-term debt agreement. It should be noted that the seventy-five-percent and the ninety-percent tests should not be applied if the lease term begins within the last twenty-five percent of the total estimated life of the asset.

According to SFAS 13, paragraph 7, if any one of the above four criteria are met, the lessee should classify the lease as a capital lease and record the acquisition of a plant asset and the incurrence of long-term debt. When the lease is classifed as a capital lease, each lease payment is viewed as containing payment of both principal and interest. Because the agreement is in substance a purchase of the property, the lessee must also record the depreciation or amortization of the property.

If none of the above four criteria are met, the lease must be classified as a simple operating lease. Under the operating method, each lease payment is expensed immediately as rent expense. There is no recognition of a plant asset, the long-term debt, interest expense or depreciation expense on the lessee's financial statements.

Financial Statement Implications: Capital versus Operating Leases. A simple review of the SFAS 13 criteria for capitalization would indicate the fact that lease provisions could easily be manipulated so as to capitalize or to avoid capitalization. However, the first and most critical point to understand in comparing the financial statement effects of a capital versus an operating lease is that there is absolutely no "real" differences between the two alternative accounting treatments because the required cash outflows are the same under either method. No matter how the lessee accounts for the lease, the required cash outflows are fixed by the agreement with the lessor and are equal to the periodic rental payments. It should be noted that the tax laws relating to the tax status of a lease as a "true" or "tax" lease versus a "purchase" are not always consistent with the criteria of SFAS 13. Therefore, the terms of the lease contract could have important tax implications and only in this sense impact the cash flows of the firm.

For tax purposes, the transfer of ownership and bargain purchase option provisions, similar to those of SFAS 13, are also used to determine the status of the lease as a purchase. However, the IRS also considers other factors that identify the economic substance of the transaction, rather than its legal form, to determine which party to the contract is the "owner" of the property for tax purposes. Therefore, there may be inconsistencies between the classification of the lease for tax and financial reporting purposes. In order to isolate the financial statement effect of the lessee's accounting alternatives, the tax implications of the lease will not be considered in the remainder of this chapter and therefore the cash flow consequences of the agreement are always assumed to be the same for both capital and operating leases. Other complexities of the tax law relating to lease contracts are beyond the objectives of this text.

Even where there are no cash flow or tax differences between the capital and the operating methods of accounting for the lease, there may be several cosmetic incentives to avoid capitalization on the financial statements of the lessee. To begin with, the use of the operating method is sometimes considered to result in off-balance sheet financing. Off-balance sheet financing refers to those cases where the noncancelable lease terms are manipulated to avoid capitalization so as not to record the long-term debt on the lessee's balance sheet. There are additional cosmetic benefits from using the operating method. In the earlier years of the lease, the sum of interest and depreciation charges under the capitalization method generally exceed the simple rent expense recorded under the operating method. Therefore, reported net income and EPS will be higher in the earlier years if the lessee can record the transaction as an operating lease.

In order to illustrate the financial statement effects of a capital versus operating lease, the following equation analysis is presented.

```
------------------------------------|-----------------------------------
            BALANCE SHEET           |           INCOME STATEMENT
------------------------------------|-----------------------------------

                      STOCKHOLDERS' | NET INCOME
  ASSETS  = LIABILITIES +  EQUITY   | OR LOSS  = REVENUES - EXPENSES
    |          |          |         |    |  |        |         |
    |          |          |         |    |  |        |         |
  ---------    |     ---------------|    |  |        |         |
  |    |       |       |       |    |    |  |        |         |
  |  NON-      |       |       |    |    |  |        |         |
  |  CASH      |    CAPITAL  + RETAINED |NET INCOME  |         |
 CASH + ASSETS LIAB + STOCK   EARNINGS | OR LOSS  = REVENUES - EXPENSES
 ----  ------  ------ --------- ---------|---------- ---------- --------
                                    ^    |  |
                                    |    |  |
                                    |<---<---<-|
=================================================================
 -Cash                              ^    |                  - Rent
  (a)                               |    |                  Expense
 (Credit)                           |    |                    (a)
                                    |    |                  (Debit)
                            |<---<---<---<---<---<---<---<-----|
=================================================================
  +Leased  +Lease                   |
   Asset    Obligation              |
   (b)       (b)                     |
  (Debit)   (Credit)                 |
=================================================================
 -Cash    -Lease                    ^    |                  - Interest
  (c)      Obligation               |    |                  Expense
 (Credit)   (c)                     |    |                    (c)
            (Debit)                 |    |                  (Debit)
                            |<---<---<---<---<---<---<-----|
=================================================================
  -Accum                            ^    |                  - Depr.
  Depr. (d)                         |    |                  Expense (d)
  (Credit)                          |    |                  (Debit)
                            |<-----<-----<-----<-----<-----<--|
=================================================================
```

(a) Entry to record the annual rent expense under an operating lease. The first and subsequent payments under the lease would be the same each year. It should be noted that there is no entry at the inception of an operating lease.

(b) Entry to record the acquisition of the plant asset and the long-term lease obligation at the inception of the capital lease.

(c) Entry to record the periodic lease payment under the capital lease. Note that each lease payment consists of a loan principal paydown and the payment of interest.

(d) Entry to record the periodic depreciation or amortization of the plant recorded asset under the capital lease.

==

The equation analysis clearly indicates that if the potential tax differences are ignored, the cash outflows are identical for the capital and the operating lease. For the operating lease the cash rental payments are recorded as rent expense. Under the capital lease, the same cash rental payment is recorded as a reduction of the outstanding lease debt and the payment of the periodic interest. In addition, there is no leased asset or lease obligation recorded under the operating lease. Therefore, if a capital lease is misclassified, off-balance sheet financing results. With the leased asset recorded under the capital lease, periodic depreciation or amortization must be charged against income. As noted earlier, the sum of the interest and depreciation charges are greater than the rent expense recorded in the earlier years of the lease. This reduces the reported income and EPS under the captial lease relative to the operating lease. The higher income and the off-balance sheet financing effects of the operating method may increase the managerial incentives to avoid capitalization.

In order to assist the financial statement user, there are extensive lease disclosure requirements under SFAS 13. The lease footnote disclosures can be used by the analyst to assess the extent of the lessee's off-balance sheet financing. The required lessee disclosures are presented in the following section.

Lessee Disclosure Requirements. Paragraph 16(f) of SFAS 13 states that for all operating leases with noncancelable terms of more than one year, the lessee must disclose the future minimum rental commitments in the aggregate and individually for each of the next five years. This schedule provides the information needed to assess future lease obligations and can be used to assess the extent of the lessee's off-balance sheet financing. In addition, the total minimum sublease rentals to be received under noncancelable agreements must be disclosed. For all operating leases the lessee must disclose the rent expense charged against income for all periods presented. This disclosure must also separately identify the amounts of minimum rentals, sublease rentals and contingent rentals. For example, for the total rent expense recorded under a retail lease, the lessee must disclose the fixed amount of the rental and the amount of the rent expense contingent on sales revenue.

If the lessee also has lease contracts accounted for under the capitalization method, several additional disclosures are required by SFAS 13, paragraph 16(a). For the capital leases in effect, the lessee must disclose the gross amount and type of leased assets held. This disclosure is important because it identifies that portion of the firm's fixed assets not owned and therefore not available for collateral. In addition, the accumulated depreciation or amortization deducted on the balance sheet and the depreciation and amortization expense charged against income must be disclosed for all periods presented in the annual report.

A schedule showing the future minimum lease payments in the aggregate and for each of next five years must be presented, net of executory costs and the amounts representing interest. By deducting the amount of the total payments representing interest, the present value of the minimum lease payments is disclosed. The present value of the minimum lease payments is the total obligation under capital lease. When the current portion is deducted, the long-term lease obligation is determined and can be agreed to the firm's long-term debt disclosures. Minimum future sublease rentals to be received under noncancelable leases, sublease rentals paid and contingent rentals incurred must be disclosed as in the operating lease requirements. Sample disclosures for the lessee are presented in Exhibit 7.1.

Lessor Accounting: A Brief Overview

Accounting for the lessor is not as controversial as accounting for the lessee, and is generally not considered a significant issue in accounting and finance. Therefore, accounting for the lessor will only be discussed briefly here.

Lease classification is also an issue for the lessor. The lessor can classify a lease agreement as either a capital or operating lease. For the lessor, the capital lease is essentially a "sale" of a plant asset or inventory. As a result, there is accounting recognition given to a long-term receivable and a disposal of a plant asset or a sale of inventory.

If the lease is classified as a capital lease for the lessor, it can be further grouped as either a direct finance lease or a sales-type lease. In a direct finance lease, the economic return to the lessor is only in the form of interest or financing income. In this type of lease, the lessee is basically providing a source of financing for the lessee. The direct financing lease is probably used most often by commercial banks and insurance companies in leasing large computer systems, airliners and other heavy equipment.

In the sales-type lease, the lessor uses the lease contract as a vehicle to market the firm's products. In this case, the lessor earns both interest or financing income and gross profit on the sale of the product. The lessor's gross profit on the sale of the product is known as dealer's or manufacturer's profit. The dealer's or manufacturer's profit is measured as the difference between the fair market value (i.e., sales price) of the product and the lessor's cost or carrying value. The sales-type lease is generally used by manufacturers or retailers of products such as automobiles and computers.

If the lease is classified as a capital lease for the lessor, the asset is sold and is removed from the books and is replaced by a long-term receivable due from the lessee. Because the asset is removed from the books of the lessor, depreciation of a plant asset is no longer recognized.

If the lessor classifies the lease agreement as an operating lease, only rental income is recognized and the depreciation of plant assets or rental equipment inventory is recorded as usual.

EXHIBIT 7.1

Sample Disclosure: The Allen Group, Incorporated: Lessee Footnote Disclosure Under SFAS 13

NOTE 9: LEASE COMMITMENTS

Property, plant and equipment held under capitalized leases were as follows (amounts in thousands):

	1986	1985
Land	$ 249	$ 528
Buildings	3,771	4,652
Machinery and equipment	860	860
	4,880	6,040
Less accumulated depreciation	(2,811)	(2,634)
	$2,069	$3,406

The Company's leases consist primarily of manufacturing facilities and equipment and expire principally between 1987 and 1993. A number of leases provide that the Company pay certain executory costs (taxes, insurance and maintenance) and contain renewal and purchase options. Annual rental expense for operating leases approximated $9,500,000 in 1986, $9,000,000 in 1985 and $7,500,000 in 1984. Future minimum payments under noncancellable leases as of December 3Γ, 1986 are as follows (amounts in thousands):

Year	Operating Leases	Capital Leases
1987	$ 7,607	$ 357
1988	6,464	357
1989	5,213	357
1990	3,307	357
1991	2,636	753
Thereafter	3,103	692
Total minimum lease payments	$28,330	2,873
Less amounts representing interest		(641)
Present value of minimum lease payments ($222,000 principal amount due within one year)		$2,232

Source: The Allen Group, Inc. 1986 Annual Report. Copyright, 1987, by The Allen Group, Inc. Reprinted with permission.

Lessor Accounting: Criteria for Use of the Capitalization Method

In order for the lease to be classified as a capital lease by the lessor, two groups of criteria must be met. The SFAS 13, paragraph 8, criteria for capitalization by the lessor are presented below.

Group I: Any one of the four lessee criteria must be met

AND

Group II: Both of the following two criteria must be met:

1. Collectibility of the required minimum lease payments
   from the lessee is reasonably assured

2. There are no material uncertainties regarding the
   amount of future unreimbursable costs to be incurred by
   the lessor under the terms of the lease.

If the lease contract does not meet any one of the four criteria from Group I and both of the Group II criteria, the lease must be classified as an operating lease.

The Group II criteria are nothing more than the accountant's criteria for revenue recognition. Due to the revenue elements built into the capital lease, it is logical to require that the criteria for revenue realization be met for a lease that is in substance a sale.

In most cases, the Group II criteria should be met. Nonetheless, there is a possibility that the lessor may not meet the Group II criteria. If the Group I criteria are met but the lessor fails to satisfy the revenue realization requirements of the Group II criteria, there would be asymmetrical accounting treatment for the lessor and the lessee. Specifically, the lessor would record the contract as an operating lease while the lessee would record the transaction as a capital lease. Not only is it illogical to have a purchase without a sale, but due to the lack of accounting symmetry both parties to the contract "own" and depreciate the same asset.

Financial Statement Implications: Capital versus Operating Leases. Ignoring possible tax differences, the cash flows are identical and are equal to the periodic rental, regardless of the accounting method used by the lessor. The same conclusion was drawn earlier in the discussion of accounting for the lessee. However, unlike the lessee the lessor may have fewer incentives to manipulate the lease terms to avoid capitalization and to achieve cosmetic accounting benefits.

Although the lessor can also force the lease classification by manipulation of the lease terms, the impact on the analyst's ability to properly determine the economic substance of the transaction may not be as critical as in the case of the lessee. Nonetheless, many lessors, particularly in the financial services industry, may prefer to capitalize so as to record a long-term financing receivable and keep certain types of plant assets off their books. For example, assets such as heavy construction equipment and jet airliners would be incompatible with the fundamental operations and the financial statement presentation of a financial institution and would provide some incentive to management to capitalize the lease and avoid recording such types of equipment on the balance sheet.

If the lessor misclassifies the contract and records the capital lease, the only balance sheet effect is the substitution of a long-term receivable for a plant asset or rental equipment inventory. The issue of off-balance sheet financing is not relevant to the financial statements of the lessor.

On the income statement, the potential misclassification would consist of the substitution of interest income and/or the gross profit on the sale for rental income. The lessor's income statement effects would generally favor capitalization in the early years of the contract. Because the effects of misclassification of the lease contract are generally not significant, lessor accounting is not a major issue for the credit and financial analyst.

Lessor Disclosure Requirements. The disclosure requirements for the lessor as listed in SFAS 13, paragraph 23, can also be useful to the analyst.

A general description of the lessor's leasing activities must be disclosed for both types of leases, capital and operating.

For capital leases, both direct financing and sales type leases, the lessor must disclose "the components of the net investment" in the finance lease which include "the future minimum lease payments to be received", net of executory costs, and any provision for uncollectable rental payments; the lessor's "unguaranteed residual value"; the deferred or unearned interest revenue; and initial indirect costs on direct finance leases. In addition, the lessor must provide a schedule showing the future minimum lease payments to be received over the next five years. The total balance of the receivable must be classified into its current and long-term components. Finally, the amount of contingent rentals included in the lessor's income statement must be presented.

For operating leases, the lessor must disclose the total cost or carrying value of assets leased or to be leased by major category of plant and equipment, and the amount of accumulated depreciation related to the leased assets. In addition, the lessor must provide a schedule of the minimum lease payments on noncancelable lease agreements in total and for each of the next five years. Finally, the lessor must disclose the amount of contingent rentals included in income for each year presented in the income statement.

A sample of the SFAS 13 disclosures for the lessor is presented in Exhibit 7.2.

LEASE ACCOUNTING ILLUSTRATED

Data for the Illustration

Accounting for both the lessor and the lessee will be illustrated in this example. For purposes of this illustration assume that on January 1, 1991, the Boston Company entered into a lease agreement with Webester Equipment Corporation for purposes of leasing new heavy equipment to be used in manufacturing. The following information is available concerning the lease contract:

EXHIBIT 7.2

**Sample Disclosure: Jiffy Lube International, Incorporated
and Subsidiaries: Lessor Footnote Disclosure Under SFAS 13**

Note K—Leases

As Lessee: The Company leases certain service center sites,
automobiles, office space, and furniture and equipment with
lease periods of 1 to 20 years. The Company pays the property
taxes, insurance and maintenance costs related to the leased
property where applicable. Rent expense under these operating
leases for the years ended March 31, 1988, 1987 and 1986 was
$5,684,918, $2,457,105 and $1,699,200, respectively.

The Company also leases certain additional service center
sites and equipment, most of which are subleased to franchisees.
The typical lease period for the service centers is 20 years, and
some leases contain renewal options. These leases are accounted
for as capital leases and are capitalized using interest rates appropriate at the inception of each lease.

As Lessor: The Company owns or leases numerous service
center sites which are leased or subleased to franchisees. The
typical lease period is 20 years, and some leases contain renewal
options. The franchisee pays the property taxes, insurance and
maintenance costs related to the leased property. Most of these
leases or subleases are accounted for as direct financing leases.

In those cases where the Company leases only land, or the
lease or sublease does not meet the criteria for capitalization, the
lease or sublease is accounted for as an operating lease.

Future minimum commitments under leasing arrangements
at March 31, 1988 were as follows:

	Amounts Payable as Lessee		Amounts Receivable as Lessor	
	Capital Leases	Operating Leases	Direct Financing Leases	Operating Leases
	(Thousands of Dollars)			
Year Ending March 31:				
1989	$ 5,292	$ 7,401	$ 8,782	$ 7,508
1990	5,292	7,163	8,782	7,553
1991	5,292	7,040	8,782	7,595
1992	5,283	6,939	8,782	7,651
1993	5,235	6,664	8,782	7,161
Thereafter	63,771	76,867	115,587	82,276
Net minimum commitments	90,165	$112,074	159,497	$119,744
Less interest	53,378		97,007	
Present value of net minimum commitments	36,787		62,490	
Less current portion	657		867	
Long-term commitments at March 31, 1988	$36,130		$ 61,623	

Source: Jiffy Lube International, Inc. 1988 Annual Report. Copyright, 1988, by
Jiffy Lube International, Inc. Reprinted with permission.

1. The term of the noncancelable lease is three years with no renewal option and no residual value at the end of the lease term. Annual rental payments are $232,819.84. The rental payments are due on each December 31, with the first payment due on December 31, 1991.

2. At the inception of the lease, the fair market value of the equipment was $600,000. The cost of the machine to Webester was $550,000. The machine has an economic life of five years, with no scrap value. The equipment reverts back to Webester upon termination of the lease.

3. The Boston Company depreciates similar equipment over a five year period using an accelerated depreciation method.

4. The Boston Company's incremental borrowing rate on actual debt with similar terms and under similar conditions is 10%. Webester's rate of return implicit in the lease is 8%.

5. All executory costs are paid by the lessor. In addition, the lessor has no material uncertainties as to the collectibility from Boston and as to any unreimbursed future costs to be incurred under the lease.

You are asked to determine the proper classification for the lease for both the lessor and the lessee. In addition, the effects of the lease on the financial statements of both parties should be determined.

Solution

Relevant Provisions of SFAS 13. Before the actual solution to this illustration is presented, several relevant provisions of SFAS 13 relating to lessee accounting will be discussed.

First, the provisions of SFAS 13 imply that the lessee should account for the asset and the liability separately. If the lessee capitalizes the lease, the amount to be recorded as an asset must be equal to the lower of the present value of the minimum lease payments or the fair market value of the property. This provision is included to prevent overstatement of the asset and is based on conservatism. Additionally, for all computations involving present values, the lessee must use the lower of the lessee's incremental borrowing rate or the lessor's implicit rate of return, if known to the lessee. The lessor's implicit rate may not be known to the lessee because the provisions of the truth in lending laws do not apply to lease contracts at this time. The lower rate increases the discounted value of the future cash flows and is used in order to prevent undervaluation of the liability in the discounting computations.

Second, if the lessee capitalizes the lease under the transfer of ownership or the bargain purchase option criteria, depreciation should be determined by using the method and life the lessee normally utilizes for similar equipment owned. The use of the lessee's normal depreciation and useful life is justified by the fact that by satisfying either the transfer of ownership or the bargain purchase option criteria, the lessee will eventually own the leased property. On the other hand, if the lease is capitalized under the seventy-five-percent or the ninety-percent rules, the lessee must return the equipment to the lessor, and actual ownership will probably not take place. In this case, depreciation would be determined by using the straight-line method over the life of the lease.

Lease Classification: Lessee. Given the provisions of the lease contract in this illustration, the transfer of ownership and the bargain purchase option criteria are not met. The seventy-five-percent test is also not met because the lease term is less than 75% of the economic life of the property. Specifically, the lease term is three years and the economic life of the equipment is five years. Hence, the lessee would have use and control of the asset for only 60% of its economic life.

The lessee would be able to capitalize this lease agreement under the ninety-percent rule. In this illustration the present value of the minimum lease payments, discounted at 8% is equal to $600,000. Because the present value of the minimum lease payments is equal to the fair market value of the property, it can be capitalized. The amount of the asset to be recorded is 600,000. It should be noted that the lessor's implicit rate of return of 8%, is used to discount the minimum lease payments of $232,819.84 because it is lower than the lessee's incremental borrowing rate of 10%.

Lease Classification: Lessor. For the lessor, meeting the ninety-percent test also means that the Group I criteria have been satisfied. As indicated in item five of the data for the illustration, the requirements for revenue recognition have been satisfied, and therefore the Group II criteria for the lessor have also been met. With both the Group I and Group II criteria satisfied, the lessor would also classify the agreement as a capital lease, and accounting symmetry results.

The lessor would also classify the lease as a sales-type lease because there is dealer's or manufactuer's profit of $50,000 (i.e., fair market value - cost or carrying value = $600,000 - 550,000).

Accounting for the Lease. Because the contract is classified as a capital or a finance lease, a loan amortization schedule must be prepared. The following loan amortization schedule could be used by both the lessor and the lessee.

Lease Amortization Schedule

Date	(a) Minimum Lease Payments	(b) 8% Interest	(c) Principal Reduction	(d) Outstanding Balance
1/1/91	-	-	-	$600,000.00
12/31/91	$232,819.84	$48,000.00	$184,819.84	415,180.16
12/31/92	232,819.84	33,214.41	199,605.43	215,574.73
12/31/93	232,819.84	17.245.11	215,574.73	-
	$698,459.52	$98,459.52	$600,000.00	-

(b) = 8% x (d).

(c) = (a) - (b).

(d) = Prior (d) - (c).

==

For both the lessor and the lessee, the total lease payments under the contract are composed of $600,000, which is allocated to the cost of the equipment, and $98,459.52, which represents the finance charges built into the lease payments.

On the books of the lessee, a plant asset and a long-term obligation in the amount of $600,000 is recorded at the inception of the lease. Each year, the lessee charges income for the 8% interest on the outstanding debt and the depreciation or amortization of $200,000 per year (i.e., $600,000/3 years).

To avoid capitalization, the estimated fair market value of the leased property could be overstated, so that the contact fails to meet the ninety-percent test and the lease could be misclassified as an operating lease. If this lease was classified as an operating lease for the lessee, the cash flows each year would be the same and equal to the annual rental payment of $232,819.84. However, the effects on the financial statements would be significantly different.

Under the operating method, the leased asset and the long-term obligation would not be recorded on the financial statements of the lessee. On the income statement, reported net income and EPS would be higher in earlier years under the operating method. To illustrate these financial statement differences, the charges against income under the capitalization and the operating methods are presented in the following summary.

==

Year	Capital Lease Annual Expense			Operating Lease Annual Expense
	Interest	Depreciation	Total	Rent Expense
1991	$48,000.00	$200,000.00	$248,000.00	$232,819.84
1992	33,214.41	200,000.00	233,214.81	232,819.84
1993	17,245.11	200,000.00	217,245.11	232,819.84
	$98,459.52	$600,000.00	$698,459.52	$698,459.52

==

As indicated in the above summary, the lessee's reported income and EPS would be higher in the first two years of the lease under the operating method. This fact, coupled with the off-balance sheet financing feature of an operating lease, provides the cosmetic accounting incentives for management to avoid lease capitalization.

For the lessor, the opposite side of the transaction is reflected and the incentives for capitalization are converse to those of the lessee. Under the capitalization method, the lessor records a sale. At inception, there is a receivable for $698,459.52, of which $98,459.52 represents deferred interest income and the balance, $600,000, is recorded as sales revenue. The inventory or asset account is reduced and cost of sales is recorded at $550,000. The difference between the gross sales revenue and the cost of sales results in the dealer's profit of $50,000. For each subsequent year, the lessor would amortize the deferred income to interest earned.

If the lease was misclassified as an operating lease, only the rental income of $232,819.84 would be recognized each year and the asset would be depreciated. Once again, only cosmetic accounting differences would result in the financial statements. The cash inflows to the lessor would be identical under either accounting method. The following summary compares the financial statement effects of a capital versus an operating lease for the lessor.

	Capital Lease			Operating Lease		
Year	Profit	Interest	Total	Rent Income	Depreciation(a)	Net
1991	$50,000.00	$48,000.00	$98,000.00	$232,819.84	$183,333.33	$49,486.51
1992	-	33,214.41	33,214.41	232,819.84	183,333.33	49,486.51
1993	-	17,245.11	17,245.11	232,819.84	183,333.34	49,486.50
	$50,000.00	$98,459.52	$148,459.52	$698,459.52	$550,000.00	$148,459.52

(a) The cost of the asset is assumed to be depreciated over the lease term using the straight-line method. (i.e., $550,000/3 years = $183,333.33/year).

As noted earlier, the capitalization method would be preferred by the lessor. Reported net income and EPS would be higher in the first year of the lease. In addition, the finance lease receivable would replace plant and equipment held for lease on the balance sheet. Lessors in the insurance and banking industries would prefer to reflect the finance receivable rather than the heavy manufacturing equipment on their balance sheets due to the incompatibility of reporting certain types of plant assets with their basic operations.

Although the previous discussion may point out some motivation for lessors to manipulate lease terms to achieve cosmetic accounting benefits on their financial statements, the key issue in credit and financial analysis is the proper determination of the economic substance of the lease transactions reported by the lessee. In the next section of this chapter, an analytical approach is presented that enables the analyst to capitalize operating leases for the lessee. This approach can assist the analyst in determining the extent of the lessee's off-balance sheet financing, and in making effective credit and investment decisions.

THE CAPITALIZATION OF OPERATING LEASES FOR THE LESSEE: A DISCOUNTED CASH FLOW APPROACH[1]

Prior to the issuance of SFAS 13, the criteria for lease capitalization were considered vague and were often criticized for enabling a significant amount of managerial discretion in the classification of the lease contract. In theory, SFAS 13 eliminated the flexibility afforded to management in the classification of leases as either capital or operating. In practice, there is a significant amount of evidence indicating that fewer leases have been capitalized by lessees since the effective date of SFAS No. 13, January 1, 1977.[2]

The key reason for the reduction of lease capitalization by lessees has been noted several times throughout this chapter. By avoiding capitalization, the lessee can keep a significant amount of debt off the firm's balance sheets. In addition, in the earlier years of the lease, the lessee would report lower profit under a capital lease due to the excess interest and depreciation charges over the simple rent expense resulting from the operating lease.

The lessee can accomplish off-balance sheet financing by manipulation of lease terms to avoid capitalization. However, this managerial behavior results in serious problems for credit and financial analysts in the assessment of the lessee's debt paying ability and in the evaluation of other financial ratios.

To determine the extent of the lessee's off-balance sheet financing, most users of financial information have utilized the information provided in the footnotes to the lessee's financial statements. As noted earlier, the lessee's footnote disclosure indicates the minimum lease payments required over the next five years and over the remaining lease term in aggregate, for all noncancelable operating leases of terms of one year or more. In order to determine the effect of operating leases on the financial statements, credit and financial analysts should incorporate operating leases into the financial statements through analytical lease capitalization methods.

A frequently used method of incorporating operating leases into a lessee's balance sheet is the rating agency method (i.e., the method used by bond rating agencies), which defines the capitalized operating lease obligation as "eight times rent expense". The annual interest component of the lease obligation is defined as "one-third times rent expense". As will be illustrated later, the rating agency approach is conservative because it assumes that all operating leases have been misclassified. In addition, the rating agency approach also tends to either overstate or understate the discounted amount of the future lease obligations.

As a result, the rating agency approach is a very tentative measure of the lease obligation and interest expense and may result in inaccurate predictionsof the financial position of the lessee.

The purpose of this section is to present an alternative approach to the determination of the extent of the lessee's off-balance sheet financing. This approach is more consistent with the SFAS 13 requirements for lease capitalization by using a discounted cash flow (DCF) methodology. In addition, this method makes better use of the lessee's footnote disclosure which was designed to provide the user with enough data to determine the financial statement impact of operating leases that perhaps should have been capitalized. As with the rating agency rules of thumb, the DCF approach is conservative in that it assumes that all operating leases were misclassified. That is, the operating leases with noncancelable terms of one year or more were classified as operating leases as a result of managerial manipulation of lease terms to avoid capitalization.

An Alternative Approach to Capitalizing Operating Leases

The illustration of lease accounting presented in this chapter indicated that according to the provisions of SFAS 13, the capitalized lease asset and obligation should be recorded at the lower of the fair market value of the asset or the present value of the future minimum lease payments. Although not discounted, the lessee's footnote information provides the future minimum lease payments required under operating leases with noncancelable terms of one year or more. This stream of payments becomes the input for the discounted cash flow (DCF) model. The future cash flows is only one of the three key variables needed to capitalize the operating leases for the lessee.

The Required Variables. To use any DCF model, three variables are required:

1. The stream of cash flows;

2. The time period over which these cash flows will be received or paid;

3. The discount rate of interest;

In the case of the operating lease footnote information, the cash flows and the time period are readily available; however, the discount rate to use may be difficult to determine. An approach for estimating the discount rate to use is presented in the following section.

Using the Implicit Average Interest Rate. One alternative discount rate may be to use the firm's average interest rate on actual debt obligations, which can be obtained easily from the long-term debt footnote disclosure. If the lessee also reports capital lease obligations, a better alternative may be to use the implicit average rate of interest incurred on the firm's capitalized leases. This rate can be calculated from the lessee footnote disclosure for capital leases. In this footnote, the lessee is required to disclose the future minimum lease payments on noncancelable capital leases. In addition, the lessee discloses the current portion of the lease obligation. The current portion disclosed is calculated as follows.

```
Current Portion In Time t  =  Lease Payment In Time t - Interest Element Time t

    CP              =        LP           -     Rate x Lease Debt
     t                        t                                t-1
```

The average discount rate is determined as:

$$\text{Rate} = \frac{LP_t - CP_t}{\text{LEASE DEBT}_{t-1}}$$

Once the average discount rate on the firm's capital leases has been determined, the minimum lease payments on the lessee's operating leases can be discounted to compute the lease obligation, the interest expense and the extent of the lessee's off-balance sheet financing.

In the next section, an illustration of the discounted cash flow approach is provided. The results of this illustration are compared to the rating agency approach. It should be noted that the discounted cash flow approach emphasizes the measurement of the effective operating lease debt. As a result, capitalized operating leases will understate fixed assets. This is due to the fact that SFAS 13 requires that the operating lease term be for less than 75% of the useful life of the asset and because the discounted lease payment must be less than 90% of the fair market value of the asset. So, while the DCF method provides the best method of measuring the effective operating lease debt, asset turnover and fixed asset turnover ratios will tend to be overstated by using this approach.

An Illustration of the DCF Approach to Capitalization Of Operating Leases

In this section, the DCF approach is applied to the lease footnote information found in the 1985 financial statements of National Data Corporation. Exhibit 7.3 below provides the National Data Corporation 1985 lease footnote information.

Calculating the Average Discount Rate. The first step in using the DCF approach is to calculate the average discount rate implicit in the firm's capitalized leases. Using the formulation presented earlier, the average discount rate is determined as follows.

Current Portion = 1986 Total Payment - Interest On Outstanding Lease Debt

$619   = $1,285   -   Rate x $4,112

$666   =   Rate x $4,112

Rate   = $666/$4,112

Rate   =   16%

Given the rate of interest, the DCF model can be applied to the footnote data disclosed. The only remaining problem is the distribution of the minimum future lease payments over the 1991-1996 period. Without any other information, the only solution is to assume a stream of cash flows for this period.

Exhibit 7.4 provides the capitalization of the operating leases for National Data

EXHIBIT 7.3

Illustration: National Data Corporation: SFAS 13 Footnote Disclosure

---

Note 6—Leases:

The Company conducts a major part of its operations using leased facilities and equipment. Many of these leases have renewal and purchase options and provide that the company pay the cost of property taxes, insurance, and maintenance.

Asset balances for property acquired under capital leases consist of the following (in thousands):

	May 31,	
	1985	1984
Buildings	$ 2,702	$ 2,702
Equipment	3,375	3,672
	6,077	6,374
Less accumulated amortization	(3,163)	(2,632)
	$ 2,914	$ 3,742

Charges to income resulting from amortization of assets recorded under capital leases are included with depreciation of owned property and equipment.

Future minimum lease payments for all noncancellable leases at May 31, 1985, are as follows (in thousands):—

Year Ending May 31:	Capital Leases	Operating Leases
1986	$ 1,285	$ 4,457
1987	1,216	4,083
1988	1,214	3,733
1989	1,094	3,302
1990	492	1,343
1991–1996	1,332	2,822
Total minimum future lease payments	6,633	$19,740
Less amount representing interest	(2,521)	
Present value of net minimum lease payments	4,112	
Less current portion	(619)	
Long-term obligations under capital leases at May 31, 1985	$ 3,493	

Rent expense on all operating leases for fiscal 1985, 1984, and 1983 was $6,278,000, $5,470,000, and $4,732,000, respectively.

Source: Alexander J. Sannella, "The Capitalization of Operating Leases: The Discounted Cash Flow Approach," The Journal of Commercial Bank Lending" (October 1989). Copyright, 1989, by Robert Morris Associates. Reprinted with permission.

National Data Corporation 1985 Annual Report. Copyright, 1985, by the National Data Corporation. Reprinted with permission.

EXHIBIT 7.4

Capitalization of Operating Leases: National Data Corporation
1985 Annual Report

		Capital Leases		Operating Leases	
Year	P.V. Factors @ 16%(a)	Reported	P.V.	Reported	P.V.
1	2	3	4	5	6
1986	.8621	$1,285	$1,108	$ 4,457	$ 3,842
1987	.7432	1,216	904	4,083	3,034
1988	.6407	1,214	778	3,733	2,392
1989	.5523	1,094	604	3,302	1,824
1990	.4761	492	234	1,343	639
1991	.4104	492*	202	1,043*	438
1992	.3538	492*	174	1,043*	369
1993	.3050	120*	37	254*	77
1994	.2630	76*	20	161*	42
1995	.2267	76*	17	161*	36
1996	.1954	76*	15	160*	31
Totals		$6,633	$4,093	$19,740	$12,724

Footnote Presentation:	Capital Leases	Operating Leases
Total future minimum lease payments............................	$6,633	$19,740
Less: deferred interest	(2,521)	$7,016
P.V. of minimum lease payments......	$4,112	$12,724
Less: current portion	(619)	(2,421)(b)
Long-term lease obligation....................................	$3,493	$10,303

Notes:
(a) Current portion = 1986 total payment − interest on outstanding balance
     $619   = $1,285   −   % × $4,112
     $666   =   % × $4,112
     %   =   16%
(b) Current portion = 1986 total payment − interest on outstanding balance
     Current portion = $4,457   −   (16% × $12,724)
     $2,421   = $4,457   −   2,036
* These are assumed cash flows.

Source: Alexander J. Sannella, "The Capitalization of Operating Leases: The Discounted Cash Flow Approach," The Journal of Commercial Bank Lending" (October 1989). Copyright, 1989, by Robert Morris Associates. Reprinted with permission.

Corporation. In column four of this exhibit, the individual cash outflows under the capital leases in column three are discounted to prove the accuracy of the average discount rate calculation. By multiplying the present value factors in column two by the reported minimum future lease payments in column three, the resulting discounted cash flows in column four amount to $4,093. When compared to the reported lease obligation of $4,112, the error is less than 1% and verifies the accuracy of the average discount rate of 16%.

Applicability to Future Lease Payments. With the accuracy of the discount rate verified, the same approach can be applied to the reported nominal minimum future lease payments reported under the firm's operating leases. The results are found in columns five and six of Exhibit 7.4. The discounted cash flow approach would result in a capital lease obligation for the operating leases of $12,724 at May 31, 1985.

The bottom section of Exhibit 7.4 presents parallel footnote information for the capital leases, as presented by National Data Corportion, and the capitalized lease information, as derived under the DCF approach. In this section, the current portion of the long-term lease obligation for the operating leases was determined to be $2,421 and the 1986 interest charge was calculated as $2,036.

Applying the Rating Agency Approach. If the rating agency approach was applied to the National Data Corporation footnote information presented in Exhibit 7.3, the capitalized lease obligation at May 31, 1985 would have been estimated at $35,656 (8 X $4,457) and the interest expense for 1986 would have been estimated at $1,486 ($4,457 / 3). It should be noted that in practice, the analyst using the rating agency approach would probably capitalize using the 1985 rent expense. However, because the DCF method uses future cash flows, the 1986 rent expense was used in the rating agency computations. When these estimates are compared with those derived in Exhibit 7.4, significant differences result.

In this case, the rating agency approach overstates the lease obligation by 180% and understates the interest expense component of the lease payment by 27% when compared with the results obtained from the DCF approach. Specifically, the rating agency approach would, in this case, significantly overstate both the debt/equity ratio and the times-interest ratio and may have a material effect on credit granting decisions and recommendations made by financial analysts.

A SHORTCUT DCF APPROACH

The DCF model presented in the previous section of this chapter is superior to the rating agency approach in that it is consistent with the SFAS 13 computations for capital leases and makes better use of the information available in the lessee's footnote disclosure. One criticism, however, may be the complexity of the computations presented in Exhibit 7.4 as compared to the rating agency method.

If the lessee also reports capital lease transactions, a "shortcut" DCF model could be used as an alternative with minimal differences in the results obtained. As noted in column two of Exhibit 7.4, regardless of the stream of lease payments, capital, or operating leases, the present value (PV) factors are the same. The constant PV factors can be factored out by calculating the average PV factor for the entire stream of capital lease cash outflows. The average PV factor can be obtained by the following ratio for the capital leases.

$$\text{Average PV Factor} = \frac{\text{PV of Minimum Lease Payments}}{\text{Total Minimum Future Lease Payments}}$$

Using the footnote information for National Data Corporation in Exhibit 7.3, the Average PV Factor is $4,112/$6,633 = .6199. The present value of the future minimum lease payments (i.e., the capitalized lease obligation) for the operating leases can be obtained by simply multiplying the average PV factor derived above by the total minimum future lease payments for the firm's operating leases. In the case of National Data Corporation, we have $19,740 X .6199 = $12,237. Comparing this amount with the lease obligation computed in Exhibit 7.4, the difference is only $487 ($12,724 - $12,237), an error of less than 5%. Therefore, the shortcut DCF model provides the same results as the more complex approach but avoids the need for detailed computations. However, to determine the current portion and the interest components, the short-cut approach requires the use of an average interest rate obtained from the long-term debt footnote.

Conclusions: The DCF Approach

This section presented a DCF approach to the capitalization of operating leases on the financial statements of the lessee. The DCF model is viewed as a superior alternative to the rating agency rules of thumb for computing the extent of the lessee's off-balance sheet financing (i.e., the lease obligation) and the interest component of the lease payment. The DCF model is more consistent with the computation of the lease obligation for capital leases under SFAS 13, and makes better use of the footnote information required by this pronouncement.

A criticism of the DCF model may be the complexity of its computations as compared to the rating agency approach. To avoid this criticism, a shortcut approach was presented which provided similar results but with minimal computational effort.

It is believed that both DCF models are an improvement over the rating agency approach for credit-granting purposes and financial statement analysis in general.

However, the DCF methodology focuses on the measurement of the effective operating lease debt, and as a result, it tends to understate fixed assets. Therefore, asset turnover and fixed asset turnover ratios will tend to be overstated. This fact simply seems to support the reality that operating leases continue to be problematic for creditors and financial analysts who seek a less complex way of measuring and understanding financial performance.

NOTES

1. This section is adapted with permission from Alexander J. Sannella, "The Capitalization of Operating Leases: The Discounted Cash Flow Approach," The Journal of Commerical Bank Lending (October, 1989) 49-55. Copyright, 1989, by Robert Morris Associates.

2. A. Rashad Abdelkhalik, Research Report: "The Economic Effects on Lessees of FASB Statement No. 13, Accounting For Leases", (Stamford, CT: FASB, 1981).

CASE 7.1. MATRIX CORPORATION: CAPITALIZATION OF OPERATING LEASES FOR THE LESSEE--NO CAPITAL LEASE TRANSACTIONS

Matrix Corporation is a leading manufacturer of equipment used for electric image acquisition, recording, processing, storage, transmission and display. Its three Optical/Electronic Business Units are Medical Imaging, Computer Graphics and Industrial Imaging.

Source: Matrix Corporation 1986 Annual Report. Copyright, 1986, by the Matrix Corporation. Reprinted with permission.

REQUIRED: Review the Consolidated Balance Sheet, Consolidated Statement of Income and the Property, Plant and Equipment and Notes Payable footnotes.

1. Capitalize the operating leases for the Matrix Corporation for 1986 using the DCF approach. Be certain to include the current and the long-term portions of the capitalized lease obligation as well as the current and the deferred interest components. Show all computations.

2. Repeat the requirements for question 1 using the rating agency approach (i.e., capitalized lease obligation = "eight times rent expense", and interest expense = "one-third times rent expense").

3. Using the results from questions 1 and 2, compute the company's debt to equity ratio, fixed charge coverage ratio and the debt to total assets ratio for 1986, after the capitalization of operating leases. Compare these results with the same ratios calculated from the company's financial statements as reported.

MATRIX CORPORATION AND SUBSIDIARIES

CONSOLIDATED STATEMENT OF INCOME
(dollars in millions, except per share amounts)

	Eleven Months Ended July 31, 1986	August 31		Twelve Months Ended (Unaudited) July 31	
		1985	1984	1986	1985
Net sales	$92.9	$93.3	$75.0	$111.0	$85.7
Cost of sales	52.6	51.5	41.2	62.2	47.4
Gross profit	40.3	41.8	33.8	48.8	38.3
Selling, general and administrative expenses	25.1	23.0	18.0	27.2	22.5
Interest expense (income), net	.2	(.3)	(.4)	.2	(.3)
Other income, net	(1.8)	(1.1)	(.4)	(1.9)	(1.2)
	23.5	21.6	17.2	25.5	21.0
Income before income taxes	16.8	20.2	16.6	23.3	17.3
Provision for income taxes	6.7	8.1	7.2	9.4	7.0
Net income	$10.1	$12.1	$ 9.4	$ 13.9	$10.3
Income per common share	$ .77	$ .94	$ .78	$ 1.06	$ .80
Weighted average number of common shares (in thousands)	13,085	12,936	12,088	13,077	12,891

The accompanying notes are an integral part of the consolidated financial statements.

Source: Matrix Corporation 1986 Annual Report. Copyright, 1986, by the Matrix Corporation. Reprinted with permission.

MATRIX CORPORATION AND SUBSIDIARIES

CONSOLIDATED BALANCE SHEET
July 31, 1986 and August 31, 1985
(dollars in millions)

ASSETS	1986	1985
CURRENT ASSETS:		
Cash	$ 1.8	$ 2.6
Marketable securities	58.1	25.5
Accounts receivable, less allowance		
for doubtful accounts of $.9 and $1.1	31.9	29.5
Inventories	31.0	29.1
Prepaid expenses and other	5.7	3.3
Total current assets	128.5	90.0
Marketable securities	27.8	6.3
Investments in and advances to 50% or		
less owned companies	—	3.7
Property, plant and equipment, less accumulated		
depreciation and amortization	20.6	16.2
Excess of cost over equity in net assets of		
subsidiaries, less accumulated amortization of		
$2.0 and $1.6	16.3	10.2
Other assets	4.1	2.9
	$197.3	$129.3

LIABILITIES		
CURRENT LIABILITIES:		
Accounts payable	$ 5.3	$ 3.8
Accrued expenses and liabilities	5.5	5.0
Income taxes	1.3	1.1
Deferred income taxes	1.5	—
Total current liabilities	13.6	9.9
Long-term debt	86.3	34.5
Deferred income taxes	3.0	2.1
Total liabilities	102.9	46.5
SHAREHOLDERS' EQUITY	94.4	82.8
	$197.3	$129.3

The accompanying notes are an integral part of the consolidated financial statements.

Source: Matrix Corporation 1986 Annual Report. Copyright, 1986, by the Matrix Corporation. Reprinted with permission.

3. Inventories   Inventories consist of:

	July 31, 1986	August 31, 1985
Raw materials	$17,500,000	$16,500,000
Work in process	8,100,000	8,600,000
Finished goods	5,400,000	4,000,000
	$31,000,000	$29,100,000

4. Property, Plant and Equipment   Property, plant and equipment consists of:

	July 31, 1986	August 31, 1985
Land	$ 1,600,000	$ 1,500,000
Buildings and improvements	11,100,000	8,500,000
Machinery and equipment	9,900,000	6,800,000
Furniture and fixtures	2,500,000	1,900,000
Leasehold improvements	800,000	600,000
Construction in progress	100,000	200,000
	26,000,000	19,500,000
Less, accumulated depreciation and amortization	5,400,000	3,300,000
	$20,600,000	$16,200,000

At July 31, 1986, the future minimum rental payments under operating leases are as follows:

Year Ended July 31,	
1987	$ 900,000
1988	700,000
1989	300,000
1990	100,000
1991 and thereafter	100,000
	$2,100,000

Rental expense for the eleven months ended July 31, 1986, and for the years ended August 31, 1985 and 1984 was $800,000, $700,000 and $500,000, respectively.

5. Notes Payable   As to short-term borrowings for the year ended August 31, 1985 (there were no bank borrowings in 1986 and 1984), the maximum borrowings at any month end was $8,000,000, the average borrowings during the year (computed on month end balances) was $3,000,000 and the weighted average interest rate was 9.5%.

6. Accrued Expenses and Liabilities   Accrued expenses and liabilities consist of:

	July 31, 1986	August 31, 1985
Salaries and wages	$1,100,000	$1,200,000
Warranty costs	1,100,000	1,000,000
Employee stock ownership contribution	1,100,000	700,000
Interest expense	900,000	100,000
Vacation	700,000	500,000
Other	600,000	1,500,000
	$5,500,000	$5,000,000

Source: Matrix Corporation 1986 Annual Report. Copyright, 1986, by the Matrix Corporation. Reprinted with permission.

CASE 7.2. MCI COMMUNICATIONS CORPORATION: CAPITALIZATION OF OPERATING LEASES FOR THE LESSEE--CAPITAL LEASE TRANSACTIONS

MCI Communications Corporation, through its four operating units, offers a full range of modern telecommunications services, both nationally and internationally. The Company's services include long distance phone service, cellular mobile telephone, paging and message services, and electronic mail service.

Source: MCI Communications Corporation 1984 Annual Report. Copyright, 1985, by the MCI Communications Corporation. Reprinted with permission.

REQUIRED: Review MCI's financial statements for the year ended December 31, 1984 and footnotes 2 and 3.

1. Capitalize the operating leases for the MCI Corporation for 1984 using the DCF approach. Be certain to include the current and the long-term portions of the capitalized lease obligation as well as the current and the deferred interest components. Show all computations.

2. Repeat the requirements for question 1 using the rating agency approach (i.e., capitalized lease obligation = "eight times rent expense", and interest expense = "one-third times rent expense").

3. Using the results from questions 1 and 2, compute the company's debt to equity ratio, fixed charge coverage ratio and the debt to total assets ratio for 1984, after the capitalization of operating leases. Compare these results with the same ratios calculated from the company's financial statements as reported.

Statement of Operations

Year Ended December 31,	1984	1983	1982
	(In thousands, except per share amounts)		
Revenues:			
Sales of communications services	$1,959,291	$1,521,460	$906,596
Operating expenses:			
Local interconnection	479,658	262,012	142,972
Facilities leased from other common carriers	343,257	273,663	104,438
Communications system engineering, operations and maintenance	263,276	184,942	117,420
Sales and marketing	240,131	157,002	85,743
Administrative and general	192,917	145,310	104,788
Depreciation	264,573	158,959	89,164
	1,783,812	1,181,888	644,525
Income from operations	175,479	339,572	262,071
Interest expense	188,545	134,277	69,141
Interest (income)	(114,644)	(76,708)	(21,602)
Provision for decline in value of telex-related equipment	49,800		
Other expense (income), net	1,244	(365)	729
Income before income taxes	50,534	282,368	213,803
Income tax provision (benefit)	(8,669)	79,456	62,388
Net income	$ 59,203	$ 202,912	$151,415
Earnings per common share:			
Primary	$.25	$.89	$.78
Assuming full dilution	$.25	$.88	$.73

Source: MCI Communications Corporation 1984 Annual Report. Copyright, 1985, by the MCI Communications Corporation. Reprinted with permission.

Balance Sheet

December 31,	1984	1983
	(In thousands)	
Assets		
Current assets:		
Cash and short term investments	$ 865,140	$1,336,011
Accounts receivable	305,190	276,002
Other	63,084	48,654
Total current assets	1,233,414	1,660,667
Communications system:		
System in service	2,259,019	1,491,709
Other property and equipment	515,877	313,231
	2,774,896	1,804,940
Accumulated depreciation	(656,138)	(364,858)
Construction in progress	495,400	350,172
Total communications system, net	2,614,158	1,790,254
Other assets and deferred charges	46,246	49,159
Total assets	$3,893,818	$3,500,080
Liabilities and stockholders' equity		
Current liabilities:		
Accounts payable and accrued liabilities	$ 500,713	$ 363,152
Accrued interest payable	66,432	65,969
Accrued income taxes	12,940	22,233
Long term debt due within one year	60,901	48,573
Total current liabilities	640,986	499,927
Deferred income taxes and other	232,573	182,769
Long term debt	1,821,138	1,697,805
Stockholders' equity:		
Preferred stock, 20,000,000 shares		
authorized, none issued		
Common stock, $.10 par value, authorized		
400,000,000 shares, issued and outstanding		
234,686,378 and 231,980,344 shares	23,469	23,198
Capital in excess of par value	789,998	769,930
Retained earnings	385,654	326,451
Total stockholders' equity	1,199,121	1,119,579
Total liabilities and stockholders' equity	$3,893,818	$3,500,080

Source: MCI Communications Corporation 1984 Annual Report. Copyright, 1985, by the MCI Communications Corporation. Reprinted with permission.

Statement of Sources of Funds Invested in Communications System

Year Ended December 31,	1984	1983	1982
		(In thousands)	
Funds provided from operations:			
Net income	$ 59,203	$ 202,912	$151,415
Items included in net income not affecting working capital:			
Depreciation and amortization	276,616	170,986	92,379
Provision for decline in value of telex-related equipment	49,800		
Deferred income taxes	(9,107)	65,202	40,142
Other	1,333	6,579	3,277
Total from operations	377,845	445,679	287,213
Funds provided from external financing:			
Increase in long term debt:			
Sale of subordinated debt		1,219,265	441,587
Capital lease obligations	139,810	19,511	12,486
Mortgages and notes payable	31,036	3,124	10,237
Increase in stockholders' equity:			
Sale of warrants with subordinated debt, net		197,105	
Other	20,339	15,506	9,460
Retirement of debt	(52,026)	(50,226)	(41,124)
Deferred gain on sale of assets	42,099	50,963	
Other, net	42,029	(31,742)	(7,870)
	223,287	1,423,506	424,776
Funds used to acquire net assets of WUI, Inc., excluding working capital of $18,584:			
Communications system			191,368
Long term debt			(20,894)
Other assets, net			6,084
			176,558
Changes in components of working capital, excluding debt due within one year (brackets denote a change representing funds employed as working capital):			
Cash and short term investments	470,871	(1,140,790)	(29,290)
Accounts receivable	(29,188)	(136,079)	(77,674)
Other current assets	(14,430)	(34,317)	(8,450)
Accounts payable and accrued liabilities	137,561	158,217	126,108
Accrued interest payable	463	46,510	7,455
Accrued income taxes	(9,293)	(2,217)	24,450
	555,984	(1,108,676)	42,599
Investment in communications system	$1,157,116	$ 760,509	$578,030

Source: MCI Communications Corporation 1984 Annual Report. Copyright, 1985, by the MCI Communications Corporation. Reprinted with permission.

Income Taxes

The Company files a consolidated Federal income tax return on a March 31 year end basis. Deferred income taxes are provided on transactions which are reported in the financial statements in different years than for income tax purposes. Investment tax credits are recorded under the flow-through method of accounting.

Earnings Per Common Share

Primary earnings per share is computed on the basis of the weighted average number of shares of common stock outstanding during each year, plus common stock equivalents arising from the assumed exercise of warrants and stock options, if dilutive. The weighted average number of shares used in the primary computation for each of the years was: 1984-234,025,124, 1983-229,163,427 and 1982-194,845,810.

Fully diluted earnings per share include additional adjustments for shares applicable to convertible subordinated debt securities that were converted during 1983 and 1982. Convertible subordinated debt securities outstanding at the end of 1984 and 1983 are not classified as common stock equivalents and have not been included in the computations since their effect is not dilutive. The weighted average number of shares used in the fully diluted computation for each of the years was: 1984-234,025,124, 1983-232,210,304 and 1982-222,959,878.

Note 2.
Lease
Transactions

The amounts included in communications system financed by capital leases are:

December 31,	1984	1983
	(In thousands)	
System in service	$373,853	$272,899
Other property and equipment	25,626	21,231
	399,479	294,130
Accumulated depreciation	(128,864)	(105,204)
Construction in progress	2,595	3,787
	$273,210	$192,713

Leases not capitalized are primarily for sites on which communications equipment and microwave stations are located, and for administrative facilities including office buildings, vehicles, data processing equipment and office equipment. In addition, during 1984 and 1983, the Company sold and leased back under operating leases 12 transponders aboard each of the Hughes Galaxy II and Galaxy III Satellites. Total rental expense for all operating leases, net of deferred gain amortization and sublease income on sale/leaseback transactions, was $65.3 million, $48.3 million and $34.0 million for the years ended December 31, 1984, 1983 and 1982.

Source: MCI Communications Corporation 1984 Annual Report. Copyright, 1985, by the MCI Communications Corporation. Reprinted with permission.

At December 31, 1984, the future aggregate minimum rental commitments for capital leases and noncancellable operating leases were:

Years Ending December 31,	Capital leases	Operating leases	Total
		(In thousands)	
1985	$ 74,671	$ 81,067	$ 155,738
1986	61,288	93,994	155,282
1987	44,770	86,161	130,931
1988	32,233	79,240	111,473
1989	26,474	76,860	103,334
thereafter	67,082	324,963	392,045
Minimum lease payments	306,518	$742,285	$1,048,803
Less-Amount representing interest	69,872		
Present value of future lease payments	$236,646		

Note 3.
Long Term Debt

Long term debt consists of:

December 31,	1984	1983
	(In thousands)	
9½% Subordinated Notes due August 1, 1993	$1,000,000	$1,000,000
7¾% Convertible Subordinated Debentures due March 15, 2003	399,180	399,180
12⅞% Subordinated Debentures due October 1, 2002	250,000	250,000
14⅛% Subordinated Debentures due April 1, 2001	125,000	125,000
15% Subordinated Debentures due August 1, 2000	52,500	52,500
Capital lease obligations at a weighted average interest rate of 9%	236,646	141,668
12½% Mortgage payable February 1, 1994	30,308	
7.9% promissory notes due in equal annual installments through 1987	13,350	17,800
Notes payable and other debt	10,986	12,051
Total debt	2,117,970	1,998,199
Net unamortized discount	(235,931)	(251,821)
Long term debt due within one year	(60,901)	(48,573)
Total long term debt	$1,821,138	$1,697,805

Annual maturities of long term debt for the five years after December 31, 1984 are: 1985-$60.9 million, 1986-$54.7 million, 1987-$42.6 million, 1988-$24.7 million and 1989-$21.2 million.

The subordinated notes and debentures are subordinated in right of payment to the Company's existing and future senior indebtedness, as defined in the respective indentures.

Total interest costs were $220.5 million in 1984, $153.9 million in 1983 and $78.2 million in 1982, of which $34.9 million, $19.7 million and $9.0 million have been capitalized.

Part III

Full Disclosure in
Corporate Financial Reporting

8

Special Income Statement Items
and Other Issues in Full Disclosure

INTRODUCTION

The income statement is the primary source of information regarding the firm's ability to generate future cash flows needed to repay debt and to make earnings distributions to stockholders. For decades, accountants have debated the appropriateness of including unusual or nonrecurring items on the income statement. The current reporting standards are essentially based on the all-inclusive concept of income. Under the all-inclusive concept, all items of profit and loss, except those events properly classified as prior period adjustments, should be reported on the income statement.

The all-inclusive concept of income has been modified over the last 20 years. With the completion of the work of the AICPA's Study Group on the Objectives of Financial Statements in 1973,[1] there has been a greater emphasis on reporting an accrual basis net income that is more closely related to the underlying cash flows of the firm. As a result of the work of the Study Group, the FASB requires that financial statements prepared in accordance with GAAP include a statement of cash flows. The cash flow statement will be discussed in detail in Chapter 9. In addition to the required cash flow statement, the accounting profession has now begun to exclude from reported income those items not reasonably expected to be converted into cash in the short run. These items are reported on the balance sheet as cumulative valuation adjustments to stockholders' equity. Some of these items discussed in previous sections of this text include cumulative gain or loss on foreign currency translation adjustments and the cumulative unrealized loss on write-downs to market for the long-term portfolio of marketable equity securities.

Aside from prior period adjustments and the cumulative valuation adjustments to stockholders' equity on the balance sheet, all other items of profit and loss must be reported on the income statement. This means that the income statement includes events and transactions that are normal and recurring as well as those that would be considered unusual, infrequent or both.

In order to assist the credit and financial analyst in assessing the quality of accounting earnings and the degree of accounting risk associated with the reported income figure, the accounting profession identifies what it considers to be unusual and nonrecurring items.

The present income statement format divides the income statement into two major sections: (1) income (loss) from continuing operations, and (2) income or loss from unusual, nonrecurring or otherwise special events and transactions. These special items are identified by a separate "net of tax" treatment on the income statement. The following income statement will illustrate the current reporting format.

```
                        Sample Corporation
                         Income Statement
                    For the Year Ended 12/31/XX


    Sales.................................................$  XXX

    Less: Cost of Goods Sold.............................  < XX>

        Operating Expenses..............................  < XX>
                                                          --------

    Income before Tax....................................$  XXX

    Less: Income Tax Expense (T).........................  <  X>
                                                          ---------

    Income from Continuing Operations...................$  XXX

===================ACCOUNTANT'S DIVIDING LINE===========================

    Gain (Loss) From Discontinued Operations -

        Net of Tax (T)..................................    XX

    Extraordinary Gain (Loss) - Net of Tax (T).........    XX

    Cumulative Effect from a Change in Accounting

        Principle - Net of Tax (T).....................    XX
                                                          ---------

            Net Income (E)..............................$  XXX
                                                          =========
```

NOTES: (T) Along with reporting Prior Period Adjustments--Net of Tax as
       an adjustment to opening retained earnings on the balance sheet,
       the matching of the portion of the total tax expense to the item
       that gave rise to the tax on the financial statements, within

the same accounting period, is known as "intraperiod tax allocation".

(E) As noted in chapter 6, EPS is usually reported below the
bottom line net income for each income statement category. That
is, EPS from income from continuing operations, EPS from discontinued operations, EPS from the cumulative effect of a change in
accounting principle would be reported along with EPS from net
income.

As noted earlier, the purpose for using this income statement reporting format
and EPS disclosures is to provide sufficient information to make a proper assessment of the quality of accounting earnings, in the aggregate and for each income
statement category. For example, income generated from normal, continuing operating activities is considered to be of higher "quality" than an extraordinary gain
because normal operating activities are frequent and recurring events that can be
used to project the future cash flows of the firm. Extraordinary items or any of the
unusual items or special events noted in the sample income statement are nonrecurring and will not generate cash flows on a regular basis. As a result, the unusual
items cannot be relied upon as a source of dividend distribution or principal and
interest payments on corporate debt.

In the following sections of this chapter, the special income statement items will
be discussed in detail. In addition, other events such as loss contingencies and related party transactions will be presented.

SPECIAL INCOME STATEMENT ITEMS

Accounting for Extraordinary Items

According to APB Opinion No. 30, "Reporting the Results of Operations",
extraordinary items are defined as those material items with a character significantly different from the normal activities of the business and would not be expected to
recur on a regular basis.

In order to operationalize the concept of an extraordinary item, Opinion 30,
paragraph 20, sets forth two specific criteria that must be met in order for an event
to be classified as an extraordinary item. To be classified as an extraordinary item,
the material event or transaction must be both:

1. Unusual in nature, and

2. Infrequent in occurrence, within the environment in which the firm operates. It is interesting to note that a major loss of inventory due to a flood, in
   an area where there is frequent flooding, is not considered an extraordinary item because of the environment in which the firm operates.

Satisfying both of the Opinion 30 criteria may be difficult in practice. In fact,
this was one of the objectives of Opinion 30. Prior to Opinion 30, the criteria for

classification of an event as extraordinary were somewhat vague and left much of the classification choice to the discretion of management. If management believed that financial statement users discounted extraordinary items, an unusual transaction resulting in large gains could be classified as part of normal operating income while large losses could be classified as extraordinary. This practice is sometimes known as "classificatory smoothing of income with extraordinary items".[2] The two Opinion 30 criteria severely limit this type of smoothing behavior.

Although the Opinion 30 criteria would be difficult to meet in practice, they would usually be satisfied in the case of any of the following three events:

1. A major casualty (e.g., fire, flood, earthquake, etc., unless these casualties are expected in the environment in which the firm operates);

2. Expropriation of assets by government;

3. Prohibition under a newly enacted law or regulation.

For example, the write-off of some obsolete inventory is an expected part of most business operations, although it may not be frequent in occurrence. As a result, it would not qualify as an extraordinary item. However, if the government (e.g., the Food and Drug Administration) prohibited the sale of a certain inventory item, and the entire inventory of this item was written down to a zero value, this loss would then qualify as an extraordinary item.

In addition to meeting the specific criteria of Opinion 30, certain events not meeting the criteria may still be classified as extraordinary if required by a specific professional pronouncement. If material, the following items must be classified as extraordinary without regard to the two Opinion 30 criteria.

1. The debtor's gain resulting from a troubled debt restructuring under the provisions of SFAS 15, "Accounting by Debtors and Creditors for Troubled Debt Restructurings" (see chapter 3).

2. Gain or loss from an early extinguishment of debt under the provisions of SFAS 4, "Reporting Gains and Losses from Extinguishment of Debt", unless the early extinguishment was made to satisfy sinking-fund requirements that must be met within one year of the date of the early extinguishment. This exception is permitted under SFAS 64,"Extinguishment of Debt Made to Satisfy Sinking-Fund Requirements" (see chapter 3).

3. Gain or loss resulting from the disposal of a significant part of the assets or a segment of the previously separate companies, now combined under the pooling of interests method, provided that the gain or loss is significant in relation to the net income of the combined entity and the disposal is within two years after the combination is consummated. The classification as extraordinary in this case is required under Opinion 16, "Business Combinations" (see chapter 6).

4. The write-off of unamortized costs of interstate operating rights subject to

the provisions of the Motor Carrier Act of 1980. The operating rights are classified as intangible assets on the books of motor carriers. The classification of the write-off as extraordinary is required by SFAS 44, "Accounting for Intangible Assets of Motor Carriers".

It should be noted that the materiality of extraordinary items must be judged individually and not in the aggregate. Extraordinary items should be presented on the income statement after the gain or loss from discontinued operations but before the cumulative effect from a change in accounting principle.

A sample disclosure of an extraordinary item by Squibb Corporation and Subsidiaries in its 1984 annual report is presented in Exhibit 8.1.

Events and Transactions that are Unusual in Nature or Infrequent in Occurrence but Not Both. In practice, there are a significant number of transactions that are either unusual in nature or infrequent in occurrence, but not both. Disposals of plant and equipment are not considered part of the normal operations of a service business. However, these events could be recurring. For example, a computer maintenance firm could turnover its fleet of automobiles every three years. On the other hand, events such as the write-off of obsolete inventory or the write-off of a receivable from a major customer may not occur frequently, but must be considered a normal part of doing business. In all of these examples, the events are special either due to their unusual nature or infrequent occurrence. Nevertheless, these events do not meet both of the Opinion 30 criteria for classification as an extraordinary item, and would not be reported as such, unless the disposal of the fleet of automobiles, the write-off of the obsolete inventory and the receivable write-off were caused by a major casualty, expropriation by government or a prohibition under a newly enacted law or regulation. If not extraordinary, the question for the accountant is how to properly report these events on the current income statement and the question for the analyst is to determine if the accountant's classification is satisfactory for a proper determination of the operating strength of the firm.

Reporting Issues. With respect to the accountant's classification question, Opinion 30 also provides guidance as to the treatment of events that are either unusual or infrequent, but not both. If the gain or loss results from a transaction that is unusual in nature or infrequent in occurrence, but not both, its income statement disclosure depends on the materiality of the item.

1. If the gain or loss is not material in amount, the gain or loss is combined with other items of revenue and expense within the "income from continuing operations" section of the income statement.

2. If the gain or loss is material in amount, the gain or loss is disclosed as a separate line item in the "income from continuing operations" section of the income statement. That is, the significant unusual or infrequent item would be presented above the "accountant's dividing line" on the current income statement.

The disclosure required in item (2) above is similar to an extraordinary item in that it results in separate presentation. However, several differences in presentation are required in order to prevent the financial statement user from "misclassifying"

EXHIBIT 8.1

Sample Disclosure: Squibb Corporation and Subsidiaries:
Extraordinary Item Disclosures Under Opinion 30

Statement of Consolidated Income

Squibb Corporation and Subsidiaries
Years ended December 31, 1984, 1983 and 1982
(Amounts in thousands except per share figures)

	1984	1983	1982
Net Sales	$1,886,037	$1,768,891	$1,660,766
Costs and Expenses:			
Cost of sales	719,402	694,323	678,472
Marketing and administrative	716,483	671,228	647,908
Research and development	150,645	141,678	122,962
Other, net	8,776	6,048	1,890
	1,595,306	1,513,277	1,451,232
Profit from Operations	290,731	255,614	209,534
General Corporate Income (Expenses):			
Interest income	40,309	51,441	60,832
Interest expense	(23,271)	(36,535)	(40,257)
Other, net	(13,586)	(8,780)	(10,624)
	3,452	6,126	9,951
Income before Taxes on Income	294,183	261,740	219,485
Provision for taxes on income	97,011	88,466	65,849
Income before Extraordinary Items	197,172	173,274	153,636
Gain on early extinguishment of debt	—	27,041	—
Loss on disposal of operations in Argentina, Brazil and Uruguay	—	(27,608)	—
Net Income	$ 197,172	$ 172,707	$ 153,636
Per Share:			
Income before extraordinary items	$3.68	$3.31	$3.01
Gain on early extinguishment of debt	—	.52	—
Loss on disposal of operations in Argentina, Brazil and Uruguay	—	(.53)	—
Net income	$3.68	$3.30	$3.01

Exhibit 8.1, continued

Extraordinary Items

Items of an extraordinary nature in 1983 were as follows:

	(Amounts in thousands)
Gain on early extinguishment of debt	$ 27,041
Loss on disposal of operations in Argentina, Brazil and Uruguay	(27,608)
	$ (567)

In December 1983, the Corporation acquired $165,000,000 principal amount of its notes in exchange for 1,019,540 shares of its common stock and $91,575,000 cash. This early extinguishment of debt resulted in a tax-free extraordinary gain of $27,041,000, or $.52 per share.

Due to the imposition of increasingly severe operating restrictions by the governments of Argentina, Brazil and Uruguay, the Corporation determined that its pharmaceutical operations in these countries were no longer viable and, accordingly, its operations in these countries had to be discontinued and disposed of. Prices for pharmaceutical products are among the most rigidly controlled in these countries, requiring special applications for price increases which, if and when granted, are inadequate to cover increases in wages and other costs. In addition, in certain cases, the governments have imposed significant restrictions on the ability of the companies to import materials and obtain financing at reasonable costs. As a result of the determination to cease operations in these countries, the Corporation recorded an extraordinary loss of $27,608,000 (with no tax benefit), or $.53 per share, for the estimated losses on the disposition of plant, property and equipment, estimated costs of severance and operating losses during the disposal period.

Source: Squibb Corporation and Subsidiaries 1984 Annual Report. Copyright, 1985, the Bristol-Myers Squibb Company. Reprinted with permission.

the item as extraordinary. To begin with, the unusual or infrequent gain or loss cannot be shown net of tax. In addition, there cannot be a separate EPS presentation for the unusual or infrequent gain or loss.

A sample disclosure of a nonrecurring write-off of goodwill on the 1984 annual report of the Whittaker Corporation is presented in Exhibit 8.2.

Analytical Issues. The issue for the credit and the financial analyst is to determine the proper treatment of the unusual or infrequent items in assessment of the future cash flows of the firm. It is clear from the Whittaker Corporation disclosures in Exhibit 8.2 that in substance, there is little difference between the nonrecurring goodwill write-off and the extraordinary loss. In this case, the credit and financial analyst should probably classify the goodwill write-off with extraordinary items when assessing the quality of accounting earnings or conducting a trend or comparative analysis over several years.

Careful examination of Exhibit 8.2 points out another problem for the analyst. The nonoperating charges and credits footnote implies that the write-down of an investment portfolio due to a decline in market value is unusual or infrequent, and should be discounted by the analyst. If discounted by the analyst, these events may be reclassified into the extraordinary category. In this case, however, the investment could be part of the firm's cash management activities and should probably be considered as part of normal operations. This is the original classification used by the accountant in the financial statements.

The previous discussion indicates that the provisions of Opinion 30 may have substituted one analytical problem for another. Prior to Opinion 30, the analyst was faced with the problem of determining if management was attempting to smooth income through the improper classification of items as extraordinary or ordinary income. With Opinion 30, the classification of events as extraordinary is relatively limited. However, the classification of a gain or loss as an unusual or infrequent item, together with the related disclosures, may result in the additional problem of carefully analyzing this information and possibly reclassifying them as extraordinary in the analysts' trend analysis or cash flow projections.

Although the provisions of Opinion 30 have resulted in a significant improvement in classification and reporting of extraordinary items, proper analysis of ususual or infrequent events remains a continuing problem for the credit and financial analyst.

Accounting for Discontinued Operations

The term discontinued operations includes the disposal of a segment of a business or a major product line. Specifically, Opinion 30 states that discontinued operations represent a segment of a business that has been sold or will be sold, spun off, or otherwise disposed of subject to a formal plan of disposal. Opinion 30 requires the disclosure of a separate income statement category entitled "discontinued operations", showing the total gain or loss from the discontinued operation, net of tax.

The total gain or loss from the discontinued operation, net of tax, consists of two components:

EXHIBIT 8.2

Sample Disclosure: Whittaker Corporation and Consolidated Subsidiaries: Disclosure of Unusual or Infrequent Items Under Opinion 30

Whittaker Corporation & Consolidated Subsidiaries

Consolidated Statements of Income

For the Years Ended October 31	1984	1983	1982
		(In thousands)	
Sales	$1,437,026	$1,602,825	$1,673,604
Costs and expenses			
Cost of sales	1,119,059	1,263,547	1,298,200
Engineering, selling and general and administrative	190,536	212,799	230,554
Interest on long-term debt	15,967	18,000	14,570
Other interest, net	(5,051)	1,904	(3,882)
Nonrecurring item—goodwill write-off	11,944	—	—
Minority interest in income of subsidiaries	19,217	41,104	28,117
	1,351,672	1,537,354	1,567,559
Income before provision for taxes	85,354	65,471	106,045
Provision for taxes (Note 6)	41,484	27,862	47,357
Net income (Note 5)	$ 43,870	$ 37,609	$ 58,688
Earnings per share (Note 2)	$3.01	$2.55	$3.77

... accompanying notes are an integral part of these statements.

Note 9. Nonoperating Charges and Credits

"Nonrecurring item—goodwill write-off" in the income statement reflects the write-off in 1984 of goodwill related to certain operating units which were disposed of during the year and of goodwill which in management's opinion no longer had value.

In addition, the following other significant nonoperating charges and credits were recorded in fiscal years 1984 and 1983. Net income was reduced during 1984 and 1983 by $6,550,000 (after tax benefit of $450,000) and $2,000,000 (after tax benefit of $1,500,000), respectively, as a result of declines in the market value of Whittaker's investment in Smith International, Inc. (see Note 5); net income in 1984 was also reduced by $6,100,000 (after tax benefit of $5,200,000) as a result of losses associated with obligations of a debtor in bankruptcy; and, as the result of a gain on the termination of a financing transaction, net income in 1984 was increased by $4,200,000 (after tax provision of $3,500,000).

Source: Whittaker Corporation and Consolidated Subsidiaries 1984 Annual Report. Copyright, 1985, by the Whittaker Corporation. Reprinted with permission.

1. The after-tax profit or loss from the results of operations of the segment disposed of or to be disposed of within an agreed upon period of time. This after-tax operating profit or loss is only determined from the beginning of the year to the date of the decision or agreement to dispose of the segment. The date on which the firm decides or agrees to dispose of the business segment is known as the "measurement date".

The first component of the total gain or loss from discontinued operations is nothing more than a condensed income statement for the discontinued segment from the beginning of the year to the measurement date. In other words, the revenues and expenses relating to the discontinued operation are removed from the continuing operations section of the income statement and the profit or loss, net of tax, is presented as a single line item in the discontinued operations section of the income statement. A footnote would include the details of the profit or loss presented in this line item. By segregating these revenues and expenses from the revenues and expenses generated from continuing operations, the user of financial statements is better able to project the recurring cash flows of the entity.

2. The actual or projected net loss or the actual net gain on the disposal of the segment. That is, the net gain or loss from the sale of the shares held as an investment in a subsidiary or from the sale of the individual assets of a segment or division, plus any after-tax operating profit or loss from the measurement date.

This second component includes any after-tax operating profit or loss of the segment (with related disclosures and excluding the applicable items of revenue and expense from income from continuing operations) from the measurement date to the actual date of disposal of the segment. This period of time is known as the "phase-out period". If the phase-out period is contained within a single accounting period, all gains and losses should be fully realized by year end and at the time the financial statements are issued. Quite often, however, there is a substantial lag between the decision or agreement to dispose of a segment of the business and the actual date of the disposal. If the phase-out period extends beyond the current accounting period, estimates of gains and losses on future disposal, as well as the estimated after-tax operating profit and loss, must be considered and accrued from the year end to the expected date of disposal. After the measurement date the operating profit or loss of the discontinued segment is considered part of the gain or loss on disposal rather than part of operations. There are two primary reasons for this treatment. First, operations of the discontinued segment may take on a significantly different character after the measurement date. Second, the actual results of operations of the discontinued segment after the measurement date could influence the selling price of the segment.

During an extended phase-out period, the realized operating profit or loss, net of tax, is always presented for the discontinued operation from the beginning of the year and the measurement date (Item [1] above). The amount reported for the net gain or loss on the disposal (Item [2] above) will always include the realized after-tax operating profit or loss of the discontinued operation during the portion of the phase-out period extending from the measurement date to year end. However, the total gain or loss reported on disposal in Item (2) depends on whether the other components of the net gain or loss are realized or unrealized.

Realized losses on assets actually sold during the phase-out period are always reported and may be increased by estimated losses on future operations and asset disposals. This amount may be reduced by projected gains on future operations and asset sales. However, an estimated future gain can only reduce a loss to zero. In other words, it cannot result in a net unrealized gain.

Realized gains on actual asset disposals are also reported and can be reduced by estimated unrealized losses from future operations and assets to be sold. However, realized gains cannot be increased by estimated unrealized gains on future operations and disposals. Therefore, an estimated net gain or a realized gain increased by an unrealized gain cannot be recognized during the phase-out period. This is a conservative approach designed to prevent the overstatement of assets and earnings. It should be noted that the accrual of a net unrealized loss can only be made if it is probable and subject to reasonable estimation. In addition, all estimates should be accrued as of the measurement date because this is the date at which the disposal decision is made by management.

The total after-tax gain or loss from discontinued operations should be presented on the income statement immediately after income from continuing operations and before extraordinary items.

Illustration: Limited Phase-Out Period. In the case of a limited phase-out period, the measurement date and the disposal date occur within the same accounting period. In order to illustrate a limited phase-out period, assume a firm decides to dispose of a business segment on March 23, 1991. The actual disposal takes place on June 30, 1991. The year end of the firm is December 31. Assume an effective tax rate of 40%.

The segment reported an operating loss of $5,000 before tax ($3,000 after tax from the beginning of the year to the measurement date). From the measurement date to the date of the disposal, the operating loss of the segment amounted to $1,000 pretax ($600 after tax). The sale of the segment's assets resulted in a loss of $15,000 pretax ($9,000 after tax). Based on the facts presented in this illustration, the disclosure on the 1991 income statement would appear as follows:

```
Income from continuing operations before tax...................$  XXXX


Income tax expense...............................................  <XXX>
                                                                 --------
Income from continuing operations after tax....................$  XXXX


Discontinued operations (Note___):


   *Loss from the operations of the Discontinued
   Segment, net of tax of $2,000 ..................$ 3,000


   *Loss on the disposal of the Discontinued
   Segment, $9,000 (net of tax of $6,000), including
   segment operating losses incurred during
   the phase-out period of $600 (net of tax
   of $400)........................................   9,600      <12,600>
                                                    --------    ---------

Net Income.....................................................$  XXXX
                                                                ========
```

Illustration: Extended Phase-Out Period. In an extended phase-out period, the measurement date and the disposal date occur in two different accounting periods. In this case, assume that the measurement date is June 6, 1991, but the expected disposal date is November 9, 1992. If the firm's year end is December 31, 1991, gains and losses on expected disposal and from future operating profit and loss from year end to the disposal date may be accrued if probable and subject to reasonable estimation. Again assume that the firm is subject to a 40% tax rate.

Assume that the discontinued segment reported income from operations of $7,200 after tax ($12,000 before tax) from the beginning of the year to the measurement date. From the measurement date to year end, the segment reported a realized operating loss of $3,600 after tax ($6,000 before tax). Due to the extended phase-out period, it was estimated that the segment would incur an after-tax operating loss of $4,800 ($8,000 pretax) from the beginning of 1992 to the expected date of disposal. The projected gain from asset disposal on November 9, 1992, is $3,000 after tax ($5,000 before tax). Given the facts presented in this illustration, the disclosure on the 1991 income statement would appear as follows:

```
Income from continuing operations before tax...................$  XXXX


Income tax expense................................................  <XXX>
                                                                  --------


Income from continuing operations after tax....................$  XXXX

Discontinued operations (Note___):

    *Income from the operations of the Discontinued
     Segment, net of tax of $4,800 ..................$ 7,200

    *Estimated net loss on the disposal of the
     Discontinued Segment, including realized loss
     on operations during the phase-out period
     $3,600 (net of tax of $2,400), estimated loss
     from operations from December 31, 1991, to the
     expected disposal date $4,800 (net of tax of
     $3,200), and estimated gain on the disposal of
     assets of $3,000 (net of tax of $2,000)........ <5,400>    1,800
                                                     --------  ---------


Net Income......................................................$  XXXX
                                                                 =========
```

Disclosure Requirements. In addition to the income statement section for discontinued operations, Opinion 30, paragraph 18, requires extensive footnote disclosures which should include:

1. A description of the operations discontinued or to be discontinued;

2. The expected disposal date, if known;

3. The expected manner of disposal;

4. The income or loss from operations and any proceeds on the actual disposal of assets from the measurement date to year end;

5. A general description of the remaining assets and obligations of the discontinued operations as of the balance sheet date.

With respect to the last disclosure requirement, Opinion 30 suggests that firms consider segregating the net assets of the discontinued operation on their balance sheets. The net assets of the discontinued operation include the remaining assets and any liabilities to be assumed by the purchaser. The classification of the net assets would be current or noncurrent depending on the expected disposal date, and not based on the original classification of the underlying assets and liabilities.

Although not mandatory, it seems appropriate to segregate the net assets of the discontinued operation. If the assets of the segment are removed from the total productive assets of the firm, management is taking a disclosure position consistent with that of segregating the segment's profit or loss from income from continuing operations. By segregating both the segment's operating income or loss and its assets from the normal, recurring operations of the firm, the resulting ratios and other financial statistics would only be based on the continuing operations of the firm, and therefore become more meaningful to the analyst.

Similarly, if the discontinued segment is represented by an equity investment in a subsidiary, it would be classified as current or noncurrent depending on the expected date of disposal.

Qualifying for Discontinued Operations Treatment. Not all disposals of business segments qualify for discontinued operations treatment. According to Opinion 30, in order to qualify for discontinued operations treatment, the results of operations, the assets, and the activities of the discontinued segment must be "clearly distinguishable", physically, operationally, and for financial reporting purposes, from the other operations, assets, and activities of the firm. Thus, if General Electric disposes of its Financial Service subsidiaries, it would qualify for discontinued operations treatment, but if Sears decides to drop its sporting goods departments, it would not qualify.

Exhibit 8.3 presents the income statement and balance sheet presentations and the required footnote information for the discontinued operations for PepsiCo, Inc. and Subsidiaries in its 1984 annual report.

Analytical Issues. Although there are adequate disclosures under Opinion 30, there are several issues to consider in the analysis of discontinued operations. To begin with, the analyst must be aware of the restatement of prior periods' financial statements in the year of the measurement date. There will be several line items on the income statement and balance sheet that will be reduced by the removal of the revenues, expenses, assets and liabilities of the discontinued segment. The segregation of these line items could result in a significant distortion and a lack of comparablity in a time series of financial ratios. In this case, the analyst may consider using the footnote disclosures to compute financial ratios both "with and without" the discontinued operation. In this way, the analyst can analytically restate the financial statements and compute ratios, etc., as if the segment was not discontinued, and restore comparability with prior years. By using the financial statements as reported, the ratios can be compared with subsequently issued financial information. It should be noted, however, that the net assets of the discontinued segment may not be segregated from the continuing operations of the firm. In this case, the analyst must carefully examine the footnote information provided in order to determine the significance of the net assets of the discontinued operation and the possible distortion of financial ratios and other statistics based on total assets, plant assets and liabilities.

Another problem for the analyst is to determine if all discontinued operations are properly identified in the financial statements. The vague criteria of Opinion 30 may result in a discontinued segment not qualifying for discontinued operations treatment on the income statement. For example, if the accountants and the management of the firm determine that a segment to be disposed of is not "clearly distinguishable" from the other operations of the firm, this segment would not be reported as a discontinued operation. Without discontinued operations treatment,

EXHIBIT 8.3

Sample Disclosure: PepsiCo, Inc. and Subsidiaries: Discontinued Operations Disclosure Under Opinion 30

CONSOLIDATED STATEMENT OF INCOME AND RETAINED EARNINGS

(in thousands except per share amounts)
PepsiCo, Inc. and Subsidiaries
Years ended December 29, 1984 (fifty-two weeks), December 31, 1983 (fifty-three weeks) and December 25, 1982 (fifty-two weeks)

		1984	1983	1982
Revenues	Net sales	**$7,698,678**	$7,165,586	$6,810,929
Costs and Expenses	Cost of sales	**3,149,940**	3,007,398	2,949,160
	Marketing, administrative and other expenses	**3,853,540**	3,629,509	3,233,050
	Interest expense	**206,956**	176,759	165,270
	Interest income	**(86,131)**	(53,650)	(49,325)
		7,124,305	6,760,016	6,298,155
Income From Continuing Operations Before Unusual Charges and Income Taxes		**574,373**	405,570	512,774
Unusual Charges	Provision for restructuring	**220,000**	–	–
	Reduction in net assets of foreign bottling operations (without tax benefit)	**–**	–	79,400
Income From Continuing Operations Before Income Taxes		**354,373**	405,570	433,374
	Provision for United States and foreign income taxes	**147,701**	134,233	220,947
Income From Continuing Operations		**206,672**	271,337	212,427
Discontinued Operations	Income from discontinued operations (net of income taxes of $14,915, $6,728 and $5,846 in 1984, 1983 and 1982, respectively)	**20,875**	12,774	11,861
	Loss on disposal (net of $500 tax benefit)	**(15,000)**	–	–
		5,875	12,774	11,861
Net Income		**212,547**	284,111	224,288
	Retained earnings at beginning of year	**1,622,550**	1,489,797	1,412,636
	Cash dividends (per share: 1984–$1.665; 1983–$1.62; 1982–$1.58)	**(156,185)**	(151,358)	(147,127)
	Retained earnings at end of year	**$1,678,912**	$1,622,550	$1,489,797
Net Income Per Share	Continuing operations	**$ 2.19**	$ 2.88	$ 2.27
	Discontinued operations	**.06**	.13	.13
	Net income	**$ 2.25**	$ 3.01	$ 2.40

See accompanying notes

CONSOLIDATED BALANCE SHEET
(in thousands)
PepsiCo Inc and Subsidiaries
December 29 1984 and December 31 1983

		1984	1983
Assets	**Current Assets**		
	Cash	$ 28,139	$ 24,434
	Marketable securities	784,684	529,326
	Notes and accounts receivable, less allowance: 1984–$31,966; 1983–$33,738	640,081	647,329
	Inventories	451,781	375,606
	Prepaid expenses, taxes and other current assets	242,181	159,247
	Net assets of the transportation segment held for disposal	143,210	149,504
		2,290,076	1,885,446
	Long-term Receivables and Investments		
	Long-term receivables and other investments	178,647	161,283
	Investment in tax leases	73,236	77,941
		251,883	239,224
	Property, Plant and Equipment		
	Land	218,231	190,942
	Buildings	819,990	732,999
	Machinery and equipment	1,988,112	1,891,046
	Capital leases	191,924	190,842
	Bottles and cases, net of customers' deposits: 1984–$11,678; 1983–$32,777	23,785	56,550
		3,242,042	3,062,379
	Less accumulated depreciation and amortization	1,079,029	1,019,000
		2,163,013	2,043,379
	Goodwill	163,904	235,768
	Other Assets	81,358	88,919
		$4,950,234	$4,492,736

See accompanying notes

366

Exhibit 8.3, continued

Note 3/Discontinued
Operations

In 1984, PepsiCo adopted a plan to sell its transportation segment, which was comprised of North American Van Lines, Inc. (NAVL) and Lee Way Motor Freight, Inc. (Lee Way). Pursuant to this plan, PepsiCo has entered into a definitive agreement to sell the stock of NAVL for cash. The sales price is the sum of a base price of $315 million and an additional amount equal to the prime rate of interest on the base price from December 31, 1983 to the closing date. If the pending sale had been consummated on December 29, 1984, a gain of approximately $197 million before-tax and $141 million after-tax ($1.47 per share) would have been produced. This gain has not been recorded because the sale is contingent on obtaining approvals from both United States and Canadian regulatory authorities, including the United States Interstate Commerce Commission. It is likely that a regulatory decision will be received in 1985.

The divestiture of Lee Way, which became final on August 6, 1984, resulted in a second quarter loss of $15.5 million before-tax and $15 million after-tax ($.16 per share). Total proceeds were approximately $22 million. The loss on the sale of Lee Way is reflected in the Consolidated Statement of Income under the caption "Loss on disposal."

The results of operations of Lee Way through June 5, 1984, the date prior to which the buyer assumed management and control, and NAVL (for the full year) are included in the Consolidated Statement of Income under the caption "Income from discontinued operations" and include:

	1984	1983	1982
	(in thousands)		
Operating revenues	$729,316	$730,350	$688,069
Costs and expenses	692,498	710,517	673,202
Interest expense (income)	1,028	331	(2,840)
Provision for income taxes	14,915	6,728	5,846
Income from discontinued operations	$ 20,875	$ 12,774	$ 11,861

The net assets of NAVL and Lee Way are carried at their historical cost in the Consolidated Balance Sheet caption "Net assets of the transportation segment held for disposal" as follows:

	NAVL	NAVL and Lee Way
	December 29, 1984	December 31, 1983
	(in thousands)	
Current assets	$236,214	$187,929
Current liabilities	164,500	141,511
Net current assets	71,714	46,418
Property, plant and equipment (net)	98,855	127,122
Other non-current assets	52,969	4,008
Non-current liabilities	80,328	28,044
Net non-current assets	71,496	103,086
Net assets of the transportation segment held for disposal	$143,210	$149,504

Source: PepsiCo, Inc. 1984 Annual Report. Copyright, 1985, by PepsiCo, Inc. Reproduced with permission.

all of the revenue, expenses, assets and liabilities of the discontinued segment would still be combined within the continuing operations of the firm. In this case, the analyst must examine the footnotes to the financial statements for information regarding the disposal of the segment and make the appropriate adjustments to the income, assets and liabilities of the continuing operations. Again, by analytically restating the financial information provided, the analyst can compute ratios and other statistics both "with and without" the discontinued segment. By excluding the discontinued segment, financial statistics would more properly reflect the expected, recurring operating strength of the firm and would provide better information for projecting the firm's future cash flows.

Accounting Changes

According to APB Opinion No. 20 ("Accounting Changes"), paragraph 6, there are three types of accounting changes. These are:

1. Change in accounting estimate;

2. Change in accounting principle or method;

3. Change in the reporting entity.

There is also a correction of an error, which is identified in Opinion 20, but is not considered to be an accounting change. For purposes of discussion, however, the error correction is identified as:

4. Correction of an error made in previously issued financial statements.

Items (3) and (4) have already been considered in detail in previous chapters of this text. A change in the reporting entity, item (3), involves the proforma disclosures of income information when there has been a business combination accounted for under the purchase method. A correction of an error made in previously issued financial statements, item (4), is classified as a prior period adjustment by SFAS 16, "Prior Period Adjustments". As previously mentioned, the prior period adjustment must be shown as an adjustment to opening retained earnings, net of tax.

A detailed discussion of items (1) and (2) is presented in the following sections of this chapter.

Change in Accounting Estimate

A change in accounting estimate involves revisions of estimates used in accounting in areas such as the bad debts expense, depreciation, depletion and amortization, and accounting for pensions. Because estimates are considered a natural part of the accounting process, changes in estimate are expected, particularly with experience and as new information becomes available. Therefore, changes in estimate are not considered significant or unusual problems by the accounting profession. Any adjustments made are "prospective in nature", whereby the new estimate is implemented in the year of the change and in all subsequent accounting periods. There is no consideration of retroactive effects and adjustments of previously issued financial statements. If the effect of the change in estimate on net income is material, it should also be disclosed in the footnotes to the financial statements.

Whenever it is impossible to distinguish between a change in estimate and a change in principle, it should be considered as a change in estimate. Similarly, changes in estimate effected by a change in accounting principle should be accounted for as a change in estimate.

Change in Accounting Principle

A change in accounting principle involves changing from one GAAP accounting method to another. For example, a switch from the accelerated to the straight-line method of depreciation would qualify as a change in accounting principle by the provisions of Opinion 20, paragraph 7. A change in accounting principle is not considered to result from a change to a GAAP method from a method that was not GAAP. Similarly, a change in principle does not result from a change in accounting method due to circumstances occuring for the first time or that were previously insignificant, such as, the capitalization or deferral of costs such as leaseholds, which were previously expensed due to immateriality. Another example is the first-time use of the LIFO method for a newly adopted product line because of the inflationary conditions of the industry in which the new product is classified.

A change in accounting principle is considered more significant than a change in estimate, and will require more extensive accounting adjustments and footnote disclosures.

The change in a GAAP method results in a violation of the consistency principle of accounting. When consistency is violated, the financial statements are no longer comparable from period to period. Nonetheless, the consistency principle does not prohibit changes in accounting method, as long as there is adequate accounting for the change and full disclosure of the change and its effects on the financial statements. Adequate accounting and full disclosure of the change are prescribed by the provisions of Opinion 20. The accounting procedures to be followed and the extent of disclosures depends on the type of change in accounting principle.

Types of Changes in Accounting Principle. Opinion 20 identifies three types of changes in accounting principle. These are:

1. Retroactive-effect type change;

2. Cumulative-effect type change;

3. Change to the LIFO method of accounting for inventory.

In a retroactive-effect type change, all prior years' financial statements presented are restated "as if" the newly adopted accounting principle had always been used.

According to professional pronouncements, there are only five types of changes in accounting principle that qualify for retroactive restatement of prior years. These are:

1. Change from the LIFO method of accounting for inventory valuation to some other GAAP inventory method;

2. Change in accounting for long-term construction contracts (i.e., percentage of completion to or from the completed contract method);

3. Change to or from the full-cost method of accounting in the oil and gas (extractive) industries;

4. Issuance of financial statements by a firm for the first time to obtain additional equity capital to effect a business combination or to register securities. This case only applies to closely held firm and can be applied only once;

5. The FASB requires that a newly adopted standard be applied retroactively.

Any change in accounting principle other than the five special changes listed above and a change to the LIFO method of inventory valuation must be classified as a cumulative-effect type accounting change.

Accounting for A Change in Accounting Principle. As discussed earlier, when a firm changes from one GAAP method to another, the consistency principle of accounting is violated. In addition, the financial statements of the firm are no longer comparable between accounting periods. The accounting profession permits changes in principle and the resulting consistency violation, as long as there is adequate accounting and full disclosure that restores comparability.

Opinion 20 requires extensive accounting procedures and disclosures which are designed to restore the comparability of financial information reporting over several accounting periods. These requirements are discussed in the following paragraphs.

Footnote Disclosures. For any type of change in accounting principle, an explanatory note is required. In the year of the change in accounting principle, a footnote is provided which generally includes the following three elements:

1. A description of or the nature of the change (e.g., "...effective January 1, 1991, the Company changed its method of accounting for the depreciation of its plant assets from the straight line to the declining balance method").

2. Management's justification for the change in principle (e.g., "...management believes that the new method of accounting better matches costs and revenues or better reflects the Company's operations"). Where the change is mandated by a newly adopted FASB standard, management's justification would simply consist of a reference to the requirements of the new FASB statement.

It should be noted that the SEC in Financial Reporting Release (FRR) No. 1 requires a written statement by the firm's accountant indicating that the new method of accounting is preferable, and the accounting firm must be consistent among clients and industries in its justification as to what is the preferable method of accounting under similar circumstances.

3. The effect of the change on net income after tax or a statement that the effect of the change was immaterial (e.g., "...net income after tax would have been $1,000,000 greater [$1.23/share] if the straight-line [the old] method of depreciation was still used").

The last footnote requirement assists the analyst in restoring comparability with prior years in that this information can be used to analytically restate the current year's reported net income to what it would have been under the previously used accounting method.

In addition to the Opinion 20 footnote disclosures, the CPA firm must modify its opinion on the financial statements. If all of the requirements mandated by the professional standards are met, the change is considered "acceptable" and the auditor issues an unqualified opinion, with a fourth paragraph indicating that a change in principle has taken place and making reference to the footnote discussed above. If the change is considered "unacceptable" (e.g., management does not satisfy all of the reporting and disclosure requirements of Opinion 20), the auditor must issue a qualified opinion. That is, the opinion on the financial statements, taken as a whole, is qualified as to consistency. This qualification requires a statement that the financial statements are prepared in accordance with GAAP on a consistent basis "...except for the change" in accounting principle. An explanatory fourth paragraph as described above is also included in the auditor's report.

Cumulative-Effect Type Change. If the change in accounting principle is classified as a cumulative-effect type change, in addition to the footnote discussed above, Opinion 20 requires the following accounting adjustments.

1. Application of the new principle in the year of the change and all future periods. This is basically prospective application of the new accounting method.

2. Presentation of the cumulative effect, net of tax, on the face of the income statement in the year of the change, between discontinued operations and extraordinary items. The cumulative effect is the combined effect of retroactive application of the new standard to all prior periods. Specifically, the cumulative effect is a current or catch-up adjustment which represents the total effect on beginning retained earnings "as if" the new method of accounting had always been used.

Because this adjustment "catches up" for all prior years, it excludes the year of the change. In other words, the cumulative effect is the total or the aggregate effect on net income and on the related asset's and/or liability's carrying value "as if" the newly adopted accounting principle had always been utililzed from the beginning of the asset's or liability's life up to the beginning of the year of the change. When the cumulative effect is used, there is no retroactive restatement of the primary financial statements so that all prior years' income statements appear as previously reported.

3. Supplementary proforma income information presented immediately below the income statement, for all years presented. The proforma information can consist of net income and/or earnings per share. The proforma net income for the current year is the same as income before the cumulative effect because the new method is actually adopted and applied in the year of the change. For all prior years presented, the proforma income information is a recalculation of the previously reported income "as if" the new method had always been used in those accounting periods. The proforma income information is actually the same as the income that would be reported under a retroactive restatement, except that the primary financial statements are not retroactively restated and appear as previously reported. In addition, the proforma information is only partial income data, and not a complete income statement.

The purpose of the proforma information is to restore comparability by enabling the analyst to compare the year of the change with all prior years presented under the new method. Of course, until there is another accounting change, these accounting periods can also be compared with subsequent years' financial statements.

A sample disclosure of a cumulative-effect type change for USX is presented in Exhibit 8.4.

Retroactive-Effect Type Change. A retroactive-effect type change requires the same footnote disclosures discussed earlier. In addition to the footnote information, if the change is classified as a retroactive-effect type change, the following accounting is required.

1. The current year's income is determined based on the new accounting principle and all prior years presented are restated on a basis consistent with the newly adopted accounting principle. The retroactive restatement obviates the need for the proforma income information.

2. The cumulative effect attributable to years prior to those presented in the annual report is reported as an adjustment to opening retained earnings on the balance sheet for the earliest year presented.

Illustration. The following data are presented primarily to illustrate a cumulative-effect change in accounting principle. At the end of the illustration, the provisions for a retroactive-effect type change will be applied.

Assume that the CSN Corporation acquired plant and equipment for $15,000 ($000's omitted). The equipment was estimated to have a useful life of five years with no scrap value. The plant and equipment was depreciated by the sum-of-the-years-digits (SYD) method. The tax rate was 50% over the entire life of the asset.

At the beginning of year four, CSN elected to switch from the SYD method to

EXHIBIT 8.4

Sample Disclosure: USX Corporation and Subsidiary Companies: Disclosure of a Cumulative-Effect Type Accounting Change Under Opinion 20

Consolidated Statement of Income — USX

(Dollars in millions except per share data)	1986	1985	1984
Sales *(Note 8, page 34)*	**$14,938**	$20,779	$21,092
Operating costs:			
Cost of sales (excludes items shown below) *(Note 13, page 36)*	**10,971**	14,598	14,574
Inventory market valuation provision *(Note 13, page 36)*	**300**	—	—
Selling, general and administrative expenses	**630**	682	639
Pensions, insurance and other employee benefits *(Notes 5 and 6, page 33)*	**105**	489	489
Depreciation, depletion and amortization	**1,559**	1,591	1,489
State, local and miscellaneous taxes	**1,242**	1,416	1,494
Exploration expenses	**168**	298	310
Restructuring charges and other unusual items *(Note 3, page 32)*	**1,457**	(30)	22
Total operating costs	**16,432**	19,044	19,017
Operating income (loss) (excludes items shown below)	**(1,494)**	1,735	2,075
Other income *(Note 9, page 34)*	**71**	190	362
Net interest and other financial costs *(Note 9, page 34)*	**(786)**	(809)	(961)
Total income (loss) before taxes on income, extraordinary items and cumulative effect of a change in accounting principle	**(2,209)**	1,116	1,476
Less provision (credit) for estimated United States and foreign income taxes *(Note 10, page 35)*	**(616)**	614	762
Total income (loss) before extraordinary items and cumulative effect of a change in accounting principle	**(1,593)**	502	714
Extraordinary items, net of income tax *(Note 7, page 34)*	**(240)**	51	79
Cumulative effect on prior years of a change in accounting principle, net of income tax *(Note 27, page 41)*	**—**	45	—
Net income (loss)	**$ (1,833)**	$ 598	$ 793

Income per common share

Primary:

	1986	1985	1984
Weighted average shares, in thousands (Note 11, page 35)	*257,821*	*245,568*	*239,399*
Total income (loss) before extraordinary items, cumulative effect of a change in accounting principle and preferred stock dividends	**$ (6.18)**	$ 2.05	$ 2.98
Extraordinary items	**(.93)**	.21	.33
Cumulative effect of a change in accounting principle	**—**	.18	—
Dividends on preferred stock	**(.35)**	(.50)	(.50)
Net income (loss) per common share	**$ (7.46)**	$ 1.94	$ 2.81

Fully diluted:

	1986	1985	1984
Weighted average shares, in thousands (Note 11, page 35)	*257,821*	*260,176*	*248,074*
Total income (loss) before extraordinary items, cumulative effect of a change in accounting principle and preferred stock dividends	**$ (6.18)**	$ 1.96	$ 2.88
Extraordinary items	**(.93)**	.20	.32
Cumulative effect of a change in accounting principle	**—**	.17	—
Dividends on preferred stock	**(.35)**	(.35)	(.39)
Net income (loss) per common share	**$ (7.46)**	$ 1.98	$ 2.81

Pro forma data, assuming the 1985 change in accounting principle were applied retroactively

	1986	1985	1984
Total income before extraordinary items		$ 502	$ 753
Per common share (after preferred stock dividends) — primary		1.55	2.65
— fully diluted		1.60	2.66
Net income		$ 553	$ 832
Per common share (after preferred stock dividends) — primary		1.76	2.98
— fully diluted		1.80	2.96

The accompanying notes are an integral part of these financial statements.

Exhibit 8.4, continued

---

27. Change in Accounting Principle

In 1985, USX adopted a change in accounting for petroleum revenue tax payable to the United Kingdom. The new method of accounting for this income tax is based on the estimated effective tax rate over the life of the Brae field. This method recognizes certain unique tax allowances proportionally over the income from the field rather than when realized for tax return purposes. Management considers the new method to be a preferred accounting practice under the circumstances, resulting in a better matching of expense with revenue and a better measurement of deferred tax liability. The cumulative effect of the change on prior years is $45 million, net of United States income tax. The effect on income for the year 1985 is as follows:

(In millions except per share data)	1985		1985
Total income before extraordinary items	$ 15	Net income	$ 60
Per common share — primary	.06	Per common share — primary	.24
— fully diluted	.07	— fully diluted	.24

---

the straight-line (S/L) method of depreciation for financial reporting purposes. The depreciation schedules for the equipment under both accounting alternatives are presented below.

Year	SYD	S/L
1	$5,000	$3,000
2	4,000	3,000
3	3,000	3,000
4	2,000	3,000
5	1,000	3,000

In order to compute the cumulative effect from the change in accounting principle, the depreciation for all prior years and the year of the change must be compared. This comparison is presented below.

	Prior Years			Year of the Change	
Method	1	2	3	4	
SYD	$5,000	$4,000	$3,000	$2,000	
S/L	3,000	3,000	3,000	3,000	
Change	$2,000	$1,000	-0-	<$1,000>	
Cumulative Effect:				Footnote Information:	
Before tax......$3,000				Net income after tax	
				would have been $500	
After tax.......$1,500				higher if SYD was still	
				used.	

The comparative financial statements and the related footnote for CSN Corporation are presented in Exhibit 8.5.

Although a balance sheet is not presented in Exhibit 8.5, the accumulated depreciation and the deferred tax accounts must also be adjusted. After making the appropriate accounting adjustments, these two accounts would be restated "as if" the straight-line method was always used. In this illustration, the accumulated

EXHIBIT 8.5

Illustration: CSN Corporation: Income Statement and Footnote Disclosure for a Cumulative-Effect Type Accounting Change

----

CSN Corporation

Income Statements

For the Years Ended December 31, 19X4, 19X3, and 19X2

	19X4	19X3*	19X2*
Revenues	$10,000	$12,000	$11,000
Operating Expenses	< 4,000>	< 8,000>	< 5,000>
Depreciation Expense	< 3,000>(SL)	< 3,000>(SYD)	< 4,000>(SYD)
Income before tax	$ 3,000	$ 1,000	$ 2,000
Income tax expense (50%)	< 1,500>	< 500>	< 1,000>
Income before the cumulative effect	$ 1,500	$ 500	$ 1,000
Cumulative effect, net of tax (Note A)	1,500	-	-
Net income	$ 3,000	$ 500	$ 1,000
Proforma Income Information	$ 1,500	$ 500	$ 1,500

* = 19X2 and 19X3 as previously reported

Note A. On January 1, 19X4, the Company changed its method of depreciation of its plant assets from the sum-of-the-years digits method to the straight-line method. Management believes that the new method of depreciation more closely reflects the economic conditions influencing the Company's operations. If the sum-of-the-years digits method was still used in 19X4, net income after tax would have been greater by $500.

depreciation account would be reduced by $3,000, from $12,000 to $9,000. This $3,000 is the pretax cumulative effect and represents the difference between the sum-of-the-years digits and the straight-line methods of depreciation. The balance in the accumulated depreciation account is $9,000, which is exactly the amount of depreciation that would have been taken if the straight-line method had always been used (i.e., $3,000 per year for the first three years).

The deferred tax liability is increased by $1,500, which is the after-tax cumulative effect. This adjustment assumes that another accelerated method, such as a Federal MACRS method, is used for tax purposes. When the firm switches to the straight-line method for financial reporting, the temporary book-tax difference is larger than if the sum-of-the-years digits method was used, and therefore more deferred taxes have to be provided.

The proforma income information is determined by retroactive application of the new standard to all prior years presented. The detailed computations for this cumulative-effect accounting change and the retroactive (proforma) application are presented in Exhibit 8.6. The exhibit also illustrates the financial reporting requirements if this change was a retroactive-effect type change.

A Change to the LIFO Method of Inventory Valuation. The last type of accounting change is a change to the LIFO method of inventory valuation. When a firm changes to the LIFO method, the cumulative effect and proforma income information are not required because it would be too impractical to determine. All that is required in this case is the Opinion 20 footnote disclosures as discussed earlier and a statement indicating that the cumulative effect and the proforma income information have been omitted and the reasons why this information has not been provided (i.e., impracticality from a cost-benefit standpoint).

It should be noted that in any case where the accountant believes that the determination of the cumulative effect and proforma income information or retroactive restatement would not be cost justified, the firm may omit these disclosures. However, a footnote must indicate that this otherwise required information has been omitted and the reasons why these disclosures have not been provided.

Rationale for Different Types of Changes in Accounting Principle. The reasons for allowing exception to the cumulative-effect type change are varied. The special treatment for a change to LIFO was allowed due to the cost-benefit argument noted in the previous section. The five exceptions that qualify for retroactive restatement were made because the profession believed that the cumulative effect adjustment for these special changes would be of such magnitude that there would be a significant effect on the net income of the firm in the year of the change and that the reported net income would be misleading. For example, a switch from LIFO to any other inventory valuation method would probably result in a significant positive cumulative effect, causing a large increase in reported net income in the year of the change.

The different types of change in accounting principle will be illustrated in Case 8.1 at the end of this chapter.

Analytical Issues. As noted throughout this chapter, the accounting and disclosure requirements of Opinion 20 were designed to restore the comparability eliminated by a change in accounting principle.

The analyst can use the footnote disclosure of the effect of the change on net income to restate the current year's income under the old accounting method so as

EXHIBIT 8.6

Illustration: CSN Corporation: Computation of the Proforma Income Information for a Cumulative-Effect Type Accounting Change

---

CSN Corporation
Supplementary Proforma Income Information
For the Years Ended December 31, 19X4, 19X3, and 19X2

	19X4	19X3*	19X2*
Revenues.................	$10,000	$12,000	$11,000
Operating Expenses.......	< 4,000>	< 8,000>	< 5,000>
Depreciation Expense.....	< 3,000>(SL)	< 3,000>(SL)	< 3,000>(SL)
Income before tax........	$ 3,000	$ 1,000	$ 3,000
Income tax expense (50%).	< 1,500>	< 500>	< 1,500>
Net income...............	$ 1,500	$ 500	$ 1,500

NOTE: If this was a retroactive-effect type change, the primary income statements would be restated as above with all years presented based on the new, straight-line method of depreciation.

to compare all years under the prior GAAP method. The supplementary income information or the retroactive restatement of prior periods' financial statements could be used to compare all years under the newly adopted accounting principle. In this way, the analyst can determine the results of operations both "with and without" the effects of the accounting change.

An analytical problem results, however, with a cumulative effect type accounting change. As noted earlier, when the change in principle is classified as a cumulative-effect type change, the cumulative effect is reported on the face of the income statement. The cumulative effect is the aggregate after-tax effect of adopting the new accounting principle in prior years. This aggregate effect is not very useful to the analyst and should probably be grouped with other unusual items. Therefore, investment and credit decisions can be improved by segregating the gain or loss from discontinued operations, extraordinary items and the cumulative effect from a change in accounting principle from the income or loss from continuing operations. In this way the analyst is better able to determine the potential operating strength of the firm and its ability to generate positive cash flows in the future.

ACCOUNTING FOR CONTINGENCIES

Introduction

FASB Statement No. 5 ("Accounting for Contingencies"), paragraph 5, defines a contingency as "an existing condition, situation or set of circumstances involving uncertainty as to possible gain (i.e., a gain contingency or a contingent asset) or loss (i.e., a loss contingency or a contingent liability), to a firm that will ultimately be resolved when one or more future events occur or fail to occur".

As indicated by the FASB's definition of a contingency, there are two types of contingencies: a gain contingency and a loss contingency. The actual accounting for the contingency will depend on its type. In general, there are three possible accounting alternatives for a contingency. These are:

1. Recognize (accrue) the contingent event in the current financial statements and disclose in the footnotes;

2. Disclose the event only in the footnotes to the financial statements;

3. Make no disclosure.

As will be discussed in the following sections, the accounting alternative actually used will not only depend on the type of contingency, but will also depend on the probability of future occurrence and the ability to estimate the amount of the contingent event.

Accounting for Gain Contingencies

A gain contingency is an uncertain right or claim, which may become a valid property right in the future. Due to conservatism, contingent assets are never recorded or accrued in the accounts and the financial statements, and are disclosed in the footnotes only when there is almost complete certainty of realization in the future. Examples of gain contingencies that may be disclosed in the footnotes to the financial statements include favorable settlements of tax disputes with the IRS or favorable settlements of litigation.

Accounting for Loss Contingencies

A loss contingency or a contingent liability is a potential obligation whose realization is dependent upon the occurrence of some future event or the failure of the event to occur. In the case of a loss contingency, all three accounting alternatives are used. The particular alternative used is dependent on the probability of occurrence and the ability to provide a reasonable estimation of the future loss.

Recognition of the Loss Contingency in the Financial Statements. An estimated loss is accrued and charged against income, and a liability is recorded or an asset is reduced if both of the following SFAS 5, paragraph 8, criteria are met:

1. Prior to the issuance of the financial statements there is evidence that it is "probable" that a liability has been incurred or an asset has been reduced as of the date of the financial statements;

2. The amount of the loss is subject to "reasonable estimation".

Common examples of loss contingencies that are accrued and reported on the financial statements are the bad debt expense and product warranty accruals.

According to FASB Interpretation No. 14 ("Reasonable Estimation of the Amount of a Loss)", paragraph 3, the term subject to "reasonable estimation" can include a range of possible amounts. When one amount in the range appears to be the best estimate at the time the financial statements are prepared, that amount is accrued. If no amount in the range appears to be the better estimate, the accountant would accrue the low end of the range and disclose the high end of the range in the footnotes to the financial statements.

Footnote Disclosure of Loss Contingencies. If the amount of the loss is not subject to reasonable estimation, but the loss is material and "reasonably possible", the loss contingency should be disclosed in the footnotes to the financial statements. The footnote disclosure should include a "description of the nature of the contingency and an estimate of the possible loss, an estimated range of the loss or a statement that an estimate of the loss cannot be made". This type of disclosure is quite common for pending litigation with uncertain outcomes and guarantees of the debt of others. A sample litigation footnote for the National Fuel Gas Company is presented in Exhibit 8.7.

Loss Contingencies Without Disclosure. If the probability of the occurrence of the loss contingency is "remote", the event may not be disclosed in the financial

EXHIBIT 8.7

Sample Disclosure: National Fuel Gas Company: Contingent Liability Disclosure Under SFAS 5

Note B—Litigation Involving Synthetic Natural Gas Purchases:

(a) The PaPUC Proceedings: The Pennsylvania Public Utility Commission (PaPUC) in an order issued August 28, 1980, found that an unspecified portion of the cost of SNG purchases made by Distribution Corporation from Ashland Oil, Inc. (Ashland) for the Pennsylvania rate jurisdiction during the period September 1, 1979, through August 31, 1980, should be disapproved and accordingly excluded from rate schedules. In a later proceeding, the PaPUC issued an order on December 18, 1981, fixing the disapproved amounts at approximately $14,000,000 with interest at the rate of 6 percent per annum from the months in which those costs were collected, through December 30, 1981, to be refunded in five equal annual adjustments to the Gas Cost Rate billing factor. Distribution Corporation appealed both orders to the Commonwealth Court of Pennsylvania (Commonwealth Court), and obtained a stay of the refund order from that court.

Cross-appeals were filed by an Erie, Pennsylvania consumer group with the Commonwealth Court with respect to the orders issued August 28, 1980, and December 18, 1981. Cross-appellants contend that (1) the approximately $14,000,000 refund ordered by the PaPUC should be increased to approximately $20,000,000; (2) the PaPUC erred in conditionally permitting Distribution Corporation to recover 50¢ per MCF for SNG not taken for the period from September 1, 1979, through the expiration of the SNG contract (i.e., approximately $3,300,000 annually until May 1984); and (3) the PaPUC should have ordered Distribution Corporation to refund approximately $56,800,000 with respect to SNG purchases for the period from July 1, 1975, through August 31, 1979.

On August 4, 1983, the Commonwealth Court reversed the orders of August 28, 1980, and December 18, 1981, and remanded (i.e., returned) the record to the PaPUC for further proceedings. Cross-appellants filed a petition with the Supreme Court of Pennsylvania requesting permission to appeal from the remand order and opinion of the Commonwealth Court. This petition was denied. While encouraged by the actions of the Commonwealth Court and the Supreme Court of Pennsylvania, neither management nor counsel can at this time determine what, if anything, may occur on remand with respect to any of cross-appellants' contentions, what may occur with respect to the PaPUC's refund order or what the ultimate outcome of any or all of these matters will be. Therefore, the Company has not established an accrual for any potential liability. The Company preserves its right to appeal any adverse determination of the PaPUC.

Exhibit 8.7, continued

(b) The Federal District Court Proceedings: In May of 1972, Distribution Corporation contracted to purchase approximately 18,200 MMCF per year of SNG from Ashland over a ten-year period ending May 1984. The cost of SNG purchases had been included in Distribution Corporation's Commission-approved rate schedules in both its New York and Pennsylvania rate jurisdictions. However, during fiscal year 1980, both the Public Service Commission of the State of New York and the PaPUC ordered Distribution Corporation to discontinue including the cost of SNG purchases in its rate schedules. Accordingly, Distribution Corporation ceased purchasing SNG from Ashland. Distribution Corporation filed appeals in New York and Pennsylvania seeking a reversal of the Commissions' orders. The New York and Pennsylvania orders have been upheld with respect to discontinuing inclusion of the cost of SNG purchases in rate schedules.

On November 18, 1980, Ashland interposed a claim in United States District Court, Western District of New York against Distribution Corporation premised upon a breach of contract. Ashland advised Distribution Corporation in mid-November 1984, that, in light of the expiration of the original contract term and market conditions believed to be in existence during the period 1980-1984, Ashland would shortly seek the court's permission to amend, formally, its claim against Distribution Corporation so as to: (1) eliminate a claim for an order compelling Distribution Corporation to resume SNG purchases; (2) reduce its aggregate damage claim from $2.90 per MCF to approximately $1.19 per MCF of SNG not taken (i.e., from approximately $53,000,000 to approximately $21,700,000 per year) during the balance of the contract term; and (3) eliminate a claim for an additional $64,000,000 in respect of damages allegedly resulting, indirectly, from Distribution Corporation's cessation of SNG purchases.

Distribution Corporation is vigorously opposing Ashland's breach of contract claim and has raised as a defense thereto, among other things, the regulatory commissions' actions referred to above. At present, pretrial discovery is in progress. Neither management nor counsel can determine the ultimate outcome of these proceedings. Therefore, the Company has not established an accrual for any potential liability.

---

statements. However, due to conservatism, most accountants would make some disclosure of the event, even if the footnote includes a statement that legal counsel and the management of the firm do not expect the loss to be realized or that the ultimate realization of the loss contingency would not materially affect the financial statements.

Exhibit 8.8 presents examples of contingency footnotes where the firm does not expect a material adverse impact on the financial statements, but still makes a disclosure.

Analytical Issues. By setting strict conditions under which a loss contingency can be recognized in the accounts and the financial statements, SFAS 5 reduced the flexibility available to management with respect to the creation of "reserves". These reserves were traditionally used by management as income-smoothing devices. For example, if management expected a sharp decrease in earnings next year, it could create a reserve for repairs and maintenance. The current addition to the reserve would be charged against income as an operating expense while the cumulative balance of the allowance (reserve) for repairs and maintenance or a liability for future repairs and maintenance would be reported on the balance sheet. By reducing this year's income, next year automatically looks better. In addition, when there is an actual cash outflow for repairs and maintenance next year or in the future, it would be changed against the allowance (reserve) or it would reduce the liability. Thus, the actual repairs and maintenance would have no effect on the income reported in subsequent accounting periods.

Although SFAS 5 significantly reduced the use of reserves in the financial statements, the analyst must still examine the financial statements for the employment of reserves as income-smoothing devices. Liberal interpretation of the loss recognition criteria of SFAS 5 (i.e., the loss is "probable" and subject to "reasonable estimation") may result in the creation of many loss reserves. Common examples include reserves for obsolete inventory and provisions for future losses.

The analytical problem with income smoothing is that it artifically shifts accrual-based accounting income between periods. This could be done to reduce the variation in the trend of accounting earnings. In addition, smoothing devices and unusual write-offs are used in "big bath" accounting. When a company is incurring large losses, write-offs of items such as obsolete inventory and previously deferred costs increase the loss even further. By increasing the loss, future recovery seems more significant. In addition, these write-offs may be a way to "clean house" because many of the items in inventory and deferred costs may have been known to be of little value, but management was reluctant to write these items off during years of marginal profitability.

The use of reserves and other unusual changes against income may also represent a signal by management that next year will result in below normal operating performance.

Regardless of the reason for the creation of the reserve or the write-off, the analyst should be aware of these items and their effect on the quality of accounting income. In the year the reserves are created or the write-off is taken, income will be understated. In the year when the events provided for by the reserve or the charge-off result in cash outflows, accounting income will be overstated. The analyst should make "qualitative adjustments" to the accrual basis income reported in these accounting periods. In addition, analysis of the cash flow statement will provide

EXHIBIT 8.8

**Sample Disclosure: Contingent Liability Disclosures Under SFAS 5:
No Material Effect on Consolidated Financial Position**

Unisys 1987 Annual Report

---

17. Litigation

There are various actions or claims which have been brought or asserted against the Company. After consultation with counsel, management does not consider such actions or claims to be material to the Company's consolidated financial position.

Source: Unisys Corporation, 1987 Annual Report. Copyright, 1987 by Unisys Corporation. Reprinted with permission.

Ashland Oil, Inc. and Subsidiaries 1982 Annual Report

**Note G—Litigation
and claims**

Numerous lawsuits are pending or threatened against Ashland or its subsidiaries, alleging claims for substantial amounts. Ashland has been advised by its law department that either there are meritorious defenses to substantially all such litigation and claims, or any liability which finally may be determined, in excess of amounts already provided for, should not have a material effect on Ashland's consolidated financial position.

Source: Ashland Oil, Inc. and Subsidiaries 1982 Annual Report. Copyright, 1982, by Ashland Oil, Inc. Reprinted with permission.

ConAgra, Inc. and Subsidiaries 1985 Annual Report

---

12. Contingencies

There was no litigation at May 26, 1985, which, in the opinion of management, would have a significant effect on the financial position of the Company.

Source: ConAgra, Inc. and Subsidiaries 1985 Annual Report. Copyright, 1985, by ConAgra, Inc. Reprinted with permission.

information regarding the cash consequences of the items accounted for by the reserve method.

Finally, if the loss contingency involves a material amount, the auditing firm may modify its opinion as to uncertainty. This modification would involve an explanatory paragraph discussing the contingency and referring to the contingent liability footnote disclosure in the financial statements. As with the accrual of the loss, the extent of modification of the auditor's report depends on the probability of occurrence of the contingency. According to Generally Accepted Auditing Standards, if the loss is "probable", the explanatory paragraph is added; if the loss is "reasonably possible", the explanatory paragraph may be added; and if the loss is "remote", there is no modification to the standard audit report.

OTHER ISSUES IN FULL DISCLOSURE

Related Party Transactions

A related party has the ability to significantly influence the policies of the company. The transactions between the related party and the company may not be objectively determined (i.e., not "arms-length"). For example, a transaction between two closely held companies, owned by the same family, would probably not be objectively determined. Therefore, the accountant must disclose the economic substance of the transaction, regardless of its legal form. According to FASB Statement No. 57 ("Related Party Disclosures"), paragraph 2, a related party footnote disclosure would include the nature of the relationship and the nature and the amounts of the transactions involving the company and the related party.

The analyst should consider the related party footnote disclosure in the assessment of the future operating strength of the firm. If a significant part of the company's revenues are generated from transactions with related parties, the firm may be less profitable than reflected by the accounting income numbers when eliminating sales to related parties.

When related parties exist, the analyst should obtain the financial statements of the related party. An examination of the long-term debt and other footnotes to the financial statements of the related party could reveal guarantees of the related party's debt made by the company. This could have a significant effect on the lending decision made by the credit analyst.

A sample related party transactions disclosure for Panco Equipment Corporation is presented in Exhibit 8.9.

Segment Reporting

In a highly diversified enterprise, it is difficult for the credit and financial analyst to assess the future profitability and cash flows of the firm using the consolidated financial statements. For example, what industry standards for working capital and other ratios should the analyst use for a comparison of these same financial statistics for a firm such as General Electric? The difficulty in the analysis of the

EXHIBIT 8.9

Sample Disclosure: Panco Equipment Corporation:
Related Party Transactions

NOTE 8 Related Party Transactions

Other Receivables include a Note Receivable from an affiliate controlled by a shareholder, officer and director of the Company. As of February 28, 1990, the long term portion of $248,042 is included in Notes Receivable and the current portion of $67,012 is included in Other Receivables. The note is payable in interest bearing monthly installments of $8,434 per month through January, 1994. Also included in Other Receivables is approximately $62,000 of other loans due from other affiliates.

In 1989, the Company entered into an agreement with an affiliate whereby the Company may utilize certain customer lists for a monthly royalty of $7,552. The agreement is cancellable at the option of either party.

Source: Panco Equipment Corporation 1990 Annual Report. Copyright, 1990, by Panco Equipment Corp. Reprinted with permission.

consolidated financial statements for conglomerate firms results from the fact that each segment or line of business provides a different risk and return contribution to the firm's overall profitability, future cash flows and growth potential.

FASB Statement No. 14, "Financial Reporting for Segments of a Business Enterprise", was issued as a direct response to these analytical problems and the demands of the financial community. SFAS 14 requires the disclosure of certain data relating to the operations of the firm in different industries and nations and in dealings with major customers.

Specifically, SFAS 14, paragraph 15, requires line of business disclosures for each "reportable segment". A line of business qualifies as a reportable segment if it is a segment representing 10% of total revenues, 10% of total profit, or 10% of total identifiable assets. The line of business disclosures required by SFAS 14, paragraphs 22 through 27, consists of the following:

1. Revenues by business segment (with intercompany transfers shown separately);

2. Operating profit by line of business;

3. Segment identifiable assets;

4. Capital expenditures by line of business;

5. Depreciation and amortization by line of business.

This segment information is usually disclosed in a separate footnote or as part of the management's discussion and analysis (MDA) section of the financial statements. The segment information provided must reconcile with the total revenues, total operating profit, total assets, total capital expenditures, and total depreciation and amortization reported on the consolidated financial statements.

A sample segment footnote disclosure for Avon Products, Inc. and Subsidiaries is presented in Exhibit 8.10.

Major Analytical Issues in the Application of SFAS 14

There are two major analytical issues in the application of SFAS 14. These involve the definition of an industry segment and the allocation of common or joint costs.

Definition of an Industry Segment. The FASB did not prescribe the procedures to be used in defining an industry segment. A firm could use SIC codes, geographic limits, legal entities or divisions. As a result, there is no standard definition of an industry segment reported under SFAS 14. Thus, the consumer products division of General Motors could be operating in a completely different industry from the consumer products division of the Chrysler Corporation. Due to this lack of guidance from the FASB, the analyst cannot easily compare the segments of different firms, even if the firms are operating in the same industry.

EXHIBIT 8.10

Sample Disclosure: Avon Products, Inc. and Subsidiaries: Line of Business Disclosures Under SFAS 14

Business Segment Data

The Company's business is primarily composed of four industry segments: the manufacture and sale of cosmetics, fragrances and toiletries; the manufacture and sale of fashion jewelry and accessories; the rental and sale of home health care equipment and the operation of nursing homes and alcohol and drug abuse treatment centers; and the sale of apparel. Operations are conducted in the United States, Europe, Latin America, the Pacific and Canada.

Operating profit consists of total revenues less cost of goods sold and marketing, distribution and administrative expenses. Interest income, interest expense and other income (deductions)—net, including amortization of the excess of cost over the fair market value of net assets of purchased subsidiaries, which are included in earnings before taxes, are excluded from operating profit.

The identifiable assets of industry segments and geographic areas are those assets used in the Company's operations in each segment and area.

Industry Segments

Year Ended December 31	Net Sales	Operating Profit	Identifiable Assets	Depreciation Expense	Additions To Property
1986					
Cosmetics, fragrances and toiletries	$1,923.8	$236.8	$1,089.1	$40.9	$ 49.4
Fashion jewelry and accessories	310.0	45.0	204.1	5.9	7.6
Health care services	431.8	65.0	731.9	26.9	59.7
Direct response	216.2	11.6	139.7	1.5	3.4
Other	1.3	—	.7	—	—
Corporate and eliminations	—	(39.7)	130.8	.4	.4
Consolidated	$2,883.1	$318.7	$2,296.3	$75.6	$120.5
1985					
Cosmetics, fragrances and toiletries°	$1,727.9	$207.3	$1,021.9	$29.9	$ 36.6
Fashion jewelry and accessories°	275.9	27.3	185.5	5.5	6.4
Health care services	261.1	51.0	345.0	16.5	40.4
Direct response	205.2	8.8	128.8	1.2	3.3
Net assets of discontinued operations	—	—	524.9	—	—
Corporate and eliminations	—	(40.1)	82.9	2.2	4.5
Consolidated	$2,470.1	$254.3	$2,289.0	$55.3	$ 91.2
1984					
Cosmetics, fragrances and toiletries°	$1,851.1	$238.1	$ 955.4	$31.6	$ 52.3
Fashion jewelry and accessories°	332.1	54.1	194.2	6.9	7.0
Health care services	159.0	22.3	194.1	10.7	26.1
Direct response	186.0	2.9	100.2	.6	4.5
Other	77.6	(.5)	—	1.1	8.2
Net assets of discontinued operations	—	—	731.0	—	—
Corporate and eliminations	(.5)	(19.8)	112.6	1.3	6.1
Consolidated	$2,605.3	$297.1	$2,287.5	$52.2	$104.2

°Cosmetics, fragrances and toiletries, and fashion jewelry and accessories have been restated to conform to the 1986 presentation.

Exhibit 8.10, continued

Geographic Areas

Year Ended December 31	Net Sales	Operating Profit	Identifiable Assets	Depreciation Expense	Additions To Property
1986					
United States	$1,855.4	$206.2	$1,568.4	$50.1	$ 89.4
Europe	343.6	36.2	215.3	9.0	15.9
Latin America	348.7	65.1	197.9	9.5	8.3
Pacific and Canada	335.4	50.9	183.9	6.6	6.5
Total international	1,027.7	152.2	597.1	25.1	30.7
Corporate and eliminations	—	(39.7)	130.8	.4	.4
Consolidated	$2,883.1	$318.7	$2,296.3	$75.6	$120.5
1985					
United States	$1,582.2	$155.4	$1,156.0	$36.0	$ 68.3
Europe	290.7	32.8	182.5	5.9	7.5
Latin America	324.2	58.4	178.6	6.4	5.8
Pacific and Canada	273.0	47.8	164.1	4.8	5.1
Total international	887.9	139.0	525.2	17.1	18.4
Net assets of discontinued operations	—	—	524.9	—	—
Corporate and eliminations	—	(40.1)	82.9	2.2	4.5
Consolidated	$2,470.1	$254.3	$2,289.0	$55.3	$ 91.2
1984					
United States	$1,639.3	$172.4	$ 943.7	$32.9	$ 68.0
Europe	332.6	27.9	161.4	6.1	9.1
Latin America	346.0	64.7	193.5	7.3	15.1
Pacific and Canada	287.9	51.9	145.3	4.6	5.9
Total international	966.5	144.5	500.2	18.0	30.1
Net assets of discontinued operations	—	—	731.0	—	—
Corporate and eliminations	(.5)	(19.8)	112.6	1.3	6.1
Consolidated	$2,605.3	$297.1	$2,287.5	$52.2	$104.2

Source: Avon Products Inc., and Subsidiaries 1986 Annual Report. Copyright, 1987, by Avon Products, Inc. Reprinted with permission.

The Allocation of Common or Joint Costs. The FASB requires the disclosure of segment operating profit after the allocation of common costs. The common or joint costs are costs incurred at the corporate level for the benefit of more than one line of business. Common costs include corporate administration, centralized data processing, corporate advertising and executive compensation.

The SFAS 14 requirement that operating profit be determined after the allocation of common costs raises problems for financial statement analysis. One issue results from the fact that there are no guidelines provided regarding the composition of the common cost pools and as to the methods of allocation. As a result of this flexibility, some firms allocate all common costs to industry segments, while others leave some or all of the common costs unallocated and charge these costs to the "corporate segment". For example, corporate interest is typically not allocated to the firm's business segments.

There is also no uniformity as to the definition of a common cost. Some firms may consider centralized data processing services as a common cost and thereby subject to allocation. Other firms may consider centralized data processing services as a pure corporate function and would not allocate costs of operating the data center to the industry segments. In addition, regardless of the composition of the common cost pool, the method of allocation selected could "shift" profit between segments, and could be used as a means of concealing the relative profitability of the individual segments from competitors.

Another problem results from the fact that there is no uniformity as to the disclosures of the composition of the common cost pool and the methods of allocation used. In general, this information is not disclosed in the segment footnote.

Due to these and other problems, segment information is generally considered "soft" data in the sense that it is significantly influenced by managerial discretion and involves a great deal of subjectivity in its preparation and disclosure. As long as the total of the segment operating profit is equal to the consolidated total on the income statement, management can manipulate the individual segment profitability. Although segment information is of low quality and results in a high level of accounting risk, it is the only line of business information available in the annual report and could be used as the starting point for a more detailed analysis of the firm.

Interim Reporting

The professional standards governing interim or quarterly reporting are found in APB Opinion No. 28, "Interim Financial Reporting". In general, the provisions of Opinion 28 require that the same accounting principles be used in the quarterly report as are used in the annual financial statements. However, there are several significant exceptions to this general rule. Two of these exceptions are:

1.   Interim reporting standards only require the inclusion of an income statement. However, the inclusion of a balance sheet and the statement of cash flows is recommended.

2. The interim financial statements differ from the annual report with respect to accounting for inventory in several key areas. First, the gross profit method of estimating inventory value can be used during interim periods. Second, interim period liquidations of LIFO layers are not recognized in the interim financial statements, if replacement of the layers is expected by year end. Finally, write-offs of obsolete inventory can be deferred.

Other issues to be considered in the analysis of quarterly financial information result from the different views of interim reporting. The two concepts of interim reporting are discussed in the following sections.

The Discrete versus the Integral View of Reporting

The Discrete View. Under the discrete approach, each interim reporting period is treated as a separate accounting period. As a result, accruals and deferrals are accounted for as if the interim period was a complete, self-contained accounting period. For example, if a company prepays a six-month insurance policy on January 2nd, it would be fully expired by year end, December 31st. However, if the firm follows the discrete view of the quarter, the firm would defer the expense at acquisition and capitalize it as a prepaid asset. The deferred asset cost would be amortized to expense on a monthly basis. Therefore, at the end of the first quarter, three months or one-half of the deferred asset is expired and would be charged to expense. The other half would be reported on the balance sheet as a deferred asset.

Although the discrete view is not favored by the APB in Opinion 28, it is still employed by many firms for certain financial statement items, such as large advertising expenditures extending beyond the quarter in which the payment was made.

The Integral View. Under the integral approach, the interim reporting period is viewed as an integral part of the annual reporting period. Therefore, items such as accruals and deferrals are accounted for by considering what would occur for the entire year. In the prepaid insurance example, the entire prepayment on January 2nd would be charged to expense immediately because there would be no asset value remaining (i.e., it would be fully expired) by December 31st. The integral view is favored by the accounting profession in Opinion 28. Although considered the preferred approach, the application of the integral view has resulted in several implementation problems in practice. Some of these problems include the following.

1. Practice has varied widely (i.e., discrete or integral treatment) in accounting for material advertising expenditures extending beyond the quarter of cash disbursement.

2. A great deal of subjectivity must be employed in recording expenses on an interim basis that require information for the entire accounting period. For example, charges against income for the bad debt provision, write-off of obsolete inventory and accrued pension expense require information for the full accounting period if reliable accruals are to be recorded.

3. In determining the income tax provision for each interim period, the amount of income for that period would not provide an appropriate level of income for determining the tax rate to use from the graduated tax rate schedule. As a result, FASB Interpretation No. 18, "Accounting for Income Taxes in Interim Periods", requires that the estimated annual effective tax rate must be applied to the year-to-date income at the end of each interim period.

4. An extraordinary item should be recognized in the quarter in which it actually occurs. However, according to FASB Statement No. 3 ("Reporting Accounting Changes in Interim Financial Statements"), paragraph 7, all cumulative-effect type accounting changes must be recognized in the first quarter in the comparative interim reports and in the quarterly income information provided in the annual report, regardless of the actual quarter in which they occur. The cumulative effect, net of tax, must be computed as of the beginning of the year, with the first quarter restated. There should be no recognition given to the after-tax cumulative effect in any other quarters. This requirement prevents the use of an accounting change for purposes of manipulation of a given quarter's reported profit or loss.

5. The EPS for each quarter must be determined as if the interim period was a discrete annual period. Therefore, each quarter "stands alone" as a discrete accounting period and all of the Opinion 15 tests involved in the EPS computation (e.g., the 20% limit in the treasury stock method, the three-percent materiality test and tests for antidilution) must be made for each individual interim period.

The implementation problems noted above will result in quarterly information that is less reliable than the information contained in the annual report. In essence, the accountant is trading off relevance for reliability. Quarterly data are more timely, and therefore more relevant to the financial statement user. However, the more timely the data, the greater the use of estimates and subjective judgements, making the interim information less reliable. If the analyst is aware of the limitations of interim financial information, quarterly reports can still be used, but used with caution.

NOTES

1. Objectives of Financial Statements (New York: American Institute of Certified Public Accountants, October, 1973).

2. Joshua Ronen and Simcha Sadan, Smoothing Income Numbers (Reading, MA: Addison-Wesley Publishing Company, 1981).

CASE 8.1. RCA: ACCOUNTING CHANGES--USE OF DISCLOSURES FOR A CUMULATIVE-EFFECT TYPE AND A RETROACTIVE-EFFECT TYPE CHANGE IN PRINCIPLE

RCA is a multidivisional business engaging in electronics, communications, entertainment, transportation services, research and development and other products.

Source: RCA 1984 Annual Report. Copyright, 1984, by RCA, Inc. Reprinted with permission.

REQUIRED: Study the RCA 1983 Consolidated Statement of Income and Retained Earnings and Footnote 2--Accounting Changes.

1. Explain the differences between the two types of accounting changes discussed in footnote 2, with respect to the impact of the changes on the three basic financial statements.

2. For the change in accounting for the Investment Tax Credit, recompute net income "as if" the flow-through method had always been used by RCA.

3. What is the cumulative effect on retained earnings from the change in accounting for the effects of certain types of regulation?

RCA
Consolidated Income and Retained Earnings

	(In millions, except per share)		
Years ended December 31	1984	1983*	1982*
Sales			
Electronic and other products	$ 5,031.6	$4,356.3	$3,885.2
Broadcasting, communications, transportation, and other services	5,080.0	4,621.0	4,130.8
Total sales	10,111.6	8,977.3	8,016.0
Costs, expenses, and other			
Cost of products	4,050.0	3,592.0	3,220.6
Cost of services	3,794.8	3,423.4	3,021.8
Selling, general, and administrative expenses	1,649.3	1,557.4	1,416.0
Interest expense (Note 7)	244.3	187.1	206.3
Investment income	(113.1)	(15.7)	(15.7)
Other income, net	(66.5)	(25.0)	(85.4)
Total costs, expenses, and other	9,558.8	8,719.2	7,763.6
Income before income taxes and special provision	552.8	258.1	252.4
Provision for VideoDisc restructure (Note 3)	(175.0)	–	–
Income before income taxes	377.8	258.1	252.4
Income taxes (Note 6)	131.4	109.8	87.7
Income from continuing operations	246.4	148.3	164.7
Income from discontinued operations (Note 3)	18.9	78.7	51.5
Cumulative effect of change in accounting principle (Note 2)	75.7	–	–
Net income	$ 341.0	$ 227.0	$ 216.2
Earnings per share of common stock			
Primary			
Continuing operations	$ 2.15	$ .97	$ 1.26
Discontinued operations	.23	.96	.68
Cumulative effect of change in accounting principle	.92	–	–
	$ 3.30	$ 1.93	$ 1.94
Fully diluted	$ 3.20	$ 1.90	$ 1.92
Retained earnings–beginning of year (Note 2)	$ 1,306.2	$1,221.9	$1,142.5
Net income	341.0	227.0	216.2
Less dividends			
$3.65 cumulative preference stock	(41.7)	(41.3)	(41.0)
$2.125 cumulative convertible preference stock	(23.8)	(23.7)	(23.6)
$3.50 cumulative first preferred stock	(.5)	(.5)	(.5)
$4 cumulative convertible first preferred stock	(3.8)	(3.8)	(3.8)
Common stock	(82.3)	(73.4)	(67.9)
Retained earnings–end of year	$ 1,495.1	$1,306.2	$1,221.9

*Restated, see Note 2.
The accompanying notes are an integral part of this statement.

Source: RCA 1984 Annual Report. Copyright, 1984, by RCA, Inc. Reprinted with permission.

2. Accounting Changes

Regulated Subsidiaries. Financial Accounting Standard No. 71, "Accounting for the Effects of Certain Types of Regulation," lists criteria that must be met in order for regulated companies to follow specialized accounting policies prescribed by regulatory authorities. Because of changes in the marketplaces in which RCA American Communications, Inc. and RCA Global Communications, Inc. operate, these companies no longer meet all of these criteria. Accordingly, effective January 1, 1984, the accounting policies of both companies were changed from those prescribed by the Federal Communications Commission to those in effect for the remainder of RCA. Previous years' financial statements have been restated for this change as follows:

	(In millions, except per share)	
Years ended December 31	1983	1982
Net income as previously reported	$240.8	$222.6
Adjustment	(13.8)	(6.4)
Net income restated	$227.0	$216.2
Earnings per share of common stock		
Primary as previously reported	$ 2.10	$ 2.03
Adjustment	(.17)	(.09)
Primary restated	$ 1.93	$ 1.94
Fully diluted as previously reported	$ 2.06	$ 2.00
Adjustment	(.16)	(.08)
Fully diluted restated	$ 1.90	$ 1.92

The effect for the year ended December 31, 1984 was to decrease net income by approximately $11.5 million ($.14 per share). The decrease in retained earnings at January 1, 1982 as a result of the restatement of prior years was $55.7 million.

Income Taxes. Effective January 1, 1984, RCA changed its accounting for investment tax credits from the deferral method to the flow-through method in order to achieve greater comparability with the accounting policies of most other companies. Under the flow-through method, investment tax credits are reflected in net income in the year the qualified investment is placed in service. Under the deferral method, credits are amortized over the estimated lives of the qualified investment.

As a result, net income for the year ended December 31, 1984, before the cumulative effect of this change, increased $8.4 million ($.10 per share). The pro forma effect of this change in 1983 and 1982 would have increased net income by $12.1 million ($.15 per share) and $25.4 million ($.32 per share), respectively. The cumulative effect of this change through December 31, 1983 increased net income in the first quarter of 1984 by $75.7 million ($.92 per share).

9

The Statement of Cash Flows: Preparation and Analysis

INTRODUCTION

The analytical problems resulting from the flexibility afforded to management within the framework of accrual basis accounting have been discussed at length in the previous chapters of this text. Nevertheless, GAAP generally prohibits the use of the cash basis of accounting for preparation of the income statement and the statement of financial position. The cash basis has been criticized because of its failure to adequately measure economic activity. In addition, the cash basis allows even greater manipulation of the results of operations through management's ability to control the timing of cash receipts and cash disbursements.

Notwithstanding the persuasive arguments against the cash basis of accounting, credit and financial analysts find cash flow information an invaluable resource in determining an entity's ability to repay principal and interest on outstanding debt and to provide a dividend return to stockholders. For years it seemed paradoxical that information regarding a firm's cash flows was excluded from the reported financial statements and the related footnotes. Without this information, much of which was dependent on internal data, the credit and financial analyst was forced to rely on crude measures of cash flow. This paradox was resolved in November 1987 with the issuance of FASB Statement No. 95, "Statement of Cash Flows".

SFAS 95, paragraph 3, requires the inclusion of a Cash Flow Statement (CFS) as one of the three basic financial statements to be provided in order to issue financial information in accordance with GAAP. The new standard became effective for financial statements issued for fiscal years ending after July 15, 1988, and supersedes APB Opinion No. 19, "Reporting Changes in Financial Position" (1971), which required the old Statement of Changes in Financial Position (SCFP).

A NEW STANDARD FOR CASH FLOW REPORTING

The Need for a New Standard for Cash Flow Reporting

SFAS 95 was issued by the accounting profession as a direct response to the recommendations of the financial community. In the early 1980s it became apparent that credit and financial analysts were increasingly dissatisfied with the funds flow information provided by the SCFP. Although Opinion 19 defined the fund as either cash or working capital, by the mid-1980's about 75% of the Fortune 500 companies were reporting the SCFP on a cash basis.[1] However, the definition of the cash fund differed widely among firms. For example, the General Electric Company defined the fund on its 1982 SCFP as cash plus marketable securities less short-term borrowings. In this case, the fund was neither cash nor working capital. The diversity of reporting practices for the SCFP made it difficult for the analyst to determine the cash flow for the individual firm both in the current year and over time, and made it virtually impossible to compare the cash flows between firms within the same industry.

Credit and financial analysts have expressed several reasons for their preference for accurate cash flow information. As implied throughout the previous chapters, accrual basis net income may not be related to the net cash flows generated from operations. This point is clear when one considers the extensive use of deferrals and capitalization of costs. In addition, working capital may not adequately reflect the liquidity of the firm. The high debt levels of many firms, particularly with increases in LBO activity and the onset of a growing trend of corporate bankruptcies since the 1980s, have made cash flow analysis an even more critical component in the evaluation of credit and investment alternatives.

The Objectives of Cash Flow Reporting Under SFAS 95

Under SFAS 95, the CFS is a basic financial statement that summarizes the cash inflows and outflows for a firm over a period of time. It is a flow statement that is used to explain the change in cash and cash equivalents (to be discussed). The statement can also be useful in explaining and reconciling many other significant changes in the financial position of the firm when the CFS is used with the other financial statements and related footnote disclosures.

Specifically, SFAS 95, paragraphs 4 through 6, established two primary objectives for cash flow reporting. The primary purpose of the CFS is "to provide information about the cash receipts and cash payments of the firm over a period of time". The first objective of cash flow reporting relates to the current operating cash flows of the firm which are associated with net income for the period and the certain working capital items on the statement of financial position.

A secondary purpose of the CFS is to provide information about a firm's financing and investing activities. These activities relate to debt and equity financing and investments in plant and equipment, as well as other current and noncurrent assets.

Both of the SFAS 95 objectives imply that the CFS should provide information needed by the analyst to assess the ability of the firm to generate positive future cash flows from operations, pay dividends, meet debt service requirements, and assess the firm's future needs for external financing and therefore its financial flexibility. Because of the inherent deficiencies of accrual basis accounting, the CFS can also assist the analyst in assessing the quality of reported net income and the level of accounting risk associated with the accrual basis financial statements.

Changes in Terminology

The new CFS requires more precision than the old SCFP in defining "cash". To begin with, the term *funds* is no longer acceptable. The members of the FASB believed that this term was too ambiguous and would promote wide diversity in practice, as was the case with prior reporting under the SCFP. Under SFAS 95, paragraph 7, the caption "cash and cash equivalents" replaces the concept of the fund. The new caption is a much broader concept than cash, and now the CFS is designed to explain the change in the firm's cash and cash equivalents.

According to SFAS 95, paragraph 8, the term "cash equivalents" includes "short-term, highly liquid investments" with original maturities of three months or less which were acquired by the firm by using cash in excess of its immediate cash requirements. It is in the sense of using excess cash that these types of investments are cash substitutes and will be converted back into cash if needed in the operating cycle. In addition, SFAS 95 includes cash equivalents within the cash concept because the acquisition and disposal of investments of this nature are considered part of the firm's overall cash management activities, and therefore should not be considered within the operating, investing and financing activities of the entity.

It should be noted that the term "original maturities of three months or less" used in SFAS 95, paragraph 8, requires that there must be three months to maturity at the time the investment is acquired by the firm. For example, a three-year treasury instrument purchased with two months to maturity qualifies as a cash equivalent, while a three-year treasury instrument acquired three years ago does not become a cash equivalent when it reaches three months to maturity. Therefore, the determination of a cash equivalent is made only at acquisition and is not modified in subsequent accounting periods. Clearly, it is management's intention at the date of acquisition and not the time to maturity that determines a security's status as a cash equivalent.

SFAS 95, paragraph 7, also requires that cash and cash equivalents on the CFS agree with the same financial statement items on the balance sheet. This requirement resulted in many firms reclassifying line items on their balance sheets. For example, the line item "cash and marketable securities" is no longer permitted. In fact, only investments such as treasury bills, commercial paper and money market funds usually qualify as cash equivalents. Short-term marketable securities such as investments in common stock and corporate debt will generally not qualify as cash equivalents and should be shown as a separate line item in the current asset section of the balance sheet.

Finally, SFAS 95, paragraph 10, requires that the firm disclose its policy regarding the definition and composition of its cash equivalents. That is, the firm should disclose the specific criterion used to classify an investment as a cash equivalent (i.e., investments with original maturities with three months or less), along with the types of securities included within this category.

Classification of Cash Flows by Activity or Function

The old sources and uses format utilized under the SCFP is no longer permitted by SFAS 95. A functional or activity format must be used under the new standard.

SFAS 95, paragraph 14, identifies three classifications of cash flow activity which are designed to meet the stated objectives of cash flow reporting. A CFS should classify cash receipts and disbursements into three major categories. These are operating activities, investing activities and financing activities.

Operating Activities. In SFAS 95, paragraph 21, cash flows from operating activities are defined as the "cash effects of economic events that enter into the determination of net income" or loss for the period, regardless of source. A firm's income statement and working capital items related to operations from the statement of financial position form the basis for net cash flows from operating activities. Although certain working capital items are related to the operating cash flows of the firm, a reconciliation to a specific line item entitled "working capital from operations" is no longer permitted under SFAS 95.

SFAS 95, paragraphs 22 and 23, indicate that cash flows from operations include the following activities.

Cash Inflows:

        -From the sale of goods and services
        -From interest and dividend income

Cash Outflows:

        -To suppliers for inventory, utilities and other services
        -To employees for services
        -To government agencies for taxes
        -To creditors for interest paid, net of amounts capitalized

It should be noted that by requiring a CFS and the determination of cash flow from operating activities, the FASB is not advocating a cash basis of accounting. As noted earlier, the accrual basis must still be used to properly measure the results of operations from economic activities. Cash flow from operations is designed to report the net cash generated from the year's economic activity, as measured under the accrual basis.

The definition of operating activities used in the CFS is not consistent with the usual concept of operating income as used in the income statement. On the income statement, income from operations excludes other income and other expense items such as interest income and dividends received. On the other hand, net cash flow from operating activities as defined by SFAS 95 includes interest and dividends received and excludes all items of revenue and expense without cash consequences.

In addition, SFAS 95 does not classify operating cash flows by source such as miscellaneous income and expense or discontinued operations. As a result, operating cash flows from the CFS cannot always be related to a specific line item on the income statement. These points will be discussed further in the analysis of the CFS.

Investing Activities. The net cash flows from investing activities generally relate to the cash receipts and disbursements from the acquisition and disposal of noncurrent assets such as plant and equipment and long-term investments, and from the acquisition and disposal of short-term investments not qualifying as cash equivalents. Specifically, SFAS 95, paragraphs 16 and 17, indicate that cash flows from investing activities should include

Cash Inflows:

    -From the sale of property, plant and equipment
    -From the sale of debt or equity investments
    -From the collection of principal on loans to others

Cash Outflows:

    -For the acquisition of property, plant and equipment, including
     interest capitalized on construction in progress
    -For the acquisition of investments in debt or equity securities
    -For making loans to others

(NOTE: Interest received and interest paid are classified as operating activities).

Financing Activities. The final classification of cash flows for a firm without foreign operations involves cash receipts and payments related to debt and equity financing, including dividend distributions to owners. According to SFAS 95, paragraphs 19 and 20, financing activities include the following cash flows.

Cash Inflows:

    -From the issuance of debt securities
    -From the issuance of common or preferred stock

Cash Outflows:

    -To redeem or retire debt securities
    -To purchase treasury stock or retire capital stock
    -To make dividend distributions to stockholders

The SFAS 95 cash flow classifications are critical to credit and financial analysis because it is the source of the cash flow and not the amount that is useful in assessing the ability of the firm to repay principal and interest and to make future dividend distributions. Specifically, cash generated from operating activities is of higher "quality" than cash generated from borrowing or from the disposal of productive assets. Thus, the rationale behind these classifications is similiar to the justification for the income statement captions "income from continuing operations" and "extraordinary items". As noted earlier, the SFAS 95 does not require cash flows to be identified with the income statement captions, so that a line item cash flows from extraordinary items, discontinued operations, etc., is not required on the CFS.

Gross versus Net Presentation for Financing and Investing Activities and the Application of SFAS 95 to Financial Institutions. Individual items within the investing and financing activities section of the CFS must be shown on a gross cash flow basis. For example, acquisitions and disposals of plant assets must be disclosed separately and cannot be netted out as either a net cash inflow or outflow. Although the FASB did not specifically exempt financial institutions from the requirements of SFAS 95, certain exceptions were permitted in paragraphs 12 and 13 to accommodate financial institutions. For example, net presentation is allowed for balance sheet items with "quick turnover and short maturities" such as short-term investments, loans receivable and demand deposits, "provided that the original maturities of these items are three months or less". A net presentation is also permitted in those cases where the financial institution is substantially holding or disbursing cash on behalf of its customers (e.g., commercial letters of credit) and for all credit card receivables. The exception was made for credit card receivables because a customer generally has the option to pay off the credit card balance within 30 days. As a result, the FASB considered these receivables to have original maturities of less than three months.

The gross presentation was originally required for all longer term assets and liabilities such as investment securities, commercial loans, real estate loans, installment loans and certificates of deposit. However, the financial commmunity generally believed that the gross presentation for transactions of financial institutions provided information of little value that was quite costly to generate and disseminate through the CFS. Therefore, SFAS 95 was amended by the issuance of Statement No. 104, "Statement of Cash Flows--Net Reporting of Certain Cash Receipts and Cash Payments and Classification of Cash Flows from Hedging Transactions". The new standard permits banks, savings institutions and credit unions to report in the CFS net cash receipts, any payments for deposits made and withdrawn, time deposits made and withdrawn, and loans made and collected. SFAS 104 became effective for fiscal years ended after June 15, 1990.

SFAS 95 was also amended by FASB Statement No. 102, "Statement of Cash Flows--Exemption of Certain Enterprises and Classification of Cash Flows from Certain Securities Acquired for Resale". SFAS 102 is effective for financial statements issued after February 28, 1989.

SFAS 102 exempts the following entities from the requirement to provide a cash flow statement as part of a full set of financial statements:

a. Defined-benefit pension plans covered by SFAS 35 and certain other employee benefit plans;

b. Certain highly liquid investment companies.

SFAS 102 also makes some minor changes in the classification of cash receipts and payments for certain transactions of banks, investment brokers and other financial institutions.

Cash Flow Classifications Involving Multiple Activities. In those cases where the cash flow classification is not clear, the FASB indicated that the cash flow classification should be based on the dominant source of the cash flow. For example, an auto manufacturer that temporarily uses vehicles for key employees, but ultimately sells the automobiles, would classify the production as an operating activity and not as an investment in plant and equipment.

Significant Events Not Affecting Cash Flows. A firm will generally engage in many significant transactions that do not have immediate cash flow consequences. For example, events such as the acquisition of plant and equipment financed by a bond issue or the declaration of stock dividend can have a significant impact on the financial position of the firm but do not have an effect on cash flow. According to SFAS 95, paragraph 32, all non-cash flow events should not be included within the CFS. However, if significant, non-cash flow events must be disclosed in a footnote or a separate schedule.

PREPARATION OF THE CASH FLOW STATEMENT: REPORTING FORMATS

There are two acceptable formats for the preparation of the CFS. These are the Indirect Method (the Reconciliation Format) and the Direct Method (the Income Statement Format). Although both methods are acceptable under SFAS 95, the direct method is preferred by the FASB, but to date is the least popular in practice.

The only difference between these two approaches is the method used to determine cash flows from operating activities. The determination of net cash flow from investing and financing activities will be identical under either reporting format.

In the determination of cash flow from operating activities, changes in working capital items such as increase <decrease> in accounts receivable, inventories, and accounts payable can be shown on a net basis. In addition, net cash flows from operating activities must be the same under either reporting format.

The Indirect Method: The Reconciliation Format

Under the indirect method, aggregate accrual basis net income from the income statement is converted to cash generated from operating activities by applying a series of adjustments or reconciling items to the net income figure. A statement of cash flows for Quaker State Corporation and Subsidiaries is presented in Exhibit 9.1. Note that cash flow from operating activities can begin with either net income or net loss.

Common adjustments or reconciling items used in the indirect format are presented below.

EXHIBIT 9.1

Sample Disclosure: Quaker State Corporation and Subsidiaries: Statement of Cash Flows--Indirect Reporting Format

Years ended December 31	1987	1986	1985
(in thousands)			
Cash flows from operating activities:			
Net (loss) income	$ (48,057)	$50,288	$45,892
Adjustments to reconcile net (loss) income to net cash provided by operating activities:			
Depreciation and depletion	39,467	35,675	36,416
Deferred income taxes and investment tax credit	(55,150)	4,000	16,000
Unusual items—noncurrent	105,356	—	—
Undistributed net earnings of Heritage Insurance Group	(4,710)	(6,757)	(4,796)
Increase (decrease) from changes in:			
Receivables	11,584	1,739	(10,284)
Inventories	6,424	13,711	(10,576)
Other current assets	1,147	(1,161)	(7,917)
Accounts payable	(3,773)	(10,753)	7,025
Accrued liabilities	3,501	(8,116)	9,094
Income taxes	(1,158)	1,196	(569)
Net cash provided by operating activities	54,631	79,822	80,285
Cash flows from investing activities:			
Proceeds from disposal of fixed assets, net	6,361	7,853	3,819
Capital expenditures, including acquisitions	(77,658)	(70,955)	(64,852)
Net cash used in investing activities	(71,297)	(63,102)	(61,033)
Cash flows from financing activities:			
Dividends paid	(21,087)	(21,418)	(19,439)
Proceeds from long-term debt	40,260	5,044	1,149
Payments on long-term debt	(415)	(2,993)	(7,373)
(Payments on) proceeds from notes payable	—	(2,750)	2,750
Other	2,365	830	1,537
Net cash provided by (used in) financing activities	21,123	(21,287)	(21,376)
Net increase (decrease) in cash and cash equivalents	4,457	(4,567)	(2,124)
Cash and cash equivalents at beginning of year	8,305	12,872	14,996
Cash and cash equivalents at end of year	$ 12,762	$ 8,305	$12,872

The accompanying notes are an integral part of the financial statements.

Supplemental disclosure of cash flow information:

Cash paid during the year for:	1987	1986	1985
Interest, net of amounts capitalized	$ 6,866	$11,673	$13,407
Income taxes	9,022	29,080	21,017

Source: Quaker State Corporation and Subsidiaries, 1987 Annual Report. Copyright, 1988, The Quaker State Corporation. Reprinted with permission.

Net income

Adjustments to Reconcile Net Income to Net Cash Provided by
Operations

Additions:

*Depreciation, Depletion and Amortization Expense
*Compensation Expense paid in Stock Options
*Amortization of Bond Discounts and Other Deferred Charges
*Increase <Decrease> in the Deferred Income Tax Liability
   <Asset>
*Losses reported on Investments accounted for under the Equity
   Method
*Losses on Sales of Noncurrent Assets and Investments
*Decreases in Current Assets Other than Investments
*Increases in Current Liabilities Other than Short-term Debt
   and Dividends Payable

Decreases:

*Amortization of Bond Premiums and Other Deferred Credits
*Decrease <Increase> in the Deferred Tax Liability <Asset>
*Undistributed Income from Investments Accounted for under the
   Equity Method
*Gain on Sale of Noncurrent Assets and Investments
*Increases in Current Assets Other than Investments
*Decreases in Current Liabilities Other than Short-term Debt
   and Dividends Payable

Net Cash Flow from Operating Activities
==

The Direct Method: The Income Statement Format

Under the direct method of determining net cash generated from operating activities, the accrual basis income statement is disaggregated and each line item is adjusted to convert that particular line item from the accural basis to the cash basis. In substance, a cash basis income statement is prepared. It should be noted that the same adjustments (i.e., reconciling items) are applied to the individual line items of the income statement under the direct method as were applied against aggregate net income under the indirect method.

According to SFAS 95, paragraph 27, at a minimum the following line items must be included in the operating cash flow section using the direct format.

* Cash collected from customers, lessees, licensees, etc.
* Interest and dividends received
* Other operating cash receipts, if any
* Cash paid to employees and other suppliers of goods and services
* Interest paid, net of amounts capitalized
* Income taxes paid
* Other operating cash disbursements, if any.

Determination of Operating Cash Flow Line Items Under the Direct Method

Under the direct method (income statement format), the accrual basis income statement is disaggregated and each line item is converted to the cash basis. The following formulas should be used in determining cash inflows and cash outflows for the minimum line items required under the direct method.

1. Cash Collected From Customers:

```
              Net Sales (Accrual Basis)
    Less <Add>: Increase <Decrease> in Net Accounts Receivable
    Less:       Bad Debts Expense
    -----------------------------------------------------------
              Cash Collected from Customers
    ===========================================================
```

2. Cash Paid for Merchandise Purchased:

The computation of cash paid for merchandise purchased requires two steps. First, accrual basis purchases must be determined from an analysis of cost of goods sold and changes in inventory balances. Second, the cash paid for the acquisition of merchandise is determined by an analysis of the change in accounts payable. The computations used in the two-step approach are illustrated in formulas 2a and 2b.

2a. Determination of Accrual Basis Purchases:

```
              Cost of Goods Sold (Accrual Basis)
    Add <Less>: Increase <Decrease> in Inventory
    -----------------------------------------------------------
              Accrual Basis Purchases
    ===========================================================
```

2b. Determination of Cash Paid for Merchandise Purchases:

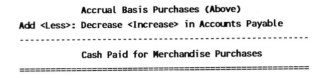

```
        Accrual Basis Purchases (Above)
Add <Less>: Decrease <Increase> in Accounts Payable
------------------------------------------------------
        Cash Paid for Merchandise Purchases
======================================================
```

3. Cash Paid to Employees for Wages:

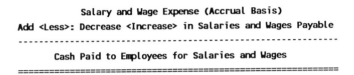

```
        Salary and Wage Expense (Accrual Basis)
Add <Less>: Decrease <Increase> in Salaries and Wages Payable
--------------------------------------------------------------
        Cash Paid to Employees for Salaries and Wages
==============================================================
```

The general formula for determining cash paid to employees for salaries and wages can be used for computing cash paid for most other operating expenses. Cash paid for prepaid or deferred expenses, interest expense and income taxes are illustrated below.

4. Cash Paid for Prepaid or Deferred Expenses (insurance expense is used to illustrate the formula for determining the cash outflow for deferred expenses):

```
        Insurance Expense (Accrual Basis)
Add <Less>: Increase <Decrease> in Prepaid (Deferred) Insurance
----------------------------------------------------------------
        Cash Paid for Insurance
================================================================
```

The line item entitled "cash paid to employees and suppliers of goods and services" on the CFS usually consists of cash paid for merchandise plus cash paid to employees for wages. It is not uncommon to combine cash paid for other operating expenses such as insurance in this line item. Otherwise, a separate line item entitled "cash paid for other operating expenses" could be utilized. In many cases, the income statement line item entitled "selling, general and administrative expenses" (SG&A) is the starting point for cash paid for operating expenses. In addition to the adjustments for changes in payables, prepaid expenses, and other assets, adjustments to SG&A would include the elimination of noncash expenses. Noncash expenses include depreciation, depletion, amortization and the bad debts expense.

5. Cash Paid for Interest:

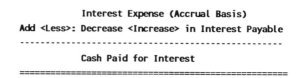

```
         Interest Expense (Accrual Basis)
Add <Less>: Decrease <Increase> in Interest Payable
----------------------------------------------------
         Cash Paid for Interest
====================================================
```

6. Cash Paid for Income Taxes:

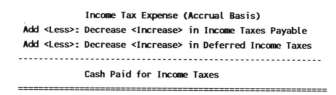

```
           Income Tax Expense (Accrual Basis)
Add <Less>: Decrease <Increase> in Income Taxes Payable
Add <Less>: Decrease <Increase> in Deferred Income Taxes
-------------------------------------------------------------
           Cash Paid for Income Taxes
=============================================================
```

Comparison of the Reporting Formats. The formulas presented above indicate that the computations under the direct method are more complex, more time consuming and therefore more costly than under the indirect approach. Nevertheless, the direct method is preferred by the FASB. The FASB justified its position by stating that a CFS based on cash receipts and disbursements is easier to understand. In addition, cash flow projections are more accurate if based on the disaggregated line items than if the total cash flow from operations is used.

A major disadvantage of the direct method is that the line items included within the operating cash flows section cannot be traced and agreed to any other financial statement included within the annual report. On the other hand, the individual reconciling items used in the indirect approach can generally be agreed to the information included in other financial statements. In addition, the indirect method is closer to the SCFP prepared under the cash format. As a result of these and other criticisms of the direct method, the indirect method is used most often in practice.

SFAS 95 Disclosure Requirements. As noted earlier, an underlying requirement of SFAS 95 is that the same net cash flow from operating activities is presented, regardless of the reporting format used. Consistent with this requirement, SFAS 95 also stipulates that there must be sufficient disclosures to enable the user to convert from one reporting format to the other. For example, if the firm uses the direct method, the firm must disclose the reconciliation of accrual basis net income and cash flows from operations as required under the indirect approach in a separate schedule or footnote. If the firm reports the CFS under the indirect method, income taxes paid and interest paid (net of amounts capitalized) must be disclosed in a footnote or a separate schedule. For both the direct and the indirect method, the firm must disclose its policy regarding its definition and composition of cash equivalents.

Foreign Currency Cash Flows Under SFAS 95. For firms with foreign operations or foreign transactions, there are two additional reporting requirements under SFAS 95, paragraph 25. First, the firms must present "the reporting currency (e.g., the U.S. dollar) equivalent of the foreign currency cash flows using the exchange rate in effect at the time related cash flows" took place or at the average rate for the year, regardless of the functional currency. This requirement involves three steps: (a) obtain a statement of cash flows in the foreign currency from all foreign operations; (b) translate into the reporting currency (e.g., the U.S. dollar) using the rate in effect when the transactions took place or at the average rate for the year; and (c) consolidate (b) with the U.S. CFS.

Under the second requirement, the effect of exchange rate changes on foreign currency cash balances is to be presented as a separate classification of cash flow activities. That is, a CFS prepared for a firm with foreign operations would appear as follows.

```
Net Cash Provided by:
    Operating Activities
    Investing Activities
    Financing Activities
    Effect of Exchange Rate Changes on Cash
----------------------------------------------------
    Change in Cash and Cash Equivalents
====================================================
```

The effect of exhange rate changes on foreign cash balances is not a cash receipt or cash disbursement, but is needed as part of the reconciliation of the net change in cash and cash equivalents for the year. Because it is not an operating, financing or investing activity, the separate caption is created. Finally, any foreign currency transaction gains <losses> are reported as decreases <increases> in the reconciliation of accrual basis net income and net cash flow in the operating activities section of the CFS prepared under the indirect method.

PREPARATION OF THE CASH FLOW STATEMENT: AN ILLUSTRATION

Exhibits 9.2 and 9.3 present the statements of income and retained earnings for the year ended December 31, 1992 and the comparative balance sheets for the Gibson Corporation at December 31, 1992 and 1991.

In addition, an examination of the footnotes to the financial statements and management's discussion and analysis revealed that during 1992, Gibson paid $130,000 in cash for new equipment and financed an additional $30,000 in plant acquisitions by borrowing the full amount on a long-term note from the manufacturer. The company also disposed of a piece of equipment for $40,000 in cash, which was also equal to its net book value. Finally, Gibson borrowed an additional $100,000 from the Country National Bank.

Given this information, cash flow statements can be prepared under both the direct and indirect reporting formats. The first step in constructing a CFS under either method is to isolate the changes in balance sheet items between 1991 and 1992. The analysis of changes in balance sheet items is presented in Exhibit 9.4.

Using the information provided in Exhibits 9.2 through 9.4, the individual line items for the cash flow from operations under the direct method can be determined. These line items are presented below ($000's omitted).

EXHIBIT 9.2

Illustration: The Gibson Corporation: Statements of Income and Retained Earnings

```
                     Gibson Corporation
          Statements of Income and Retained Earnings
              For the Year Ended December 31, 1992
```

```
Sales...........................................$500,000

Less: Cost of Goods Sold:
      Inventory 1-1-92.............$230,000
      Purchases.................... 300,000
                                  ----------
      Cost of Goods Available
      for Sale...................$530,000
      Less: Inventory 12-31-92.....<350,000>
                                  ----------
            Cost of Goods Sold.....................<180,000>
                                                  ---------
Gross Profit on Sales...........................$320,000

Less: Operating Expenses:

      Selling, General & Administrative
      Expenses.....................$ 40,000
      Depreciation Expense......... 120,000
      Income Tax Expense........... 60,000
      Interest Expense............. 20,000
                                  ----------
            Total Operating Expenses...............<240,000>
                                                  ---------

Net income.......................................$ 80,000
Retained Earnings 12-31-91........................ 360,000
Less: Dividends................................... <30,000>
                                                  ---------
Retained Earnings 12-31-92.......................$410,000
                                                  =========
```

EXHIBIT 9.3

Illustration: The Gibson Corporation: Statement of Financial Position

---

Gibson Corporation
Statements of Financial Position
At December 31, 1992 and 1991

Assets:	1992	1991
Cash	$ 70,000	$ 50,000
Accounts Receivable	80,000	26,000
Inventory	350,000	230,000
Prepaid Expenses	100,000	74,000
Plant Assets	500,000	400,000
Accumulated Depreciation	<300,000>	<200,000>
Total Assets	$800,000	$580,000

Liabilities and Stockholders' Equity:		
Accounts Payable	$ 40,000	$ 10,000
Accrued Income Taxes Payable	90,000	80,000
Long-Term Debt	160,000	30,000
Capital Stock	100,000	100,000
Retained Earnings	410,000	360,000
Total Equities	$800,000	$580,000

EXHIBIT 9.4

Illustration: The Gibson Corporation: Analysis of Changes in Statement of Financial Position (Balance Sheet) Items

Gibson Corporation
Analysis of Changes in Statement of Financial Position Items
For the Year Ended December 31, 1992

Assets:	1992	1991	Change
Cash	$ 70,000	$ 50,000	$ 20,000
Accounts Receivable	80,000	26,000	54,000
Inventory	350,000	230,000	120,000
Prepaid Expenses	100,000	74,000	26,000
Plant Assets	500,000	400,000	100,000
Accumulated Depreciation	<300,000>	<200,000>	<100,000>
Total Assets	$800,000	$580,000	

Liabilities and Stockholders' Equity:			
Accounts Payable	$ 40,000	$ 10,000	$ 30,000
Accrued Income Taxes Payable	90,000	80,000	10,000
Long-Term Debt	160,000	30,000	130,000
Capital Stock	100,000	100,000	-0-
Retained Earnings	410,000	360,000	50,000
Total Equities	$800,000	$580,000	

1. Cash received from customers during the year:

```
Sales.................................$500
Less: Increase in accounts receivable..< 54>
                                      ------
Cash collected from customers..........$446
                                      =====
```

This illustration points out one of the problems in constructing a CFS from published annual reports. Specifically, much of the actual CFS is based on internally generated information which is not disclosed in the annual report. In this case, the bad debts expense is not disclosed. As a result, it cannot be used to determine cash collected from customers and it cannot be deducted from operating expenses as an adjustment for noncash expenses. Overall, the cash flow from operations will not be affected by the misstatement. However, the individual line items will not be correct. Therefore, if the analyst converts from the indirect to the direct format the resulting operating cash flows will generally be correct, but the individual line items may only be approximate.

2. Cash Paid to Suppliers for Merchandise:

```
Cost of goods sold.....................$180
Add: Increase in inventory............. 120
                                      -----
Purchases (accrual basis)..............$300
Less: Increase in accounts payable..... <30>
                                      -----
Cash paid to suppliers for merchandise.$270
                                      =====
```

3. Cash Paid for Operating Expenses:

```
Selling, general & administrative
expenses...............................$ 40
Add: Increase in prepaid expenses...... 26
                                      -----
Cash paid for operating expenses.......$ 66
                                      =====
```

4. Cash Paid for Income Taxes:

```
Income tax expense.....................$ 60
Less: Increase in deferred taxes.......  -
Less: Increase in taxes payable........<10>
                                      ------
Cash paid for income taxes.............$ 50
                                      =====
```

Because the balance sheet does not reflect any liabilities for interest or dividends, it can be assumed that interest paid is $20,000 and cash dividends paid equal $30,000.

The additional information provided can be used to explain or reconcile the changes in certain account balances. For example, the cost of plant assets sold can be determined as follows ($000's omitted).

Plant Assets:

```
Beginning balance.....................$400
Add: Capital expenditures.............. 160
Less: Ending balance...................<500>
                                       -----
Cost of plant assets sold.............$ 60
                                       =====
```

Similarly, the accumulated depreciation removed on the disposal of the plant asset can be determined as follows ($000's omitted).

Accumulated Depreciation:

```
Beginning balance.....................$200
Add: Depreciation expense.............. 120
Less: Ending balance...................<300>
                                       -----
Accumulated depreciation removed on
the disposal of plant assets...........$ 20
                                       =====
```

Therefore, the net book value of plant assets removed on the disposal is equal to $40 (i.e., cost - accumulated depreciation = $60 - 20), which is consistent with the additional information provided earlier.

The CFS for the Gibson Corporation prepared under the direct format is presented in Exhibit 9.5. The supplementary schedules and required disclosures for the direct method are presented below ($000's omitted).

EXHIBIT 9.5

Illustration: The Gibson Corporation: Statement of Cash Flows-- Direct Reporting Format

---

```
                        Gibson Corporation
                 Statement of Cash Flows (Direct Method)
                   For the Year Ended December 31, 1992
```

Cash Flow From Operating Activities:

```
        Cash received from customers................$446,000
        Cash paid to suppliers and employees........<270,000>
        Cash paid for other operating expenses......< 66,000>
        Interest paid, net of amounts capitalized...< 20,000>
        Income taxes paid...........................< 50,000>
                                                    ---------
            Net cash provided by operating activities........$ 40,000
```

Cash Flow From Investing Activities:

```
        Proceeds from sale of facility..............$ 40,000
        Capital expenditures........................<130,000>
                                                    ---------
            Net cash used in investing activities.............< 90,000>
```

Cash Flow From Financing Activities:

```
        Proceeds from issuance of long-term debt....$100,000
        Cash dividends paid.........................< 30,000>
                                                    ---------
            Net cash provided by financing activities.........  70,000
                                                              ---------
    Net Increase in Cash and Cash Equivalents...................$ 20,000
    Cash and Cash Equivalents, 1-1-92...........................  50,000
                                                              ---------
    Cash and Cash Equivalents, 12-31-92.........................$ 70,000
                                                              =========
```

---

1. Reconciliation of Net Income and Net Cash Provided by Operating
   Activities:

   Income from continuing operations...................$ 80

   Adjustments to reconcile net income to net
   cash flow provided by operating activities:

       Depreciation expense....................$120
       Increase in accounts receivable........ <54>
       Increase in prepaid expenses........... <26>
       Increase in inventory...................<120>
       Increase in accrued taxes payable...... 10
       Increase in accounts payable........... 30   < 40>
                                               ----- -----
   Net cash provided by operating activities...........$ 40
                                                        =====

The above reconciliation is also provided in the operating cash flows section of
the CFS prepared under the indirect method.

2. Disclosure of Significant Noncash Investing and Financing Activities:

   Equipment with a value of $30,000 was purchased through the issuance
   of a long-term note in the amount of $30,000.

3. Accounting Policy for the Definition of Cash Equivalents:

   For purposes of the statement of cash flows, the Company considers
   all highly liquid debt instruments purchased with a maturity of three
   months or less to be cash equivalents.

The CFS for the Gibson Corporation prepared under the indirect method is
presented in Exhibit 9.6. The supplementary schedules and required disclosures for
the indirect format are presented below ($000's omitted).

1. Supplemental Disclosure of Cash Flow Information:

   Cash paid during the year for:

       Income Taxes.......................$ 50
                                          =====
       Interest (net of amounts
       capitalized).......................$ 20
                                          =====

EXHIBIT 9.6

Illustration: The Gibson Corporation: Statement of Cash Flows-- Indirect Reporting Format

---

```
                        Gibson Corporation
                 Statement of Cash Flows (Indirect Method)
                   For the Year Ended December 31, 1992
```

Cash Flow From Operating Activities:

Net income...$ 80,000

Adjustments to Reconcile Net Income to Net Cash
Provided by Operating Activities:
      Depreciation Expense.........................$120,000
      Increase in accounts receivable..............< 54,000>
      Increase in prepaid expenses.................< 26,000>
      Increase in inventory........................<120,000>
      Increase in accrued income taxes payable.... 10,000
      Increase in accounts payable................. 30,000   < 40,000>

        Net cash provided by operating activities........$ 40,000

Cash Flow From Investing Activities:

      Proceeds from sale of facility...............$ 40,000
      Capital expenditures.........................<130,000>

        Net cash used in investing activities.............< 90,000>

Cash Flow From Financing Activities:

      Proceeds from issuance of long-term debt....$100,000
      Cash dividends paid..........................< 30,000>

        Net cash provided by financing activities........ 70,000

Net Increase in Cash and Cash Equivalents...................$ 20,000
Cash and Cash Equivalents, 1-1-92.......................... 50,000

Cash and Cash Equivalents, 12-31-92........................$ 70,000

2. Supplemental Schedule of Noncash Investing and Financing Activities:

Same as under the direct method.

3. Accounting Policy for the Definition of Cash Equivalents:

Same as under the direct method.

AN ANALYSIS OF THE CASH FLOW STATEMENT

As indicated in the previous sections of this chapter, the CFS is a key analytical tool for both the credit and financial analyst. There were several reasons noted why the CFS is critical to any successful analysis. However, the analyst must be aware of the problems involved in the analysis of the CFS. The following sections present the analytical advantages and disadvantages of the CFS as required under SFAS 95.

Usefulness of the Cash Flow Statement

There are many analytical advantages of using the CFS required by SFAS 95. First, the CFS summarizes all cash flow information regarding operating, financing and investing activities. Although this information could probably be obtained from other financial statements and footnote disclosures, the CFS proves to be more useful in that it provides this information in a single, concise statement that avoids the difficulties involved in reconstructing cash flow information from multiple sources. In addition, by providing a CFS that clearly specifies the sources and uses of cash by activity, the analyst can better identify the cash effects of the key transactions of the firm and can understand the underlying economic substance of events reported under the accrual basis. By forcing the definition and classification of cash flows, SFAS 95 enables the analyst to avoid other crude and inaccurate measures of cash flow such as net income plus depreciation.

Second, although the indirect method is used most often in practice, the disclosures required by SFAS 95 enable the analyst to convert from the indirect method to the direct method. If the analyst prefers the direct format, this conversion will become necessary in most cases. The conversion from the indirect to the direct reporting format will be illustrated in Case 9.1 at the end of this chapter.

The direct method is preferred by the FASB and is generally preferred by most credit and financial analysts. As noted earlier, when forecasting future cash flows, the use of a disaggregated time series will result in more accurate projections than if aggregated data are used. In addition, credit and investment risk are closely related to fluctuations in the individual components of cash flow from operating activities. If the indirect format is used, only fluctuations in the total operating cash flow are available. Therefore, the conversion to the direct method should be performed in most credit and investment analyses.

Third, due to the problems with accrual basis net income, cash flows from operations may be a more reliable measure of operating performance in credit and investment analysis. For example, increases in sales and net income may not enhance the firm's ability to meet scheduled debt payments and to make dividend distributions if sales and net income are not converted into cash. It is for this reason that many financial analysts compute a measure of the quality of accrual basis net income. The quality of earnings is measured by the ratio of operating cash flows to net income. In addition, many bond rating agencies and investment banks evaluate debt coverage by both a times-interest-earned ratio and a ratio of cash flow to long term debt or total debt.

Some Analytical Problems

In addition to the benefits of using the CFS, there are several analytical problems that the analyst must consider in the assessment of the credit and investment risk of the firm.

To begin with, and most important, the analyst must not place undue reliance on the firm's operating cash flows. Accrual basis net income measures economic activity; operating cash flows do not. Operating cash flows can only be generated from the economic activities of the firm. Therefore, operating cash flows must be analyzed in conjunction with the examination and analysis of the other financial statements and the related footnote disclosures.

Second, the analyst must be aware of the inconsistencies in terminology and presentation between the CFS and other information contained in the annual report. As noted earlier, net cash flows from operations includes dividend and interest income, but excludes all items of profit and loss devoid of cash effect. On the income statement, the term operating income excludes other income such as dividends and interest. Thus, the term "operations" has quite different meanings for the two financial statements. In addition, SFAS 95 does not require the identification of cash flows from unusual sources such as discontinued operations, extraordinary items and the cumulative effect from a change in accounting principle. Again, it is difficult to relate cash flow items to the line items of the income statement. Similarly, because the CFS only reflects the cash consequences of transactions, the statement will not always articulate well with changes in line items on the statement of financial position. For example, if there are dividends payable, dividends paid on the CFS will not agree with the total dividend declaration on the statement of retained earnings. In the same way, a full understanding of other key changes in the statement of financial position may require additional information such as noncash acquisitions of plant and equipment.

Fourth, in converting from the indirect to the direct method, many inaccuracies can result due to the lack of disclosure of internal information. For example, the change in accounts payable is generally used to adjust the cost of sales in deriving cash paid to suppliers. However, the balance in accounts payable may actually relate to the acquisition of goods and services other than inventory. Similarly, the bad debts expense is generally not disclosed in the footnotes to the statement of financial position. Without this information the analyst cannot accurately convert sales to cash collected from customers. The cash paid for operating expenses will also be misstated because of the inability of the analyst to exclude the noncash bad debts expense. It should be noted that although the individual line items will be only approximations, the net cash flow from operating activities should be correct.

If the analyst prefers to convert from the indirect to the direct format, care must be taken not to ignore the possible signals contained in the individual reconciling items used in the indirect method. For instance, a decrease in prepaid expenses such as rent, insurance or supplies results in an adjustment that increases cash flow. However, a decrease in the acquisition of items such as operating supplies could signal an expected slowdown in future operations. Therefore, knowledge of the relationships between the CFS and the other financial information provided as well as familiarity with the operations of the firm and the industry are critical for making sound investment and credit decisions.

An analysis of financing and investing activities also requires additional sources of information. Although these activities indicate the sources of financing, both internal and external, and how earnings are reinvested, the analyst needs to consider the signals regarding expansion or contraction of future operations. Disclosure of the type of capital expenditure is not required by SFAS 95. Therefore, additional information is needed to identify the exact areas of acquisition and disposal of plant assets and if there are noncash acquisitions and disposals.

If expansion is financed by debt or additional equity, the analyst must consider the availability of future cash flows. The long-term debt and stockholders' equity footnotes must be examined in order to determine the extent of future debt service, preferred dividends in arrears and scheduled mandatory redemptions of debt and redeemable preferred stock. Given these commitments, the bottom line net cash flow may not be "free" for use in future operations.

The above discussion indicates that the analyst must never lose sight of the fact that a proper analysis of cash flow can only be made within the overall analysis of the firm. The overall analysis requires additional information from the annual report and other sources such as economic and industry publications.

NOTES

1. Donald E. Kieso and Jerry J. Weygandt, Intermediate Accounting, 6th edition (New York: John Wiley & Sons, 1989), 1139.

CASE 9.1. AMERICA WEST AIRLINES, INC.: THE CASH FLOW STATEMENT --CONVERTING THE INDIRECT REPORTING FORMAT TO THE DIRECT REPORTING FORMAT

America West Airlines, Inc. is a certificated major carrier operating a fleet of 89 aircraft at December 31, 1989: 2 Boeing 747s; 10 Boeing 757s; 69 Boeing 737s and 8 de Havilland DHC-8s. The Company provides service to 54 destinations throughout the continental United States, Hawaii and Canada primarily through hubs in Phoenix, Arizona and Las Vegas, Nevada.

Source: America West Airlines, Inc. 1989 Annual Report. Copyright, 1989, by
America West Airlines, Inc. Reprinted with permission.

REQUIRED: Using America West's 1989 Balance Sheets, Statements of Operations and Statements of Cash Flows (Indirect Reporting Format), prepare the Operating Cash Flows Section of 1989 the Statement of Cash Flows using the direct reporting format.

AMERICA WEST AIRLINES, INC
BALANCE SHEETS
December 31, 1989 and 1988

ASSETS

	1989	1988
	(in thousands)	
Current assets:		
Cash and cash equivalents	$ 66,780	$ 63,490
Short-term investments	12,877	4,958
Accounts receivable, less allowance for doubtful accounts of $1,058,000 in 1989 and $826,000 in 1988	66,360	44,904
Expendable spare parts and supplies, less allowance for obsolescence of $1,444,000 in 1989 and $1,010,000 in 1988	22,467	17,857
Prepaid expenses	26,940	15,063
Total current assets	195,424	146,272
Property and equipment (notes 2, 10 and 11):		
Flight equipment	564,590	419,684
Other property and equipment	150,827	118,138
	715,417	537,822
Less accumulated depreciation and amortization	129,679	77,546
	585,738	460,276
Equipment purchase deposits	28,051	10,113
	613,789	470,389
Restricted cash (notes 9 and 10)	6,640	7,300
Other assets	20,032	15,516
	$835,885	$639,477
LIABILITIES AND STOCKHOLDERS' EQUITY		
Current liabilities:		
Current maturities of long-term debt (note 2)	$ 28,864	$ 20,717
Accounts payable	64,363	37,422
Air traffic liability	71,242	63,017
Accrued compensation and vacation benefits	11,232	9,078
Accrued interest	12,298	7,269
Accrued taxes	14,718	12,167
Other accrued liabilities	11,591	4,208
Total current liabilities	214,308	153,878
Long-term debt, less current maturities (notes 2 and 9)	301,300	264,336
Manufacturers' and deferred credits	48,624	37,293
Other liabilities	10,842	5,504
Convertible subordinated debentures (note 3)	173,608	120,483
Stockholders' equity (notes 2, 3, 5, 6, 7, 8 and 11):		
Preferred stock, $.25 par value. Authorized 50,000,000 shares:		
Series B 10.5% convertible preferred stock, issued and outstanding 291,149 shares; $5.41 per share cumulative dividend (liquidation preference $15,000,000)	73	73
Series C 9.75% convertible preferred stock, issued and outstanding 73,099 shares; $1.33 per share cumulative dividend (liquidation preference $1,000,000)	18	18
Common stock, $.25 par value. Authorized 90,000,000 shares; issued and outstanding 17,232,498 shares in 1989 and 15,500,150 shares in 1988; subscribed 493,000 shares in 1989	4,431	3,875
Additional paid-in capital	145,293	127,478
Accumulated deficit	(42,395)	(60,322)
	107,420	71,122
Less deferred compensation and notes receivable — employee stock purchase plans (note 5)	20,217	13,139
Net stockholders' equity	87,203	57,983
Commitments and subsequent event (notes 3 and 10)		
	$835,885	$639,477

Source: America West Airlines, Inc. 1989 Annual Report. Copyright, 1989, by America West Airlines, Inc. Reprinted with permission.

AMERICA WEST AIRLINES, INC.
STATEMENTS OF OPERATIONS
Years ended December 31, 1989, 1988 and 1987
(in thousands of dollars except per share amounts)

	1989	1988	1987
Operating revenues:			
Passenger	$935,200	$743,261	$559,181
Cargo	28,648	16,972	8,861
Other	29,561	15,442	7,405
Total operating revenues	993,409	775,675	575,447
Operating expenses:			
Salaries and related costs	249,715	185,377	135,741
Rentals and landing fees	197,568	169,350	131,950
Aircraft fuel	141,095	109,156	106,051
Agency commissions	71,346	54,216	40,085
Aircraft maintenance materials and repairs	18,590	27,001	25,578
Depreciation and amortization	54,117	42,257	28,218
Other	212,862	170,177	143,179
Total operating expenses	945,293	757,534	610,802
Operating income (loss)	48,116	18,141	(35,355)
Nonoperating income (expenses):			
Interest income	10,782	6,531	6,963
Interest expense	(43,769)	(38,016)	(23,181)
Gain (loss) on disposition of property and equipment	(167)	1,569	5,855
Other, net (note 10)	5,078	(472)	43
Total nonoperating expenses, net	(28,076)	(30,388)	(10,320)
Income (loss) before income taxes and extraordinary items	20,040	(12,247)	(45,675)
Income taxes (note 4)	7,237	—	—
Income (loss) before extraordinary items	12,803	(12,247)	(45,675)
Extraordinary items:			
Gain on retirement and exchange of subordinated debentures, net of income taxes of $3,750,000 (note 3)	—	17,858	—
Utilization of net operating loss carryforward (note 4)	7,215	3,750	—
	7,215	21,608	—
Net income (loss)	$ 20,018	$ 9,361	$ (45,675)
Net income (loss) per share:			
Income (loss) before extraordinary items	$ .61	$ (.92)	$ (3.85)
Extraordinary items	.39	1.43	—
Net income (loss)	$ 1.00	$ .51	$ (3.85)

AMERICA WEST AIRLINES. INC
STATEMENTS OF CASH FLOWS
Years ended December 31, 1989, 1988 and 1987
(in thousands of dollars)

	1989	1988	1987
Cash flows from operating activities:			
Net income (loss) before extraordinary items	$ 12,803	$ (12,247)	$ (45,675)
Adjustments to reconcile net income (loss) to cash provided by (used in) operating activities:			
Extraordinary credit resulting from utilization of net operating loss carryforward	7,215	—	—
Depreciation and amortization	54,117	42,257	28,218
Amortization of manufacturers' and deferred credits	(2,547)	(1,586)	(623)
(Gain) loss on sale of property and equipment	167	(1,569)	(5,855)
Other	188	190	173
Changes in operating assets and liabilities:			
Decrease (increase) in short-term investments	(7,919)	195	4,359
Decrease (increase) in accounts receivable, net	(21,456)	21,448	(19,292)
Increase in spare parts and supplies, net	(4,610)	(3,102)	(8,641)
Increase in prepaid expenses	(11,877)	(16)	(5,114)
Decrease (increase) in other assets and restricted cash	(3,856)	13,678	771
Increase (decrease) in accounts payable	26,941	(3,682)	23,684
Increase in air traffic liability	8,225	25,868	15,513
Increase in accrued compensation and vacation benefits	2,154	5,417	283
Increase in accrued interest	5,029	471	2,247
Increase in accrued taxes	2,551	2,968	4,332
Increase in other accrued liabilities	7,382	1,315	2,373
Increase in other liabilities	5,338	1,904	1,538
Net cash provided by (used in) operating activities	79,845	93,509	(1,709)
Cash flows from investing activities:			
Purchases of property and equipment	(179,552)	(138,067)	(319,143)
Increase in equipment purchase deposits	(17,938)	(5,254)	(409)
Proceeds from disposition of property	992	34,048	79,825
Proceeds from manufacturers' credits	27,312	16,246	29,705
Application of manufacturers' credits	(15,634)	(10,300)	(4,600)
Net cash used in investing activities	(184,820)	(103,327)	(214,622)
Cash flows from financing activities:			
Proceeds from issuance of long-term debt and convertible subordinated debentures	137,643	82,040	184,846
Repayment of long-term debt and capital leases	(40,780)	(32,380)	(50,651)
Deferred gains on sale and leaseback transactions	2,200	—	2,332
Proceeds from issuance of common stock	12,052	4,424	36,396
Purchase of common stock	(1,177)	—	(1,111)
Preferred dividends paid	(1,673)	(1,672)	(1,673)
Net cash provided by financing activities	108,265	52,412	170,139
Net increase (decrease) in cash and cash equivalents	3,290	42,594	(46,192)
Cash and cash equivalents at beginning of year	63,490	20,896	67,088
Cash and cash equivalents at end of year	$ 66,780	$ 63,490	$ 20,896

Source: America West Airlines, Inc. 1989 Annual Report. Copyright, 1989, by
America West Airlines, Inc. Reprinted with permission.

Appendix
Solutions to Cases

SOLUTION: CASE 2.1 JOHNSON AND JOHNSON AND SUBSIDIARIES

----

1. Determination of the LIFO Reserve

	1983	1982	Change
Inventory at:			
FIFO Cost.....................	$1,115.2	$1,090.5	
LIFO Cost.....................	< 992.2>	<957.5>	
LIFO Reserve............	$ 123.0	$ 133.0	< $10.0>

2. 1983 Financial Information Converted to the FIFO Basis

   (a) Cost of Goods Sold (CGS)

	1983
CGS - LIFO as reported..............	$2,471.8
Add: Decrease in the LIFO Reserve..	10.0
CGS - FIFO as restated..............	$2,481.8

   (b) Earnings after tax under FIFO (restated)

                                          1983

LIFO pretax earnings as reported...$ 724.1
Less: Decrease in the LIFO Reserve.   <10.0>

FIFO pretax earnings as restated...$ 714.1

1 - Effective tax rate
    (1 - (235.1 / 724.1)).......... x .6754

Net income after tax before
extraordinary items under FIFO.....$ 482.3
                                        =========

(c) Earnings per share (EPS) before extraordinary items under FIFO

Weighted average number of shares = Net income / EPS

                                  = $489.0 / $ 2.57 = 190.27 shares
                                                      =============

EPS before extraordinary items under FIFO = $482.3 / 190.27 = $2.53 per
                                                                 share

3. Financial Ratios

		LIFO	FIFO
		--------------------	---------------------
	Current Assets	$2,457.1	($2,457.1 + 123.0)
Current Ratio =	------------------ =	------------	--------------------
	Current Liabilities	$ 923.8	$ 923.8
	=	2.7 to 1	2.8 to 1
		========	========
	CGS ⸳	$2,471.8	$2,481.8
Inventory Turnover =	------------ =	-----------------	-----------------------
	Average	($957.8 + 992.2)	($1,090.5 + 1,115.2)
	Inventory	----------------	--------------------
		2	2
	=	2.5 Times	2.25 Times
		==========	===========

$$\text{Holding Interval} = \frac{360 \text{ Days}}{\text{Inventory Turnover}} = \frac{360}{2.5} = \frac{360}{2.25}$$

$$= 144 \text{ days} \qquad 160 \text{ days}$$

Although not significantly different from the FIFO basis in this case (probably due to the decrease in the LIFO reserve), the results presented above exhibit the general effects of using LIFO when determining the basic financial ratios. LIFO tends to

1. Understate liquidity (i.e., the current ratio);

2. Overstate inventory turnover.

SOLUTION: CASE 2.2 MATRIX CORPORATION
----

1. Analysis of the Current Portfolio

	7/31/86	8/31/85

Balance Sheet (Note: Only Funds and
Equity Securities are valued at
Lower of Cost or Market [LCM]):

Marketable Equity Securities (MES) at Cost.....................................	$58,200,000	$25,500,000
Less: Allowance to reduce MES to market.	<100,000>	-
Marketable Securities at LCM............	$58,100,000	$25,500,000
	===========	===========
Retained Earnings (To Balance--See Income Statement analysis below)...	<$100,000>	-
	===========	===========

Income Statement:

Other Income (Expense) Classification: Unrealized Loss on Write-down to Market.............................	<$100,000>	-
	===========	===========

Cash Flow Statement: No Effect
----

2. Analysis of the Noncurrent Portfolio

Balance Sheet:	7/31/86	8/31/85

Marketable Equity Securities At Cost.................................	$28,100,000	$ 6,500,000
Less: Allowance to reduce MES to market.	<300,000>	<200,000>
Marketable Equity Securities at LCM.....	$27,800,000	$ 6,300,000
	=============	=============

Stockholders' Equity Section:

Cumulative Unrealized Loss...............   <$300,000>   <$200,000>
```
                                          ==========       ===========
                                              |                  |
                                              |------------------|
```

1986 Unrealized Loss recorded as a reduction
of total Stockholders' Equity.........................<$100,000>
```
                                                      ==========
```

Income Statememt: No Effect

Cash Flow Statement: No Effect

----

3. 1986 Disposals of Marketable Securities

     Assuming that the Certificate and Time Deposits were Disposed of:

                Balance 1985...................$10,000,000
                Balance 1986................... <3,300,000>
```
                                            ------------
```

                Costs removed on disposal.....$ 6,700,000
```
                                            ==========
```

     Impact on the Cash Flow Statement:

                Cost of investments disposed
                of in 1986....................$ 6,700,000
            Add: Realized gain on disposal..... 1,500,000
```
                                            -----------
```

                Cash inflow on disposal.......$ 8,200,000
```
                                            ===========
```

SOLUTION: CASE 3.1 J.C. PENNEY COMPANY, INC.

----

1. Determine the Market Rate or Yield on the Zero Coupon Notes

   Because the notes were issued at a price that was 33.247% of par value, the discount factor is simply .33247, for a present value of an amount of $1. That is, there is only one cash flow, the maturity or face value of $200,000,000, and there is no cash or coupon interest. Therefore, there is no annuity relating to these notes.

   On a present value of an amount of $1 table, the discount factor of 33.247% falls between 7% and 8%. By linear interpolation, the semiannual yield is approximately 7.125%. This is 14.25% annually, which agrees to the disclosure for the current maturity of the zero coupon note.

   Based on the information provided in this case, the zero coupon notes sold at a price of $66,494,000 (i.e., 33.247% x $200,000,000).

2. Amortization Table for the Zero Coupon Note

===

Date and Number	(a) 7.125% Effective Interest	(b) Outstanding Balance
5/1/81 n = 0	-	$ 66,494,000
11/1/81 n = 1	$ 4,737,698	71,231,698
5/1/82 n = 2	5,075,258	76,306,956
11/1/82 n = 3	5,436,871	81,743,827
5/1/83 n = 4	5,824,278	87,568,075
11/1/83 n = 5	6,239,225	93,807,300
5/1/84 n = 6	6,683,770	100,491,070
11/1/84 n = 7	7,159,989	107,650,968
5/1/85 n = 8	7,670,131	115,321,099
11/1/85 n = 9	8,216,628	123,537,727
5/1/86 n = 10	8,802,063	132,339,790
11/1/86 n = 11	9,429,210	141,769,000
5/1/87 n = 12	10,101,041	151,870,041
11/1/87 n = 13	10,820,074	162,690,115
5/1/88 n = 14	11,805,420	174,495,535
11/1/88 n = 15	12,432,807	186,928,343
5/1/89 n = 16	13,071,657	200,000,000

Notes: (a) Because there is no cash interest, the total effective interest is the discount amortization. The total effective interest is equal to 7.125% multiplied by the beginning outstanding balance of the debt

(b) The outstanding balance of the debt is equal to the beginning balance plus the discount amortization (i.e, the total effective

interest)

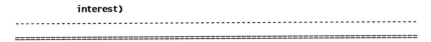

The balance of the zero coupon notes at January 28, 1989 can be verified as follows:

Balance at November 1, 1988 (n = 15 per above table).....$186,928,243

ADD: Accrued interest for 3 months (i.e., November, December
and January) $13,071,657/2................................   6,535,828

Current maturity of the zero coupon note per footnote....$193,464,171
                                                         =============

This is approximately equal to the $194,000,000 disclosed in the footnote at January 28, 1989 (i.e., or fiscal 1988 according to the footnote).

3. Determination of the market rate or yield on the 6% debentures

The debentures were issued at 42.063% of par value or at an issue price of $84,126,000 (i.e., $200,000,000 x .42063).
$84,126,000 is the sum of the present values of the future cash flows relating to the debt. In this case, the future cash flows are a lump sum amount at maturity of $200,000,000 and annuity interest of $6,000,000 (i.e., 6% / 2 x $200,000,000) semiannually for 50 interest periods (i.e., 25 years payable semiannually). To find the yield, interpolation is necessary to solve for the present value factors that equate the future cash flows to the selling price of $84,126,000.
The interpolation results in an approximate effective yield is 7.425% semiannually or 14.85% annually. The proof is provided below

Future Cash Flow	x	P.V. Factor @ n = 50, i = 7.245%	=	Present Value
$200,000,000	x	.02784	=	$ 5,568,000
6,000,000	x	13.0930	=	78,558,000

	Issue Price of the 6% Debentures			$84,126,000
				==========

or $84,126,000
      --------------- = 42.063%
      $200,000,000   =======

The annual yield of 14.85% seems reasonable because it falls within the range of 13.5% to 15.1% disclosed in the long-term debt footnote.

SOLUTION: CASE 4.1 EMERY AIR FREIGHT

----

1. Verify Effective Tax Rates

	1984	1983	1985
Income Tax Expense	$24,583	$20,526	$ 3,872
Effective Tax Rate = ─────────── =	─────────	─────────	───────
Pretax Income	25,468	45,512	14,078

(handwritten: 56,468)

2. Income Taxes Paid in 1984 (Cash Outflow for Taxes)

Taxes payable 1/1/84...............$ 3,897
Current tax provision.............. 22,555

Total due...........................$ 26,452

Less: Taxes payable 12/31/84.............. <11,668>

Cash outflow for taxes..............$ 14,784
                                   =========

NOTE: The disclosure of cash outflow for income taxes is now a requirement for the cash flow statement under SFAS 95.

3. Reconciliation of the Net Increase in Deferred Taxes for 1984:

	Deferred Tax Liability (Noncurrent)	Deferred Tax Asset (Other Assets) (Current)
Balances at:		
December 31, 1984........	$ 21,395	$ 4,575
January 1, 1984..........	<17,496>	<2,704>
Increase in 1984.........	$ 3,899	$ 1,871

Net increase in the 1984
Deferred Tax Account.......................$2,028
                                   =======

4. Estimation of Depreciation and Amortization for Tax Purposes

	1984	1983	1982
Excess Tax Depreciation:			
(Book-tax Diff./Tax Rate)...$5,375/.435		$6,335/.451	$6,442/.275
	= $12,356	= $14,057	= $23,425
Add: Book Depreciation......	23,901	18,624	15,693
Tax Depreciation............	$36,257	$32,671	$39,118

5. A review of Note 6 indicates that there are several temporary differences that are reversing. Specifically, tax depreciation is increasing only slightly from the current additions to property, plant and equipment. Therefore, unless the Company increases capital expenditures even further in the near future, reversal may take place and may result in an additional tax liability. Deferred credits and other temporary book-tax differences have already reversed and reduced the deferred tax provision in 1984 resulting in additional taxes paid currently. If this trend continues, the deferred tax liability will become current in nature and will result in cash outflows in the short run. In this case, the analyst may view a portion of the deferred tax liability as a real obligation for income taxes in subsequent accounting periods.

SOLUTION: CASE 5.1 XEROX CORPORATION

----

1. Reconciliation of the Finance Subsidiaries Stockholders' Equity with the Investment in Financial Services Businesses at Equity for 1984

Stockholders' Equity 1/1/84 (12/31/83)...............$2,016.9

1984 Acquisition: Van Kampen Merritt, Inc.
Original Cost = Carrying Value - Net Income
(170.6 - 20.5)....................................   150.1

1984 Subsidiary Net Income............................   67.7

Subtotal..$2,234.7

Less: Dividends from Crum and Foster, Inc............   <35.0>

Less: Change in the market value of the long-term
      portfolio of marketable securities which was
      deducted from stockholders' equity and not
      net income......................................   <22.7>

Less: Rounding errors (possibly due to immaterial
      dividend distributions not disclosed in the
      footnotes)......................................   < 1.9>

Stockholders' Equity of the Finance Subsidiaries.....$2,175.1

Xerox Percentage Ownership............................ x 100%

Carrying Value of the Investment in Financial
Services Businesses...................................$2,175.1
                                                      ========

2. Consolidating workpaper to consolidate the majority-owned subsidiaries
----

	Xerox Corp. 1984	100% of Finance Subs	100% of Other Subs	Elimination & Adjusting Entries	Minority Interest	Proforma Consolidated
Current Assets..	$3,739.2	$6,400.1	$ 672.4	<6.1>(d)		$10,805.6
Noncurrent Assets..........	3,369.9	1,409.6	568.7	-		5,348.2
Investments at Equity..........	2,175.1	-	-	<2,175.1>(a)		-
Other Investments.....	252.9	-	-	<252.9>(b)		-
Intercompany Receivables.....	-	234.0	-	<234.0>(c)		-
Total Assets....	$9,537.1	$8,043.7	$1,241.1	<2,668.1>	-	$16,153.8
	========	========	========	==========	========	==========
Current Liabilities....	$2,451.1	$4,357.5	$ 608.5	<234.0>(c)		$ 7,183.1
Long-Term Debt.	2,985.0	1,511.1	192.7	-		4,688.8
Intercompany Payables.......	-	-	6.1	<6.1>(d)		-
Stockholders' Equity.........	4,101.0	2,175.1		<2,175.1>(a)		4,101.0
			433.8	<252.9>(b)	$ 180.9	180.9
Total Equities.	$9,537.1	$8,043.7	$1,241.1	<2,668.1>	$ 180.9	$16,153.8
	========	========	========	==========	======	==========

(a) Entry to eliminate Xerox Corporation's investment account against the
    stockholders' equity of the financial service subsidiaries.
(b) Entry to eliminate Xerox Corporation's investment account against the
    stockholders' equity of the other subsidiaries and to record the minority
    interest.
(c) and (d) Entries to eliminate intercompany receivables and payables.

NOTE: The financial statement groupings for the first three columns of the
      consolidating working paper are presented on the following pages of the

solution.

Financial Statement Groupings for the 1984 Proforma Consolidation
----

Xerox Corporation:

        Current Assets: given on the balance sheet...........$3,739.2
                                                             ========

        Noncurrent Assets:

                Total Assets......................$9,537.9
                Less: Investments at equity............<2,175.1>
                      Other investments................<   252.9>
                      Current assets (above)...........<3,739.2>

                        Noncurrent assets..........................$3,369.9
                                                                   ========

        Current Liabilities (given on the balance sheet).....$2,541.1
                                                             ========

        Common Equity (given on the balance sheet)...........$4,101.0
                                                             ========

        Long-Term Debt:

                Total Liabilities and Common
                Equity............................$9,537.1
                Less: Current liabilities (above)......<2,451.1>
                      Common equity (above)............<4,101.0

                        Long-Term Debt..........................$2,985.0
                                                                ========
Finance Subsidiaries:

        Intercompany receivable (given in footnote)..........$ 234.0
                                                             ========
        Noncurrent Assets:

                Excess cost, etc. (Goodwill).....$1,033.9
                Add: Other assets....................   375.7

                        Noncurrent assets..........................$1,409.6
                                                                   ========

Current Assets:

```
        Total Assets....................$8,043.7
Less: Noncurrent assets (above)........<1,409.6>
      Intercompany receivable (above)..<  234.0>
                                        ---------
        Current assets...........................$6,400.1
                                                 ========
```

```
Stockholders' Equity (given in footnote).............$2,175.1
                                                    =========
```

Long-Term Debt:

```
      Notes Payable....................$1,231.4
Add: Deferred Taxes...................   279.7
                                       --------
        Long-term debt...........................$1,511.1
                                                 =========
```

Current Liabilities:

```
        Total Equities...................$8,043.7
Less: Long-Term Debt (above)...........<1,511.1>
      Stockholders' Equity (above).....<2,175.1>
                                        ---------
        Current liabilities.......................$4,357.5
                                                 =========
```

Other Subsidiaries:

The following accounts are given directly in the footnote:

```
        Current assets................$ 672.4
                                      =======

        Noncurrent assets.............$ 568.7
                                      =======

        Current liabilities...........$ 608.5
                                      =======

        Stockholders' equity..........$ 433.8
                                      =======

        Intercompany payables.........$   6.1
                                      =======
```

Long-Term Debt:

    Other Noncurrent Liabilities.....$ 46.4
    Add: Long-Term Debt................... 146.3

       Long-term debt.............................$ 192.7
                                                  ========

3. Analysis of Selected Financial Ratios: Xerox Corporation versus Proforma
Consolidation in 1984

              Xerox Corporation   Proforma Consolidation
         ----------------------------   ----------------------------------
Debt/Equity ($2,451.1 + 2,985.0)/$4,101.0 ($7,183.1 + 4,688.8 + 180.9)/4,101.0

               = 1.33   = 2.94
               ====   =====
                          Change = +122%
                          ==============

Debt
Ratio   ($2,451.1 + 2,985.0)/9,537.1 ($7,183.1 + 4,688.8 + 180.9)/16,153.8

               = 57%   = 75%
               ===   ===
                          Change = + 31%
                          ==============

Working
Capital $3,739.2 / 2,451.1 $10,805.6 / 7,183.1

               = 1.5 to 1   = 1.5 to 1
               ============   ===========
                          No Change
                          ===========

SOLUTION: CASE 5.2 McCORMICK AND COMPANY, INC.
----

1. The Purchase Method of Accounting for Business Combinations

The Purchase Method is the fair market value approach which should be compared to the Pooling of Interests Method, the book value (i.e., historical cost approach).

Parts (a), (b) and (d):

The differences in asset valuation and current and future operating results will be due to the probable increases in depreciation and amortization and cost of sales under the Purchase Method. Under the Purchase Method, goodwill is recognized and assets (e.g., both fixed assets and inventory) are revalued at fair market value (FMV). As a result, depreciation and amortization expense will typically increase, reducing reported income.

In this case, goodwill is amortized over a 40-year period. Specifically, reported income will be reduced by $1,077,500 per year (i.e., $43,100,000/40 years). However, there are no tax or cash flow consequences for the amortization of goodwill. In addition, if other assets are undervalued, there will also be a write-up to FMV. This could increase depreciation expense or cost of goods sold, and reduce reported book income. Further, if assets are disposed of at their "stepped-up" bases, a loss will be increased or any gains will be reduced.

Under the Pooling of Interests Method, there would be no asset revaluation. Therefore, when compared to the Pooling of Interests Method, the Purchase Method is generally the income-reducing accounting method.

Part (c):

If we assume that newly issued voting common stock is exchanged for 90% of the voting common stock of the acquired company, but if another of the Opinion 16 criteria for a Pooling of Interests is violated, the combination would be accounted for under the Purchase Method. However, if this specific criterion was not violated, the acquisition would be accounted for as a Pooling of Interests. Under these assumptions, the two methods might be considered alternatives. If newly issued voting common stock is used to effect the combination, the transaction would result in identical cash flows. However, as noted above, there could be substantial differences in reported accrual basis net income.

It should be noted that the method of accounting for the business combination does not affect the tax treatment of the transaction. This point is illustrated in the following summary:[1]

Type of Combination	Accounting Valuation		Income Tax Valuation	
	FMV	Historical Cost	FMV	Carryover Basis
Nontaxable Purchase	X			X
Taxable Purchase	X		X	
Nontaxable Pooling		X		X
Taxable Pooling		X	X	

2. Under the Purchase Method, the combined results of operations are only reported as of the date of acquisition (i.e., from June 1984 to November 30, 1984). However, for comparative purposes, the footnote disclosure provides proforma income information from the beginning of each period presented.

In 1983, McCormick reported EPS of $3.22 without Paterson Jenks, plc., and $3.21 with the subsidiary consolidated on a proforma basis. This information seems to indicate that the immediate effect of the acquisition on consolidated income is insignificant.

3. The Purchase Method was required in this case because the combination was effected by a payment of cash and notes. It was not a "stock-for-stock exchange". The use of cash and notes violates one of the 12 criteria required by Opinion 16 for a Pooling of Interests. Therefore, the violation prohibits the use of the Pooling Method, and the Purchase Method must be used.

NOTES

1. Samuel Laibstain, "Income Tax Accounting for Business Combinations", The CPA Journal (December, 1988). p.34.

SOLUTION: CASE 6.1 SEAGRAM COMPANY LIMITED

----

1. Recomputation of 1987 Primary EPS

   Hypothetical proceeds on the assumed exercise of stock warrants:

   $37 x 3,498,500 = $129,444,500
              =============

   Limitation on treasury stock acquisitions:

   20% x 95,494,856 = 19,098,971 shares
                      =================

   Maximum number of treasury shares that can be purchased:

   $129,444,500
   ----------- = 3,236,113 shares
   $40 Avg. Mkt.   ================
        Price

   The maximum number of treasury shares that can be purchased is
within the 20% limitation. Therefore, all of the hypothetical proceeds are
used on the acquisition of treasury stock and there are no excess proceeds to
retire debt or invest in government securities, commercial paper, etc.

   Incremental and weighted average number of common shares:

   Assumed issuance of shares on the exercise
      of the stock warrants....................... 3,498,500

   Repurchase of treasury shares................... <3,236,113>

   Incremental shares..............................   262,387

   Weighted average number of common shares
      (see footnote #5)........................... 95,112,193

   Shares for primary earnings per share........... 95,374,580
                                                    =============

            $423,458
   Primary EPS = --------- = $4.44/share = $4.45/share.
            95,374   ==========   ==========

   NOTE: The $.01 error could be due to lack of information concerning
the LYONS. Without the necessary yield and average Aa corporate bond rate

information, it cannot be determined if the LYONS qualify as CSEs. In addition, even if the LYONS were common stock equivalents, the after-tax interest savings from the avoidance of the discount amortization charges could not be readily determined.

2. Recomputation of 1987 Fully Diluted EPS

Maximum number of treasury shares that can be purchased:

$$\frac{\$129,444,500}{\$67 \text{ Year End Mkt. Price}} = 1,932,007 \text{ shares}$$

Again the maximum number of treasury shares that can be purchased is within the 20% limitation. Therefore, all of the hypothetical proceeds are used on the acquisition of treasury stock and there are no excess proceeds to retire debt or invest in government securities, commercial paper, etc.

Incremental and weighted average number of common shares:

Assumed issuance of shares on the exercise of the stock warrants.........................	3,498,500
Repurchase of treasury shares.....................	<1,932,007>
Incremental shares................................	1,566,493
Shares issued on the assumed issuance of the LYONS...	1,992,801
Weighted average number of common shares (see footnote #5).............................	95,112,193
Shares for fully diluted earnings per share......	98,671,487

$$\text{Fully Diluted EPS} = \frac{\$423,458}{98,671} = \$4.29/\text{share} = \$4.30/\text{share}$$

Again, the $.01 error is probably due to the incomplete treatment of the LYONS (i.e., failure to include the net of tax interest add-back assuming the conversion of the LYONS at the beginning of the period).

3. The 3% Materiality Test

Basic or Unadjusted $423,458
     EPS   = ----------- = $4.45/share
                      95,112   ============

Note: Unadjusted EPS is the same as Primary in this case.

3% Materiality Test:

    $4.45 x 97% = $4.32/share
                  ============

    $4.30 < $4.32.
    ==============

CONCLUSION: Because fully diluted EPS is less than 97% of the unadjusted EPS, dilution is considered material (i.e., dilution is greater than 3%) and therefore a dual presentation is required.

SOLUTION: CASE 7.1 MATRIX CORPORATION

----

1. Capitalization of Operating Leases: The DCF Approach

Year	Nominal Cash Flows	PV Factor at 9 1/2% per Debt Footnote	Present Value
1987	$ 900,000	.910	$ 819,000
1988	700,000	.830	581,000
1989	300,000	.760	228,000
1990	100,000	.690	69,000
1991	60,000	.630	37,800
1992	40,000	.575	23,000
Totals	$2,100,000		$1,757,800 (a)

Proforma Footnote Disclosure:

Minimum Lease Payments..........$2,100,000
Less: Deferred Interest Expense....... <342,200> (Plug)

Present Value of Minimum
Lease Payments..................$1,757,800 (a)

Less: Current Portion................. <733,009> (b)

Long-Term Lease Obligation......$1,024,791
                                    ===========

(b) Current Portion = 1987 Total Payment - Interest on Outstanding
                                           Balance of the Debt

           = $900,000   - (.095 X $1,757,800)
           = $900,000   - 166,991
           = $733,009
                 ========

2. Rating Agency Approach. (NOTE: In practice, the analyst may use the 1986
   rent expense. However, because the DCF model uses future cash flows
   in its computations, the 1987 rent expense will be used in the Rating
   Agency Method as well).

```
Capitalized Lease Obligation = 8 x Rent Expense
   $7,200,000              = 8 x  $900,000
   ==========


   Interest Expense        = 1/3 x Rent Expense
      $300,000             = 1/3 x   $900,000
```

3. Ratio Analysis

		Capitalized Operating Leases	
Ratio	As Reported	Rating Agency Approach	DCF Approach
Debt/Equity	102.9 / 94.4	(102.9 + 7.2) / 94.4	(102.9 + 1.8) / 94.4
	= 1.1 to 1	= 1.2 to 1	= 1.1 to 1

Fixed Charge
Coverage   = (EBT + Rent + Interest) / (Rent + Interest)

$$\frac{(16.8 + .8 + .2)}{(.8 + .2)} \qquad \frac{(16.8 + .8 + .2)}{(.2 + .3)} \qquad \frac{(16.8 + .8 + .2)}{(.2 + .2)}$$

```
   = 17.8 to 1            = 35.6 to 1           = 44.5 to 1
```

Debt to
Total Assets

$$\frac{102.9}{197.3} \qquad\qquad \frac{(102.9 + 7.2)}{197.3} \qquad\qquad \frac{(102.9 + 1.8)}{197.3}$$

```
   = 52%                  = 56%                 = 53%
```

NOTE: In the fixed charge coverage ratio, the 1987 lease interest is used as an estimate for 1986. The actual 1986 lease interest would have to be obtained from the capitalization of operating leases from the prior year.

SOLUTION: CASE 7.2 MCI COMMUNICATIONS CORPORATION
----

1. Capitalization of Operating Leases: The DCF Approach

    Using the shortcut approach, the average discount factor is obtained
from the footnote information for capital leases:

                              PV $236,646
    Average PV Factor = ------------------- = -------- = .772046
                       Nominal Cash Flows $306,518   ========

    Capitalized Operating = Nominal Cash Flows   Average PV
       Leases   for the Operating Leases x   Factor

       $573,078   = $742,285   x   .772046
       ========

    Proforma Footnote Disclosure:
                                          Capital   Operating
                                          Leases   Leases
                                        ------------ ------------

         Minimum Lease Payments.............$306,518 $742,285
    Less: Deferred Interest Expense.......... <69,872>   <169,207> (Plug)
                                        ----------- ----------
         Present Value of Minimum
         Lease Payments....................$236,646 $573,078

    Less: Current Portion.................... <53,373> (a)   <29,290> (b)
                                        ----------- ----------
         Long-Term Lease Obligation.........$183,273 $543,588
                                        ========== ========

    Current Portion Computations:

    Current Portion = 1985 Total Payment - Interest on Outstanding Debt

    Capital Leases:
                    = $74,671   - ($236,646 x 9% (c))
                    = $74,671   -   21,298
                    = $53,373 (a)
                          =======

Operating Leases:

=	$81,067	-	($573,078 x 9% (c))
=	$81,067	-	51,577
=	$29,290 (b)		

(a) and (b) Intrapage cross-references.

(c) The long-term debt footnote indicates that the weighted average rate of interest on capitalized lease obligations is 9%.

2. Rating Agency Approach (NOTE: In practice, the analyst may use the 1984 rent expense. However, because the DCF model uses future cash flows in its computations, the 1985 rent expense will be used in the Rating Agency Method as well.)

Capitalized Lease Obligation = 8 x Rent Expense
        $648,500   = 8 x $81,067

Interest Expense   = 1/3 x Rent Expense
        $27,023   = 1/3 x $81,067

3. Ratio Analysis

		Capitalized Operating Leases	
Ratio	As Reported	Rating Agency Approach	DCF Approach
Debt/Equity	2,695 / 1,199	(2,695 + 648) / 1,199	(2,695 + 573) / 1,199
	= 2.3 to 1	= 2.8 to 1	= 2.7 to 1
Fixed Charge Coverage	= (EBIT + Rent) / (Rent + Interest)		
	(175 + 65)	(175 + 65)	(175 + 65)
	(65 + 188)	(27 + 188)	(52 + 188)
	= .95 to 1	= 1.12 to 1	= 1.00 to 1

```
Debt to
Total Assets      2,695              (2,695 + 648)         (2,695 + 573)
                 ----------         ----------------      ----------------
                  3,894              (3,894 + 648)         (3,894 + 573)

              =   69%              =    71%               =    73%
                 =====                  =====                  ======
```

NOTE: In the fixed charge coverage ratio, the 1985 lease interest is used as an estimate for 1984. The actual lease interest for 1984 would have to be obtained from the capitalization of operating lease calculations from the prior year.

SOLUTION: CASE 8.1 RCA

----

1. Types of Accounting Changes

Accounting for Regulated Subsidiaries. This event was accounted for as a retroactive-effect type accounting change. In this case, all prior years have been restated to give effect of the change in accounting principle. In other words, the new accounting method has been given retroactive application to all years presented.

Accounting for the Investment Tax Credit. This change was accounted for as a cumulative-effect type accounting change. Here, there is no retroactive application of the new accounting principle to prior periods, although supplementary proforma income information is provided.

Rather than giving retroactive application of the change to all prior periods, the effect of the change on all prior periods is aggregated and is reported as the cumulative effect, net of tax, on the face of the income statement in the year of adoption of the new accounting standard.

2. Recomputation of Net Income "As If" the Flow-Through Method Had Always Been Used

	1984	1983	1982
Net income as reported...............	$341.0	$227.0	$216.2
Deduct: Cumulative Effect...........	<75.7>	-	-
Subtotal........................	$265.3	$227.0	$216.2
Proforma effect of the change (see footnote 2).....................	-	12.1	25.4
Net income as restated under the Flow-through method.................	$265.3	$239.1	$241.6

3. The Cumulative Effect for the Retroactive-Effect Type Change

For a retroactive-effect type accounting change, the cumulative effect is presented as an adjustment to the opening retained earnings on the balance sheet of the first year for which retroactive application of the new accounting method is given.

In this case, footnote 2 indicates that the cumulative effect of the restatement to the new accounting method is a decrease of $55.7 million in retained earnings at January 1, 1982.

SOLUTION: CASE 9.1 AMERICA WEST AIRLINES, INC.
----

1. Line Item Computations for Cash Flows From Operating Activities

```
Operating Revenues..................................$993,409
Less: Increase in Accounts Receivable--net........ <21,456>
                                                   ---------
      Cash Collected from Passengers...............$971,953
                                                   =========


Salaries Expense...................................$249,715
Less: Increase in Accrued Wages................... <2,154>
                                                   ---------
      Cash Paid for Salaries.......................          $247,561


Aircraft Maintenance and Supplies.................$ 18,590
Fuel.............................................. 141,095
Add: Increase in Inventory (parts, etc.).......... 4,610
                                                   ---------
      Purchases...................................$164,295

Less: Increase in Accounts Payable............... <26,941>
                                                   ---------
      Cash Paid for Inventory, Parts and Supplies..          137,354

Rentals and Landing Fees..........................$197,568
Agency Commissions................................ 71,346
Other Operating Expenses.......................... 212,862
Add:  Increase in Prepaid Expenses................ 11,877
      Increase in Other Assets & Restricted Cash.. 3,856
Less: Increase in Air Traffic Liabilities......... <8,225>
      Increase in Other Accrued Liabilities....... <7,382>
      Increase in Other Liabilities............... <5,338>
                                                   ---------
      Cash Paid for Other Operating Expenses......          476,564
                                                            ---------
      Cash Paid to Employees and Suppliers...............$861,479
                                                         =========
```

```
Other Nonoperating Income--Net.....................$  5,078
Amortization of Deferred Credits...................  <2,547>
Other Income.......................................    188
Interest Income....................................  10,782
Less: Increase in Short-Term Investments..........  <7,919>
                                                     ---------

     Cash from Other Income--Net...................$  5,582
                                                     =========


Interest Expense...................................$ 43,769
Less: Increase in Accrued Interest................  <5,029>
                                                     ---------

     Cash Paid for Interest........................$ 38,740
                                                     =========

Income Tax Expense.................................$  7,237
Less: Increase in Accrued Taxes Payable...........  <2,551>
      NOL Carryforward Benefits Realized on
         Income Tax Returns.......................  <7,215>
                                                     ---------

     Net Cash Received from Income Taxes...........$ <2,529>
                                                     =========
```

2. Restatement of Cash Flows From Operating Activities under the Direct
   Reporting Format

   Cash Flows From Operating Activities:

```
     Cash Collected from Passengers................$971,953
     Cash Paid to Employees and Suppliers.........<861,479>
     Cash Received from Other Income--Net.........  5,582
     Cash Paid for Interest.......................< 38,740>
     Cash Received for Income Taxes...............  2,529
                                                    ---------

     Net Cash Provided by Operating Activities....$ 79,845
                                                    =========
```

Bibliography

Abdelkhalik, A. Rashad. Research Report: The Economic Effects of Leasees of FASB Statement No. 13, Accounting for Leases. Stamford, CT: FASB, 1981.

American Institute of Certified Public Accountants. Objectives of Financial Statements. New York: AICPA, 1973.

Bernstein, Leopold A. Financial Statement Analysis: Theory, Application and Interpretation. 4th ed. Homewood, IL: Richard D. Irwin, Inc., 1989.

Blumstein, Michael. "Pros and Cons of Defeasance." The Wall Street Journal (January 12, 1984): D8-D9.

Coopers and Lybrand. Executive Alert. New York: Coopers and Lybrand USA Communications Department (May, 1985): 12-15.

Dieter, Richard. "Is Now the Time to Revisit Accounting for Business Combinations." The CPA Journal 59 (July, 1989): 44-48.

Financial Accounting Standards Board. Accounting Standards Current Text: General Standards as of June 1, 1990. Norwalk, CT: FASB, 1990.

_____. Accounting Standards Current Text: Industry Standards as of June 1, 1990. Norwalk, CT: FASB, 1990.

_____. Statement of Financial Accounting Concepts No. 1, Objectives of Financial Reporting by Business Enterprises. Stamford, CT: FASB, 1978.

Kieso, Donald E., and Jerry J. Weygandt. Intermediate Accounting. 6th
ed. New York: John Wiley & Sons, 1989.

Laibstain, Samuel. "Income Tax Accounting for Business Combinations."
The CPA Journal 58 (December, 1988): 32-40.

Mohr Rosanne M. "Unconsolidated Finance Subsidiaries: Characteristics and
Debt/Equity Effects." Accounting Horizons 2 (March, 1988): 27-34.

Pfeiffer, Glenn M., and Robert M. Bowen. Financial Accounting: A Casebook.
Englewood Cliffs, NJ: Prentice-Hall, 1985.

Praiser, David B. "Financial Reporting Implications of Troubled Debt."
The CPA Journal 59 (February, 1989): 32-39.

Ronen, Joshua, and Simcha Sadan. Smoothing Income Numbers: Objectives, Means,
and Implications. Reading, MA: Addison-Wesley, 1981.

Sannella, Alexander J. "The Capitalization of Operating Leases: The
Discounted Cash Flow Approach." The Journal of Commercial Bank Lending
72 (October, 1989): 49-55.

"Statement on Financial Instruments Disclosures." News Report. The
Journal of Accountancy 170 (June, 1990): 19-20.

U.S. Congress. Senate. Banking, Housing and Urban Affairs Committee.
The Competitive Equality Banking Act of 1987. 100th Cong., 2nd sess.,
1987. S.790.

Index

About the Author

ALEXANDER JOHN SANNELLA is a Certified Public Accountant and Assistant Professor of Accounting at the State University of New Jersey, Rutgers, Campus at Newark. His articles have appeared in such publications as the *Journal of Accounting, Auditing, and Finance* and the *Journal of Commercial Bank Lending.*